THE MYSTERIOUS AFFAIR AT THE MET

The Mysterious Affair at the Met

Priscilla Plays in High Cotton in the World of Highly-Valued Works of Art

CITIOFBOOKS, INC.

3736 Eubank NE Suite A1

Albuquerque, NM 871113579

www.citiofbooks.com

Hotline: 1 (877) 3892759

Fax: 1 (505) 9307244

Ordering Information:

Quantity sales. Special discounts are available for corporations, associations, and others who purchase in bulk. For details, contact the publisher at the address above.

Printed in the United States of America.

ISBN13:   Softcover   979-8-89391-438-2

            eBook   979-8-89391-439-9

            Hardback   979-8-89391-440-5

Library of Congress Control Number: 2024924779

Cover Design by Jina McGriff

Paragraph dividers by iStock clipart ID: 500019543, Daxi

Logo Design by John Simms

Web Administrator Toure Jones at demonstr8d.com

THE MYSTERIOUS AFFAIR AT THE MET

Priscilla Plays in High Cotton in the World of Highly-Valued Works of Art

M. J. Simms-Maddox, Ph.D.

M. J. Simms-Maddox, Inc. ~ Salisbury, NC US

ALSO BY M. J. SIMMS-MADDOX, Ph.D.

THE PRISCILLA SERIES
Priscilla Engaging in the Game of Politics

Mystery in Harare: Priscilla's Journey into Southern Africa

Three Metal Pellets

Special Envoy 1: Priscilla Journeys into Arab Islamic Territory

BOOK REVIEWS
Maqoma: The Legend of a Great Xhosa Warrior
by Timothy Stapleton, 2016

FOREWORDS
Can't Complain: God Is Good to Me, My Story
Felecia Todeh Wesley, 2020

For Momma, Hazel B. Owens Simms.

Contents

Dedication   v

Prologue   viii

1. Amiss at the Met   13

2. Until Further Notice   22

3. Stallions Racing   30

4. The Breakthrough   38

5. Welcome to 'The City'   50

6. The NYC Branch Office   62

7. Uncovering Deception   69

8. All-In in New York City   80

9. Some Must-Do Personal Business   94

10. Back at Bow Lake   108

11. The Whole Damn… Sordid Truth   116

12. Rendezvous at Poughkeepsie & Recruiting
    the Woman Once Known Only as "Sally"   126

13. A Striking Resemblance   137

14. An Unlikely Acquaintance   144

15. An "Unauthorized" Plan, for Sure   150

16. A French Mystery Novel   160

17. The Man Who Was, In Fact, Artemis Thibaut   168

18. Shopping in Gay Paree &
    Raid at New Rochelle 178
19. Under Wraps 189
20. Seafarers in Mykonos 201
21. Just One More Day 213
22. Raid at the Manhattan Mansion, and Then ... 224
23. The Fashionista & You've Got that Wrong 238
24. A Celebration of Life 248
25. A Bernhardt Welcoming 260
26. The Invitation 268
27. And Associates, Incorporated 273
28. A PR Charade 284
29. Finders' Fees 292
30. Put a Sock in It, Iggy 299
31. No! You Can't Be 307
32. The Special Edition 320
33. And Who're *You* Wearing 327
34. Oh, But You Really Should 340
35. Another of Life's Seemingly
    Unbearable Circumstances 351
36. Ship My Belongings, Such as They Are 366
37. Wrapping Up Loose Ends 383
38. Like a Page From *National Geographic* 397
39. Coming Out, Macy's Good News &
    "The Boys" in Croatia 404
40. The Masquerade Ball 414
41. Medical Appointments,
    Speaking Engagements ... *Oh, My!* 425
Epilogue 438
Acknowledgments 442
About the Author 444

PROLOGUE

In the city that never sleeps, the howling gales and torrential spring rains were a deluge. It was Wednesday of the fourth week in May, and it rained and rained in New York City, along with the whole northeastern American seaboard. It was a cold rain, too, unusually cold for May. But people were still out and about, dressed in rain hats, trench coats, and other waterproof wear. They held umbrellas to shield themselves from the gale and the pouring rain. Some held newspapers and attaché cases over their heads. Some scurried about playfully, whereas others sloshed through puddles of water on the sidewalks, the side streets, and the alleyways. Tourists, however, drifted in and out a myriad of shops and restaurants and showplaces such as museums and theatres, any place to escape the pouring rain.

A favorite destination—even for New Yorkers—was the venerable Metropolitan Museum of Art. On this particular day, "the Met," as it was generally known, was experiencing an unusually large number of visitors. The colossal structure at 1000 Fifth Avenue and 82nd Streets occupied nearly a city block of some of the most highly-valued square footage in the world. Visitors had their choice of viewing over two million works of art spanning five millennia of cultures, something from nearly every-where. But some among them were up to something quite different than viewing the magnificent works of art; rather, they had something more sinister on their minds.

Around three o'clock in the afternoon of that same day, the Met's surveillance cameras' lenses captured "a mysterious-looking couple" amid the multitude of visitors strolling about the museum galleries. The pair were dripping wet in their matching taupe Burberry trench coats. Just as the two of them were walking past *Soleil dans le Ciel de Saint-Paul,* a masterpiece of Marc Chagall, a large tourist group—who, oddly enough, all wore distinctive red-and-white-striped vinyl raincoats—seemed to converge around them. Then the woman in the taupe Bur-berry turned around and bent down as if she were searching for some-thing on the wet floor. The lenses of one surveillance camera focused on the tightly-spaced crowd—and, too, provided a few unfocused frames of wet pants legs and stockings and boots and galoshes of the large tourist group in their red-and-white-striped raincoats. And meanwhile, the male member of "the mysterious-looking couple" opened the right flap of his trench coat, as if he, too, were searching for something. Then he pulled out what looked like a big red silk handkerchief, leaned over, and—as the woman appeared to continue searching for something on the wet floor—tapped the woman's shoulder. As she looked up at him, he opened wide that large handkerchief—which was bigger than a scarf, actually, but not as big as a banner—as if he were showing her something he wanted her to notice. In so doing, he effectively concealed from the surveillance camera lenses not only some of the large tourist group but also the Chagall painting on the wall behind them.

Meanwhile, the camera recorded a surprised expression on the woman's face as she gazed at whatever had caught her interest behind that sizeable red silk handkerchief. A second or so later, the man took the woman by the hand and helped her back to her feet. Then, not just "the mysterious-looking couple," but also the large tourist group, walked out of that particular camera's range, as they were submerged elsewhere in the interminable galleries of the gigantic museum.

For the time being, as many more tourists swarmed about the Chagall gallery, the surveillance camera continued recording the *Soleil dans le Ciel de Saint-Paul,* which still appeared to hang in its proper place on the wall.

So began what later came to be called "The Mysterious Affair at the Met." And before it would all end, the illustrious P.J. Austin-Bernhardt, *PR consultant extraordinaire*—and intelligence agent—would be called upon by the Met to help avert some of the deceit, fraud and skullduggery that could easily become the scandal of the decade, if not of the century.

THE MYSTERIOUS AFFAIR AT THE MET

1

Amiss at The Met

Met authorities were first aroused that something was amiss with a Chagall masterpiece—and possibly other highly valued works of art—shortly after "the mysterious-looking couple" and the tourists in the red-and-white-striped vinyl raincoats had disappeared from any of the cameras' lenses, or after they had already vacated the premises of the Met.

But the wake-up call did not come from a high-tech source but rather from a keen-eyed volunteer docent who used a low-tech tool—her eyes—to register that there was something not quite right about the *Soleil dans le Ciel de Saint-Paul.* More importantly, she had the audacity to speak up.

Only seconds after "the mysterious-looking couple" had disappeared, this attentive volunteer docent approached one of the security guards. She pointed to the Chagall, which happened to have been a favorite of hers. "Sorry to tell you this," she said. "And it's probably nothing. But something's not right. This painting looks a little strange. *Different*. It just doesn't, you know, look *right* to me."

The guard's initial instinct was to dismiss her. Then he studied her for a long moment. *Young. Untrained. Inexperienced in the world of high art*, he must have thought of her. He stared at her museum volunteer badge, swiveled his head toward the painting, and then did what he had been trained to do if there was even a remote possibility that any of these priceless works of art were at risk. Swiftly, he grabbed hold of a thick, tightly woven rope barrier—which resembled those mobile chrome and rope dividers that movie theatres use to corral crowds lined up for the next feature—and cordoned off the Chagall Gallery. Then he told himself to try to speak authoritatively. He wanted to be careful not to sound panicked and shrill, but speak loud enough so that everyone in the gallery could hear:

"Attention! Attention!" he bellowed. "This is security. Stay where you are! No one may enter or leave this gallery until the authorities arrive." Then he lifted the radio affixed to his Velcro-padded shoulder, pressed a button, and intently hissed into the speaker: "Code A! High alert in the Chagall Gallery! This is a high alert!"

The response from his headpiece was immediate: "Message received. *Code A* confirmed!"

Then the guard spoke in an equally loud and authoritative voice to the museum visitors:

"Away from the gallery exit, people!" He herded the stunned, dripping-wet visitors toward the center of the gallery. "Take your time. No reason to panic. But move, everybody, please move!"

But as his eyes looked up to where the ceiling met the wall, so, too, did everyone else's eyes look up. Bewildered. The visitors watched as a heavy metal grille dropped down from the ceiling to the floor, effectively locking them inside the gallery.

"No!" someone screamed frantically.

"We're locked in!" muttered someone else.

"At the Met, of all places!" yet another visitor screeched.

In the frantic next hour, many things happened in many parts of the museum. Before anybody inside the Chagall Gallery knew anything else, several security personnel arrived. One among them unlocked the metal grille and then he and two other security officials entered. The other security personnel remained outside the gallery and directed onlookers away from the cordoned-off area. Before long, the security officials inside the gallery had developed a rhythm whereby they first introduced themselves, interviewed each visitor, and then searched each of them as well as any of their possessions. They then collected contact information if there was a need to question anyone further. It all went relatively smoothly, save for the fact no one told the visitors what had happened to lead to their detention and their being interviewed and searched in the first place.

While the security personnel interviewed, searched, and collected contact information from the stunned visitors, two curators surrounded the Chagall. One of them took photographs. The other touched the masterpiece with his glove-covered hands as both anxiously conferred with the other. Then, the one who was examining the masterpiece with his gloved hands said, "Hmm, we'd better examine it more closely."

At that, the two curators continued examining the *Soleil dans le Ciel de Saint-Paul* but decided to wait a while before removing it. After all, they did not wish to create any suspicions that something was the matter with that particular masterpiece.

Nearly an hour after the security alert, shortly after 4:00 in the afternoon, the somewhat startled museum visitors who had been locked inside the Chagall Gallery were allowed to leave, not that everyone was excited about going back out into the howling gales and the torrential rains.

"But, anywhere," someone from among the departing, disgruntled visitors said, "is better than in *here*."

As things stood, behind closed doors in the museum's upper-level executive suites, the issue was only just beginning. Although their telephones rang off their hooks, the angst-ridden executives ignored them. They preferred first to listen to preliminary reports of what had happened. They were particularly concerned with the report that the museum security had issued a "high alert" code in the Chagall Gallery near the *Soleil dans le Ciel de Saint-Paul* painting. Had the masterpiece been tampered with? Were art thieves on the prowl? Was it even a certainty that one of the other masterpieces was at risk? Underlings, such as the security guards and the volunteer docent, prayed that they had acted properly, while the executives prayed that they themselves would not be held accountable for whatever had happened. Yet, they all knew that something was terribly wrong. They just did not know what the matter was.

This was especially the case with the one who sat at the apex of the organization, for this particular executive was especially at risk. And he knew it, too.

Met Executive Director Shane Carpenter was fully aware that he bore the brunt of whatever the matter was. It was his role to do all that he could to protect the reputation of one of the world's most highly recognized museums. A tall, fairly handsome, and distinguished-looking man, he bore a striking resemblance to the movie star George Hamilton.

But Shane was rather pale in complexion and did not possess the stunning suntan as did Mr. Hamilton. Moreover, he was transgender, but not too many people were aware of his sexual preference. Indeed not that he and the chairman of the board of trustees carried on such a relationship. Besides, this was New York City in the early 1990s, and no one gave a darn about who anybody else slept with, anyway.

Moments ago Shane had fielded several telephone calls from some of the most aggressive journalists assigned to the metropolitan art beat. He had wondered, when *The Times* reporter was the first to get to him: *How'd they get wind of this and so fast? Those reporters! Art, they cover art. But they act like they're investigating organized crime. Why are they always so on top of everything bad?* A few minutes later *The Daily News* called, then *Newsweek* and *Time Magazine.* Of course someone must have tipped them off about the Met's "high alert." They all wanted to know what sensational happening had triggered that "high alert."

As it so happened, and it all happened pretty quickly, Shane had also thought about what he would tell his boss, Ignatius Devoe, the chairman of the board of trustees. He so hated that the chairman had a tendency to involve himself in the museum's operations when, as board chair, his primary role centered on policy, not administrative affairs. Solving what generated the "high alert" was Shane's responsibility, but he already knew that the chairman would put himself into the mix. So Shane set about first averting any suspicions that something bad had happened as best he could.

He told the news reporters: "For insurance purposes, from time to time, the museum conducts tests—in the form of emergency drills—to test our security system," which seemed to allay the immediate concerns of the inquisitive newsmen and -women. Although what he said had been true, technically, he knew he could not tell them the whole truth, not at this time. Shane knew how to do his job, and he was good at it, too. Even so, he knew that the newsmen and -women would come at him again.

Next, he found himself staring at the phone for a long New York minute, but that no longer rang. *Good*, he thought. Now that the first wave of reporters had ebbed, he briefly wondered what he should do next. *Should I write a short press release about this erstwhile "emergency drill?"* He decided against doing that. Taking the initiative, any initiative on this kind of matter, was usually a mistake. He would try to brazen this one out and not call any more attention to it than need be.

Then, back to how he would craft his take on the situation with his boss, who was also his lover. Then, almost immediately, he decided to give it to him straight. He called Board Chair Ignatius Devoe and held his phone a safe distance from his ear because he knew that "Iggy," as he called him affectionately, would be yelling at the top of his lungs.

Shane allowed Iggy some time to vent. Then he brought him up to speed with what he knew.

First, he told his boss what the volunteer docent had said to the security guard. Then he told him what the security guard had done. But when Shane said that he himself had told the news reporters: "For insurance purposes, from time to time, the museum conducts emergency drills to test our security system," Chairman Devoe settled down somewhat—no more panting and heavy breathing into the telephone line, either. So Shane felt that, just as he had averted suspicions with the news reporters, he had just succeeded in averting any presumably irreparable harm to the Met with the chairman of the board.

During a moment of silence on the part of the board chairman, who routinely rubbed his head at its receding hairline and bit his stubbed fingernails, Shane absently smoothed down his elegant Armani blazer over his slim hips. He adjusted his already perfectly knotted tie. Then, calmly he continued. "You know, sir, Chagall's *Soleil dans le Ciel de Saint-Paul* does look somewhat strange."

"Hmm," Iggy mumbled because that was the first time that he had heard of that. But before he could comment further, the executive director continued briefing him.

"So I asked our curators to take a look at it; and, they're already examining it, pending confirmation of its authenticity. Or is that validation of its provenance?" Shane paused because he knew the chairman knew that he referred to the two curators who specialized in such works of art as those that had been created by Marc Chagall, Oscar-Claude Monet, and Paris Bordone.

Nevertheless, Shane already knew there was more to the story. He may not have known exactly what that was, but he instinctively knew there was more. So he told all that he knew, in a manner of speaking.

Fully in his role as executive director, he finally removed his personal feelings, when he said, "Mr. Chairman," much more assertively than before, "this is the third such incident in as many months."

"What!" The chairman was himself more irate than before. For sure, this was the first time he had heard of this.

However, Shane continued as if the chairman had not spoken in such an astonished tone of voice. He elaborated:

"Mr. Chairman, we've also noticed that Monet's *La Promenade* and Bordone's *Diana and the Two Nymphs* seem a little strange, as well. And, well, sir, security is on the prowl for a 'mysterious-looking couple' who did something peculiar in the Chagall Gallery this afternoon." There, now, Shane had told the board chairman everything that he knew.

So undone was the chairman that he hung up his telephone without nary another word. That was the signal that both men now knew the next step was one the chairman was not eager to take.

While the board secretary called the twenty-two other board members for an emergency meeting at six-forty-five that evening, Shane set out for updates on what was what, and then he made a mad dash downstairs to the museum. As he made his way through the dripping-wet visitors, he eventually reached the Chagall Gallery, where he paused for a moment to collect his bearings. He straightened his blazer and necktie again. Then he approached one of the many security guards for a personal escort to the masterpiece in question. After seeing the two curators taking photographs and examining the masterpiece, and that it still hung in its proper place, he headed to a back room in the museum where the surveillance equipment was housed.

As he appeared in the vicinity of the surveillance equipment room, someone among the security personnel spotted him right away. So he radioed to the others inside the room: "Mr. Carpenter is here."

Once inside the room, the security personnel, who were examining the few frames of footage of "the mysterious-looking couple" for the umpteenth time, beckoned to Shane to join them. As he took a seat and watched the same footage that the security personnel had watched so many times before, one of them remarked: "Sir, for the life of me, I can't figure out what that couple was up to."

"Hmm," Shane said. For he had no idea who either one of the couple was. Nor could he fathom the meaning behind the prank with that big red silk handkerchief. He also noticed that the man and the woman in the footage had skillfully tilted their heads at angles that had shielded much of their faces. In addition, he noticed that, although the man had worn a tam-ó-shanter—one of those like Beatniks used to wear—the surveillance cameras' lenses did capture what appeared to have been a thin moustache over his lips. As for the woman, the security personnel assumed that her tinted eyeglasses, thick bangs, and long red hair had probably been a disguise. It had been along those lines that the couple had been deemed "mysterious." One of the best surveillance systems in the business had failed to capture their facial images. Well, maybe not one of the best in the business because it did not even possess a facial imaging feature.

Nevertheless, Shane somehow knew that those few frames of surveillance footage lay at the heart of this mystery. But little did he know that once Chairman Devoe caught a glimpse of those few frames, he would know for a certainty about the heart of this mystery. Oh yeah, Iggy's past transgressions were about to catch up with him and, in so doing, threatened to snare the unsuspecting Shane right along with him.

Not long after Shane returned to his office, and before Chairman Devoe called him to attend the emergency board meeting, he placed an urgent call to someone whom he knew the board would approve of in helping to avert what he now sensed could easily become the scandal of the decade, if not the of the century. Yet, he kept this particular action to himself.

2

Until Further Notice

Around 7:00 that evening, Ignatius Devoe gaveled the opening of an emergency meeting of an overly anxious assemblage of some twenty-three men and women, himself included, of every imaginable sector of New York's high society. Somewhat flushed from the events of the past three hours, he patted his forehead to his receding hairline with a big white cotton handkerchief. Then, right before he spoke, there was an outpouring of questions and declarations about the many rumors some board members had already heard.

"Was there *really* a theft of a Chagall?" shouted someone.

"Why'd you have to call a state of 'high alert' in the first place?" asked another board member.

Yet someone else with much disenchantment said, "I'm not liking any of this."

The chairman waved his stout hands to generate calm. Then, after a moment or two, he found himself looking in the direction of his executive director. "Shane, please bring everyone up to date on the events of the day."

It was then that the assemblage calmed down. They all turned their attention to the executive director, but not before one of them said in a not-so-subtle commanding tone of voice, "Yeah, Shane. Enlighten us."

Shane stood up in the most relaxed, though stoic state, and spoke as if he were giving his usual report to the board. But this particular report had nothing to do with prospective donors or new and exciting exhibitions; instead, a report about events that dealt with artwork possibly having been tampered with, maybe even stolen.

"The events of the day started with a conversation that one of our able volunteer docents had with a security guard," he said, and then he told them about the cordoning off of the visitors closest to the Chagall Gallery, and the interviewing and searching and collecting of their contact information.

But when the nearly five-feet-nine-inches tall, stout man of nearly immaculate aplomb interrupted Shane and mentioned the few frames of footage that showed "the mysterious-looking couple" pulling that prank with the big red silk handkerchief, even the twenty-two other board members knew something more sinister was afoot.

Yet, no one said a word. They all put on their best poker faces as they remained quiet and listened to what else the executive director and the board chairman had to tell them.

"Thank you, Shane," Chairman Devoe said with an element of gratitude. Then he continued. "Everyone, this is, in fact, a state of emergency. Marc Chagall's *Soleil dans le Ciel de Saint-Paul*, Oscar-Claude Monet's *La Promenade*, and Paris Bordone's *Diana and the Two Nymphs* may already have been compromised." He paused. "Worse still, the authentic paintings may even have been stolen." Then he shook his head of thinning black hair and said, "So, while we authenticate the three paintings and determine whether any others may have been tampered with, maybe even stolen, we remain in a state of 'high alert.'"

At that, the chairman paused and asked for any questions.

Once again, no one said a word; and since the board members already knew the purpose of the emergency meeting, they simply waited for the chairman to tell them their course of action.

The chairman expounded.

"After careful consideration, I have authorized our executive director to retain the public relations services of P. J. Austin and Associates, Inc. to handle our public response to what could turn out to be, for us, the scandal of the decade, if not of the century. And from what our sources tell us, Ms. Austin-Bernhardt is well on her way to setting up a branch office right down the street from us in Bryant Park." All right, so Chairman Devoe said all of that as if Priscilla had been his choice in the first place when, in fact, his announcement was his way of obtaining board approval for something that Shane had already done. But the chairman was unaware of this at this time. But he was also signaling to Shane to contact Priscilla unless, of course, the board had another recommendation. Meanwhile, his recommendation for Priscilla's firm met with overwhelming board approval.

"Really!" Attorney Macy Stoner exclaimed as she could not contain her excitement. But why hadn't Priscilla told her that she was setting up shop in New York? With an effort, she resisted blurting out her girlfriend's name: *PJ*!

Attorney Stoner was not the only board member who expressed satisfaction with the chairman's recommendation.

"Excellent choice," said someone else.

"Indeed," echoed another.

With a burst of enthusiasm, "Only the best for the Met," said a third. By this point, the board members had begun to relax somewhat.

Chairman Devoe knew his board. He rightly sensed that he had the unanimous consent in selecting Priscilla's PR firm to handle any public reaction to the impending scandal. And there having been no objections, he added, somewhat peevishly, "But I'm told even though she's not cheap—not in the least inexpensive—we need to seal the deal with her before word spreads that she is opening a branch office in the City. Apparently we won't be the only ones wanting to snap her up."

"But first, some clarification," said Nicholas Diubaldi, another attorney serving on the board. "First things first, before we turn this into a public relations circus. What about our own insurance agency?" But when he asked whether the Met was covered for all eventualities on this matter, pretty much every one of the others turned up their noses. For, it was their practice not to quibble over costs for what they just knew would be good quality service. Nicholas did not care. As a finance committee member, he had a fiduciary responsibility to justify all expenditures, even those for the highly esteemed P. J. Austin and Associates, Inc.

The chairman responded to Nicholas' question about the insurance agency first, "Indeed," he said. Tersely, he nodded and, with relief, added, "They've already got their dogs on the scent. And I can assure you, of course, we are covered."

Then he picked up with the part about the PR firm: "But under such precarious circumstances, we need to amp up our own PR and our own investigation into this mysterious affair. That's why I think we'll benefit from the highly esteemed and *discreet* services of Ms. Austin-Bernhardt, not to mention her excellent relationship with the media."

Quite cheerfully, a confident Attorney Stoner interjected, "And her impeccable resourcefulness, too. You know, the media call her, 'America's Little Sweetheart.'"

Chairman Devoe allowed himself a small smile of satisfaction. The meeting was, after all, going just as he had hoped it would. But, as he let down his guard just a smidgen, lowered his head, and spoke in a near whisper: "My God, I *cannot believe* this is even happening, and on my watch, at that."

Then, as he lifted his head and scanned the faces of the others, one among them bellowed, "*Your* watch! What about *us*?"

Then Gaylord Millsap Omiros, the board member who sat to the right of the chairman, said the two words that were on everyone's mind: "Joint liability!" For they were all aware that each of them, Gaylord included, was accountable for any breach in the museum's security, including not only the possible tampering with but maybe also the possible theft of these three highly valued works of art.

But Chairman Devoe, who had much with which to reckon, was not about to let them get bogged down in terrors strung from mere speculation. He'd had a darn good meeting. Met all his accomplishments. Allayed the concerns of this board. So, hastily he declared, "There being no further business, this emergency meeting of the board of trustees for The Metropolitan Museum of Art is adjourned."

As he hammered his gavel down on the conference table, this time he muttered under his breath, "Until further notice."

At the start of the next business day, Chairman Devoe met with his executive director, whose office was down the corridor from his office.

"Get P.J. Austin on the phone, right away," he said and sank on a chair opposite Shane's desk.

Shane had been the primary "source" that the chairman had alluded to during the emergency board meeting the night before. For the time being, however, he pretended not to have already contacted Priscilla's PR firm. He played along with his boss and pretended to call her office.

But before he picked up his telephone, he asked Iggy, "Apart from all those news stories about Ms. Austin-Bernhardt, what else do you happen to know about her?"

"Oh, nothing much," Iggy said and continued. "Just someone who's been put through it. You know, abducted to some Godforsaken place in Africa, married to one of the wealthiest men in New England … that kind of stuff." He shrugged and, just as quickly added, "Oh, yes, how could I forget? She's the one all those terrorists tried to kill back when she worked on the president's election campaign. Come to think of it," he said, "I remember her quite well."

"All right, Iggy," Shane said as he noticed his boss was in a more pleasant manner than he was the day before. "But you don't seem to know much about her ability as a PR person, for which, I'm told, she's pretty darn good: 'the woman is good at her game,' not to mention 'she's worked in the political arena,' too."

Then Shane pretended to call the information operator for the telephone number for "P.J. Austin and Associates, Inc. in Ohio," a locale for which even he knew his boss was unfamiliar.

"Yes, operator," he said, "the number for P.J. Austin and Associates, Inc. in *Columbus*, Ohio?" Then, he said, "Yes, I'll hold." He pretended to write down the telephone number he already had because he had called the number last evening; and he had also spoken with Priscilla's able assistant, Julia Cahill.

He then pretended to have gotten someone on the line.

"Yes, Ms. Cahill," Shane said after pretending that Julia had answered the telephone and given him her name. "This is Shane Carpenter, executive director at The Metropolitan Museum of Art." After pretending that Julia had said something more, he then said, "Yes. Our board of trustees has asked me to inquire about the availability of your public relations services for a delicate matter we're facing. More precisely, possible forgeries, maybe even theft."

Then Shane peered across the way at Iggy and pretended that he was listening to Julia asking follow-up questions. "Hmm." "Yes, that's right," he said more than a few times.

But he and Julia had talked shortly before the board had met the day before when she'd told him, "Mr. Carpenter, we might be in the nation's heartland, but we're not exactly off the grid with happenings in New York. And 'yes,'" she had told Shane, "we're acutely aware that something is amiss at The Met." She had then paused, especially after having sensed the urgency of the call. *It's not every day that one receives a call from The Metropolitan Museum of Art's executive director. This is a live one for sure! And we haven't even opened up our branch office yet.* Then she'd said, "I'm fairly certain that PJ will get back to you on this. Give her a day or so."

Shane had then expressed his appreciation, after which their conversation had ended.

At this very moment, though, he still pretended that Julia was on the line and said, "All right then, Ms. Cahill. We'll wait to hear back from Ms. Austin-Bernhardt. Thank you so very much."

Then he pretended that she had said, "Goodbye."

"And good day to you, too, Ms. Cahill."

"My goodness, Shane," Iggy said as he rose from the edge of his seat. "That was quick!"

"Yes, boss, I told you that that woman's firm was among the best there is." For a brief moment though, he thought about the many times that he had saved his boss's bacon, in a manner of speaking. *Enough already,* he must have thought as he then waved him away.

As it so happened, to Shane's way of thinking, and Iggy's, too, Priscilla was being brought on board to help avert much harm to the museum's image. But little did either of them know that she would be equally instrumental in helping to solve the mystery behind the impending scandal as well.

3

Stallions Racing

Priscilla sat astride Mystique, the chocolate-colored stallion that had become her favorite mount at her in-laws' Bow Lake estate. She gazed off into the distance, where the undulating New Hampshire hills rolled into the horizon and beyond. She wished it were as easy to see some clear pattern in the ups and downs of her own life, which had changed so much in the four months of her marriage. *So this is what trials and tribulations are all about,* she wondered—*much more than I could ever have expected. Why, even our honeymoon—wonderful as it was!—had ended almost before it had begun! Then I was off again, this time to Arab Islamic territory, when. somehow, my Darling Carlton contracted amnesia.*

Amnesia, she thought again. *How the hell does one contract amnesia from sitting behind a frigging desk at Langley?* she pondered for the umpteenth time. Why, even she knew better than that ridiculous story that

Carlton's friends had concocted, something about him having fallen and hit his head. But Priscilla knew that it was only a matter of time before she would learn the truth, which was exactly what happened, only later, much later.

For the time being, though, Priscilla was not at herself—greatly distressed, off-kilter, even edgy—which was so unlike her.

She shifted in her saddle. She so yearned to chase away her misgivings, to be off, to gallop anywhere that was not here. Dubai! Harare! Even Columbus, which she especially regarded for years as her home, rather than here at her in-laws' New Hampshire home. And she just hated pondering and wondering as she sat in this saddle. She was decisive, a woman of action. But here she was: aimless, mulling, sitting astride this powerhouse of a stallion, not off and galloping like both she and Mystique were born to do.

She sat erect in the saddle, her riding posture perfect. On this particular day, she donned her OSU-Buckeye sweatshirt and blue denim jeans, not her elegant black tailor-made riding clothes and the jodhpurs. Nor did she wear the traditional headgear because she loved the feel of the brisk New England wind blowing through her light brown hair, which, on this day, she wore pulled back and pinned up in a clamp. But her favorite part of the attire was her dark chocolate-colored riding boots, which she had a habit of smoothing with her hands. She loved the feel of the leather, not to mention the color, dark chocolate!

But riding her favorite stallion had not been enough to keep her fully engaged and soak up her prodigious energy. Instead, she found herself spending lots more time than usual pondering what to do about her predicament. Mostly, she thought about married life, which was not exactly as she had thought it would be. Sometimes, it was hard enough to be sure about her profession, let alone this new status in life that she had apparently assumed with her marriage vows. Was she still what some called her—*a PR consultant extraordinaire*—or was she a politician, or an intelligence agent, or some kind of action heroine? She smiled at the thought of being an action heroine. P.J. Austin, action heroine! Her dormant exuberance emerged and coursed through her for the first time in a long time. She laughed out loud. Still, she wondered whether she had found, or lost, not her true passion, but the very essence of her life.

As she continued sitting astride Mystique on top of that New Hampshire hill and staring toward the horizon in the uncertain early morning light, Priscilla returned to her wayward, uncertain thoughts. Although everyone was always telling her that she was a woman of many talents, she somehow knew that she was not yet doing whatever she was meant to do. For she already intuitively understood that just becoming known as a *PR consultant extraordinaire* did not necessarily fulfill her heart's desire. She sensed, vaguely but surely, that her PR projects were no longer what she once thought of as "earthy," although she was not quite able to articulate what that meant. She was aware, however, that she did not quite relish her work as she once did. Could it be that she was right on the cusp, almost—at last—finally coming into her own, discovering her true calling, as it were? If only she could determine with finality what that "true calling" was.

She recalled a significant conversation she had once had with her father not long before he died. Nelson had been not only an admirable man of God and leader of men but also a great storyteller in his own right. What they had shared had not been so much an unwelcomed encounter but rather one in which a loving father shares precious thoughts about his life and his hopes for his beloved daughter: "It would please your mom and me both, Priscilla, if you start living your life to please yourself." She remembered how fondly he smiled as he'd added, "And, be happy, Priscilla." Priscilla had understood he had said that because, up until then, she'd spent most of her young life trying to please her parents, especially her authoritative minister-father. A decade later, here and now, she found herself wrestling over whether she had transferred her tendency to please her parents to that of pleasing her darling Carlton.

Resolutely she turned her thoughts from her intelligence agent-husband back to her own *professional* heart's desire. There was, indeed, one thing that she truly enjoyed, one thing that she would unwittingly do at a moment's notice. She possessed a penchant for politics. But it had never crossed her mind whether she would ever seek a public office herself. And she was not about to let herself wander into that particular wilderness now, either. Despite the many years that she had studied political science, that she had taught political science, that she had served as a legislative aide for a state senator, that she had worked as a political campaign consultant and as a marketing consultant to a presidential hopeful and, now that she served as a special agent "in service to her country," she had never really considered running for public office herself.

And not today, either, she thought. Nor was she about to consider that everyone who knew her recognized that political trait in her. In this, as in many other ways, Priscilla still did not see herself the way others did.

Exhausted from so much introspection, she was just about to flick the reins and lead Mystique off into an exhilarating, fast gallop back to the stables when she thought she saw something silhouetted on the horizon. She shaded her eyes with her hand. *Someone else is out riding this morning.* So she waited a moment to see who it was. Then she laughed out loud as the approaching figure before her unveiled himself. Why, she would recognize him anywhere: tall, broad shoulders, well-shaped legs, and thick, long, wavy locks of black hair in a ponytail underneath his helmet. The figure approaching was her Darling Carlton!

As Carlton approached, Priscilla remembered with much sadness how—during the course of his stay at the Johns Hopkins Bayview Medical Center—she had sat in the same uncomfortable metal chair in the same drab room where she tried daily, unsuccessfully, to convince her husband that she was, in fact, his wife, and where he had tried daily, unsuccessfully, to convince her otherwise.

Time and time again, he had said, "How many times do I need to tell you, I don't know you, beautiful woman, and I'm sure you're somebody's wife, but I'm not even married?"

Early on, Carlton's medical team had advised Priscilla to seek psychiatric counseling to help her cope with the situation that involved her husband's condition. So she occasionally met with Dr. Robert Chisholm, her PTSD specialist. Why, after what she herself had just experienced on her recent trek into Arab Islamic territory, she, for sure, needed psychiatric counseling. But now this! Whatever the situation was with her husband, simply threw her off-kilter. Not at herself; at least she had someone with whom she could talk about her problems. And so it was that, once again, Dr. Chisholm had served a significant role in Priscilla's life.

As her Darling Carlton came closer, Priscilla reflected on how timely the arrival of her and Carlton's longtime friends and associates in the intelligence realm had been. They had all assembled at her and Carlton's Georgetown condo, where the men had played poker, smoked cigars, and drank beer, and where the women had all sat in the kitchen while Priscilla had made a mess of a seafood salad. It was there that the pathway forward had crystallized for her. That was when she had decided to get her husband released from the hospital and take him home to Bow Lake to "more familiar surroundings." In so doing, however, the doctors had given her one month to try and bring back his memory, or return him to the Baltimore facility where he would be committed to long-term care.

She put her frustrations into words: "My God!" she cried out. "We've only been married *four* months. Why can't he remember our wedding? Our short honeymoon and all those fabulous gowns he had made exclusively for me? Please, dear God," she prayed. "Bring my Darling Carlton back to me."

Three weeks had already passed, and although there had been momentary improvements or glimpses of restorative memory, mostly, though, Carlton still was a stranger. With less than one week to spare, either his memory would be restored, or he would automatically be committed to a nursing home, maybe for good.

"I don't think so," Priscilla said out loud with an air of certainty.

She dug her heels into Mystique's side, and the horse galloped forward at full throttle. Priscilla told herself that it was now or never. Her optimism was restored. Or, was that her prayer had been answered? She just knew her Darling Carlton would *have* to remember.

The two of them galloped toward each other on their stallions.

Although Priscilla had just prayed, she still tried hard not to get her hopes up or even make too much of his presence. He still did not recognize her. Or so she thought.

Carlton smiled at her and called out. "My goodness, you seem so familiar. But for the life of me, I can't say how I know you."

As she swallowed her disappointment, still she thought, *Well, at least that's more than it's been.* But then she said, "Oh, that's okay, Carlton. Why not just admire the scenery with me."

Dr. Chisholm had accompanied the couple to Bow Lake, where he impressed upon Priscilla and the rest of the Bernhardt household how crucial it was not to pressure the patient in any way.

But Priscilla could not resist the temptation, just this once, to talk about more than she had been told she should. She was tired of playing by the rules that the medical team had prescribed. It was high time that she nudged her husband a bit. So that was what she did.

"You know, Carlton, I think you used to ride out here when you were a youngster with your sister Arvana and some of your friends and, a short time ago, with Germane, my nephew when he visited with us here. Anyway, your sister told me that you guys used to swim nude in that lake over there, behind those trees." She pointed, and then she laughed. "Oops! I wasn't supposed to say all that." But Priscilla knew precisely what she was doing.

"Oh?" Carlton looked where she pointed and then wrinkled his forehead. "Why not?"

Priscilla was beyond desperate for a resolution to his illness, and Carlton had no way of knowing it, but she had just put him on a short leash. But she responded to his query anyway: "Your shrink told us to let you come back around on your own and *not* to prompt you, which I guess is what I just did."

Carlton stared at Priscilla. And although she could tell he was trying very hard to remember her, she tried to pretend she was comfortable with his staring at her like that, so intense.

Then, in a more serious tone than before, he said, "Are you *sure* you and I don't know each other?"

"Well, I know *you*," she said while evading all the questions she saw in his searching eyes. "But until *you* recognize me on your own, well…."

Priscilla shrugged as if this were not the most important thing in her whole life. Then she succeeded in sounding almost casual when she changed the subject. "How 'bout racing back to the house?" Without giving him a chance to respond, she pulled the reins of her horse, turned Mystique around, and took off as if someone were in hot pursuit.

Carlton accepted her challenge, "All right, beautiful woman." And just as quickly, he followed suit.

Faster and faster they raced.

Priscilla let out a peal of laughter, and then, so, too, did he. Carlton was ahead most of the way. But since somewhere down deep in his memory, he might have known that his horse was faster than hers and that Priscilla loved to win at everything, so right at the end of their race, he allowed her horse to win.

Like most happenings at the Bernhardt estate, Priscilla's and Carlton's horse race had been observed by others in the family. Carlton's mother and father, watching from a second-story window of the mansion, and many among the household staff from just outside the French doors that led to the portico, even the psychiatrist, all watched the suddenly exuberant couple.

And from what they all saw, Carlton was racing toward a breakthrough.

4

The Breakthrough

That night, over dinner at the Bernhardts of Bow Lake, there was much, much more cheer to celebrate.

While everyone laughed and talked, Carlton suddenly, in fact, began experiencing a series of the primary breakthroughs that his family had so desperately desired. He looked at Lady Chelsea, that charming woman of understated elegance seated at the head of the table, and thought, *Mother.* Maybe he had actually said that aloud because she gave him a startled look. But when he smiled at her, she patted her watery eyes with her cloth napkin and wiped away tears of joy.

Then, one by one, he looked at Father, his surrogate father—Ramses—and then his grandparents—Poppa and Marlena. He nodded and smiled at each of them, too. And every one of them saw the expression on his face and understood that their beloved Carlton knew them—that he finally knew who they were and what they meant to him.

Next, he surprised his family and friends as he rose to his feet, walked to one end of the dinner table, and kneeled knee-high to Grandma Marlena. She rubbed his head—a particular sign of family affection—and ran her hands through his thick, long locks of wavy black hair. Then Poppa extended his hands for him to kiss, and he kissed them, while the others at the table shed tears of joy and "oohed" and "aahed."

Then Carlton walked to Ramses, who sat proudly erect in his high chair across from the table. He laid his head on the older man's shoulder. Ramses rubbed his head and ran his hands through the younger man's hair. Then he wept tears that the son he had raised knew him once again.

Next, Carlton then walked to the other end of the table, knelt knee-high, and reached for Lady Chelsea's open arms. She grabbed hold of him and openly wept for joy. As she, too, ran her hands through his hair, Father came and embraced his wife and son.

Still on his knees, he looked across the table at Dr. Chisholm. "Doc," he said, "thank you for a job well done. But tell me, how's our girl doing?"

The doctor grinned, aware now that his patient recognized Priscilla, too.

Finally, Carlton headed toward his wife. "My, my, you sure are a beautiful woman."

But unlike the others at the dinner table, Priscilla was not ready to receive her husband. She stared at him, frozen with shock. His sudden breakthrough was more than she could handle. She simply could not believe that her husband had finally recognized her. She blinked and then kept staring at him. But no one in the family, as they watched and waited, dared to urge her to accept this for what it was: the long-awaited breakthrough. These precious moments, they all knew, belonged to Carlton and Priscilla, alone. It was up to Priscilla to come to terms with her husband's recovery on her own.

Calmly she patted her lips with her napkin and, unable to stop her impulse to flee, she stood. "Sorry, folks, but I need to excuse myself."

Intently Carlton, and everyone else, followed her with their eyes as she turned and walked out of the dining room. They all listened to the sound of her footsteps ascending the colossal marble staircase.

For once, no one commented. Everyone realized that Priscilla needed some time and space to deal with what was happening.

Father ended the momentary silence and asked for confirmation of what he and the others had assumed was the breakthrough they had so desired. "Son," he said, "does this mean you *know* who we are?"

Carlton held his hand on his heart. "Yes, Father, I *know* who you all are. You are my family, and Missy is my wife." His voice dropped to a whisper. "The love of my life."

Everyone at the dinner table shouted cheers of jubilation. There were hugs and toasts and slaps on the backs. The family and their guests and the household staff shared a long-awaited reunion with Carlton Elliott Bernhardt, the son of the master of the household.

Before the night of revelry was over, Father prayed a prayer of thanksgiving to God.

As it so happened, for Carlton and one other, the night was still young.

Not long after he had gone upstairs and seemed to have retired to his bedchamber, he walked across the way to Priscilla's suite. Since Carlton had had amnesia, he and Priscilla had not slept together as husband and wife, hence the separate bedchambers. As he approached her bed, he noticed that she lay fast asleep. So he knelt beside her bed and prayed a prayer of gratitude. He thanked God for curing him of his amnesia and bringing him back home from the mission in Yemen "relatively" safe and unharmed, save for his bout with amnesia. Then he planted a moist kiss on Priscilla's lips.

Her eyes opened, but she was still half asleep. "What—?"

Carlton kissed her again.

"No. It can't be," she said and burst into tears.

Carlton kissed his wife yet again. Tears of joy flowed freely down her face.

Then her husband picked her up in his arms and carried her back across the corridor to his bedchamber. He set her on the edge of the bed and held her in his arms for a long time. Neither one of them spoke. Then Carlton asked, "Missy, was it hard being around me when I didn't even know you?"

"Oh, Carlton, my darling, I don't much care to remember any of that. I'm just glad to have my husband back."

The newlyweds then kissed some more, and one thing led to another, and the next thing either of them knew, a servant was opening their drapes, and another was rolling in two breakfast trays. Carlton and Priscilla were about to enjoy the honeymoon they had never had—at least not as it should have been—at the palatial Bernhardt estate of Bow Lake, of all places.

Later that same morning, after Priscilla and Carlton made love again—as if for the very first time—Priscilla slept for three more hours before really awakening.

Afterward, she went into the shower of her Darling Carlton's master bathroom. As she stood for a long while beneath the gushing showerheads, she realized this was the first time in nearly five months that she had been able to relax thoroughly.

As she felt the warm water gushing and smashing against her body, she was ever so grateful that her Darling Carlton's memory had been restored. "Thank you, dear Lord." Tears filled her eyes.

As she washed the tears from her face and the mucous from her runny nose, another thought occurred to her, something she had been considering all along. It was time to put her secret plan into action.

She adjusted one of the knobs on the shower stall to lessen the water's thrust and then picked up a bottle of shampoo. As she lathered her hair, she considered it had been a mere seven years since she had first set out on her own in her PR business. But she had never been content to keep doing something simply because she was good at it. She so yearned for something more. She rinsed the suds out of her hair. Then she thought about how she had only served as an intelligence agent for three years. But she had to admit that she enjoyed the excitement of her life as a special envoy: all the interesting people she had met, all the wonderful places she had visited, even all the horrible encounters with people that her nephew Germane once called "the bad guys." Oh, how, she relished the sheer rush of an occasional storm! But as she turned off the several knobs inside the shower stall and felt the water dripping from her head to her feet, she knew she had yet to do what she really wanted to do. Or even, what that was! But she was getting there.

As she reached for a towel to cover her head, she noticed the initials CEB embroidered on the linen and was reminded where she was, at her husband's family estate at Bow Lake, New Hampshire. For a moment, when she had allowed herself to think of what she always thought of as "my secret plan," she had forgotten where she was. Often, when enmeshed in deep thoughts about work, Priscilla had no sense of time, space, or place.

But now she wondered exactly how she would reveal her secret plan to the love of her life. And what if he were unwilling to support her plan?

Then, as she dried herself off, she heard a female staff calling out to her from Carlton's bedchamber. "Is Madame PJ dressed? May I bring you anything?"

Priscilla crossed into the bedroom to see which staff it was. "Oh! It's you, Melissa. And how are you today?"

"Melissa's fine, Madame PJ. Let me help you dry off." She hurriedly grabbed hold of one end of the towel and began drying Priscilla's backside. Momentarily she stared at the scars on Priscilla's neck and right shoulder that she sustained from the terrorist attack back during the presidential election campaign.

Sensing that Melissa was staring at her scars, Priscilla turned around and looked into her eyes. "Oh, Melissa, Girlfriend, I've long since learned to live with all that. Mostly though, it's just good to be alive." She smiled but then said firmly, "Stop fussing over me. I'm just fine."

Before Priscilla could say another word, Melissa said, "I can bring your clothes in here if you like." She dropped her end of the towel, went out of the bedroom, and quickly returned with garments over one of her arms and Priscilla's newly-polished riding boots in her other hand.

Priscilla smiled as Melissa helped her dress. "How'd you know what I'd like to wear today?" Priscilla had yet to understand that good household staff were first and foremost acutely aware of their masters' and mistresses' likes and dislikes. Melissa had already observed that the new mistress liked simple, understated clothes and was fairly consistent in her attire, and cuisine, too.

"Why, Madame PJ," she said, "everyone scrambles to serve you. You're so easy to please."

Priscilla looked surprised. *Easy to please*? *Really*? Was that how she seemed to the household staff?

Melissa helped Priscilla don her undergarments. Then she held open a gray silk blouse for her to put her arms through and helped her pull a matching cashmere sweater over her head and arms. Finally, she helped her pull up a pair of woolen slacks and then her riding boots. Melissa had correctly assumed that Priscilla would want to go riding after breakfast.

Priscilla eagerly headed downstairs, where she expected to see the whole family and all of the servants assembled, ready to tease her for sleeping late. But when she walked into the family room, she saw only Father and Lady Chelsea.

Father approached her almost immediately. He held her close. He smelled her hair. "Fresh out of the shower, eh?"

Priscilla returned his smile, thinking how handsome Carlton would probably look when he reached his father's age, early-to-middle seventies. He had that same thick wavy hair, nearly touching his shoulders, but with a splattering of gray around the edges, and his alluring Mediterranean complexion was smooth, barely any wrinkles in sight. *Great genes.*

"My favorite daughter-in-law. You're such a godsend. Bless you, my child. Bless you." Then Father released his hold of her and left her alone with his wife.

Priscilla stood still in her tracks as Father retreated. "Goodness gracious! What was that all about?"

Lady Chelsea smiled but did not answer the question. "Hungry?" Then she gently led Priscilla down the corridor to the dining room.

As Priscilla obliged, she was not sure what she had done to be fussed over. But then she remembered how, when she first met Lady Chelsea and Father, she felt like she was being moved about a virtual game board. This time she did not resist. But she did ask where Carlton and everybody else were.

"Carlton's out with Ramses on the grounds. Carlton wanted to see everything and also speak to all the staff. They'll be out for the remainder of the day."

"And our shrink, Dr. Chisholm?"

"I believe he's touring the winery. Then I think he's going downtown for some reason or another." Lady Chelsea patted Priscilla's arm. "So it's just the two of us."

Since Priscilla wanted to break her silence about her secret plan—to open her new business venture in New York City—she readily agreed. "Wonderful! And have I got something to tell you!" But she had yet to surmise that her mother-in-law had something to tell her, too.

As they proceeded toward the dining room, Lady Chelsea expressed her gratitude to Priscilla for helping with Carlton's recovery from amnesia. She added that she and the whole family wanted the newlyweds to be as comfortable as possible while Carlton completed his recuperation and while Priscilla "got back to her old self again."

Priscilla thought that was kind of all of them, and she said as much. "You are so kind." But then her eyes widened as they entered the dining room and she saw the buffet overflowing with an assortment of seafood: shrimp, lobster, and crabmeat, as well as onion soup, cheeses, nuts, fruits, various kinds of bread, and both wine and hot drinks.

Lady Chelsea gently kissed her cheek and said, "A bountiful breakfast for a young woman who has shown forth herself beyond measure."

"Oh, Lady Chelsea, you shouldn't have," Priscilla said, sounding like her nephew Germane when what he really meant to say was, "Gee, how'd you know what I really like to eat?"

Lady Chelsea's social skills were usually so acute that she had a sixth sense about how to engineer every little conversation. But this time she failed to understand that Priscilla only had eyes and ears for the buffet, so as she broached the subject she was intent on discussing, soberly she said, "PJ, we *know*."

But Priscilla was studying the spread—*Hmm. What do I eat first?*—and hardly listening. "You know *what*?"

"PJ, President Hollingsworth called us. He shared just enough information with Father and me to let us know how proud he is of what he called your 'service to your country.'" Lady Chelsea paused and looked meaningfully at her daughter-in-law. *Service! Country!* Father himself had similarly been acknowledged by another president for his own "remarkable service to his country."

Besides, Lady Chelsea and Father were astute enough to know that the United States President did not just make casual telephone calls and meaningless compliments. She and Father were also aware that the president knew lots more than Priscilla did about the Bernhardts' tradition of government service. On that note, she also assumed it would be a while before Priscilla found out about all that. But for now, it was important that this newest member of their distinguished family begins to understand that they shared a certain noblesse oblige at the highest level.

However, Priscilla was more interested in gobbling down the seafood than hearing about family secrets about service to their country. She picked up a piece of shrimp and popped the whole thing in her mouth. She loved seafood above all foods. She could not resist another piece and then a third. "Hmm. Hmm. Good!" She said at one point. Then she filled a big plate with more shrimp and lobster and crabmeat before sitting down and tucking into it.

For a quick moment, she looked up from her overflowing plate and said, "I am so sorry, Lady Chelsea. You wanted to talk, and here I am feeding my face. But I had no idea how hungry I was." Then she held a cup of steaming hot tea to her lips and blew on it.

As Lady Chelsea dotingly smiled and watched her eat, she thought about how discreet she was: that Priscilla could not break her vows of silence about her work as a government intelligence agent.

But Priscilla was remembering that Lady Chelsea had said something about the president having called. *The president phoned! Not another mission!* She remembered when she first arrived with the amnesiac-ridden Carlton and told everyone that she was refusing all calls, especially from Washington, D.C. She had wanted to expend all her time and energy helping her "darling Carlton" recover. But she also thought, *Surely they don't expect me to go off on another mission?* Then another thought: *Nah, the president never calls me himself. Those calls always come from inside the agency.* By "the agency," she meant the CIA. She relaxed. But, man alive, did she keep stuffing her face with that delectable seafood!

To let on that she had been listening, she blurted out: "Please don't tell me that those folks from Washington are trying to reach me. If any of them calls back, including the president, I'm not in, OK?"

Lady Chelsea, however, was patient. "PJ, dear, finish with your luncheon and then let's talk. There's something I need to tell you."

Priscilla absently nodded and replenished her plate. Eventually, she pushed away from her plate. "So, tell me. What's on your mind?"

"PJ," began her mother-in-law, "Father and I could not be happier that you've joined the ranks of the long-standing Bernhardt tradition *in service to your country.*"

Priscilla dabbed at her lips with her large cloth napkin and stared thoughtfully at Lady Chelsea. She now knew that somehow her in-laws had found out, or maybe even had just guessed, that she was an agent of sorts with the United States government. She supposed they must have already known, at the least had suspected, for quite some time about Carlton's service as well. But what exactly had her mother-in-law meant when she said that Father, too, had been "in service our country?" She had also said something about a "Bernhardt family tradition." Either way, Priscilla was not about to press the issue. At least now she had some clue as to why Father had been so affectionate with her in the family room, that it was not just about how she had aided in Carlton's recovery from amnesia. At least some of it had related to her in-laws' knowledge that she was somehow involved in government service. At that, Priscilla smiled to herself. But she knew something else. Carlton had told not just his parents but the kitchen staff, too, about her love for all things sea-food.

But there was one more surprise in the offing.

"I'm a little surprised," Priscilla eventually said, "that no one told me until now about the president calling. I guess they took my orders not to be disturbed by any phone calls very, very seriously. But tell me, am I right in assuming that there was only that *one* call from the White House? Any other calls I need to know about?"

"Just the one from the president," said Lady Chelsea. But then she stopped and reconsidered. "Oh, yes, my dear. I am so sorry, but yes. I forgot to tell you that late last night, when you and Carlton were … engaged upstairs, there was one other phone call. Julia called from your office in Ohio. Come to think of it, and she said it was 'very important and that you'd want to hear about this one.' But we thought, you know, that you and Carlton, well…." Her voice trailed off.

Priscilla's eyebrows rose. That particular message caught her attention. "Julia? Very important?" She pushed further away from her plate. Her teacup situated beside her plate raddled as she pushed her chair away from the table and stood up abruptly.

Lady Chelsea stared at Priscilla. She wondered whether she and the other family members had made a mistake not telling her about Julia's call. Then she watched as Priscilla sprinted out the dining room without even excusing herself, at that.

5

Welcome to 'The City'

Panting from having raced up the colossal marble staircase and then down the corridor to her bedchamber, Priscilla picked up the telephone from the nightstand. She dialed the numbers to her Columbus-based home office. She got reception.

"*Julia? Julia!*" she shouted, "What's going on?" Without allowing Julia to respond, she said, "Lady Chelsea just told me about your call."

But before Julia answered Priscilla's questions, she said, "So very good to hear that Carlton has recovered. Can't get any better news than that."

"Oh, Julia. You're so thoughtful. I suppose whoever answered your call must have briefed you on Carlton's recovery?"

"Yes, Girlfriend. Now to answer your question," she paused for special effect. "Brace yourself, kiddo. We're on, and that's in New York City, too!"

"*On*, to what?" Priscilla interrupted Julia.

"The Metropolitan Mu—"

"The Metropolitan *what!*"

"The Metropolitan Museum of Art!" Julia laughed. "Yes, The *Met* wants to sign on."

"My goodness. Julia! What could *possibly* be going on at the *Met*?"

"International fraud. Possible art theft, too." Julia snickered.

Priscilla remained quiet. She wanted to hear more.

"Girlfriend," Julia said, "this is high-cotton crime. Right up your alley, eh? And, oh yeah, someone named Shane Carpenter said, 'The Met needs a public relations consultant of *your* discretion.'"

"Really!"

"'Really.'"

Priscilla thought about her new client. She also thought about how little she knew about art. Or so she thought.

Priscilla felt somewhat intimidated for a moment. *Why, I've never even been inside the Met! How the devil am I going to represent a client about whom I am so unfamiliar? And all those highbrow board members? Yikes*! Then, before she knew it, she remembered that she did know a little something about art, well, more than a little something. Just three years ago, while attending a regularly scheduled meeting of the Bernhardt Foundation for Boarding Schools for Zimbabwean and South African Girls, she and Carlton visited the Chapungu Sculpture Park. She smiled as she recalled how amazed she had been at the sight of all those humungous stone sculptures on the park grounds; some depicted human forms, whereas others were abstract works of art. She learned of famous artists she had never heard of before, such as Joram Mariga, "the father of Zimbabwean sculpture." Mostly though, she remembered a massive figurative sculpture by Joseph Ndandarika, titled *Magic Bird.* Ndankarika had worked in the tradition of Michelangelo, who believed that spirits inhabited rock formations and that, as sculptors, they unleashed the soul in the stone. And so, too, did the Shona believe that spirits inhabited stone and other elements of nature. Then she remembered the tour guide telling her that another artist, namely John Takawira, had created a much smaller stone carving of serpentine, a regal Bateleur Eagle—Zimbabwe's national emblem—presented to Pope John Paul II.

Priscilla's confidence gradually restored when she remembered, again with a smile, when she and her mom, Liza, had visited the Holy Land and toured the Grand Egyptian Museum on the Giza Plateau near Cairo's pyramids. It was there they had seen that incredibly magnificent, fully intact sarcophagus of King Tut and that impressive gold mask, among numerous other artifacts and antiquities.

More recollections surfaced. The Sistine Chapel, the Palace Versailles, and many other well-known sites of unique art came to mind.

As it turned out, Priscilla's momentary intimidation had been just that, momentary. But suddenly she remembered something more. She remembered that Senator Callahan, and later, Carlton had often admonished her and insisted: "Act like you belong," and she was about to do just that.

And so it was that at this particular juncture, what she really liked was the sound of "international art fraud. High society, wealth, white-collar crime!" The international press corps would be all over it. What a launch for the opening of her branch office in New York City! What a feat for a public relations consultant heretofore known as *a PR consultant extraordinaire.*

By this point, Priscilla sat on the edge of her bed. She held the telephone tightly and listened while Julia brought her up to date on the situation at the Met. For a long time, she listened as Julia described the curious scene with the "mysterious-looking couple." Then she nearly laughed out loud at the story about the volunteer docent having noticed something "strange, something that just did not look right" about Chagall's *Soleil dans le Ciel de Saint-Paul.* She listened more intensely as Julia told her about the call from Shane Carpenter, someone who Julia noted seemed to downplay the events of the day, but who had added, "'But, just in case, the museum would prefer to err on the side of *proactivity*, hence this call to *your* firm. Our sources,'" Julia concluded Shane's message, "'tell us that Ms. Austin-Bernhardt is known for *discretion.*'"

"Hmm," Priscilla put her curiosity into words. "Sounds to me like we've got a scandal in the making." She stopped talking.

After a momentary silence, Julia asked, "Missy? You still there?"

"Yeah. Give me a moment." Then, tersely, she rattled off a list of instructions. Julia should call Shane back. Priscilla would reserve her contact until later, maybe when the matter of fees was on the table, but not now. At this point, she wanted to behave as if she had already signed on and was preparing for a press conference to address the matter head-on. *Yeah*, she thought. That was her customary way of doing things. She decided to wrap the situation at the Met together with her Midtown Manhattan PR branch office rollout and let the new branch manager make the announcement.

"Julia," she ended her instructions, "tell the new branch manager we're looking at one week tops."

Finally, she hung up the telephone.

She stared into space as her mind continued to race. Everything was happening much faster than she had anticipated. The Met was one hell-of-an-impressive client. She knew she had to play this one just right.

Besides, she knew how ludicrous it would be for her to rush to the City this morning. And she certainly did not wish to appear too eager. Or too available. The groundwork had already been laid. She had just ordered Julia to put her junior staff in place, this Ruth woman as branch manager, and another—whose name she could not remember—as office manager. With Julia on-site, all was well.

Priscilla thought about all that she had done over the course of the past four weeks while her darling Carlton was recovering from his bout with amnesia. But she had yet to reveal her new business venture to the folks here. Why, she had not even told anyone about how Julia had shuttled back and forth from Columbus to New York, getting everything ready for whatever event or new client happened into her new PR firm.

Julia had found excellent office space and secured an equally excellent skeletal staff. Priscilla was also pleased that Julia had already informed the new staff about the case at the Met. She was even more pleased when she learned about the comparatively peerless background of Ruth Steiner and her connections with the world of "highly-valued works of art," as Priscilla was prone to say of masterpieces. She was particularly excited, delighted was more like it, that she had just given Julia the go-ahead for what might best be construed as the Opening Act in what was rapidly becoming known as "the mysterious affair at the Met."

She wore her customary smirk as she thought about how New Yorkers would react to what was about to happen. Then she heard herself saying, "You go, Girl!"

Priscilla would later reflect on the first press conference, which she deemed the Opening Act about "the mysterious affair at the Met." And even though she herself had not been there, she was perfectly content with Julia's handling of everything, especially her selection of this Ruth Steiner as her second-in-charge. Although Ruth's résumé was outlined in the press kit, most reporters who covered the New York art beat already knew much of her story. She was a fourth-generation New York City family with deep roots in the garment industry through the family business, Steiner Clothiers. More importantly, many reporters already knew her from her previous work with the media. But her résumé as a credentialed arts scholar was most impressive: Columbia University, the University of Oxford, and the Sorbonne, as well as a stint at the Hebrew University of Jerusalem where she had studied art and archaeology and honed up on her Hebrew. Nor did it hurt that she had experience at the Louvre and, more recently, as a fine arts consultant to various museums.

The atmosphere in the Met boardroom could not have been more intense. Anger and imperious demands filled the space. Normally this was not the kind of reception that Priscilla cultivated with news reporters. She typically conducted such sessions in a relatively large open and public space, but not this time. This time she had told Julia to instruct Ruth to set the press session up in the Met's boardroom, the reason for which would soon be made plain to all concerned.

"In so doing," she had told Julia, "this way, we control the setting, and possibly the way the message is imparted." She had also intimated, "Besides, we don't want anybody getting the wrong idea, you know, that something really bad has happened. We also kinda want the selected group of reporters to think there's something *special* about them."

To say the news reporters were a tad upset with the delay in starting the press conference and that they had not seen any of the respective parties—P.J. Austin-Bernhardt, Ignatius Devoe and Shane Carpenter— would be an understatement.

"My God, it's going on a quarter of an hour past the start time! What gives?" an irate news reporter from a local television station shouted amid the others assembled.

"Yeah. And where's P.J. Austin-Bernhardt? Shouldn't *she* be here?" said another reporter.

"PJ? What of Ignatius and Shane? I haven't seen the likes of either of them," yet someone else blurted out.

While the anxious gathering of news reporters fretted, Ruth exited Ignatius Devoe's executive office, where Julia had compiled the final documents for the session. Besides, Iggy was not there, anyway.

As Ruth strolled down the corridor, as casually as she could, she could not help overhearing some of the outcries from inside the boardroom.

Impressively garbed in her black pantsuit—another takeaway of Priscilla's influence in terms of branding—she held her breath as she soon stepped inside the boardroom. She paused for a moment and let her eyes scope the assemblage. Then she stepped to the head of the conference table where a press kit and her statement were positioned on top of a small lectern.

She picked up one of the sheets of paper, but put it back down because some of the news reporters were still blurting out questions and making unfounded statements about the situation at the Met. The next thing she knew, she raised her hands high, palms facing outward, and shook her head. She spoke as calmly as she could under the apparently cantankerous circumstances.

"Good people, the sooner you calm down, the sooner we can begin *or not*." With those last two words, even the most boisterous among them shut up.

In control now, Ruth then said, "May I ask your patience, as Alfrieda—the newly hired office manager at P.J. Austin and Associates, Inc.'s Manhattan PR branch office—passes out some information that is *not* in your press packets."

While Ruth set the stage for what was plainly something unexpected by the news reporters, many of them ripped open their press packets, scanned through the documents and spoke out loud, some even unknowingly.

"Interpol!"

"MI5!"

"You have got to be kidding me!"

Ruth could see the expressions on the reporters' faces brighten. Their eyes glistened, too. So, continued setting the stage:

"By now you're all aware that we were careful not transmitting any of this information over the wire service. This material, as you can now see, is sensitive information." Ruth nodded at the astonished expressions of the reporters hurriedly leafing through the material. "The international intelligence community is involved. Why," she caught her breath and continued, "even you can appreciate the gravity of the situation."

"All I ask is that you allow me to walk you through the series of events as they've been shared with me. For, only this morning was I cleared to share this information with you, which is partly the reason for the seeming 'delay in this press conference.' And I swear to you…." Ruth stared at the astonished expressions of the select gathering of approximately twenty-odd, mostly white male news reporters who represented the various media, some even the international news outlets, as they continued anxiously leafing through the redacted documents that Alfrieda had just given them.

Ruth paused again to let what she had just said sink in, that the redacted documents they held in their hands bore the insignia of international law enforcement *and* intelligence agencies: "Interpol," "MI5," "CIA," "DGSE," "EYP," and "FBI."

Thrill replaced tension. The news reporters knew they were onto one heck of a story.

Except for the sound of pages turning, sudden silence permeated the boardroom.

Ruth cleared her throat.

As she began summarizing the story behind what had recently happened at the Met, she occasionally referred to museum officials, such as Ignatius Devoe and Shane Carpenter, but not a single word about Priscilla's whereabouts. Instead, she concentrated on the meaning of the redacted documents in the press kit. While Priscilla probably would have made a grand, ad-libbed story-telling of this background, Ruth, perhaps wisely, instead chose to read from her prepared statement, which was among the materials that Alfrieda had just handed out.

With a small smile, she began. "This is a long story, and a fascinating one. But it's complex. So we hope our press release and the supporting materials provide ample background for what you might need."

Then she read aloud:

> Our story begins in the mid-1940s during Nazi-occupied Paris, France. A young man named Thibaut Francois Moreaux, once heir to one of the wealthiest Parisian families, embarked on a criminal career involving highly-valued works of art. As he became known, Thibaut Francois set up his atelier in Montmartre, the 18th arrondissement of Paris, where some of the most eminent creative artists and writers, such as Vincent Van Gogh, Pablo Picasso, and Ernest Hemingway, had once lived and worked. But Thibaut Francois's work was forgery, and it involved Nazi cooperation and Jewish exploitation. His scheme began with high-quality forgeries or missing or stolen works of high value. He was aware of the Nazis' confiscation of

artwork from European museums and private art collectors, especially that of Jews. And he knew of the Nazi's smuggling operation to Austria and Germany, as well as to Asia, America, and other parts of the world, that, despite the so-called Nero Decree, which ordered the destruction of all German possessions, if Adolf Hitler died or Germany fell.

Then, as if she were mindful of something more, she looked up and went off script: "Never mind the role played by the Soviet Union near the end of World War II."

And although the reporters, perplexed as they were, looked from one to another, Ruth nodded at Alfrieda, who pressed a button on a projector. The reporters then turned their attention to three colorful images that were projected on the big screen while Ruth continued:

So here you see that Thibaut Francois took advantage of what the Nazis had done, confiscating art masterpieces, primarily from Jewish estates, and then forging them. He bilked the Nazis, too, which is why he'd earned a reputation as being 'shrewd and disreputable.' For he'd somehow managed to steal some of the previously stolen Jewish collections from the Nazis, forge excellent reproductions, and then sell both the authentic paintings, as well as the 'excellent reproductions' to art collectors the world over—which included Asia, South America, and right here in America.

While Ruth talked, the news reporters' eyes were glued to the three paintings labeled "Picassos" on the big screen. So now they knew about at least three of the paintings in question. Ruth continued her remarks:

> Chief among those targeted paintings were these three: *Nude: Green Leaves and Bust*, *Bullfight: Death of the Toreador*, and *The Death of Casagemas*.

Ruth took a deep breath as she neared her conclusion. Then she finished what Priscilla and the international law enforcement officers and the intelligence officials had authorized her to report.

> Hear me now. I realize this is a lot to absorb at one go of it. But the fascinating part is that both the 'excellent reproductions' and the authentic masterpieces— were sold all over the world, and some ended up in museums. And until now it has been anybody's guess who has the high-quality fakes and who has the genuine masterpieces.

She exhaled. "And *that*, everyone, is what 'the mysterious affair at the Met' is all about."

At no point did Ruth even mention the three masterpieces in question at the Met. The closest her presentation connected to the Met was her report about the "shrewd and disreputable" Thibaut Francois. Neither did any of the reporters pose follow-up questions about what had brought on the "high alert" in the first place. They didn't even press her about Priscilla's apparent absence. Plainly, having focused on the big picture overshadowed all else.

Then, finally, with a big grin on her face, Ruth said, "That concludes our press conference, and, as my new boss is prone to saying, 'when we know more, so, too, will you.'"

Then she did a casual about-face and left the boardroom, followed by reporters screaming out questions.

Later that same day, Priscilla called her new second-in-charge and congratulated her on "a job well done," and for what Julia had said was a "great debut performance."

Ruth thanked her new boss and told her what had happened shortly after her quick exit from the boardroom. She told Priscilla about how she had sprinted through the massive museum and across the marble floor of the main lobby, past the octagonal-shaped reception station, and lumbered out onto the sidewalk, where she had leaned against the wall of the façade, and finally taken a deep breath.

"PJ, I don't know how you do it," Ruth eventually said. "I'd just given those bastards the story of a lifetime, and they still weren't satisfied."

Priscilla laughed and said, "Ruth, the more information you give reporters, the more they want to know. Welcome to my world!"

6

The NYC Branch Office

As the Bernhardt private jet coursed through the sky from New Hampshire to New York City, Priscilla stared out her window at the big fluffy white clouds. Ever so introspective, her mind wandered deep and discursive.

It had been a week or so since Ruth's press conference at the Met, and Priscilla could not quite let go of her lingering attitude about this "shrewd and disreputable" fellow—Thibaut Francois. She quietly pronounced his name and thought, *Whatever.* She thought about how she had not shared all of what she knew with Ruth, nor with anybody else, not by a long shot. Specifically, Priscilla had intel that suggested the descendants of at least three of those collectors of fine art somewhere in North America, South America, and Asia were uncertain whether they even possessed the "excellent reproductions" or the genuine Picassos.

And she knew that, although the descendants of those same three families had been aware of Thibaut Francois's treachery—for nearly five decades—they had never once publicized the fact that they even possessed these particularly questionable works of art.

Yet Priscilla surmised that, given recent revelations in the media, mainly from Ruth Steiner's press conference, it might be increasingly difficult for the descendants holding those paintings to keep their worries to themselves. Those who possessed Picasso's *Nude: Green Leaves and Bust, Bullfight: Death of the Toreador,* and *The Death of Casagemas* were probably wondering how to authenticate their particular Picasso discreetly. But Priscilla seriously doubted that any of them would come forth and admit to their concerns. What they would do, more likely, was wait another fifty-odd years before trying to sell whatever they had, fakes or masterpieces.

As she thought about it, Priscilla could care less about who had the fakes or the masterpieces. Ruth's press conference had accomplished her purpose of diverting attention away from whatever had happened at the Met on that cold and rainy day in May. Instead, now, reporters were hot on the trail of the nefarious Thibaut Francois, as well as a new character—his son Artemis Thibaut—who had come to light just yesterday, along with what sounded like three more at-risk paintings. Great! Mission accomplished! But she reflected that even she still had no idea of the scandal's dimensions and the extent of the shrewd and disreputable Thibaut Francois's role. Other than this unholy father and his son Artemis Thibaut, who knew how many forgeries there actually were?

"Hold that thought," she said to herself because just then, the flight attendant was at her side, noting that the flight would be landing soon. It was time to fasten her seatbelt.

Priscilla put aside her ruminations about the looming art scandal and prepared to disembark.

New York City! Here I come!

As Priscilla, in high spirit, strutted Bette Davis-like down Fifth Avenue toward her new Midtown Manhattan office, little did she know about the eager New York City news reporters who had already been staked out more than a block away from her new office at the intersection of Forty-Second Street. They approached her, waving their microphones and with their cameras rolling. For nearly half a long New York City block, Priscilla simply smiled into the cameras' lenses, occasionally saying, "Good morning, everybody. How's it going?" A couple of times, she even pointed her index finger at an unnamed news reporter and said, "And a-top-of-the-morning to you." She used that ploy to avert suspicion that something was in the offing. But she knew that tactic would not stave them off for long.

"Ah, come on, PJ, give us your take on 'the mysterious affair at the Met,'" a newspaper reporter begged.

At that, Priscilla stopped her casual stride. "Okay, folks, since I'm new to the New York City beat, how 'bout we establish some protocols? I'm sure you're aware, I like to speak to the news media in one setting. *And* I like reporters to introduce themselves when addressing me. Then, after we get better acquainted, we can dispense with the formalities."

The eager New York City news reporters recorded every word she spoke, and they took close-ups of her smiling face, too.

"All right, Ms. PJ. I'm David Horowitz with *ABC News*. Can you give us your take on 'the mysterious affair at the Met?'?"

Still smiling, "Thank you, David Horowitz, with *ABC News*." Then, as politely as she could, she pointed to the revolving door behind him, which that reporter seemed to have unintentionally blocked. Quickly then, he and the other eager reporters immediately opened up a way for Priscilla and everyone else to enter. Then, just as she was about to walk through the revolving door, she turned back around and gave David and the other reporters something else they appreciated.

"Sorry for the delay," she said. "But please give me some time—an hour, maybe—to check in with my staff." She stepped aside and allowed yet more people to enter through the revolving door. "Then meet me back here in the far eastern sector of the lobby." She pointed to her right, winked, and added, "I've already secured clearance for you to set up your camera equipment in that space. But please do *not* violate that privilege. This is, after all, a *private* office building, so we need to govern ourselves, accordingly." Then she concluded with her famous declaration: "Deal?"

"*Deal*," each of the eager reporters shouted back.

"Heck, yeah, lady. Heck, yeah."

These New York City news reporters had heard from their colleagues in other parts of the country that Priscilla was fairly "approachable," but now they were about to experience her "approachability" for themselves.

While Priscilla and many others walked across the lobby floor toward the impressively designed bronze elevators, the eager news reporters flocked where she had indicated and set up their camera equipment.

Meanwhile, seven floors above, Priscilla did not try to conceal her satisfaction as the elevator opened to her new fully-furnished office, which was almost identical to her Columbus-based home office. This was hardly by accident. Julia had sent Ruth and Alfrieda photographs and floor plans from their Ohio headquarters. It had not been hard to decorate her New York office in kind.

Priscilla stepped over the threshold and exuberantly whirled round and round. Then she stood still and took a longer look at what she could see: the welcoming front desk, the firm's name painted gold on the wall, the well-appointed reception area. The color scheme was just like back in Columbus, and so, too, were the furnishings.

Ruth Steiner cleared her throat. She was standing in front of her new boss. They had spoken on the telephone, but she was shy at this first in-person encounter. "I'm Ruth," she said. "And that's Alfrieda, your new office manager, there at her desk."

"Hello, Ruth! Alfrieda!" Priscilla bestowed a welcoming smile on the two women. "So pleased to meet you. I trust we are going to be doing great things together."

Then Ruth continued, "Does this suit Dr. P. J. Austin-Bernhardt's taste? I hope you don't mind, but we thought, that is, Alfrieda and I, that it was more appropriate to install a small dry bar instead of your Baldwin piano here in the reception area. What do *you* think?"

"My goodness," was all that Priscilla could say for a moment. Then, "This all looks wonderful. And, well, I feel so at home here. Even without the piano." She turned to Ruth. "You can drop the formalities. No doctor labels, either. Please, just call me PJ. Or Missy."

Then Ruth looked over at Alfrieda, who now stood behind Priscilla. The two women raised their thumbs in not-so-subtle glee. Both were aware of Priscilla's high-profile persona, but neither had ever worked with her before. But they sensed that already they were off to a great start, indeed.

Other than the dry bar, the only other major difference between her Columbus-based home office and her new office in the City were the floor-to-ceiling mahogany bookshelves. And they were full of books. Earlier, when Priscilla had interviewed Ruth on the phone, they had talked about their shared love of the PBS *Masterpiece Mystery* series and Sir Arthur Conan Doyle, Agatha Christie, Zora Neale Hurston, Nelson DeMille, Ian Fleming, Elizabeth Peters, J. R. R. Tolkien, and Evelyn Waugh. Those authors were represented in this collection, along with the classics of fine art. Ruth had understood how Priscilla liked to close her own information gaps, and evidently she had guessed that her new boss might appreciate her loaning her some of her art books on Bordone, Chagall, and Monet.

When she noticed Priscilla examining some of the spines of the books, she said, "I took the liberty of loaning you a few books on fine art from my collection during my studies at the Sorbonne."

Priscilla smiled with appreciation. "Oh, Ruth, you're so very thoughtful."

Then she heard the boom of a familiar masculine voice. "And so, our boss is back!"

"Jordy!" Priscilla spun around and then ran and gave him a hug.

"My, my, careful now," he said, taking care to hide his surprise that this woman, who generally did not like people touching her, was so warmly and freely touching him. "We don't want the hired help to get the wrong impression."

"Oh, Jordy, it's so good to see you here!"

"Come with me, Miss Prissy," Jordy said as, arm in arm, he steered her away from Ruth down a corridor. Not only were they old chums from back at Prendergast High School, but they had worked together when Jordy and "the other boys" had served as high-powered lobbyists back during Priscilla's time in the Ohio Senate, not to mention their association as government agents of sorts.

As she walked away with Jordy, she looked back over her shoulder at Ruth and said, "We'll talk later."

Then, as they continued along the corridor of the U-shaped office space bordering the south side of the building, Jordy pointed out offices that had already been furnished in preparation for the arrival of "the boys" and the other members of Priscilla's new business venture. He pointed to a larger corner office flooded with light from windows on two sides. "Miss Prissy, since yours is the name and face of the new agency, yours is the biggest and first office in the entire setup. And Ruth's office is right next to yours."

Then Jordy said something Priscilla had not expected, "Tommy's office is next to yours on the other side." He paused, rightly assuming she might have other ideas about the arrangement of the offices.

"But Jordy, I just assumed that Carlton's office would be close—"

At that, Jordy cut her off. "Which is," he explained, "exactly why we thought it best to put him as far away as we could." Tentatively he smiled. By "we," he had referred to his associates in the clandestine CF unit of the CIA—Tommy, Angel Onslow, Carlton, and himself, that is, Jordy. "Things being what they are between the two of you. I mean, married and all, you need a little breathing room on the job." Jordy was well aware that he was the only one among their group of friends and associates who could get away with treating Priscilla in such a familiar way because of their longstanding association.

Priscilla nodded. Clearly "the boys" from the special operatives unit with the CIA, which she had been working with for some years, had already assumed they were part of her new setup. *Fine by me*, she thought, *at least for now. Why not integrate their intelligence-gathering and security expertise in this new branch office?* Then she thought, *We can work out the details later.*

After she thought about what Jordy had just said, uncharacteristically, she relented. "I suppose you do have a point." She sighed. "Oh, all right, then."

Visibly relieved, Jordy quietly said, almost to himself, "Thank goodness that's over with."

7

Uncovering Deception

Jordy led Priscilla back to her office. It was time to get down to business.

"Missy, I need to bring you up-to-date on the goings-on at the Met." Ruth was already seated in one of the high-back, striped-silk upholstered chairs in front of Priscilla's desk. Jordy slouched down in the matching chair beside her.

As Priscilla walked around her desk and sat in her executive swivel chair, Jordy spoke somewhat authoritatively when he said, "Take a look at the contents of the folder in front of you."

Priscilla opened the folder and saw photographs of the "mysterious-looking couple" that had been retrieved from the few frames of footage in the museum's surveillance cameras.

"Now," Jordy insisted, "take a look at their *real* photos and the attachments."

While Priscilla did as Jordy instructed, she felt her pulse quicken. Her temperature rose, too, especially when she saw the familiar insignia for Interpol, the DGSE (French intelligence), the EYP (Greek intelligence), the CIA, the FBI, and MI5 inscribed on letterheads containing the original photos of that same couple. Then, leafing through the dossiers, she saw the names of some persons of interest in the case: Ignatius Devoe, a.k.a. Ignatius Devonshire; Gaylord Millsap Omiros, a.k.a. Gaylord Millsap; Thibaut Francois, a.k.a. Thibaut Francois Moreaux; and Artemis Thibaut, a.k.a. Artemis Thibaut Millsap Moreaux. There were others, too, who were suspected of being involved in some way, including close associates of certain members of the Met's board of trustees. She read that the so-called "mysterious-looking couple" had been identified as Artemis Thibaut and Adrienne Hopkins, a.k.a. Arianna Cooper. Both were notorious criminals, known for art forgery and theft of some of the most priceless art in the Western world.

This time, when Priscilla returned to that listing of persons of interest, she read aloud the one name that had shocked her the most: "Ignatius Devoe." She could feel her blood heating up and rushing to her head; her earlobes burnt even more. Shane Carpenter—the executive director at the Met and the one who had contacted Julia to engage Priscilla on this case—worked for Ignatius Devoe, the Met's board chair. At that very moment, she realized that Shane, and Ignatius for sure, and possibly the whole darn board of trustees at the Met, had knowingly deceived her. She was not amused. *Surely, someone on that doggone board already knew this.* Her eyes narrowed. *What's their bloody game? What's this mess all about, anyway?*

Nervously, Ruth, observing the changes in her boss's demeanor, spoke her piece, anyway. "PJ," she began, "maybe it's best that you *not* mention any of this to the New York City press corps. In fact," she continued, "we were sort of hoping to—"

Jordy cut in before Ruth could finish her sentence.

"You see, Priscilla," he said, "we've yet to confirm whether any of the three works of art have, in fact, been tampered with, or even stolen." Jordy was the only one among the newly formed agency who occasionally called Priscilla by her given name; she likewise sometimes slipped and called him by his high school nickname, Bart.

Priscilla eyed the two of them, who were obviously bracing for her to go berserk or something of the sort. Instead she nodded, took their concern as a much-needed warning, and pulled herself up short.

"So-o," she asked, "are we looking at a possible switch?" Then she answered her own question, "Nah, not enough time to have switched the paintings. But what if?"

"'What if' what?" Ruth asked as her antennae rose.

"What if our two bandits know something that we don't know?" Priscilla postulated, "Such as the fact that they're such good forgers that the Met doesn't want anyone to know the three works of art under review are, in fact, forgeries?"

"Since that has yet to be confirmed … not so sure where you're going," Jordy said.

This time, Ruth, acutely aware of the dark side of even highly reputable museums, expounded. "I think I know, Jordy," she said without even meeting his eyes, "I've heard that sometimes a museum may choose not to reveal to the public when highly-valued works of art have been tampered with, or even stolen. Ergo, 'now you see it, now you don't.'"

"No-o!" Jordy blurted out.

By this point, Priscilla was coming to terms with the realization that, in all probability, at least some of the Met's board of trustees had not been forthcoming with her. She felt a sort of nausea set in. *But why?* Silently she pondered the reason for Ignatius Devoe's and Shane Carpenter's deception. She did not know the board members well enough to determine which ones were in on this shady deal. But since she did not want to share her suspicions with Jordy and Ruth just yet, she did her best to hang in with the rest of their conversation.

After listening to the other two puzzling out possible scenarios, Priscilla spoke again. "Here's an idea." She proceeded as if she were laying out a logical argument in a college debate. "Seems to me that maybe museums err on the side of discretion. If word ever leaked that some highly-valued works of art have, in fact, been tampered with, or, heaven forbid, stolen, there goes that museum's reputation as a good steward. So the staff, and the board, maybe keep quiet while their insurance agents go on the prowl to reclaim the original artwork." She looked from Ruth to Jordy. "I've got a funny feeling we might have such a case on our hands. 'Cause something just doesn't feel right." Mentally, she reproached herself: *There, now, I've finally let on that I know I've been deceived.*

"*Now* I get it," Jordy said. "And suppose the museum is pressing Artemis Thibaut and Adrienne Hopkins to return the originals, and this pair is *not* pleased about that. So, maybe they're forcing the Met's hands—with that little red, silk handkerchief prank—to take them more seriously."

"I like how you're thinking," Ruth said, eyeing him with new respect.

But more was coming as Jordy's honed intelligence-gathering instincts kicked into full gear. "Meanwhile, how far back do we need to examine the museum's surveillance footage? I'd like to see the original, full footage. That scanty stuff they gave us from that chilly, dreary, rainy day in May produced nada."

"I agree, Jordy. I do agree with you on that note," Priscilla said. "But the operative question is: how do we proceed *without* letting on to them that we're even *onto* them?"

Then, Ruth provided an answer that seemed to bring some closure to both of their concerns: "We *could* insist they provide us with the *minutes* of their board meetings from, say, the past *three* or more years."

Priscilla and Jordy gave each other a knowing look.

"Do it," Priscilla ordered.

"Consider it done," Jordy added. Usually Priscilla flinched whenever someone used that expression, which her former boss, Ohio Senator Daniel P. Callahan, had often used. But not this time. This time she gave Jordy a pass, so to speak.

After the threesome figured out what they thought they needed to start solving the case—which, by the way, would turn out to be easier said than done—they began concocting a story to feed to the eager New York City news reporters. They had to take care that it was a good enough story so that the media could chew on it for a while.

Then, most unexpectedly, Priscilla stood up abruptly and declared: "I've got it!" She picked up one of the sheets of paper containing the international intelligence agencies' insignia with the authentic photograph of Artemis Thibaut. Then she looked at a photo in the Met's directory. She waved Artemis Thibaut's photo in the air and said, "This is the connection. Artemis Thibaut *Millsap* Moreaux is related to Gaylord *Millsap* Omiros, one of the board members!"

Somewhat apologetic, "Oh, but PJ," Ruth said, "just because they have similar last names does *not* mean they're *related*."

But Ruth lacked Priscilla's and Jordy's intelligence-gathering prowess. For Priscilla had not based her declaration on the simple fact the two people shared similar last names. That really would have been merely circumstantial. Instead, what had mattered to her was that there, before her very eyes, was an unmistakable *resemblance* between the two men.

Jordy leaned over and peered down at the sheet of paper that Priscilla held in one hand and the photo that she pointed to in the Met's directory that lay open on her desk. Then he gave voice to what Priscilla's eyes had seen. "This resemblance is too much of a mere coincidence."

He stood beside Priscilla and arranged the two images, side by side. Gaylord Millsap Omiros' photo was one among the twenty-three board members in the Met directory that Ruth had assembled for her previously. As Jordy continued examining the two pictures, his mind raced back to his earlier examination of the photographs when he, too, had thought that he had seen doubles. But that was when the photos were separated. Then, he said, "Looks to me that they could easily be *twins*."

Then he asked Priscilla if he could use her phone. When she nodded, he said, "Give me a minute." Jordy dialed the familiar number of one of his contacts at the CIA headquarters at Langley.

Ruth meanwhile leaned over and stared at the two photographs: "Oh, how'd I miss that?"

"Well, Girlfriend," Priscilla said matter-of-factly, "someone once told me, 'We often overlook the obvious.'"

In short order, Jordy had all the validation he needed to confirm Priscilla's declaration.

But just then they heard someone banging on Priscilla's office door.

Priscilla wore an expression of having been rudely interrupted but said, "Enter."

The door to her office flung open, and none other than Macy Stoner, the kinetic, prominent defense attorney, also one of Priscilla's very best friends, burst into Priscilla's office as if she had been expected. Priscilla rushed to Macy and hugged her warmly. The two women laughed and softly slapped each other's cheeks.

Macy tugged at the lapels of Priscilla's stylish, black, pin-striped signature pantsuit. "New, eh? California? New York? Ohio? Paris?"

"Loehmann's, White Plains."

"I haven't shopped at Loehmann's in nearly three months. Next time, call me."

Ruth and Jordy stared in amazement as these two highly reputable, formidable females behaved like old chums and made plans to go, of all places, *shopping* together.

Priscilla settled back in her chair while Macy assumed some kind of standing power position, bracing herself behind Jordy's chair. She eye-balled him. "So, you're here, too? What gives? You're setting up some sort of detective/security/intelligence agency?

The others smiled blandly, but nobody answered until Priscilla finally broke the silence.

"Macy, pardon my manners. I think introductions are in order."

But Macy proceeded as if she were correcting her friend. "I think we all know one another. Hello, Ruth."

"Hi, Macy," Ruth said.

But Priscilla was not deterred. "Ruth, as Jordy and I are well aware, this is the illustrious Defense Attorney Macy Stoner, known to many as 'the best gosh-darn criminal defense attorney this side of the Granite State.' But I don't think either of you knows that she's also a *member* of the board of trustees at the Met."

Ruth and Jordy repeated in near unison, "*The board of trustees at the Met!*"

"Indeed." Priscilla smiled. She reckoned her colleagues had simply overlooked the familiar names and faces in the Met board directory, such as Macy Stoner and even the board chair Ignatius Devoe. And well, they had.

But there was more to all of this, and this time Jordy was the one who nursed secrets. With Macy among them, this was not the time to tell Priscilla and Ruth—as he had been about to—that he had already had his security team bug Shane Carpenter's office along with a few other offices at the Met. He would let Priscilla know this, of course, even though he suspected she had already surmised that this security measure would have been one of his first acts as soon as Priscilla's firm had been engaged. It had been easy enough to arrange during his preliminary interviews regarding the museum's security system. So Jordy had already listened to conversations between Shane and Ignatius. At the time, however, he had not grasped the fullness of what he had overheard and how it might have related to the case before them. He would have to listen to the tapes again.

Nonetheless, for the time being, as he observed the closeness between Priscilla and Macy, Jordy reminded himself to keep his counsel close. This case had its complexities. *Too many close ties*, he thought. And Jordy was right; man alive, was he right!

But Macy was already off and running in another direction. She gave Priscilla a big smile as if she had some news for her.

Out with it, Priscilla thought.

Macy's smile widened. "I hope I caught you before your meeting downstairs with the press." But her frankness quickly dissipated when she said, "I only just learned about your new business venture and all."

Yeah, sure you did, Priscilla, Ruth, and Jordy all must have thought.

They already knew about the Met board meeting back in May—which Macy had attended—when it was announced that Priscilla's firm would be engaged to handle the PR on the case. So the three of them were aware that Macy had just stretched the truth. But of course no one said a word about this blatant lie. They were even aware of Macy's awareness of the press conference held by Ruth a short while ago.

Priscilla smoothly took over. "So Macy, good as it is to see you, what've *you* got for *us*?"

Without batting an eye, Macy boldly announced: "PJ, folks, I've been retained by Gaylord Millsap Omiros. It seems there just might be a case filed against him." She paused. "By the Met's board of trustees." Then she nodded similar to the way she did in courtrooms when she was about to lower the hammer and said, "So I, myself, have temporarily stepped down from the board, until further notice, that is, while I represent Gaylord."

They all stared at her. One of Priscilla's best friends had just announced that she was representing Gaylord Millsap Omiros, a person of interest in this case. Now they were all sure that they were onto something big, really big. So they all tightened their best poker faces and allowed Macy to roll on with whatever else she wanted them to know.

As it so happened, they also all realized that Macy, *unknowingly*, had just confirmed Priscilla's observation about the remarkable resemblance and the possible relationship between Artemis Thibaut Millsap Moreaux and Gaylord Millsap Omiros.

While Macy rolled on, the others wisely kept their mouths shut, and Priscilla thought, *Poor Macy. She has no idea what she's just walked into.*

But when Macy asked Priscilla if she had leased an apartment in Manhattan yet, and then, without waiting for a reply, offered "to put you in touch with a couple of good realtors in the area. Then again, I do know of a quaint lit—"

Finally, Priscilla cut her off.

"Ah, come on, Girlfriend. Did you forget already? I'm a married woman now. I can't just go off doing whatever I please anymore. But since you asked," Priscilla said with her customary smirk, "I do have my eyes on a nice little brownstone." She paused for effect. "In Harlem!"

Macy's mouth dropped open. "No! *Harlem*?"

"Uh-huh, but not a peep out of you until I have a chance to share it with Carlton."

"Well, I'm sure even Carlton knew about your independent ways *before* he married you." But Macy quickly recovered. "Harlem, eh? Let me know when the deal is done. I'll arrange a little housewarming."

By then, Ruth was enjoying the interaction, which reminded her of the dynamic in that old "I Love Lucy" television show. Lucy and her friend Ethel were always up to something about which their spouses were unaware.

But as Macy was heading for the door, she turned back around and said, "Free for lunch? I can treat you to a hot dog with sauerkraut."

Happily, Priscilla said, "I accept."

Then Ruth and Jordy watched Priscilla wave goodbye to her friend as she strutted out of Priscilla's office as dramatically as she had first entered it. And to think, Priscilla did not even play poker, but she played a pretty darn good hand with Macy that time.

Nor had she ever been as cognizant as she was at this minute that her PR role was the perfect façade for what she had secretly become, a government intelligence agent of sorts—a part that she was about to play to the hilt.

Finally, alone together, Priscilla and Jordy briefly conferred. He told her about the listening devices he had placed in the Met offices and that he already had what he hoped was some good intel on Shane and Ignatius. Then, confident that they both agreed on his marching orders, he went back to his office and mapped out a preliminary plan. His goal was to obtain some high-level intel on the "mysterious-looking couple" who had tampered with, maybe even stolen, three highly-valued works of art from the Met.

But Priscilla herself had one more task before leaving her new seventh-floor office suite to meet with the eager New York City news reporters in the lobby of the private 500 Fifth Avenue office building.

After that bombshell revelation that her own high-profile persona was being exploited by the folks over at the Met, she went on the offense.

Priscilla called Shane Carpenter and shared with him what she had decided she would say.

She let Shane *think* she would allay any public concerns about a controversial exhibition coming to the Met.

But nothing could have been farther from the truth.

So when Shane contacted the board of trustees chairman and reported what Priscilla had just told him, Chairman Devoe was pleased.

"Good job, Shane," Iggy said. Then he repeated himself. "Good job."

And so it was that everyone geared up for what no one knew would be the fallout.

8

All-In in New York City

Priscilla and Ruth exited the elevator into a chaotic scene. Reporters, even some paparazzi, were everywhere. Loud frenzy prevailed through-out the lobby of what Priscilla had earlier cautioned was a *private space*. Yet, while most of the reporters and the photographers and the camera crews clamored for their preferred space, somehow, the two women made their way through the crowded, chaotic eager New York City press corps as many of them shouted questions at them, as finally they made their way to the stage that had been set for their presentation.

Priscilla was up for the challenge, and Ruth was a quick learner.

As others not involved with the press conference continued coming and going through the busy office building's revolving doors, they could not help noticing all the commotion. Some of the more curious joined in and made their way to the stage that had already been set up for the media event. Meanwhile, Alfrieda handed out press kits throughout all of it, although many reporters did not even bother opening them.

At the center of it all, Ruth stood proudly beside Priscilla as together they prepared for her first event with the New York City press corps.

The onlookers ogled Priscilla, familiar to many of them and others in the television viewing audience. They whispered among themselves, sharing her name and what they knew had made her so well-known. Both she and Ruth cut dashing figures in their professionally-tailored black pantsuits. They stood behind a batch of microphones facing a multitude of news correspondents, some of whom waved their hands and yelled out questions, with their cameras flashing and rolling.

Then a voice—one that was dimly familiar to most of them—took over:

> Thank you so much for being so patient. [Priscilla holds her signature legal pad and an ink pen, but rarely does she read from her notes. She waits until finally, there is a measure of silence.]
>
> Good morning. I'm P. J. Austin-Bernhardt. This morning, I greet you as the newly-retained PR consultant for the board of trustees at The Metropolitan Museum of Art. I'm still somewhat new to all this, having signed on with the Met less than a month ago. And, believe it or not, I only just learned about this so-called 'mysterious affair' after conferring with my staff.
>
> [Priscilla throws her head back and speaks sternly.] Just this morning, I learned about the concern on the part of the board of trustees that one of its members may have served in violation of one of the

standards of the board's code of ethics. I speak of the standard that prohibits membership by someone with familial ties to someone known to have forged, tampered with, or maybe even stolen highly-valued works of art. You will find the exact wording of that particular standard in your press kits.

Then the curious onlookers continued watching in fascination as Priscilla paused and the news reporters looked simply baffled.

"Wow! We never saw that one coming." One of the reporters flushed. He had not wanted anyone else to hear that.

Another voice emerged from the crowded group of news reporters. "Hey, yes, it's right here in the press release."

Then the lobby grew quiet again as Priscilla continued:

Specifically, I was informed that Gaylord Millsap Omiros, a junior board member and a fashion designer in his own right, has tendered his resignation pending an investigation into allegations that he may possess such an affiliation. I was also informed that he expressed utter shock and even shed tears as he handed in his letter of resignation. (Priscilla, in truth, is making up this part of the story to engender some sympathy for Gaylord.)

Several news reporters started raising their hands at that unexpected news, but Priscilla appeared to be staring straight through them. When the reporters saw that she was nonresponsive to their raised hands, they frowned. Some even mumbled and dropped their hands.

During that somewhat uncomfortable interval, Priscilla never once changed the stern expression on her face.

Finally, she continued:

> I have been informed further that Gaylord Millsap Omiros loves his work on the board and that his former colleagues have, to the person, offered only words of praise for him. Why, even Chairman Ignatius Devoe has said, 'This entire episode, though in its early stage, is regrettable. This could not have happened to a better person.'
>
> 'We look forward to clearing up this discrepancy and welcoming Gaylord back onboard.' (Once again, Priscilla was lying. Or was she just making this stuff up along the way?)
>
> [Priscilla now portrays a pleasant expression and pretends that she has forgotten something.] Oh, pardon me. The day is quickly approaching when the face and voice you see and hear in connection with P. J. Austin and Associates, Incorporated will be that of the woman standing beside me, my new second-in-charge for the New York City branch office: Ruth Steiner.

Priscilla stepped aside and gestured to Ruth. As reporters once again waved their hands in the air and even shouted questions, Priscilla continued to ignore them as she gracefully stepped aside and allowed Ruth to speak.

Ruth said:

Thank you, *Dr.* Austin-Bernhardt. I know that you rarely, if ever, use your academic credentials, but I'm one of those women who is proud of you. People need to know that you bring a lot to the table, and that includes a Ph.D. in political science. [Ruth smiles and then gravitates to her message.]

A long time ago, while my great-grandfather was peddling wares up and down the streets of Harlem, Dr. P. J. Austin-Bernhardt's great-grandfather was farming a 300-acre estate of cotton, sweet potatoes, and peanuts, overseeing sharecroppers in Canton, Mississippi. Then, four generations later, the woman we know as 'PJ' was born in Clio, South Carolina, to James Nelson Austin, an itinerant Methodist minister—who traveled about many rural, impoverished Southern parishes—and Liza Meeks, a seamstress.

Ruth could tell from the expressions on the faces of the New York City press corps that she still held their undivided attention, and she also noticed, as did Priscilla, that they no longer waved their hands in the air.

"Well, now," Ruth and Priscilla heard some of the news reporters saying, "we didn't know about any of that, either."

Ruth rolled on:

The Austin family eventually settled in Prendergast, New York, where, for the first time, PJ attended racially integrated public schools. From there, she enrolled in historically black, church-sponsored Livingstone College in Salisbury, North Carolina, and earned a bachelor's degree in government. She went on to The Ohio State University, where she earned a master's degree and, later, a doctor of philosophy degree in political science. She then taught political science at Florida A&M University in Tallahassee, and it was from there, she signed on as a legislative aide to Ohio state Senator Daniel P. Callahan.

As Ruth filled in some of the gaps about Priscilla's earlier life, she and Priscilla heard one of the reporters saying, "So that's the backstory." Then Ruth said:

> Now, for something more directly related to her PR work for the Met. P. J. Austin-Bernhardt is not new to the arts community. She has served on local arts and culture boards, and she comes from a family of creative artists. Her mom, Liza Austin, has published a book about her life as the wife of a Methodist minister and her many travels. Liza Austin has also written numerous poems, one of which was set to country music. PJ's only brother, Nelson, Junior, is a regionally-acclaimed fine artist. One of her sisters publishes children's books; another is a graphic artist, and another, a gourmet chef. Why, nearly all her family are artistic. Well, maybe not PJ, but she *is* a very good writer and PR person.

There was appreciative laughter from the reporters.

> The rest is well-documented by you all in the media. And that includes her tumultuous time in Africa

to her work on the Hollingsworth Presidential Election Campaign. It includes, too, her work on the Bernhardt Foundation for Boarding Schools for Zimbabwean and South African Girls, as well as those horrific assassination attempts on her life. And don't forget those stunning images of her in those Oscar de la Renta gowns—made exclusively for P. J. Austin-Bernhardt—that she wore at the Hollingsworth Presidential Inauguration.

Ruth and Priscilla watched as several news reporters nodded their heads as if they were acutely aware of those news stories. Then they heard someone saying, "Man, has that woman been put through it."

But someone else moved the event right along. "But why's she in New York City?"

"Why indeed!" An animated Priscilla stepped back up to the podium beside Ruth.

"After the Hollingsworth Presidential Inauguration, I decided it was high time to sink my teeth into something else. So, I surmised, if that "New York, New York" song is true—*that if you can make it* here, *you can make it anywhere*—then, I'm all-in." She beamed. "Besides, I absolutely *love* this place. So, listen up, New York City! I'm all-in." Priscilla repeated those last words loudly and with much cheer and animation. She waved at the television-viewing audience, raised her arms as high as they could go, and then repeated herself, again: "Yes, I said, 'New York City, I'm all-in.'"

While she spoke, many applauded and cheered. But for those who knew Priscilla best, particularly her family and close friends watching on

TV, they could hardly believe their eyes. Where was the stoic and indifferent Priscilla who they all knew and loved? Who was this enthusiastic woman?

Then Ruth began her wrap-up:

> I'm sharing all this with you, as well as my unabashed honor to work with my new boss because I am proud that she chose me as her top aide. Ah, come on, guys, already I'm challenged just keeping up with her, whether walking or talking.

There was much laughter, followed by applause.

Interestingly, none of the usually aggressive New York City news reporters asked follow-up questions about what everybody was calling "the mysterious affair at the Met." Mostly they already had their scoop of the day—Gaylord Millsap Omiros being investigated for possible ethics violations on the Met's board of trustees. And they had a lot to chew on from what Ruth had told them about Priscilla's earlier life and her family history, too.

Priscilla and Ruth basked in the applause, held their clasped hands up high in the air, and said, "Thank you all for coming. We look forward to a good working relationship. Thank you!"

At that, the press corps took a collective deep breath and began collecting their materials and equipment. Aside from the headlines about this new ethics scandal at the Met, the big takeaway was their sense that Priscilla really was "approachable" and someone they could deal with on an ongoing basis. Besides, they all now knew *why* the illustrious P.J. Austin-Bernhardt had opened a "branch" PR office in the City, so they had something to talk about among themselves, as well. Whether she accepted it or not, Priscilla's indeed had become a household name, not only in Ohio but in so many other worlds. If only Priscilla saw herself the way other people saw her!

David Horowitz with *ABC News* was so enamored with her that he reported in his 9:00 o'clock nightly broadcast: "P.J. Austin-Bernhardt, the international PR sensation, is already taking New York City by storm. Her charming wit and forthrightness are refreshing. No frills and no fluff, either. This morning, she revealed that Gaylord Millsap Omiros, a junior Met board member and prominent New York fashion designer, has stepped down from that museum board of trustees, at least for now. His future rests on a Met investigation into his alleged family ties to someone who, we are learning, *might* possess a criminal record related to art forgery, maybe even theft."

Horowitz added: "But Dr. Austin-Bernhardt reassured us that Met Board Chairman Ignatius Devoe and the other board members still stand solidly behind Gaylord Millsap Omiros, so much so that they anticipate the matter to be resolved in his favor."

Then the reporter laughed and said: "By the way, for those of you who wanted to know whether P.J. Austin-Bernhardt uses a legal pad and an ink pen, well, see for yourself." [The screen showed the footage of Priscilla holding her signature legal pad and an ink pen.]

But as it turned out, Ruth also showed forth her PR skills. For she had spun a story so smoothly that the news reporters believed that there was a personal connection between her and Priscilla, and they bought her not-so-subtle introduction of Priscilla as just an ordinary woman who made good. At least for now, never mind that no one bothered to ask about Priscilla's recent marriage to a member of New England's royalty—Carlton Elliott Bernhardt. However, the Bernhardts of New Hampshire were not known as a family that interacted with the media. Rarely, if ever, did Father or Lady Chelsea speak to reporters. Moreover, although Priscilla's various exploits had long been media fodder, she herself was not known for discussing her personal affairs in public, either.

As the television news reporters made their reports on camera and the print professionals scrambled out the revolving doors, Priscilla and Ruth headed back toward the impressively designed, bronze elevators. Silently they waited for the elevator. When the doors finally opened, they could hardly wait for the riders to disembark before they dashed onboard. Ruth pressed the button for number seven, and both women breathed sighs of relief when the doors closed behind them. On the seventh floor, they strolled out of the elevator as if all were well.

Meanwhile, as he watched Priscilla and Ruth addressing the press corps on the small television in his office at the Met, Shane Carpenter thought he might be losing his mind or, at the very least, was having a heart attack. He felt his heart pounding and wiped perspiration off his handsome face. He ignored the constant ringing of his telephone. He also thought about jumping off the George Washington Bridge. *Then again*, he thought, *what the hell, I'll just take the punches.*

Shane tried and failed to grasp his new awareness that this Priscilla woman was cleverer than he or any of the other board members had assumed. But, he asked himself, how could he have known that? But Shane, and Iggy and the other board members, were not the first to assume that PR consultants were not exactly the most intelligent beings. But then he let what was really bothering him rise to the top of his consciousness: *Iggy isn't gonna like this one bit*! It is unclear whether he would have been cheered or even more worried if he had known that, at this very moment, Iggy was himself stomping about his own office in his art gallery, where he all but cursed Priscilla's name.

The woman in question was, at the same exact moment, settling into the gulf of her executive swivel chair at her desk in her new fully-furnished office in Midtown Manhattan. Priscilla pursed her lips and reflected on this morning's happenings, mainly during her meeting with Ruth and Jordy, and it first became clear to her that she had been deceived from the very beginning by Met Chairman Ignatius Devoe. That man, she now knew, had deliberately chosen her to represent his board because—in addition to her high-profile persona—he felt that he could feed her whatever information he wanted and that she would run with it. *Well,* she thought, *that man, Ignatius Devoe, was about to learn that she was her own person and that there was almost no end she would go to get even with people like him.* He and his disreputable forces had intentionally deceived her, and she would make sure that this would haunt not only him, Ignatius Devoe, but Shane Carpenter, too, and whoever else, for weeks, maybe even months, to come.

Priscilla reached for a sheet of her executive stationery. She picked up her stylishly engraved black ink pen. Even-tempered, her pen chased her thoughts. Her straightforward, poignant, handwritten note read:

> Shane,
>
> I do not take kindly to being deceived. Next time, you and your confederates on the board will find yourselves knee-deep in the very crap that you yourselves have created. I hope I have made myself clear. And by the way, I have yet to deposit the two-million-dollar retainer. Let me know how you wish to proceed.
> *PJAB*

Less than half an hour later, a private courier delivered Priscilla's handwritten note to Shane Carpenter's office at the Met. But there was a slight tussle when the courier refused to hand over the missive to

Shane's assistant and instead insisted on following his client's instruction that he, "Deliver the note only to Mr. Carpenter, personally."

When finally he did so—although Shane appeared reluctant to receive it—the courier waited for a tip until finally Shane pulled out the center drawer of his desk, took out a fiver, and handed it to the young man. The courier looked at the fiver-dollar bill, crumpled it, and shoved it in his pants pocket as he uttered, "The lady gave me a Jackson."

Shane was too discombobulated to register the courier's snide remark. He still perspired, and his hands still shook as he reached across his desk for a letter opener. He slid the blade through the back flap of the envelope and removed that short handwritten note.

No! Shane thought. *Oh, no*! He tried to figure out a way to avoid telling Iggy about this note. But finally he braced himself and placed the call that he did not wish to make.

"Sir," he began, then paused. The very direness of her missive was reflected in his unusually formal address. "Shane here," he said, even though, of course, Iggy knew his voice. Cautiously he explained how he had gotten this note, then he read it aloud, and he could not stop himself from holding the telephone as far away from his ear as his long arm could stretch.

Shane's caution was in order.

Iggy ranted and screamed so many obscenities into the receiver that Shane almost dropped the telephone. His head ached from Iggy's raspy voice. He had long been aware of Iggy's terrible, uncontrollable temper. This time, however, he seemed more incensed than ever before.

After a while, Iggy's rant simmered. He was not breathing as heavily any more. Finally, he spoke in a relatively normal tone of voice. "What can you possibly say to me now?"

"Sir, Ms. Austin-Bernhardt is onto us?"

"Tell me something I don't know."

Shane dared to ask, "What about the two-million-dollar retainer? Is she refusing it or what?"

"Use your head for once," Iggy ranted. "Of course she'll keep the damn retainer. The question is, whether she'll use it to help *us*?"

Iggy was demonstrating the side of him that Shane had long since had his fill. But Shane let him delve into the gutter anyway.

"Shit, Shane, that woman has our asses over a flame. How the hell can we fire her after that dang-blasted All-American Girl press conference? We're stuck with her now. Plus, she's got Ruth Steiner onboard. Added to all that, Macy's representing Gaylord. We really are in a pickle jar." Then he thought about it some more and said, "No, we're up the damn creek with our pants down."

Shane struggled to keep his wits about him. He hated it when Iggy started using such raw language. He even wondered where someone of Iggy's social station had acquired such a vocabulary. Shane's socio-economic status fit right into the New York art world with his background—having attended a particular boarding school, the right college, not to mention his family's connections to the art world; Shane was part of New York City high society, whereas Iggy was always waiting on Shane to take the lead or tell him what to do. As for Iggy, apart from his bragging all the time about the stint he spent in the Montmartre, Shane never knew much else about his background. And more than once he had asked himself how he had ended up in a personal relationship with this man. Then, before he knew it, he said in a near whisper, "Well, Sir, maybe it's time for another rendezvous of sorts. Shall I put in for our usual rooms at the Highland-on-the-Hudson Resort?"

Without nary another word, Met Chairman Ignatius Devoe had just authorized his executive director to set up a secret meeting with what turned out to be their seven board collaborators at what they considered to be a secure site that they had used before at a hotel upstate near Poughkeepsie.

But if only they had known that someone else was listening in on their telephone conversation, they might not have been so sanguine. Not so far away from their offices, the words "Highland-on-the-Hudson" were being repeated, and a squad of technicians was already en route to set up their state-of-the-art surveillance equipment, which included listening devices as well.

Jordy soon conducted a conference call with "the boys": Tommy, Carlton, Angel, and Onslow. Their other life together as special operatives was about to come in handy to help Priscilla solve "the mysterious affair at the Met." From the eavesdropping devices that Jordy and his team had planted in Shane's and Iggy's offices, they were already aware that seven of the Met's twenty-three board members were part of this nefarious plot.

"Game on," they all said in near unison.

But not even "the boys" knew what Priscilla had decided to do next.

9

Some Must-Do Personal Business

Although outwardly she engaged in a whirlwind of activities from her New York City office, Priscilla played what really was on her mind close to her vest over the next few days. She interviewed key members of the Met's board and a few of the museum's major donors. Then, with Ruth's able assistance, she immersed herself in the previous three years of the board's minutes, as well as the voluminous documents about the organization's practices and procedures for rotating exhibited artwork. Several times, too, she reviewed the few frames of footage of that "mysterious-looking couple" from the museum's surveillance tapes.

Finally, after intense meetings with Ruth and Jordy, she telephoned Shane Carpenter.

"I'm going away for two weeks, give or take a couple of days. Got some must-do personal business." She reassured him, "Ruth Steiner knows what to do in my absence. Besides, I'm only a phone call away."

Then she dialed Bow Lake and asked for the Bernhardt's private plane to pick her up and take her back to the estate.

Lady Chelsea and Father were as stunned as Shane Carpenter had been when Priscilla shared her plans for the next fortnight. She had returned to pack and make sure that all was well with her in-laws. But she would be off again the following day.

"Oh, but PJ, you can't be serious!" Lady Chelsea said. "We thought you were just settling in at that new office of yours in New York."

"Lady Chelsea," Priscilla spoke in a kind but firm tone of voice: "I've got some personal business to wrap up. A few loose ends need straightening out and trimming."

But Lady Chelsea was not accustomed to her desires being so dismissed. "I don't understand. Does this have something to do with Carlton? Are you two at odds?"

Priscilla smiled but with thin patience. "Darling Carlton and I are just fine." Her smile warmed. Carlton had managed to extricate himself from his desk job in Washington, D.C., for a few marvelous days with her in New York. The two of them had shared a grand time. So many restaurants and clubs! So many people to see and places to go! He had loved being involved again with "the other boys" from the special operatives' unit. But he was used to Priscilla's comings and goings. Of all the people in her life, Carlton had been the least resistant to her sudden announcement that she was going off solo for two weeks.

Priscilla understood, however, that Lady Chelsea, as always, needed special handling. And although she had no intention of divulging every detail of her plans, or, in fact, any more details at all, she took care that this particular conversation remained as pleasant as possible. "Well, now, favorite mother-in-law of mine," she said, careful that her tone was a statement, not a question, "surely, you can spare me for a couple of weeks." Then her voice became more assertive: "But I have a special request. If those folks from Washington call, *I am not in,* and you certainly *do not know where I've gone.*" Priscilla knew perfectly well that her intelligence supervisor at Langley could contact her through her cellular phone, her New York office, or, if all else failed, that darn tracking device they had implanted in her lower back. But she had a sense that they would still be leaving her alone. They were allowing her more quality time to heal from her traumatic experiences from her Middle Eastern mission, including her agent-husband's recovery from amnesia.

The next morning, Priscilla was off!

She carried a lightweight carry-on bag and rode a taxi on the first leg of her personal journey, a thirty-mile trip southwest of Bow Lake to the New Hampshire Correctional Facility for Women in Goffstown. She would be visiting Carlton's sister Arvana, held in this minimum-security facility for women in substance abuse recovery.

Priscilla milled about the welcome station and attached her visitor badge to her jacket's lapel. She completed her registration card and handed it to the attending officer along with her driver's license. Then she wedged her large shoulder bag into a locker in the waiting room. She knew from previous visits not to risk having anything on her that was banned, such as a nail file.

Then, before she went through the metal detector, she, as usual, informed the security officers that she had an "electronic" implant in her lower back and was again relieved that this was not a problem. She was pleased, too, that today the visitor's room was not crowded; she would not have to wait to see Arvana. She patted the bulging pocket of her jacket. Security had already cleared her Ziploc bag filled with photographs. Arvana loved receiving pictures from her family and friends.

But as Arvana came through the door to the visitor's room, Priscilla was aghast. Her sister-in-law had always been slim, but now she looked like she had lost so much weight that she was anorexic.

Arvana's first words, reading the look on Priscilla's face, were blunt, "I'm having difficulty adjusting to the cuisine here." Faintly she smiled, which was a big deal. Unlike Priscilla, who could be as transparent as a pane of glass, Arvana rarely let her emotions show. But on this particular day, she held her arms wide open, and she and Priscilla hugged. But they quickly pulled apart, aware that they were only allowed to touch and hug for a few seconds.

The two of them sank down at a table, and Arvana talked and talked. When Priscilla handed her the photos, she took the Ziploc bag without even opening it. And she did not miss a beat of whatever it was she was saying, either.

Arvana was so very glad to see Priscilla. "My, my, Miss Prissy looks like a woman in love. How is my dear sweet brother, anyway?"

"Oh, Arvana, my Darling Carlton is fine, especially now that he's come back to us. When he had amnesia, I thought I'd lose my mind."

Arvana continued on as though she were the one visiting and consoling Priscilla. "PJ, everything will be all right." Then again, tentatively, she smiled. "You and Carlton belong together. And you do look like a woman in love." For a telltale moment, she looked wistful. Arvana had already been serving her prison term at the time of Priscilla's and Carlton's wedding. Then she added, "Oh, yeah, how's married life?"

As Priscilla smiled and listened to whatever Arvana seemed so intent on saying, she examined the face of the woman whom the Bernhardt family had assumed would come unglued in prison. But it seemed to her that, for the first time since she had known her, Arvana was at peace with herself. Then she asked the question she most wanted to know. "How are you handling withdrawal?"

"There are no drugs in here, that's for sure. Some prisons, maybe, but they make a fetish of it here. It hasn't been easy, not at all. I'm having a rough go of it. But I'm so glad you asked." Arvana took her eyes off Priscilla, but only for a moment. It was as if she gave her next words some thought before reciting them. She blinked. "When Mother and Father visit, they never even talk about my drug addiction. You know how Lady Chelsea is about things like that! I guess she and Father just pretend I don't have a problem." She smiled, for the first time, as though she really meant it. "But I like you, PJ. You're so open and forthright."

Priscilla nodded, aware that she had just been paid a genuine compliment. Then she got right to the point of her visit. "Are they treating you okay?"

"PJ, when I first came here, I thought I would die. Then, gradually, I met some of the other women and learned about their particular situations."

This was Priscilla's first lengthy and substantive conversation with Arvana since her imprisonment. It was maybe too soon to come to a conclusion like this, but it seemed to her that her sister-in-law had begun to grow from the selfish, self-centered jetsetter she once had been. *And so soon*, Priscilla thought.

"And then I realized," Arvana was continuing, "that no matter what happened to me here, it would be nothing compared to what many of these women have already endured. Missy, you wouldn't believe their stories! So hard. Life has been so very hard for so many of them!" Intently Arvana leaned forward. "And so I've been thinking, when I get released, I might start a program for women who've been abused, as well as for those of us who're narcotics addicts." Arvana sighed. "Addicts! Which I and the rest of us will be for the rest of our lives." Then she looked into Priscilla's curious eyes as if she half-expected her sister-in-law would question her sincerity. But when she said, "How does that grab you?" Priscilla nearly fell out of her chair because she had never before heard Arvana speak in such common parlance.

But just as quickly, she responded: "My goodness, Arvana, how you've grown!"

Arvana appeared much surer of herself than how Priscilla remembered her. But she worried that coming at her like this might be somewhat of an imposition. But Priscilla was wrong in her thinking, and Arvana would soon correct her.

As she continued talking about her plans to start the new program, she caught Priscilla's attention, even more when she said, "I'll use my own money to get the program started. But I'll need some help because I don't know a thing about operating such a program."

Priscilla nodded. Arvana had never worked a day in her life, so she certainly was unfamiliar with setting up a community program as ambitious as one involving mental health counselors and addiction specialists. But she was surprised that Arvana had the self-awareness of how much help she would need, especially in the initial phases, and she was about to get another surprise, too.

Arvana's voice sounded hesitant, even humble. "Do you think your friend Julia, from back in Ohio, might want to work with me?"

Caught completely unawares, Priscilla's eyebrows rose. "Let me look into it. I'll sound her out. And, well, maybe you might like to write to her about all of this, too. I'll give you her address."

Arvana's smile broadened. "Oh, I have it. We've already been keeping in touch. She's special, that Julia."

Priscilla reflected about one afternoon before her wedding, back in Ohio, when she and Julia talked about what Lady Chelsea often called Arvana's "predicament," the term that the Bernhardts used when they referred to Arvana's imprisonment. Julia, when she first visited Bow Lake, had gotten to know Arvana before her sentencing. The two of them had seemed to hit it off. At the time, too, Julia had provided Lady Chelsea with some information that she thought might be useful during Arvana's eventual transition back into society.

Priscilla had her misgivings about her sister-in-law's plan. She also felt somewhat caught between her best friend and her sister-in-law. Julia was such a straight arrow, and Arvana, well, she had long been very bent. But then she remembered the blessings of grace. *Maybe*, she thought, *Oh, well, what would life be without its challenges?*

Just then, however, a shadow fell over her. Priscilla became aware of a somewhat imposing security guard wearing a big pistol in her hip holster. The woman was staring their way.

But Arvana was ahead of this curve, too. She had already stood up and held out her arms for a farewell hug.

Priscilla fought back the tears. She accepted Arvana's warm embrace but just as quickly pulled away from her. Then she waited for Arvana to disappear behind the heavy steel door that the security guard held open.

As she walked back to the lobby, she wiped tears from her eyes and used her jacket sleeve on her runny nose. For once she did not mind that strangers caught a glimpse of her weeping. She collected her belongings from the locker, handed her badge back to the attending officer, and accepted the return of her driver's license. Then she walked back outside the facility and climbed back into the taxi she had kept running. She had engaged him previously to take her to the Merrimack Airport.

As they pulled away from the prison, Priscilla gave a forlorn little wave. She had not even told Lady Chelsea that she was going there. But for Priscilla, this visit was personal. She had simply wanted Arvana to know that she loved her. As far as Priscilla was concerned, her "personal business" was just that, personal. Moreover, she felt that "straightening out and trimming loose ends" was the right thing for her to do, now that she had essentially embarked on a new stage in her life.

Priscilla's next stop was San Francisco to visit Ellen, her eldest and perhaps dearest sister.

On a cross-country commercial flight, she anticipated spending two-and-a-half days with Ellen. Of all her siblings, Ellen was the one who had been the most influential in Priscilla's development, especially in cultivating her ability to take care of herself. Ellen had told her years ago: "You'll know when it's time to get up, get off the merry-go-round, and move on with your life. You'll feel it down deep within. That's when it's time to act, Priscilla, even if you don't know how you'll feed yourself. That's your natural instinct talking to you, one of God's ways of guiding you. Follow it, Priscilla. Follow your natural instinct."

Priscilla understood as she stared out at the all-forgiving fluffy white clouds. *And that's exactly what I'm trying so desperately to do.*

The sisters spent the first day at Ellen's Victorian home, just up the hill on Forty-Seventh Street, adjacent to the Bay. They talked and ate pizza, junk food, and Priscilla's favorite seafood; they also drank beer, wine, and bourbon. Like Priscilla, Ellen also loved all sorts of seafood! At one point, when Priscilla felt overly stuffed, she and Ellen went for a walk on the beach and watched the seagulls swoop up and down the shoreline. They also watched people roller skating on the pathway parallel to the Great Highway.

During Priscilla's brief visit, Ellen's assistant looked after the six high-achieving, developmentally disabled men who lived in her group home on the first floor of her three-story house. One morning, when Priscilla observed the men having breakfast and then heading out to the curb to catch buses to their jobs, she was taken completely unawares. "Why, they're just like everyone else."

Ellen did not comment. Instead, she thought, *Priscilla still sees the world through rose-colored lenses*, and she was not so sure that Priscilla even knew about the kinds of programs available for high-achieving autistic men. So she just let her younger sister talk and, well, display her glaring ignorance.

The sisters spent their second day together on a boat ride to Alcatraz and then to beautiful Sausalito, which Priscilla had previously loved visiting. She pretended to enjoy what Ellen thought was a little walk this time, but what Priscilla described as "a hike on the hillside." But what she really loved was shopping in the exquisite nearby boutiques.

A hallmark of their relationship had always been Ellen expressing tremendous satisfaction in her younger sister's development. And this time, too, Ellen did not disappoint. "Look how far you've come, *Dr. Priscilla*. My goodness! Who would've thought? You actually helped elect a president of the United States. And now, you're married to one of the wealthiest men in America—and one of the most handsome, too. You go, girl! Daddy would be so proud of you! As are we all."

But what most delighted Ellen was that Priscilla had thought enough of her to pay her a special visit in the first place.

Priscilla's third stop was Cheyenne, Wyoming.

"I just had to visit you, Girlfriend," she said to Cathy, her former classmate from her undergraduate years at Livingstone College.

"I still can't believe you're here," her old friend kept saying. "Who would've thought that you would ever do all that you've done! You've become known for world travel, service on a prominent family foundation board, and working on a presidential election campaign. And, you're married to one of the richest men in America, too!"

"Cathy, please." Priscilla was slightly embarrassed.

"Same ole Priscilla. Not one to blow your own horn. Girl, apart from how happy you look, you're the same ole girl. And I couldn't be happier for you."

"Oh, Cathy, I just needed to see you and catch up on old times and tell you that I'm starting a new business venture in the City. That is, New York City."

"Wow, I always knew you had the makings of someone great, but I never, ever imagined all this."

Priscilla grinned. "Well, now, Girlfriend, Carlton and I, and a few of our friends are going to give it a whirl. Who knows, it just might work." That was about all she said about her new business to her former college classmate and friend. For some reason, she just knew that Cathy would not understand what she was really up to—her being an intelligence agent and her new PR firm's scale. *Times change*, she thought, *and so do we all, well, some of us.* Yet, it did not take her long to realize that Cathy also sensed that the two of them had outgrown each other. So Priscilla changed the subject from her current life to that of their time together at Livingstone College. Otherwise, they had so little in common that Priscilla struggled to keep the conversation going.

But then, before her ole friend left for the airport, Cathy pleaded: "Oh, Priscilla, please don't ever forget me. Promise me!"

Priscilla hugged Cathy. Then, for the last time, she departed her friend's home and her life.

Her next flight was to St. Louis, Missouri, for a more meaningful homecoming in nearby Sills Creek, Illinois.

She hired a limousine for the hour-long drive to Sills Creek. As the black stretch limo pulled up in front of her mother's modest dwelling, it attracted onlookers from all over the semi-rural community. This was a far different arrival from when two female federal agents arrived in a black sedan with news that Priscilla had been shot and was in the ICU at the Harlem Hospital Center. This time Liza's friends, neighbors, and relatives all hurried to her home with cries of jubilation. Somehow, they all knew that this could only be Liza's famous daughter Miss Prissy.

As the driver held open the door for Priscilla to step out, she was met with much clamoring and cheering from her mother's friends, neighbors, and relatives. Priscilla stood still for a moment and soaked it all in. Then she made her way through the growing crowd and walked up the concrete steps to the small porch, where Liza stood with her hands characteristically covering her mouth. This gesture indicated she was experiencing much emotion. Priscilla gave her mom a warm and well-received hug. Then mother and daughter went inside the house and closed the door behind them.

Liza led the way to the kitchen, and Priscilla sat down at the table. Liza shared the goings-on about her friends, neighbors, and relatives as she prepared a welcoming meal.

Then Priscilla opened her shoulder bag and handed Liza an envelope containing several blank checks. "Momma, these are for whatever you might need."

Liza did not seem the least bit surprised at the gift. But as she filled Priscilla's plate, she was content for the moment just to watch her daughter tuck into her lunch. It was a blessing from God that this daughter had always had such a hearty appetite. But then she said, "Oh, Child, I don't need anything. As long as you children are safe and comfortable, I'm good." Then she sighed. "Oh, Priscilla, I realize my little home is not like that great big mansion you live in now. But this is *my* home, and you're always welcome. And I'm not leaving here, either."

"But Momma, I didn't mean to suggest—"

There came a loud, boisterous voice. "Aunt Priscilla!" Germane was jubilant, although he was nearly out of breath from running. "So it *is* true! You *are* here!"

Priscilla and her favorite nephew hugged and kissed and wept tears of joy.

Then he pulled away. "How long will you be here?"

"At least overnight."

His open face fell. "Can't you stay a little longer? I mean, I told my friends they could come and see you. Everybody wants to meet the woman who worked on the Hollingsworth Presidential Election Campaign and who now lives in a great big mansion."

"Oh, Germane, you're so sweet yet so young." She noticed that he had grown since her wedding, a mere six months ago.

"Your Aunt Priscilla has other business to tend to," Liza cautioned him.

Then Germane ran to his bedroom, picked up his telephone, and called some of his friends. Soon, the house filled with what seemed like half the neighborhood, between his friends and Liza's friends, neighbors, and relatives, too.

Priscilla, still ensconced at the kitchen table, rolled her eyes. "Oh, well, Momma, so much for a private moment." Yet she did manage to share her latest news: her in-laws, her life as a married woman, and her opening a PR office in New York City.

That night, after Priscilla fell asleep in Germane's bed, while he stretched out on the sofa, he woke and crept into his bedroom. He took pictures of his aunt sleeping and recorded the sound of her snoring, too. The next morning he ran into the den and proclaimed to everyone: "See, I told you, my Aunt Priscilla snores in her sleep."

As Priscilla prepared to leave, Liza told her how pleased she was with her surprise visit. She added proudly, too, that mostly she was pleased that Priscilla had thought enough of her to visit her humble abode, even unexpectedly, at that. For Liza had feared that her daughter might have grown ashamed of her humble roots. It soothed Liza to see that that was not so. And although Priscilla still regarded Prendergast as her home and Sills Creek as the home of her mother and grandparents, she would always be the first to tell people from whence she came.

Still, Priscilla could not help wondering if her mother might need a better and more comfortable home. Yet wisely, she tucked away that concern for another time.

But before she left, Liza hugged her. "Girl, you sure look good. I mean, I've never seen you look so happy. Tell Carlton that I expect you to stay this way." Then mother and daughter hugged each other again, and this time they held that embrace for a long while.

Priscilla had one final stop.

As her airplane flew over Ohio, for a moment she regretted not stopping in Columbus. But she knew she would have to return there sometime soon and make some decisions about whether to keep her headquarters open there. Yet, looking down at this state where she had done so much and grown so much, too, she thought about how dramatically her life had changed since she had first gone to work for Senator Callahan. She recalled how she had built her public relations firm, become actively involved in the realm of intelligence-gathering, and married a man she passionately loved. And now, here she was, making another life-altering decision, creating another business venture, this time, in New York City.

Then, as the regional carrier entered western New York airspace and descended onto the Chautauqua County Airport, which also served Prendergast, she welled up inside. Prendergast would always hold pride of place with her as her home.

Priscilla hired a taxi and rode the short distance on Highway 17J to the Lake Charles Cemetery. She got out of the taxi and walked to lot number ten, section twenty-six, location fourteen, grave number twenty. The marker read: "James Nelson Austin, December 17, 1909 – May 18, 1981."

"Well, Daddy," she said, as she knelt beside her father's grave, "it took me a while, but I suppose I finally made it. I'm living my life to please me, and I have a darn good man beside me, too. His name is Carlton Elliott Bernhardt, and I'm certain you'd approve of him. Not only does he treat me well, but he's good all around. By the way, I'm back in New York. But this time in the City, that's New York City, and I absolutely love it."

As she continued talking and sitting beside her father's gravesite, she noticed a few other people visiting the graves of their loved ones. She felt a cool breeze blowing and smelt the fresh scent of flowers on a gravesite nearby. Priscilla smiled as she reflected on how proud her father would be of her. *If only you were here*, she thought. Then, "If you could see me now," she said aloud.

Finally, she rose to her feet and walked away as if all were well.

In a kind of daze of grief, she then visited Amber, her longtime friend and former high schoolmate. The two chums spent the greater part of the day catching up, and then she visited with Amber's parents, Mr. and Mrs. Joseph Washington. They laughed and reminisced about the girls' shenanigans during their high school years, including the infamous street fight Priscilla engineered the summer before twelfth grade. But mostly the Washingtons talked about all that they had gleaned about Priscilla over the past four years from television news broadcasts.

"Priscilla, my dear," said Mrs. Washington, with tears streaming from her eyes, "we're all so very proud of you. And to think we knew you back when." Then she laughed. "Child, my, how you've grown!"

10

Back at Bow Lake

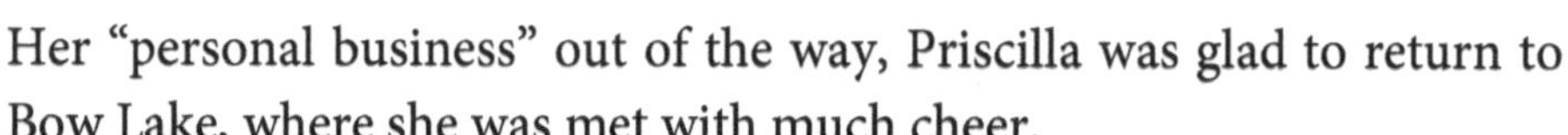

Her "personal business" out of the way, Priscilla was glad to return to Bow Lake, where she was met with much cheer.

"My dear darling PJ," Father said, "we missed you so very much, young lady." He took out a big white cotton handkerchief and pretended to blow his nose.

Lady Chelsea threw her arms around Priscilla and patted her back.

Priscilla reflected that she would never understand why her mother-in-law had been so concerned when she informed her that she was going off on personal business. But she had hoped that her in-laws had had a glimmering now of what Carlton had meant when he told them some time ago that she was not "cut from the same cloth as Lady Chelsea and Liza and many other women." Priscilla was definitely her own person, and when she said that she had "some personal business to tend to," that was what she meant. Back at Bow Lake now, everything was fine, where she was also now back to her new normal, in a manner of speaking. But more importantly to Priscilla, she hoped that the Bernhardts might be beginning to understand that, as a woman of agency, she did pretty much what she wanted to do, and without apology or explanation, for that matter.

However, she was curious that no one at Bow Lake said a word about her new business venture or about the latest news that had been all over the television about "the mysterious affair at the Met." Yet, she decided to take that as a blessing.

Later that afternoon, Priscilla had some time alone. Father and Ramses were out walking about the property. Lady Chelsea had gone to one of her many fundraising meetings; she had begged Priscilla to join her, but she had begged off, saying she needed to rest a bit after all that traveling. No one else, not even the household staff, seemed to be around, either.

So Priscilla went to her bedchamber, thinking that she was tired and that, for once, she might actually take a nap. But she was restless and found herself pacing.

Her "personal" time away from work was almost up. In two more days, she intended to return to her New York office. But she was surprised that no one involved in the Met case had called her while she was away. She had thought that she might have heard from Ruth, and especially from Shane Carpenter. And what of "the boys?" Should she be bracing herself for what she suspected would be bad news when she finally did return to her office in the City?

As she continued pacing, her thoughts shifted back and forth, from one loose end to another. How would she handle the situation with Macy, especially after having outed her client—Gaylord Millsap Omiros—during her press conference? Macy was a darn good friend, and Priscilla really did not want to hurt her. Somehow she would have to make things right with her.

Priscilla told herself to stop pacing the floor. Instead, she plopped down in an easy chair and gave herself permission to focus on what apparently was on her mind: "the mysterious affair at the Met." What had been happening while she was away? Her mind roamed over various possibilities, and for the second time in a few minutes, she focused on Jordy, Tommy, and "the other boys." While she was away, she assumed they had all continued in their discreet intelligence-gathering—eavesdropping was more like it. She assured herself that they still must be unaware that she had not exactly kept them abreast of every facet of her complex and multi-layered action plan.

Suddenly, an unsettling thought struck her. If she were holding back from them, were they also holding back on her? Were they up to some mischief on their own? She knew how they were. They were hardly likely to continue to be content with the narrow scope of action she had authorized for them. She recalled that she had instructed Jordy to surveil Shane's and Iggy's offices at the Met and at Iggy's art gallery, too. But she had given little thought, and certainly no authorization, for any additional assistance from "the other boys." As far as she was concerned, solving "the mysterious affair at the Met" was *her* project, not a shared venture with "the boys." But all that was a tad sticky. Awkward, too. She supposed she had not spent as much time as she should have in defining *their* limited roles in *her* new company. She doubted, also, if they were comfortable taking orders not only from a woman but from a woman for whom they had often served as her protectors while she carried out her "service to her country." There was a definite change in their power relationships. As it turned out, Priscilla was not only new in her work with "high-cotton crime," as Julia put it, but also in her role as "the woman-in-charge" in her new business venture with "the boys."

Priscilla sighed. There was a lot of potential for misunderstandings. She supposed she would have to address this sometime soon, but not just now.

Her mind soon seized on a related issue: surveillance. Jordy was not the only one who had hidden listening devices at the Met and other locations connected to Shane and Iggy.

Long before going off on her personal business, Priscilla had exercised her own intelligence-gathering prowess. When she had first interviewed Iggy and Shane at their offices at the Met—so long ago, it now seemed—she had surreptitiously placed listening devices inside their attaché cases. What had made that so easy was that both men had carelessly left their cases open on their desks, not having the faintest idea that Priscilla would even touch them. At this very moment, here in her Bow Lake home office, a tape reel connected to her listening devices rolled inside one of her desk drawers. Father had long since given up his private space for Priscilla's use for her home office, one of his and Lady Chelsea's endeavors for her and Carlton to make Bow Lake their new home.

At the thought of the tape recorder in her office there, Priscilla sprang to her feet. That's what she should do! Check and see if anything interesting was happening with Shane and Iggy. She ran up the corridor, back down the massive marble staircase, across the foyer, and down the corridor that connected to what was once her father-in-law's study, her new home office at Bow Lake. She pulled out the bottom drawer on the left side of her desk. She pressed the "play" button on the recorder.

The first thing she heard was bickering and snarls. Two high-pitched male voices. She sorted them out. "Shane," she said once. Then, "Nah, that's—" Then, "What's that noise in the background?" It sounded like they were in a car, and they were arguing. She heard one of them mention a hotel near Poughkeepsie. She squinted her eyes as if they could hear. She overheard the two men talking about a rendezvous with some other board members somewhere in the vicinity of Poughkeepsie; of *all places*, she thought.

She sat back into the gulf of Father's comfortable leather executive high-back chair, focused hard, and could almost see the men who she started calling "the two twerps."

Shane and Iggy sped past Yankee Stadium on the Major Deegan Expressway, heading northeast on Interstate 87. Iggy sat in the passenger's seat, and Shane was behind the wheel of his 1986 Volvo 740 station wagon. All the while, Iggy, who was in an apprehensive mood, talked so fast that Shane got edgy, too, which caused him to veer in and out of their lane. More than once, other drivers honked their horns at them. Some even yelled profanities.

This trip was not, in fact, the pair's only recent trek upstate to rendezvous with their accomplices on the Met board. In vain, they had made this journey two weeks ago, before Priscilla went off on what Shane thought was *that selfish personal errand of hers*. But, as it so happened, half their people had not gotten the message, and a few more of the others just had not shown up. So they had rescheduled the meeting for today.

Having to do this all over again did not improve Iggy's temper. As he got more and more out of control, he started punching Shane in the shoulder, waving his hands in the air, and hollering at the top of his lungs. At one point, Shane, who had about had it, almost gave in to his impulse to slam on his brakes in the middle of all the fast-moving traffic. But he caught himself just in time and resumed a safe and steady pace. Besides, nobody motors like a student driver in great-grandma's Rambler while amid the bumper-to-bumper, fast-moving traffic of the Major Deegan Expressway.

When finally Shane had had his fill of Iggy's ranting and hitting him on his shoulder and shouting, he somehow managed to shove Iggy away from him. His composure restored. Then, just as quickly, he snapped.

"Iggy, I hear you. All right. So stop hitting me and shouting in my ear. I'm sitting right next to you."

Although Iggy stopped hitting Shane, he continued ranting and pouting. "Shane," Iggy whined, "I can't afford any negative publicity. Once word leaks, I'm damaged goods. People will picket my gallery and—who the hell knows? —even burn my artwork." In addition to chairing the Met board, Iggy owned and operated Ignatius Devoe's Art Gallery. He was known for hosting exhibitions for struggling artists and was one of the most celebrated art patrons not just in New York City but in the Montmartre quarter in Paris as well. But Iggy's heart—and his head, too—ached at the possibility of losing his most cherished role as chairman of the board of trustees at the Metropolitan Museum of Art. Iggy dropped his head in his hands. His shoulders shook as he pretended to cry.

But Shane thought he knew his boss and lover well. So he ignored Iggy's crocodile tears and instead suggested a way out:

"You could just come clean, you know. Maybe we can figure out a way to use PJ in this. Besides, what do we have to lose? She already knows we deceived her."

With each word that Shane spoke, Iggy not only raised his head from his hands, but he stared at Shane as if he was insane, or something close to it. Then he put his thoughts into words.

"What the—! Are you *crazy*?"

Shane continued ignoring Iggy. But then, he persisted.

"Why not call and tell her the whole, damn, bloody, sordid story?"

"Shane, have you lost your frigging mind? Tell her the *truth*?"

"Indeed, Iggy. Call me naïve. Call me crazy. But sometimes, if you put your cards on the table, someone else picks them up. You must know that a central tenet of PR is: 'Above all else, be forthright and upfront.' Besides, now that PJ's on board as our PR girl, she also has a stake in resolving the matter. Not to mention that two-million-dollar fee. And if my instincts are correct, even though we did deceive her, she wishes us no ill will."

"Oh, Shane, talk about a tangled web!" Iggy Devoe hung his head low in his hands again and, this time pretended to be ashamed. For, in fact, Iggy indeed did have much about which to be ashamed.

It had been while listening to this part of the two men's conversation that Priscilla suddenly realized that they were, in fact, twerps. More importantly, she now suspected that Shane had no notion of just how deeply entrenched Iggy was in "the whole, damn, bloody, sordid story."

Shane and Iggy had long since veered off the Major Deegan Expressway onto the Saw Mill River Parkway, east of the long, meandering Hudson River. They continued north on New York Highway 9, just past Ossining—home to Sing Sing Prison—toward Croton-on-the-Hudson.

Since Shane had absolutely no desire to continue arguing with Iggy, he looked in his rearview mirror, switched from the fast lane into one of the slower right lanes, which was still relatively fast, and steadied his pace to a less hurried tempo. Then he looked at his wristwatch and said, "We're making pretty good time." It was a fast seventy-mile drive-time to the Highland-on-the-Hudson Resort near Poughkeepsie.

But Iggy was not finished ranting. Shane's crazy idea to "come clean" with Priscilla had truly irked him. "Don't forget, we're not dealing with some damn PR test case. This is my *life* and my *reputation*."

Shane tried not to bite, but he gave into temptation and let it rip: "My dear Iggy, there's no easy way of putting this, so here goes: You knew all that back when you jumped in feet first." Shane took grim satisfaction in finally saying what needed to have been said in the first place. Iggy had long since dug his own grave, as it were, and now, he was begging Shane to help him dig out of it.

Poor Shane. Iggy's deep, dark secret was about to come to light, and it was substantially more damaging than anything Shane had ever before imagined.

Priscilla found much amusement in listening to this expletive-studded conversation between the two twerps. She had even perked up when Shane suggested they "come clean" with her. *Not such a bad fella, after all,* she had thought. *But it's a shame about that Iggy.*

At one point, the two carried on so frantically that Iggy's voice had risen to a scream. It was then that Priscilla had hastily turned down the volume on the recorder. She also wondered where else Jordy had placed his listening devices. Obviously in Shane's car, and Iggy's too. For sure, under their desks in their offices and somewhere in the Met boardroom. She also thought, *And for sure, in Iggy's art gallery.*

Priscilla chuckled to herself and wondered if both she and Jordy were listening to this same conversation just now, albeit from listening devices they'd planted separately. It all seemed so funny to her.

Then, she figured, *Surely "the boys" and I are on the same path in this regard.*

11

The Whole, Damn... Sordid Truth

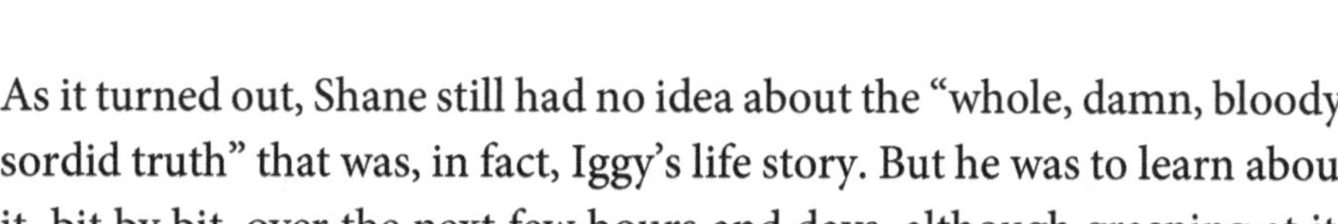

As it turned out, Shane still had no idea about the "whole, damn, bloody, sordid truth" that was, in fact, Iggy's life story. But he was to learn about it, bit by bit, over the next few hours and days, although grasping at its many twists and turns and seemingly endless complexities often still left him confused about this man whom he thought he knew, and with whom he had even shared his affection.

The story goes something like this:

During the late1940s, a struggling, twenty-something sketch artist named Ignatius Devonshire, a.k.a. Ignatius Devoe, often nicknamed "Iggy," crossed paths in Paris with one Thibaut Francois Moreaux. Those who knew this fellow well—primarily, to their chagrin—were more likely to consider him both shrewd and disreputable. But when Iggy first met him, he had no idea how unsavory a man he was. Iggy did not know that Thibaut Francois was the son of one of the wealthiest families in Paris and that his parents had disowned him for some of his less-than-admirable traits. Nor did Iggy know that Thibaut Francois had stopped using his "Moreaux" surname when he set out on his own and established an art atelier in Montmartre.

Iggy created very good sketches in terms of his craft—and was versatile, mastering the finer points of expressionism, cubism, and even romanticism. But Iggy was less accomplished in painting finished works—which happened to have been Thibaut Francois's specialty. When Thibaut Francois noticed how good his young, newfound friend's sketches were, he often finished them off himself and then began selling the finished artwork, but with his name inscribed on them. Since he funneled a portion of the proceeds from each sale to Iggy, the young sketch artist was first satisfied with the arrangement. Before long, though, Iggy soon understood that this arrangement had no future for him in his own work as an artist. Then, just as he was about to pack up his meager belongings and return to the States and start anew, something happened to change his mind.

But by then, Iggy and Thibaut Francois had become fast friends in the collaborative world of struggling young artists living and working together in Montmartre, hanging out together, dreaming of the day when they sold significant pieces of their artwork or acquired a reputable, affluent patron. They were part of the long tradition of such relationships, including renowned artists and writers like Vincent Van Gogh, Ernest Hemingway, and Pablo Picasso.

One day, when Iggy was milling about Thibaut Francois's art studio, he happened upon what looked to him like a Picasso painting, leaning in plain view at the front of a stack of paintings against a wall. As he examined the painting more closely, he realized that it was not an original Picasso, rather an excellent reproduction—a forgery—of the acclaimed artist's work. Then Iggy noticed some draped paintings clustered on a long makeshift wooden table. He removed the draping and, to his astonishment, he saw five more "excellent reproductions"—forgeries—of Picasso masterpieces. But then he sensed the presence of someone else nearby.

"Ah, Iggy," said Thibaut Francois. "I see you've uncovered some of my latest work."

Somewhat confused, Iggy shook his head. "Nah. This can't be," he said as he continued staring at the forged paintings.

"Sorry, young man," said Thibaut Francois. "But things being what they are in the real world, with your uncovering my masterpieces…." He let his voice trail off. Then, in a sharper tone, he said, "I need you to keep quiet about what you've discovered."

Iggy's eyes narrowed and his forehead creased. "But Thibaut, you're an *excellent* artist. You don't need to do this. Forgery isn't art; it's a crime. Besides, aren't you the least bit concerned about what will happen to you if you get caught?"

Thibaut Francois shrugged. "You're so American. So naïve."

Stunned. Iggy again shook his head. But this time it was unclear if he was saying "no" or simply trying to shake off his own scruples.

The two men talked some more, and Thibaut Francois opened a bottle of good quality red vintage, and the two of them began drinking. Before long, Iggy understood that all Thibaut Francois was concerned about was what he could fetch from selling the "excellent reproductions" of Picasso's artwork. He referred to the cost of his atelier, the food, and the copious wine he routinely purchased: in short, the lifestyle that Iggy had grown accustomed to had been from the proceeds from the forgeries.

And so it was that Thibaut Francois had captured Iggy's acquiescence to becoming his accomplice in one of his most lucrative criminal art schemes.

Sometime later, Thibaut Francois opened up concerning the more far-reaching dimensions of his skullduggery, a crucial part of which occurred primarily during France's Nazi occupation.

"You know, Iggy," the older man said, "the Nazis have confiscated—stolen was more like it—some of the best art from museums all over France and beyond. They have taken masterpieces, too, from private collectors, especially Jews, located all across Europe. And they've even smuggled some of them for safekeeping to Asia, America, and other parts of the world. Those guys hedged their bets, too. Whether Hitler would conquer the world quickly became inconsequential. For, today, who's to know where some of those stolen masterpieces are, anyway?"

Iggy nodded. He had heard whispers about some of the missing masterpieces. "Yes, I know about all that."

"But did you know that I'm not the only one creating 'excellent reproductions?' You see, Iggy," Thibaut Francois rolled on: "it may be a long time before anyone gets wind of what the Nazis have done."

Iggy was in a muddle. What exactly did Thibaut Francois mean? He still smarted from being called "naïve." So, cautiously, Iggy asked him how he knew all this.

Thibaut Francois poured generous glasses of more red wine. "Let's just say; I have my sources."

From then on, Iggy and Thibaut Francois were in business together. One thing led to another, and before long, Iggy began sketching some of the confiscated masterpieces, after which Thibaut Francois applied the finishing touches and produced even more "excellent reproductions."

As Iggy started getting a more significant share of the profits, he liked not having to worry about money so much anymore.

But as the no-longer-financially-struggling sketch artist settled into his new life of art forgery, Thibaut Francois still had not shared yet another profitable scheme of his criminal enterprise.

But it was not long before he let Iggy in on that secret, too.

Sometimes, when he was short on funds, Thibaut Francois would set up his easel off the Rue du Chevalier de la Barra in Montmartre, or along the Champs Elysees, or on a clearing near the Eiffel Tower and painted portraits of mostly female tourists. If Thibaut Francois, a handsome man, thought the women had money, he would try to seduce them into coming to his studio, where he sometimes could charm them into allowing him to paint them in the nude. Then, after finishing the painting, he would intimidate them—blackmail was more like it—into "paying me my asking price," or he would display their nude portraits for sale.

Since many Parisian women knew of this awful way of his, they had kept away from him and his art studio. But the tourists, especially the gullible American girls and women, became his most unwitting targets.

One such woman who Iggy came to know was New York socialite Miriam Millsap, the only child of the prominent and wealthy Artemis Millsap III of Manhattan. As it so happened, Miriam really did come to admire Thibaut Francois, and for him, the feeling was mutual. But what he, in fact, had most admired about Miriam was her wealth. So Thibaut Francois courted her, made passionate love, and painted many, mostly nude, portraits of her. But when Miriam told him that she was pregnant and that she wanted to marry him, an emphatic Thibaut Francois told her: "Marriage is out of the question."

Meanwhile Miriam gave birth to twin boys.

The infants were identical, save for two different birthmarks. One child bore a pink smudge-like permanent marking, approximately two inches in diameter, on his inside right wrist, and the other, a pink streak of similar dimensions on the nape of his neck. Both had their mother's blonde hair and their father's striking blue eyes.

When Miriam said that she wanted to take the babies home to meet her parents, Thibaut Francois, for once, was agreeable.

But in the spring of 1947, Miriam's parents had been outraged when their daughter, her French lover, and their twin baby boys arrived at their Manhattan residence. They could not countenance that their daughter had given birth out of wedlock. Within the first week of their visit, Miriam's mother, the epitome of New York high society, died suddenly of heart failure. Then, although Miriam's father had intended to adopt both baby boys, Thibaut Francois insisted on keeping one for himself. Since Artemis Millsap III had been so distraught over his wife's sudden death, he'd eventually agreed to Thibaut Francois's demand, that, despite his daughter's objection.

What Miriam did not know, however, was that Thibaut Francois had already extorted a handsome sum from her father *not* to display her nude portraits for sale and *not* to inform the New York City tabloids that she had given birth to twins out of wedlock.

Then, after he had consummated his disreputable business with her father, Thibaut Francois returned to Paris with his payoff along with one of his twin baby boys, Artemis Thibaut Millsap Moreaux. But Miriam had not returned with them.

Meanwhile, like many of the well-to-do, Artemis Millsap III had been resourceful, as he sought a way to rectify the situation with his daughter.

He took Miriam and the other twin baby boy to Greece, where he had long-standing business interests and positive relationships with some of his colleagues there. He arranged for Miriam's marriage to the only son of one of his associates, shipping magnate Demetrios Omiros. The latter, unbeknownst to Artemis Millsap III, had previously adopted his only child because he and his wife had been unable to conceive.

But Artemis Millsap III did not tell his friend Demetrios the truth about his grandson's paternity. Instead, to preserve his daughter's honor and her reputation, he concocted a story.

He told Demetrios: "Shortly after the war, both the parents of this child were killed. When my daughter Miriam heard about the tragedy, she adopted the baby herself," a story the shipping magnate and his son—Demetrios Omiros II—had both believed. Even though neither father nor son knew the child was a twin at the time, they did have their suspicions that Miriam was, in fact, the child's biological mother.

As it turned out, the son had already fallen in love with Miriam and had asked her to marry him before long and, when that was accomplished, agreed to adopt the baby boy.

As for Miriam, although she had been spared public humiliation from having born twin boys out of wedlock—as well as from having posed nude—she so longed for her other son, and she still had feelings for Thibaut Francois.

Over the ensuing years, back in Paris, Thibaut Francois eventually confided the whole, sordid, tangled story to Iggy, who had at first been appalled. But once again, Iggy failed to act on his scruples. By then, the two men had enough money to sustain the livelihood that they had both grown accustomed to.

But even then, Thibaut Francois still had not told Iggy *all* that he had done.

Perhaps wisely, he had not confided to Iggy that he himself had discreetly arranged for his twin sons to meet and get to know each other over the years. Thibaut Francois had anticipated that the boys would eventually grow fond of each other, that they might possess a natural affinity, that one day they would be old enough to make their own decisions, and that there was no telling what else they might eventually decide to do together. Mainly, he reckoned someday, down the road, even he might be able to use his twin sons' relationship to continue feathering his own nest.

Meanwhile, another dynamic had developed, this time concerning young Artemis Thibaut. It happened from the time that the little boy had first picked up a paintbrush that Iggy had taught him how to sketch, and Thibaut Francois had taught him how to forge artwork. As the young man grew up, he became as good a sketch artist as Iggy and as good an art forger as his father. And like his father, Artemis Thibaut also possessed an irresistible and reciprocal attraction to women, especially affluent American women.

The other son, Gaylord Millsap Omiros, grew up in Greece, mastering another talent as a designer of women's fashion—and he was darn good at it, too.

But as the twin boys grew into adulthood, something else became apparent. Artemis Thibaut tended to stutter, whereas Gaylord tended to blink his eyes in a kind of nervous twitch. Those traits were most evident whenever either one of them was angst-ridden. Mostly, though, since they had been raised separately, no one gave much thought to the young men's traits. But the day would come when discernment of their characteristics would be essential in distinguishing one from the other.

And so it was that for over some twenty-odd years, Artemis Thibaut eventually learned about his lineage from his twin brother and his father. He knew that his mother was Miriam Millsap Omiros, the only child of the prominent and wealthy Artemis Millsap III of Manhattan and that she was married to Demetrios Omiros II, the son of a Greek tycoon who bore the same name.

But Artemis Thibaut knew much more, for his father had confided the particularities of his "excellent reproductions" and about how the real masterpieces had been confiscated by the Nazis. He told his son about how he had extorted handsome sums of money from unsuspecting art collectors and how he had extorted mostly wealthy American women in exchange for "not displaying their nude portraits for sale." Moreover, and unfortunately for Iggy, Thibaut Francois also told his son about how Iggy had created the sketches that eventually became the finished forgeries that he, Thibaut Francois, that is, had ultimately sold to unsuspecting art collectors all over the world.

Late in the summer of 1972, Iggy was finally ready to strike out on his own and to lay to rest his long and profitable, though criminal, partnership with Thibaut Francois. Iggy had even assumed theirs would be an amicable parting.

As he bid Thibaut Francois and his son Artemis Thibaut a fond farewell, he was unaware that the son was privy to all his dark secrets. Nor did it occur to him that the son, like his father, was not averse to using what he knew was to his advantage. Poor Iggy.

Time passed.

By the time the twins reached their early forties, Artemis Thibaut was acutely aware that his twin brother Gaylord and friend-of-the-family Iggy were members of the prestigious Metropolitan Museum of Art trustee board. Iggy was the chairman. He also knew that at least seven other Met board members were somehow connected with his father's extortion racket involving those nude portraits and that they had, over all these many years, paid his father handsomely to keep quiet about that sordid business.

Yet, it had never once occurred to Iggy that Artemis Thibaut, whom he had nurtured all his young life, might not always be so inclined to treat him like family.

12

Rendezvous at Poughkeepsie & Recruiting the Woman Once Known Only as "Sally"

Meanwhile, back in rush-hour traffic on the highways in New York, Shane and Iggy continued motoring toward the Highland-on-the-Hudson Resort, and Priscilla continued eavesdropping on their revealing and sensational conversations.

The seven confederates on the Met board also continued journeying separately to that resort near Poughkeepsie.

Half-heartedly, Shane and Iggy continued debating whether it was high time to share the true story of Iggy's disreputable past. For over a dozen years, and many more years than that as an esteemed member of the New York City art community and the Montmartre Art District in

Paris, Iggy had managed to conceal all this from the fifteen other board members.

"What now?" Iggy mused aloud. He was approaching his seventy-first birthday. In his personal life here in New York City, he had finally risked coming out of the closet and had found Shane. He glanced over at his partner. He was old enough and tired enough now to value having a companion with whom to share his life. But could he trust him with so many as-yet-unshared secrets? After all the betrayals in his life, he was no longer sure who he could trust. But he did want to keep Shane as clean as possible; in his heart, he wanted to protect him, too. Yet, here he was, his professional life so at risk, on the cusp of exposure and possible criminal indictments, and maybe even convictions. What really hurt was that soon the outward glow of all he had worked so hard to polish—his impressive leadership at the Met, in the New York City art community, and back in Montmartre—might soon be forever tarnished.

Haltingly, Iggy finally dared to share with Shane more disturbing details about how his past had now begun to unravel their present fortunes. Then the two of them tried to assure each other all was not lost.

Now, they knew for sure, the not-so-mysterious-looking couple who had visited the Met on the day of the howling gales and torrential rains in May were about to make their move.

But Shane and Iggy did not know that Artemis Thibaut was as shrewd and disreputable as his father, Thibaut Francois—now deceased—had been. Iggy bit his stubbed fingernails in high anxiety, and Shane scratched the crown of his balding head. As they neared their rendezvous at the Highland-on-the-Hudson Resort, they dreaded what they feared could be a final showdown with Iggy's seven accomplices on the Met board.

Pity they did not know that their newly retained PR consultant was privy to every word they uttered, as she listened ever so attentively to the tape recording of their conversations.

Nah, Priscilla thought. She sighed, thought for a moment, and then reached for the telephone. She ordered the Bernhardt private plane. It could not be helped. She had felt this spat about her having traveled to take care of some "personal business" was finished, but no. She hurriedly scribbled a note for Lady Chelsea that she would leave with one of the servants for delivery to the lady of the house later. Then she went back upstairs to her bedchamber and packed a small carry-on case for what she estimated would be an overnight stay at her Midtown Manhattan office and then back to the Midwest again. She had already planned this extra trip, which could not be helped at this juncture. But she would have to act quickly to take advantage of what she had just overheard between Shane and Iggy.

Priscilla arrived at her Midtown Manhattan PR office approximately three hours later and was approaching Ruth's office. The door was open, and Priscilla called out a greeting as she stood on the threshold.

Startled, Ruth looked up. Priscilla was still off on whatever her "personal business" had been the last she had heard. But there she stood. Tentatively Ruth smiled. She was doing her best to learn to roll with Priscilla's flow. "Ah, you're back."

"Briefly," said Priscilla." Just wanted to tell you that I've got to disappear again. But this time, just for a couple of days."

Ruth nodded. She was learning not to ask questions of her mercurial boss. "How can I help?"

"Wish me luck." Priscilla grinned. She was liking Ruth more and more. Then she told her about a change that was coming. "I'll be bringing back one more new associate. I think you'll like her."

"Sure, we need to build this agency. Anything I can do to get ready for her arrival?"

At that, Priscilla just knew she could count on Ruth. But she raised her eyebrows just the same. "We'll need some office space for her. Pry one of the smaller offices from Jordy's pals. Suggest that two of them share a space."

"No problem," Ruth said, although she was not so sure that that was the case. The role and stature of "the boys" here were yet other mysteries she still did not understand about her new job. But she would roll with it just the same as she recalled her interview with Julia, who'd cautioned, "'Missy can be curt and clear. So don't take it personally.'"

Priscilla turned on her heels and started back up the corridor to the elevator when she paused because she noticed Jordy's door slightly ajar. She heard voices and then stuck her head inside the door.

There was a welcoming chorus. "Hey! If it isn't Miss Prissy!"

She tried to hide her surprise. Not just Jordy but Carlton, too, as well as Tommy and Angel, were bent over a large architectural rendering spread out on Jordy's desk. But it seemed to her as if "the boys" all looked a little guilty about something.

"Ah," she said, "am I interrupting?"

But just as quickly, Carlton had taken her in his arms and planted a kiss on her cheek.

"Never, my love," he said.

She stepped away from his embrace and waited in vain for her husband, or one of "the other boys," to volunteer why they were here together pouring over that drawing. And she also wondered what that drawing was. Then she wondered what Carlton was doing here in New

York when she thought he was buried at his desk in D.C. But when they all grinned at her and kept silent and did not pursue the matter, she knew she would find out about all this later. "Maybe," she told herself.

For now, however, she proceeded with something she actually did want to mention to her husband. She fished in her shoulder bag and took out a business card, which she handed to him.

"Darling, when you get a chance, find some time to contact this realtor. I've picked out a lovely Harlem brownstone. Pop by and check it out. I do hope you like it, too. I plan on signing the lease when I return, but not before you check it out. Okay?"

Yet when Carlton flushed, she almost wished she could call back her words. Belatedly she thought, *Now what*? Was he embarrassed at yet more evidence of how independent she was? Was she ever going to get this married stuff right? But blithely she decided not to say anything more. Carlton would have to figure out how to handle this one himself.

But then, as she turned away to leave, she remembered what she had intended to tell Jordy.

"Guys, I'd love to catch up with you, but not just now. I have another run to make, just for a couple of days this time. Hold down the fort, will ya?" Without waiting for their reactions, she firmly closed the door to Jordy's office and made for the elevator.

An hour or so later, Priscilla sat in the departure lounge at LaGuardia Airport, waiting to board an American Airlines commercial flight. Somehow, some technical wizard she had privately engaged had previously connected her cellular phone to her recording devices. A few moments ago, after she checked for any voicemail messages, she had then connected to her recording device when she heard Shane and Iggy wrapping up their long-drawn-out drive to Poughkeepsie.

They had driven past Peekskill, then past Wappingers Fall onto South Road into Poughkeepsie. Shane had parked his Volvo station wagon. Then the two men had joined a small group of tourists trekking over the Hudson on what was purportedly the longest pedestrian bridge in the world. As they walked, they continued talking, only less intense than when they had been in the car. Priscilla imagined them staring at what she fancied must be a beautiful sunset over the river.

Then she heard Shane reminding Iggy how fortunate he was. "Iggy, you'll be just fine. Trust me. But you're going to have to *come clean* with the others and with Ms. PJ, too. Are we clear on that, now?"

Priscilla knew that silence has often been the best way to consummate deals, and so it had been that day with Iggy Devoe. Yet she did wonder whether Iggy had shaken or nodded his head.

After stretching their legs a bit more, the pair returned to their car and drove the remaining short distance to the exclusive Highland-on-the-Hudson Resort. There, they had waited for their seven confederates from the Met board to arrive. They had both been aware that this would be a difficult encounter and that they had to bring effective closure to the whole mess.

Priscilla boarded her American Airlines flight. Once seated, her mind drifted. She knew she had to find out what "the boys" had been examining on what appeared to have been an architectural rendering. She did not like the thought of them maybe expanding their roles in the Met case. Then she put that thought out of her mind and focused again on the whole "sordid" story that Iggy had just shared with Shane. But she also thought about how, at some point, she needed to clue Macy in on the big picture. *But not just yet*, she thought. *Later, maybe tomorrow.*

She reached into her shoulder bag and pulled out her legal pad. She leafed through it until she found her current list of things to do. She focused on the top item: "Sign lease for the Harlem brownstone." She nodded. Of course that would have to wait until she got back to New York. Then she wrote down another item: "The boys": "What drawing were they studying?" Then she gazed at the last item on her list: "Track down the woman once known only as "Sally." Well, that's what she was doing.

Priscilla could trust Ruth to assist her with the ongoing PR for the Met case, but she needed someone with intelligence-gathering prowess to help with the more complex aspects of the case—and that was the specialty of this woman she was on track to hire. She had used her CIA contacts to locate "Sally," so now all she had to do was convince her to join her new agency.

Her flight time to Oklahoma was over six hours, not counting a layover in Dallas. But the captain was instructing the passengers, "Buckle your seatbelts. We're readying for landing."

"It's about time," Priscilla fussed. She reached for her shoulder bag and prepared for landing.

Shortly after landing, Priscilla was in and out of the airport terminal quicker than it had taken her to reach the American Airlines gate back at LaGuardia. The next thing she knew, her taxi stopped in front of a three-tiered stuccoed building. Priscilla entered the Tulsa City Hall. Soon she was asking the receptionist, who seemed to fade into the wall of the drab-colored lobby, where she could find Laverne Macon. This, she now knew, was the actual name of the woman who once, back in southern Africa, had been known to her only as "Sally."

"Is she expecting you? Shall I tell her whose calling?" The receptionist looked up and smiled. But then she squinted and took a second look at Priscilla.

"My name is P.J. Austin-Bernhardt, and, 'no,' Ms. Macon is not expecting me." Priscilla was not exactly surprised at the receptionist's double-take. She remembered similar encounters during her first time in southern Africa. Until now, however, she mainly had forgotten how much she and "Sally" resembled each other until now.

The receptionist once again smiled and pointed to a large round clock on the wall behind her, whose digital numbers read 4:54 p.m. "I could ring her, but she'll be coming off the elevator in a moment or two."

"Go ahead, ring her anyway." Priscilla stared at the clock. She had not given any thought to the two-hour time difference. She wanted the woman once known only as "Sally" to join her new business venture, and that was that. Mission-oriented: time, place, space, and even travel were mere incidentals to her. Priscilla said matter-of-factly, "Sorry, but I've just come from the airport. I hadn't figured in the time difference here."

After she contacted Laverne Macon by telephone, the receptionist told Priscilla, "Ms. Macon said that she'd meet you here. So, please, have a seat."

As Priscilla took her seat, she thought about how the receptionist spoke with what sounded like a Southern drawl. Priscilla had not expected that in Oklahoma, which she had pegged for the Midwest, but which was, in fact, in the Southwest. *Oh well*, she thought. But then she remembered that she had not heard Sally speaking with any accent.

So, as Priscilla sat facing the elevators, she noted that she was the only person waiting in reception as she leveled her spine against one of the modern leather steel-framed chairs. Then, all at once four elevators opened, and many people raced out of them. But none of the people approached her, and she did not see anyone who resembled the woman she had known as "Sally." As she waited, Priscilla wondered how this woman would be at discerning the differences between identical twin brothers Gaylord Millsap Omiros and Artemis Thibaut Millsap Moreaux. And she remembered Sally once having said, "Mother Nature imbues each person with idiosyncrasies that only a mother can discern." She had added that, no matter how much training she had undergone to pass for Priscilla, "I could never altogether duplicate your particular idiosyncrasies."

The elevators continued to disgorge office workers until, finally, Priscilla spotted someone oh-too-familiar-looking. She watched the woman walking cautiously in her direction. But then the woman stopped dead in her tracks. Although some people bumped into her, she still did not move. She just stared at Priscilla.

For that brief moment, Priscilla wondered whether this unexpected visit and invitation to join her firm were not such a good idea, after all. But then, with much glee on her face, she watched as the woman rushed her. Priscilla stood up as Laverne grabbed hold of her in a tight embrace.

"PJ! My God, how'd you know how to find me?"

Priscilla had not anticipated such warm and friendly reception, especially since she had never experienced such from this woman before. But here she was, behaving as if Priscilla were a long-lost friend. But in preparation for this encounter, Priscilla had prepared a tall tale about how she had learned about "Sally's" real identity in the first place. But Laverne Macon never once asked her that question. So Priscilla never once had to lie about how she had come to know her real name, not to mention how to find her.

Nevertheless, Priscilla was pleased that her instincts had served her correctly. She had been afraid that, after four long years, "Sally" might not want to see her again—much less team up—especially after what had happened inside the Rustenburg Platinum Mine in South Africa. But Laverne Macon was pleased with her unexpected visit and said as much.

"I never *ever* stopped thinking about you, and I certainly never imagined we'd meet again." But then her expression turned blank, as it seemed her intelligence-agent persona had kicked into gear, "So, what gives, Miss Prissy?"

As the two women stood tightly together, onlookers stared, apparently wondering at the resemblance. *Were they relatives, maybe even twin sisters?* some of them must have been thinking.

"Why? Why are you here, PJ?" Laverne's voice sounded eager.

Now for the big question, Priscilla thought, but then, after a brief awkward silence, "Is there someplace where we can talk? In private? There's so much I have to tell you."

"Of course," Laverne took her by the arm. "Come with me."

As the two women emerged from the office building, Laverne peppered Priscilla with questions. "Want something to eat? Where are you staying? Why are you even *here*?"

Priscilla's only reply was, "I'll answer all your questions when we get someplace private."

They soon faced each other across a table in a diner, where they talked and talked, and where onlookers stared and stared at them because of their striking resemblance. Priscilla eventually asked Laverne to join her and "the boys" and others in her Midtown Manhattan PR office.

Laverne did not need to think it over. "Yes!" She bellowed gleefully. Then she added that she could not have been happier to accept.

At last they were at a nearby Holiday Inn. Priscilla booked it for one night, and Laverne headed off to do whatever she had to do. She was to return just after four in the morning, and the two of them would be off to the small airport in Tulsa to catch an early morning flight back to LaGuardia by way of Dallas.

Priscilla dragged herself up the stairs to her second-story room. Once inside, she plopped down on top of the bedspread and fell fast asleep in the same black pin-striped pantsuit that she had worn on the flight to Oklahoma. When Priscilla awoke, it was 3:00 a.m. Laverne was knocking on her door. Soon they were in a taxi headed for the airport.

13

A Striking Resemblance

Not many hours later, Priscilla and Laverne were chatting as Laverne unpacked in a bedroom at Priscilla's and Carlton's apartment at the Waldorf Astoria on Park Avenue. The couple had leased the spacious apartment in the swanky hotel until they could find a place of their own, but, for the time being, Priscilla had invited Laverne to stay with them.

Priscilla confided that she was finally living out her dream. "I've always," she said, "wanted to live in New York, 'the City,' that is. My goodness, you have no idea how much I've dreamed of all this."

Laverne grinned. "The closest I've ever come to New York is flight layovers or the television series *Green Acres*."

Then they laughed her Elly May Clampett laugh that was a perfect echo of Priscilla's.

Noting the similarity, Priscilla told herself that she had made a wise decision, after all, bringing the woman once known only as "Sally" back into her life. Laverne was happy, so Priscilla was happy. She liked to bring cheer to someone other than herself.

But Priscilla had no idea that already the ever-alert New York media had glimpsed the two of them, first at LaGuardia and then as they had entered the lobby of the hotel, and that they had been baffled at the sight of *two* P.J. Austin-Bernhardts.

And just think, Priscilla had not even put her little scheme into action.

That afternoon, Priscilla took Laverne along with her to meet the realtor who held the lease for the Harlem brownstone. Although Carlton was not with her and had not seen the property, Priscilla signed the papers and collected the keys anyway. Then, like lightning, like always, she contacted a contractor recommended by the realtor and proceeded to instruct him about how she wanted to renovate the place.

Then she and Laverne headed back to Midtown. At her office, Priscilla introduced Laverne to Alfrieda and Ruth. The two look-alikes kept a straight face and pretended they did not notice how surprised Alfrieda and Ruth were about their striking resemblance.

Then Priscilla walked Laverne down the corridor to Jordy's office, where all "the boys"—Tommy, Angel, Jordy, Onslow, and Carlton— were assembled again. As one, their jaws dropped when Laverne strolled in behind Priscilla.

"Howdy, fellas!" Priscilla bellowed as she tried to sound like a Western cowboy of sorts.

"Allow me to introduce our new associate. Laverne Macon, say 'hello' to 'the boys.'" Of course Priscilla already knew that Laverne had worked with Carlton four years ago on that decoy caper in southern Africa. But "the other boys" were only vaguely familiar with her when she went by the name of "Sally."

Yet gamely, they all leaped to their feet and hooted and high-fived. They slapped one another's shoulders, too.

Then Carlton whispered to his wife. "What's going on, Missy? How'd you two connect? I mean—"

But Laverne intervened before Priscilla could answer.

"Now, now, Carlton, my friend. Let's be a little discreet. Besides, I, just like you, can work in the private sector."

While she talked, Carlton stared intensely into Laverne's eyes and asked, "But are you *sure* you want to do this?" Although Carlton had no idea what Priscilla and Laverne were up to, he and "the other boys" could not help behaving like the special operatives they were; once a special op, always a special op. However, Laverne and Priscilla were one step ahead of "the boys," which they would find out about later, much later.

Laverne nodded as she returned Carlton's stare.

"I'm quite aware of the ramifications of my actions, just as I'm sure you fellas are of yours." All the while she spoke, this was the only time she used her Southern drawl. Otherwise, she spoke with a Midwestern accent.

At that, all the guys looked at one another and chorused, "We do what we must," which was their old code during that African caper for bringing out the P. J. Austin look-alikes. Only this time, to their knowledge, there were no plans in the works for any P. J. Austin look-alikes. So, they all wondered, *What's Miss Prissy up to?* But since Carlton had gone along with this, so, too, did they.

Then, with no setup whatsoever, Priscilla blurted out:

"By the way, my Darling Carlton, I've signed the lease to our brownstone."

Carlton's mouth dropped open. Then when she handed him his key, he almost let it fall from his hand, but not before she added, "And I've asked Laverne to stay with us at the Waldorf until we can find her an apartment of her own. Hope that's okay with you."

Poor Carlton. He flushed and would not meet anyone's eyes, not Priscilla's, and not his friends'. Although he was embarrassed, he was not humiliated. He had come to accept that his Miss Prissy would never cease to amaze him, and she pretty much never did.

While Priscilla took Laverne by the arm and led her back down the corridor, Tommy tried his best to smile. But then he said, "Well, Bro', you knew what you were getting into when you married her."

Angel shook his head and chimed in, "Women."

At that, "the other boys" all nodded.

As Priscilla and Laverne neared Ruth's office, she apparently had heard them coming.

She called out, "Welcome back again, PJ! Ready to tell me what you're up to?" Ruth had spent enough time with Priscilla to know when something—and in this case, *someone*—was in the wind. She took a good hard look at the new recruit. *A dead ringer for the boss.* Now, *what has PJ cooked up?* Their resemblance, Ruth just knew, was no sheer coincidence.

Priscilla told Ruth that "Laverne possesses tremendous research skills and majored in psychology in graduate school," but she said no more. Then Ruth led Priscilla and the new hire to the office she had commandeered from "the boys." She left the two of them there smirking and emitting that crazy Elly May Clampett laugh of Priscilla's. She shook her head at having to listen to that hillbilly laugh in stereo. But she was smiling as she went back to her office because she just knew Priscilla was up to something and that she would tell her about it in due time.

Laverne spent the greater part of her first night in New York City getting up to speed on her new job. She studied the several documents that the others had read earlier. She listened to the tape recordings of Shane's and Iggy's conversations as they drove to the Highland-on-the-Hudson Resort near Poughkeepsie. Among Priscilla and her other associates, Laverne was the least familiar with art and the Met, or any other museum, for that matter. But she was brought to the table because of her keen sense of dealing with deceptive behavior, and, already, she knew *There was a lot of that in this case.* To herself, she ticked off all those who engaged in deception: Iggy, Shane, and their seven confederates on the Met board; that heretofore "mysterious-looking couple" who had visited the Met on the day of the howling gales and torrential rains in May; and especially the twins Gaylord Millsap Omiros and Artemis Thibaut Millsap Moreaux.

But Laverne wondered why Priscilla had evidently decided not to have either Ruth or "the boys" listen to those revealing recordings of Shane's and Iggy's conversations in the car. When she had asked Priscilla if the others were in the know, Priscilla had said, "Now is not the time to bring anyone else into our inner sanctum, not even 'the boys.'" She supposed Priscilla had her reasons. Again Laverne leafed through the documents and listened to particular parts of the recordings. She was intent on doing her best to help Priscilla solve what everyone was calling "the mysterious affair at the Met."

As for her striking resemblance to Priscilla, it did not take rocket science for Laverne to realize that she would be posing as Priscilla throughout much of the ensuing mission. And by the look on Ruth's face, Laverne suspected that even she had figured out that much.

But none of them knew yet just how all this would play out.

Laverne nodded to herself. Priscilla had found a way to put the New York City press corps, including the paparazzi, off her tail. She would almost always be somewhere other than where their cameras' lenses were flashing and rolling. Laverne smiled. If it had worked back in southern Africa, surely it could work here, too.

A couple of days later, Ruth took a most unexpected telephone call early in the workday.

"Shane Carpenter here."

"Good morning, Mr. Carpenter," she said in a warm and friendly tone. "And how are we today?"

"Come on, Ruth. It's me, Shane."

Although he could not see her face, Ruth smiled. Of course she had long been acquainted with Shane and almost everybody who was any-body in the New York City arts community. But a healthy dose of for-mality was in order as this case unfolded. Then she said, "Good morning, Shane. How can I help you?"

Shane cut to the chase: "Are we screwed, or what?"

Somewhat taken aback at the coarseness of his language, even so, she spoke as bluntly as she could.

"PJ said to tell you that she had to disappear for a short while, but for you and Iggy to know that, upon her return, you will have her undi-vided attention. And, in fact, she's back already."

"So she's not still pissed with us?"

Ruth sighed heavily. Shane could hear her displeasure.

Her voice turned frosty.

"If I were you and Ignatius, I'd prepare to put all my cards on the table. And I do mean all. 'More plainly put,' and I'm using the boss lady's words now, 'the only way we can help you is if you bring your laundry bag.' Get my drift?" Then Ruth hung up her telephone.

Iggy had been standing in front of Shane's desk at the Met while he talked to Ruth on the telephone. So when he saw Shane hang up his telephone, and without even saying "Goodbye," he said, "Well, Shane, out with it. What'd PJ have to say?"

"That was not PJ. It was Ruth Steiner."

"*Ruth!*"

"Indeed. She repeated that PJ said to tell us, 'The only way we can help you is if you bring your laundry bag.'"

Iggy let out a hiss and then leaned forward to say more.

But by this point, Shane had had enough of Iggy's ranting. Nor did he wish to listen to a diatribe.

"See," he said, "I *told* you, we must *first and foremost* 'be forthright and upfront.'" Then Shane waved his boss away. "I've got other business to attend."

Iggy stared at Shane. *How and when did my executive director get the upper hand, even for a moment?*

But Shane had already staved him away.

14

An Unlikely Acquaintance

Priscilla spent the remainder of the week at her Harlem brownstone, much of the time conferring with Mr. Hunter of Hunter Contractors of Harlem. With utter confidence, she instructed him on everything from which walls to break down, which to paint, and which bathrooms needed wallpaper and which needed to be restored to the original subway tile. Neither did she fail to tell him where to point-and-tuck the brick veneer.

As she commanded this and that, she recalled how Carlton had first objected when she told him that she herself intended to work with the contractor on the renovations. But he had soon relented when she informed him about how she used to help her father make repairs to their home and their rental property in Prendergast and how she and her siblings used to help paint and make window treatments in their home. She also shared how she had helped Jonathan Morgan, her former fiancé (the one who was gunned down so tragically at the altar), negotiate contracts with the architect to renovate the historic First Church in Columbus.

Priscilla assumed that it must have been around then that Carlton had realized she needed something to do other than what she had begun to refer to as "that darn desk job" at her new Midtown Manhattan office. But she had also sensed that Carlton had been sensitive enough to notice that she was excited about working on something that she could simply lay claim to. She remembered telling him that she needed "to touch and feel the dirt and the grime."

Mostly, she'd felt herself drawing closer to him when he'd said, "Go for it, Miss Prissy. It's all yours, anyway." Besides, he had begun to understand that when she was happy, he was, too.

Early that week, working on her new Harlem home, Priscilla kept watching out the windows and on the front steps, observing her neighbors and other passersby. Occasionally she had paced up and down the street and around the corner to familiarize herself with her new neighborhood. However, it was not long before realizing that this part of Harlem was not as inviting as she had assumed. She had envisioned herself residing in the very community where some of her favorite Harlem Renaissance artists and writers had once lived and worked. She particularly admired the literary works of Zora Neale Hurston and Langston Hughes. But, just as the Montmartre art district of Paris changed over the decades, so, too, had Harlem. Whenever she waved at her neighbors, no one waved back. When she knocked on doors and tried to introduce herself, the doors were often slammed shut in her face. Such a lack of welcome reminded her of what had happened in a housing project in Tallahassee during her time at Florida A&M University after being involved in a car accident. After being released from the hospital, she had gone looking for the women who had rescued her. Instead of welcoming her with open arms, doors had been shut in her face. Nobody would even accept her gratitude, yet she believed that in Harlem, just as in Tallahassee, there was always the potential for at least one person to break ranks and open the door to friendship and relationship.

A few days later Priscilla took a break from painting her kitchen. She liked working on her own house, especially painting walls. She had brewed a pot of coffee, lit up her occasional cigarette, and turned on her radio. Shortly after that, she thought she had heard someone, or something, in her living room. She knew that Mr. Hunter and his men were working upstairs and that, so far as she knew, she was the only one on the first floor.

Casually she called out, "Who's there?" But no one answered. Then she heard someone, or something, falling on the floor. So she got up from the kitchen table and headed boldly to the front of the house.

Imagine her surprise when she saw a child, maybe seven or so years of age, swooshing and sliding in crème-colored paint on the hardwood floor of her living room. The more the youngster tried to get up, the more he kept swooshing and sliding in paint puddles. When finally he looked up and saw Priscilla standing over him, he blurted out, "Lady, I didn't do this. Honest. I was only trying to see what you were doing up in this big house, all by yourself, when, out of nowhere, someone poured paint on me."

Priscilla did not know whether she was more amused at the sight of this young man in the paint puddles or by the tall tale that he had just spun about how he—and the paint—had gotten there in the first place. Then, "Give me a minute," she said, "we've got to clean you up." She went upstairs and told Mr. Hunter what she had found in her living room. He stopped what he was doing, collected some cloths and paint thinner, and followed her downstairs.

It took the two of them more than a few minutes to wipe off most of the paint from the young man and the floor. During that time Priscilla asked the youngster his name any number of times, but to no avail. But when she said that she would run a bath for him, he suddenly remembered his name.

"Jules, Ma'am, I'm called Jules McCorkle. I live down the street with my mom."

Then, after Mr. Hunter wiped paint off the young fellow's face for the umpteenth time, he said, "My, my, what a handsome young man." He grinned at the youngster, and then he looked at Priscilla and said, "I'll leave you to your new friend."

"Jules, Ma'am," repeated the lad. "I'm called Jules McCorkle."

As Mr. Hunter made his way back up the stairs, he turned around and said, "Missus Austin-Bernhardt, just call out if you need me again."

"Okay, and thank you, Mr. Hunter," she said, as both she and the contractor continued grinning at the sight of the young man who, now that she could see his face, reminded her so much of a younger version of her ebony-hued favorite nephew. Like Germane, Jules had ginger freckles on his cheeks and a kind of kinetic energy, too.

Yet Priscilla shook her head, troubled that Jules, whose clothes were still drenched in paint, did not seem the least concerned about his situation. "Young man, we have got to get you out of these wet clothes. And you need to soak in a warm bath, too. You don't want that paint sticking to your body. It can be very uncomfortable on your skin."

But what the childless Priscilla did not know was that young male children do not appreciate "girls" bathing them, much like her nephew Germane had disapproved. So the more she talked, the more the boy relented. The next thing she knew, Jules, still covered in crème-colored paint, was making a mad dash out her front door. Priscilla ran after him and stood on her front steps. She watched him running all the way home and turning into one of the other brownstones on the street. At least now she knew which house was his.

Although she could hardly know this, her unlikely new acquaintance would be her only friend in the neighborhood for a long time. When Priscilla first purchased the house, she had merely wanted to restore her brownstone to its original glory. But she had been and continued to be determined to make a go of it and become part of this community, too. In time, her certainty and persistence would be rewarded. She and Carlton would gradually get acquainted with a few of their neighbors, and they would slowly begin to enjoy their life together here, too. But it would take a while.

While Priscilla renovated her Harlem brownstone, back in Midtown, "the boys" continued surveilling the comings and the goings-on of Shane and Iggy, along with the others who had already become the usual suspects in this case: the seven confederates on the Met board, the heretofore "mysterious-looking couple" from the incident at the Met on the day of the howling gales and torrential rains in May, and the twins Gaylord and Artemis Thibaut. But Onslow was not among "the other boys" on that aspect of this particular mission because Carlton—without Priscilla's knowledge—had solicited his help in providing the much-needed security for Priscilla, Mr. Hunter, and his crew while they renovated the property. In his so-called day job, Onslow, like Jordy, worked as a broker on Wall Street, and his wife Laura worked on the faculty in antiquities at Columbia University, so Onslow knew Harlem well.

And so it was that Onslow had dispatched his security detail to provide round-the-clock surveillance and security for Priscilla and the others in the Harlem brownstone over the ensuing weeks, which turned into months. While the unsuspecting Priscilla moved about as if she had not a care in the world, all the while, she remained unaware that Carlton and "the other boys" had required Mr. Hunter to agree to the presence of the security detail before they approved him as the project contractor.

As a result, Onslow's security detail was on the case, whether Priscilla sometimes fell asleep at her kitchen table or forgot to lock her doors or close her windows. Some of his men perched on her front steps, and others crouched beneath her windows. Yet others sauntered up and down the street and around the nearby corners. Some carried concealed heavy weaponry, such as those big knives and big pistols they had with them during Priscilla's first time in southern Africa. It was a sign of the times that in 1990, Onslow's security detail did not attract neighborhood attention because many American cities had crime watch groups, some perhaps matching the firepower of his well-armed security detail.

Through it all, Priscilla remained oblivious not only to Onslow's security force but also to the presence of narcotics and prostitution, and even gun violence, in her new neighborhood, even though such happenings could not have been more obvious. Despite all that had happened in her life, particularly in the past few years, she still saw the world through what her siblings and her mother called "rose-colored lenses." To them, that essentially meant that Priscilla saw what she wanted to see and heard what she wanted to hear. Ah, Priscilla! Her good fortune was that her new family and circle of friends provided the surveillance and the security necessary to live out her storybook lifestyle. But the day would come—and soon—when all the money and the protection in the world would not comfort or shield her from the one thing she desired most.

And when she least expected it, too.

15

An "Unauthorized" Plan, for Sure

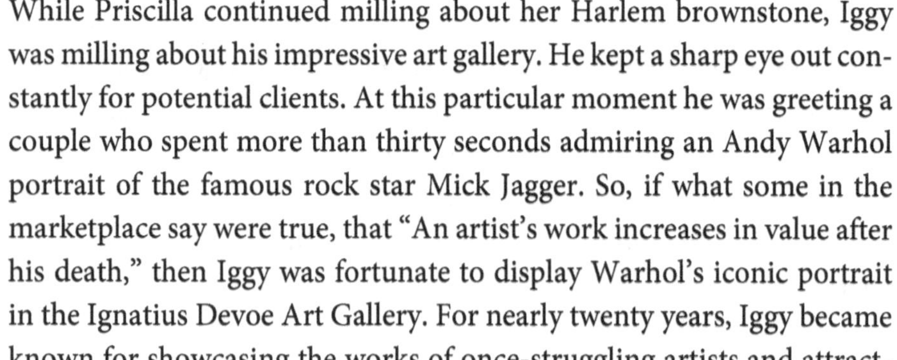

While Priscilla continued milling about her Harlem brownstone, Iggy was milling about his impressive art gallery. He kept a sharp eye out constantly for potential clients. At this particular moment he was greeting a couple who spent more than thirty seconds admiring an Andy Warhol portrait of the famous rock star Mick Jagger. So, if what some in the marketplace say were true, that "An artist's work increases in value after his death," then Iggy was fortunate to display Warhol's iconic portrait in the Ignatius Devoe Art Gallery. For nearly twenty years, Iggy became known for showcasing the works of once-struggling artists and attracting a clientele of relatively high net worth.

Iggy soon turned his attention to another possible client, who seemed engrossed in another painting in his gallery.

"I see Monsieur is captivated by this particular fine piece." But no sooner than he'd gotten those words out his mouth the man who Iggy addressed as "Monsieur" turned around and showed him his whole face. Iggy flinched and then flushed; he felt his blood rush to the top of his earlobes. Then he thought his heart would drop out of his chest, but it did not. He thought he was going to faint, but he did not faint, either.

While Iggy stood gasping for air, the man called out in a distinct French accent, holding his right hand high to his chest, "Someone get this man a drink of water. Or we might call 911."

As some other customers came to Iggy's rescue, the man with the distinct French accent disappeared.

Moments later, Iggy was on the phone in the office of his art gallery.

"Shane, I tell you, it *was* Artemis Thibaut. He was right here in my shop. I knew he wanted me to know that he was the one who performed that silly trick with the red handkerchief at the Met back in May. But now this! The wretched bastard!" Iggy ground his teeth together. He was so agitated that he never wondered why he had assumed his gallery visitor was Artemis Thibaut and not his twin Gaylord, someone Iggy knew well from the Met's board of trustees. It would have been easy, after all, for Gaylord to put on a fake French accent. But Iggy was so traumatized from all that had recently occurred that he had simply assumed that this had been the twin who was his worst nightmare.

But Iggy had been wrong. The visitor who had just spoken with the distinct French accent was not Artemis Thibaut. He had, in fact, been his twin brother Gaylord faking that French accent. If Iggy had been able to keep his wits about him, he could easily have discerned the pink birthmark on his inside right wrist. But Iggy's paranoia had gotten the better of him. Or was that the worst of him?

As it turned out, the twins had played a prank on Iggy to put the feds and the international intelligence authorities off the tail of Artemis

Thibaut. It was, too, the beginning of an ongoing scramble of identities for the twins, and it mightily contributed to much of the confusion.

At least in the short run, their prank worked.

Still on his telephone, "Oh, Iggy," Shane said while Iggy talked and talked, unable to stop babbling about how terrified he still was from what he believed was Artemis Thibaut's visit to his art gallery. His anxiety was contagious. Since Iggy could not see him, Shane tried to calm himself by taking a deep breath and letting it out slowly. Then he said, "You know, Iggy, we might need to contact the authorities, after all."

But just as Shane spoke those last words, an unexpected visitor appeared at the threshold of his office. The figure came in and stood in front of his desk. Then he took the handset from Shane's hand and pressed the receiver, effectively disconnecting the conversation between the two men.

Aghast, Shane simply stared at the unwelcome visitor.

When his line went dead on the other end of the phone, Iggy yelled: "What the—?"

Iggy yelled not at Shane but an intruder who was suddenly standing over him, too. But apart from pulling his thick, long shoulder-length black hair back behind his right ear, Jordy said not a word; instead, he smiled a slow smile of pure menace.

Back in Shane's office at the Met, Tommy Wozniah glowered at Shane, who was, in fact, himself a tall man.

"What the— and who the—?" Shane snapped. Then he shuddered at the look on the taller, nondescript man who wore a stubbed brown ponytail and whose hand remained pressed on his telephone receiver.

"Who *I* am is of no concern to you," said Tommy, who, of course, along with Jordy, were "the boys" from Priscilla's PR firm.

"But," Tommy continued, "if I were you and your friend, Iggy, I'd do exactly as instructed." Then, to the point, he told Shane that Artemis

Thibaut was wanted by the FBI and the international intelligence community for art forgery and theft, after which he asked him, "Do you want to be spared all that is due you for *your* part in creating this mess in the first place."

When Shane mutely nodded, Tommy told him what he must do.

Jordy meanwhile was giving similar instructions to Iggy across town in his office at the Ignatius Devoe Art Gallery.

At the same time, Laverne was learning the surveillance operations' inner workings that "the boys" had set up at the Met and elsewhere. She noticed that everything connected to what "the boys" thought of as their "central command center" in Priscilla's Midtown office on Fifth Avenue. She learned that CF Agent Angelo Delgato was their commanding field agent. When not giving orders and taking messages, he listened in on conversations between Iggy and Shane at their offices at the Met through the listening devices that Jordy had planted some time ago. She also learned that Onslow provided security detail for Priscilla and Mr. Hunter and his construction crew at her Harlem brownstone. Carlton was the only one among them who did not play a significant role in this mission because, as he moved back and forth from Washington, D.C. to New York, he had to keep abreast of his ongoing work as a congressional liaison. Besides, at this point, even his cohorts knew he was too close to Priscilla, anyway. That much Laverne had already figured out for herself.

If only "the boys" had known that, while they carried out their "unauthorized" plan, Laverne, well, she eavesdropped on the lot of them.

Priscilla had long since given her tape recorder to Laverne, who mainly concentrated on listening to the unsuspecting Iggy and Shane, both who almost always carried their attaché cases with them. Although Laverne could not see either Iggy at his art gallery or Shane at his office at the Met, she was listening as Jordy and Tommy separately discon-nected their calls.

She was able to monitor what "the boys" were up to because she had discretely placed a listening device under the front lip of Jordy's desk when Priscilla had introduced her to them. She did so without authori-zation from her new boss because she knew the ways of "the boys." She was a more seasoned intelligence agent than Priscilla, and she knew Priscilla needed all the help she could get. Therefore when Laverne up-dated her on what she had been doing, Priscilla could not have been more impressed.

So, as "the boys"—who were now calling themselves "and Associ-ates, Incorporated," as part of Priscilla's new firm—put their "unauthor-ized" plan into action, they inadvertently snared Shane and Iggy. In so doing, they gave Artemis Thibaut, or so they thought, just enough rope to continue moving about freely before he would eventually get tangled up in his own scheme. The "game" really was "on," at least for the "and Associates, Incorporated." But so, too, was it for Artemis Thibaut.

On a beautiful sunny day in the latter part of June, Priscilla basked in her and Carlton's Waldorf Astoria apartment, soaking in a warm bub-ble bath that had been drawn for her in a Bella Casa cast-iron, claw–foot bathtub. As she thought about her scheme to ensnare Iggy and Shane—along with their seven confederates and that "mysterious-looking cou-ple" who'd visited the Met on the day of the howling gales and torrential rains in May—it suddenly occurred to her that she first needed to rescue Iggy and Shane before she began her real end game. She wanted to avert irreparable harm to the reputation of the Met but also to that pair that she had begun to call, almost affectionately, "the two twerps." But she held no such affinity towards Artemis Thibaut. *For his abuse of all those women,* she thought, *let him rot.* Whether that was her feminist instinct kicking into gear, she could care less. But little did she know that the day would come when her attitude towards Artemis Thibaut would be tempered. At this point, however, she was still unaware of the unauthorized plan of "the boys," who had already inadvertently snared the very people she had set out to rescue. Perhaps Iggy had been prophetic, after all, when, en route to the rendezvous near Poughkeepsie, he had said, "Talk about a tangled web!"

Priscilla rose from her bubble bath, reached for a big fluffy peach-colored towel, and commenced drying herself off. Then, she thought, *Time to get on with it*. She donned her favorite powder-blue jogging outfit and then called Ruth and Laverne. But she made a point of cautioning them not to tell "the boys" where they were going.

When Ruth and Laverne arrived at the Waldorf, Priscilla served them wine along with shrimp, a leafy green salad, crackers and cheese, and an assortment of nuts. As the women nibbled and enjoyed friendly girl talk about the décor of her new Harlem brownstone, Priscilla finally turned to the matter at hand, their mission at the Met. She started by asking Laverne to brief Ruth about what had been revealed in the taped recordings of Iggy's and Shane's conversations and their rendezvous at the Highland-on-the-Hudson resort near Poughkeepsie with their seven Met board confederates.

Ruth was so shocked that she almost dropped her glass of wine. She had known Iggy and Shane for what seemed like a lifetime, and she had, therefore, understood better than Priscilla and Laverne the probable impact of the two men's sharp practice on the New York art world.

Priscilla attempted to pacify her.

"Ruth, I can easily see your anxiety. And I, too, think we need to find a way to avert too much damage to those two twerps. I certainly mean them no ill will. And even though Iggy dug his own grave, we want the Met's reputation to emerge with as little damage as possible. So we have *got* to find a way to pull Iggy *and* Shane—and their seven confederates, too—out of the worst of the consequences I see coming. So, there. Now you have it. That's our *real* dilemma."

Priscilla finally confirmed what "the boys" had suspected all along. Her primary purpose was a PR issue. She wanted to resolve "the mysterious affair at the Met" from a humanitarian perspective and, of course, to retrieve the stolen artwork. She was far less concerned with collecting intel to prosecute Iggy and Shane, although she had less concern for consequences impacting Artemis Thibaut.

As for the seven questionable members of the Met board, Ruth was even more shaken to learn about the extortion racket that they'd been subjected to for more than two decades for merely having posed nude for Thibaut Francois long ago in Paris. She could not believe her ears when Priscilla shared how that nefarious father and son had lured wealthy and unsuspecting American tourists to their Parisian art studio.

"Oh, no!" was all Ruth could say. Then, "That's terrible, just terrible!" Then she wiped a tear from one of her eyes.

"Yes, Ruth," Priscilla said.

Priscilla drained her wine glass and poured another for herself and the two other women. Finally, it was time to share her game plan. She lowered her voice to a whisper. "So this is," she said, with the air of telling an intriguing bedtime story, "what I have in mind."

Even though she did not tell Ruth about her intention of using Laverne as a decoy as a critical element in her plan, Priscilla was aware that Ruth already suspected that Laverne's striking resemblance to her had to figure into whatever Priscilla had in mind. But Ruth still had no idea about how that would fit into solving the mission's puzzle.

Priscilla took a sip, rested her glass on the table, and began: "Now...."

Priscilla ushered Ruth and Laverne, who she now regarded as her lieutenants, out of her apartment. It was time to bring another friend, Defense Attorney Macy Stoner, into the game. She dialed her number and held the phone away from her ear. Macy's speaking voice was loud and sharp. Priscilla braced for what might best be described as a howling gale gushing through her telephone.

"My God, PJ!" Macy shouted into the telephone receiver. "It's been one whole month since you fingered my client, Gaylord, at that charade of a press conference. Are you ready to fill me in on what's *really* going on? Or are you going to let Gaylord bleed out, probably on camera?"

While Macy shouted through the telephone receiver, Priscilla thought about how dramatic she could be at times. Then again, she realized that her friend did deserve a good vent.

"Macy, Girlfriend," Priscilla began again, this time in as pleasant a tone as she could. "How the devil are you?" Without expecting a response, she murmured, "I guess I've been a little preoccupied with my Harlem fixer-upper."

Then, she asked, "Macy? You still there?"

"*Damn it* all, Missy!" Macy was still booming away. "Cut to the chase. I'm not one of your toy soldier boys."

Priscilla got the message. Macy was beyond pissed off with her.

"All right, Mace," Priscilla used her friend's nickname, which, at this moment at least, suited her perfectly. Her friend could be brutal, hence the nickname "Mace." "Meet me at Nathan's Hot Dog kiosk, down the street on Park Avenue. You know the one. Say, twenty minutes, give or take?" Both women hung up their telephones.

Priscilla power-walked in her jogging suit through Waldorf Astoria's main lobby out into Park Avenue's hustle and bustle. She passed people walking dogs, some with leashes pulling a half-dozen or more canines prancing and romping about. She was glad that, in her big Jackie

O-style sunglasses, no one recognized her. She joined the ebb and flow of other pedestrians hurrying about as if they were late for appointments. She glanced at a large clock on a nearby office building. "Ah, twelve more minutes to get there."

Elbows raised and pumping, she picked up her pace and even bumped into some people, as if they had gotten in her way. Welcome to New York City!

But after meeting up with Macy at the hot dog stand, she found herself pleading with her friend.

"Oh, Mace, *please* trust me. Gaylord must *not* be forewarned. He has got to appear to be stunned by the news that he has a twin brother and that his twin brother is wanted by the feds and the international intelligence authorities for art forgery and theft."

At the time, Priscilla was unaware of the twin brothers' continuing close relationship and that Gaylord had always assumed that his brother had committed petty crimes in the art world but never anything as significant as forgery and theft. Nor was she aware that all that was about to come to a head.

Even as Priscilla devoured her hot dog covered with sauerkraut, she continued to pressure Macy not to overreact.

"And, as far as Iggy and Shane are concerned, we'll deal with them later. But first and foremost, we need to arrange for the capture of Artemis Thibaut. He's the bad seed."

Macy was not buying her argument just yet. She was angrier than she had been before they had met up. She stomped away from Priscilla.

A little later that afternoon, Macy was even more enraged when, just after meeting Priscilla at the hot dog kiosk, she got wind of a press conference that Ruth was convening at the Met. *My God*! Macy winced. *Surely, she could have told me about another press conference.*

But what Macy did not know was that Priscilla had indeed put her own game plan in effect. Besides, in Priscilla's way of thinking, she had just forewarned her friend about something she maybe should not have in the first place. Just like Macy had to protect her client's best interests, so, too, did Priscilla, whose client was the Metropolitan Museum of Art. Perhaps Jordy had been correct earlier when he surmised how complicated this case was turning out to be.

16

A French Mystery Novel

Once again Ruth Steiner was at the press conference podium in the Met boardroom, serving as the primary spokesperson for P. J. Austin and Associates, Inc. Already, in its first moments, she had galvanized the sensation-seeking New York City press corps by linking the developing scandal at the Metropolitan Museum of Art with the fortunes of unsuspecting fine art collectors in Asia, North America, South America, and yet-to-be-named other markets. At stake, she had revealed were the validation of the provenance *and* the authenticity of certain masterpieces, including works by Picasso, Monet, and Chagall.

Ruth paused in her presentation to raise a glass of water to her lips. She had intended to take a sedate sip but instead gulped it. She usually could breeze through events like this, but being on live television unnerved her. This news conference was being broadcast live by one of the New York television stations.

Oh no, she thought, *live TV!*

She began her opening remarks by speaking more conversationally, but now, as her wont, she read from prepared remarks. First she concentrated on the mysterious event that had occurred the previous spring in the Chagall Gallery of the Met:

> On Wednesday of the fourth week in May, an observant volunteer museum docent noticed something peculiar in the Marc Chagall Gallery during the howling gales and torrential rains. She particularly pointed out that the *Soleil dans le Ciel de Saint-Paul* 'looked somewhat strange.'
>
> This observation triggered her suspicions because, only days earlier, she had noticed something similarly odd with two other paintings: Oscar-Claude Monet's *La Promenade* and Paris Bordone's *Diana and the Two Nymphs*.
>
> When reports of the docent's concerns reached the administration, curators were called in to examine the three paintings in question. Alarm ratcheted up when it was determined that the three paintings did appear to have been tampered with—and perhaps were even forgeries. Then, Ignatius Devoe, the Met's board chairman, convened an emergency meeting of the trustees, who, in turn, authorized an investigation by their insurance agency.

Ruth paused for all that to sink in. She scanned the assembled media representatives and duly noted that the news reporters had edged forward in their seats. They were clearly excited. She took a deep breath and continued:

> But something else had happened on that day in May. A museum surveillance camera had captured some unusual images in the gallery where the Chagall in question had been hanging. Curiously, one couple had opened a large red handkerchief, blocking the Chagall for a few seconds. There had also been a large tourist group in the gallery simultaneously, all wearing red-and-white-striped vinyl raincoats.
>
> Later, when the museum conducted its investigation, one of the security guards said that that scene—that bizarre big red handkerchief and those singular tourists in the red-and-white-striped raincoats—reminded him of *The Thomas Crown Affair*.
>
> To be sure, the investigators concluded that both the red handkerchief and the red-and-white-striped raincoat crowd had functioned as some kind of diversion or even a signal of sorts.

Ruth looked up from her script and met the eyes of some of the curious news reporters.

> But a diversion from what or a signal to whom, and why? she queried.

She waited for the murmurs of the news reporters to subside and then continued.

> Nothing was stolen from the museum. So our best guess is that whoever was involved had merely wanted to divert attention away from whatever 'the mysterious-looking couple' was up to in the first place.
>
> Upon closer scrutiny of the museum surveillance footage, investigators determined that the man who had held up that red handkerchief bore a striking resemblance to one Thibaut Francois Moreaux. If you recall, back during our press conference on this matter in early June, we told you about this notorious mastermind behind an elaborate scheme of forgery, theft, and extortion. We told you that Thibaut Francois had even outwitted the Germans during the Nazi Occupation, that he stole, forged, and sold some of their stolen artwork around the world, including Asia, Austria, America, South America, and elsewhere. But the man in the museum's surveillance footage could not have been Thibaut Francois because he had died several months previously at his home in Paris.

Again Ruth paused, this time for special effect. Then she continued:

> Enter the federal and international intelligence authorities. They, mainly the French, connected the dots: the man in the museum surveillance footage was,

in fact, one of the *sons* of the infamous Thibaut Francois (Moreaux) and Miriam Millsap, the daughter of Artemis Millsap III of New York City.

So silent was the room that Ruth could have heard a pin drop, and so, too, could the television viewers in their homes and offices. By this time that audience included Defense Attorney Macy Stoner, who was beginning to understand why her friend had been so guarded in their conversation at the hotdog stand.

Back at the press conference, Ruth signaled to Alfrieda, who proceeded to distribute the text of what Ruth was about to say.

"Bear with me, please," she said. "This gets a little complicated. But you can follow along with what my assistant is handing out right now."

As the reporters bent over their handouts, Ruth began reading:

> Miriam Millsap first met Thibaut Francois while on holiday in Paris in the late 1940s. The couple had an affair. In 1947, Miriam became pregnant and gave birth to twin boys, after which she and Thibaut Francois brought their twin baby boys home to meet her parents here in Manhattan.
>
> During their visit, Thibaut Francois extorted a vast sum of money from Artemis Millsap III in exchange for his silence that Miriam had given birth to twin boys out of wedlock, among other things.
>
> Then Thibaut Francois took one of his infant twin sons back home to Paris, where he registered him as Artemis Thibaut Millsap Moreaux. As his son grew up there, Thibaut Francois taught him how to forge and steal highly valued works of art.

Ruth stopped reading.

Then she said, "Let me give you some more background. Some perspective, actually. Remember that we're talking about incidents that happened in 1947. Such was the stuff of scandals, especially for the socially prominent, like the Millsaps of Manhattan."

Her gaze noted the incredulous and some shocked expressions on the news reporters' faces. She even heard a few of their voices, as they could not resist whispering loudly to their fellow reporters.

One said, "Incredible."

Another said, "Who would've thought!"

A third shook her head and said, "Reads like a French Mystery novel to me. At the least, a *Masterpiece Mystery*!"

When the hubbub died down, Ruth continued reading from the handout:

> Meanwhile, Miriam Millsap married the son of Greek shipping magnate Demetrios Omiros. The couple named her twin son Gaylord Millsap Omiros and raised him here in New York City and Mykonos.
>
> As some of you know, Miriam's father, Artemis Millsap III, died three years ago.
>
> And as we speak, Miriam and her husband, Demetrios, are being interviewed by international intelligence officials at their home in Mykonos.
>
> As for Gaylord Millsap Omiros, well, he has already given up his seat on the board of trustees at the Met, pending an investigation into his association with someone who has tampered with or maybe even stolen, highly-valued works of art. He presently is at

his Manhattan residence where he is probably learning about all of this news for the first time, that is, that
his *birth* father was the notorious Thibaut Francois,
that he has a *twin* brother, and, that the federal and
international intelligence officials want his twin
brother for art forgery and theft of highly-valued
works of art.

Ruth paused in reading her script. She looked out at the reporters. But none of them asked a single question. The New York City press corps simply waited for her to continue reading her fascinating tale:

> Earlier, some of you asked about the whereabouts
> of Ignatius Devoe and Shane Carpenter. Both men are
> working with federal and international intelligence of-
> ficials to authenticate the three paintings at the Met
> and any other paintings at other museums here and
> abroad. Mr. Devoe and Mr. Carpenter are also work-
> ing with directors and curators for other reputable
> museums in Asia, Europe, South America, and a few
> other places, anywhere that Thibaut Francois is be-
> lieved to have tampered with and maybe even stolen
> and sold art masterpieces.

Ruth folded her hands on the podium in finality.
"So there you have it." She paused briefly. "As PJ likes to say, 'When we know more, so, too, will you.'"

But then she added, "But I did want to alert you that the next time that you learn anything remotely related to *this* matter, such communications might come directly from the federal and international intelligence officials identified in your press packets."

Finally, with tremendous relief, Ruth said, "Thank you for coming and good day."

17

The Man Who Was, in fact,
Artemis Thibaut

At the Millsap Manhattan mansion on Sutton Place in New York City, Defense Attorney Macy Stoner sat in the parlor with the man she and the three federal intelligence agents believed was Gaylord Millsap Omiros. Chief among the federal officials was FBI Agent Marvin Rothschild. As it so happened, they had all watched Ruth's televised press conference at the Met.

"Gaylord"—who, unbeknown to the others in the parlor was, in fact, his twin brother Artemis—was a handsome man of nearly forty-two years of age. He pretended to be ignorant of several key assertions revealed at the press conference, including that he had a twin brother, that his mother had borne him out of wedlock, or that his birth father—and his twin, too—were notorious art forgers and thieves. But Artemis was a gifted liar. He had no trouble pretending that his entire life was crumbling around him, that he had been deceived by the very people he loved most, and that now he did not know where to turn or what to do.

The more FBI Agent Rothschild and his colleagues questioned the man they believed was Gaylord—and who was, in fact, Artemis Thibaut—the more convinced they were this man had not the slightest clue about what he had just learned. For Artemis Thibaut, like his father before him, was a darn good actor, too.

As Macy watched "Gaylord," she said, "Well, my friend, at least now you know about your connection to Thibaut Francois Moreaux and Artemis Thibaut Millsap Moreaux." She thought to console him.

"But none of us controls our lineage."

But he responded tartly. "Ever heard the expression, 'ignorance is no excuse of the law?'"

Macy replied. "*Au contraire*, Gaylord. We're not talking about 'the law.' The issue is whether *you violated* the Met's code of ethics. And I submit to you that you did *not*. You never knowingly or intentionally associated with Thibaut Francois, or Artemis Thibaut, for that matter. Why, you yourself only just learned about all this, and *them*, too, from the televised press conference." If only Macy had known.

While Macy and "Gaylord" continued talking, two federal agents wearing jackets that displayed FBI in big block letters set about searching the lavish mansion for documents, such as passports and bills of sale—and especially for possibly stolen artwork. They collected birth certificates, trust funds, and last wills and testaments. They also retrieved artifacts, portraits, and other works of art, anything that might otherwise connect Gaylord to his biological father, Thibaut Francois, or his twin brother Artemis Thibaut.

But one investigator—CF Agent Laverne Macon—was not with the others on Sutton Place for the interrogation and search. She alone, among the federal and international intelligence officials, had already closely examined the birth certificates and other documents that pertained to the twins. But she kept to herself what she had previously discovered until she felt the time was nigh to share it with Priscilla. *All in due time*, she thought as she memorized documentation she'd found that distinguished the twins from each other. "In due time," she smiled and repeated to herself.

As Priscilla's look-alike, Laverne was amused that so much in this case hinged on the identical twins. Already she had altered her appearance to seem even more like Priscilla. Today and every day, she dressed like Priscilla in understated, elegant outfits, mostly pantsuits and stylish high heels that she'd borrowed from Priscilla's wardrobe at her Waldorf apartment. She pulled her hair back and put it in a clamp, and she wore thick black horn rims, which hid her brown eyes but highlighted those distinct high cheekbones of the Austin clan. Added to all that, she carried a clipboard with a legal pad and a pen from time to time. So whenever people saw her, they merely assumed that she was, in fact, P.J. Austin-Bernhardt.

Laverne and Priscilla also, it so happened, shared American Indian heritage. Laverne, who was part Choctaw, sported a naturally tan complexion. During African American slavery, some of Priscilla's Austin ancestors had taken up with and married Choctaw. Over time they had blended into the African slave population in Mississippi—not to mention those who passed as white. But many of Laverne's ancestors had been forced out of Mississippi during the infamous Trail of Tears and walked some 500 miles, eventually settling in Oklahoma. So it was that

Laverne and Priscilla had more in common than their striking resemblance. They shared a common genealogy in their race and ethnicity.

It was back in Tulsa when the two women had shared a meal at that diner and talked late into the night that Laverne had filled Priscilla in on their shared background. She said that documentation exists about how, "during both World Wars, at least nineteen Choctaw served the United States Army admirably. Along with the Navajo in World War II and the Korean and the Vietnam wars," Laverne had shared that "our ancestors were what was called 'code-talkers,' radio operators who broadcasted secret information in their native language. During the Second World War, even the Germans couldn't break the code. And just think, at the time, we weren't even considered American citizens."

At that, Priscilla remembered the time when she had attended the reception for then-presidential hopeful Fleetwood Marshall Hollingsworth at his family's Choctaw Ridge Resort. *Now*, she thought, *I'm finally filling in the gaps in some of my own family histories.*

But Laverne did not confide to Priscilla that she, too, could *speak* "the code," for she was fluent in her Choctaw ancestors' language—another reason that she was so invaluable to the "unauthorized" CF unit of the CIA. But this was something that Priscilla would eventually learn about, but later.

Back inside the Millsap Manhattan mansion, FBI Agent Rothschild interrupted the conversation between Defense Attorney Stoner and her client "Gaylord"—the man who was, in fact, Artemis Thibaut.

"Sorry," he said, "but my men need the keys to the desk drawers and the cabinets. And the wine cellar, too. Also, do you happen to know the combination of the safes, the one in the office and your grandfather's bedchamber?"

"My goodness," said the man they assumed was Gaylord. "I haven't looked in Grandfather's safes in years." He lied. But he left the room and soon returned with several keys, which he handed to the investigators. He also gave Agent Rothschild an index card that contained the combinations to the two safes.

Agent Rothschild did not tell Gaylord that his men had already obtained copies of documents pertaining to his grandfather's investment portfolios, bank accounts, and other personal effects validating the paternity of the twins' biological father, Thibaut Francois Moreaux. These documents, along with other papers, documented that Demetrios Omiros II was Gaylord's adoptive father.

When "Gaylord" sat back down in a chair near Macy, he stared into her eyes to try to determine whether she could detect any difference between him and his twin. He thought of himself as slightly intuitive, yet it seemed that she had no clue about his true identity. So he continued with his charade, only this time he upped the ante—and perhaps ought to have been awarded an Oscar for his performance.

He told Macy what he thought the real Gaylord might have said in his position. "Macy, do you *really* think I want to return to the Met's board of trustees, or any other board, for that matter?" Without waiting for an answer, he turned to Agent Rothschild and said with hauteur, "And as soon as you fellows finish rummaging through my life, I'm going to take a much-needed vacation away from all this and what I once thought was a fairly privileged life. I might even give up my citizenship. I need to think all this over."

Macy thought that she felt "Gaylord's" pain and that this was his grief and pain talking. For Macy had correctly assumed that the Gaylord she knew would not give up his American citizenship so cavalierly. But she was beginning to feel a certain uneasiness about this man sitting next to her. The Gaylord she knew was more thoughtful, warm, and did not have a cold streak in him. But she dismissed her reservations, telling herself that she was jumping to a wrong conclusion.

"All right, Gaylord, but I hope you let me clear up your part in all this *before* you go and do something foolish. And just in case you're wondering, you're still on my A-list. I don't much care who your daddy is, or was—or your brother, either." She patted her client's hand and turned to the FBI Agent. "Will there be anything else?"

"Well, Counselor, since you asked," Agent Rothschild said. "There's still the matter of a medical examination. You know, blood tests, DNA, and all. We'll also perform a thorough accounting of his finances, interview his friends and acquaintances, investigate his fashion house business, as well as any passport activity. The works." He made a faint smile. "But, come on, Attorney Stoner, you know the drill."

She nodded.

Of course, the feds and the international intelligence officials were aware that "Gaylord," like his biological father, was not only a creative artist but also a businessman. In addition to his volunteer work on the board of trustees at the Met, the investigators would also be looking into the Gaylord Fashion House, with shops in Paris, Milan, Mykonos, and Rio de Janeiro.

Macy then thanked the FBI agent for explaining the extent of the American and international intelligence officials' investigations.

"You just spared me having to tell my client what else was coming. So, Agent Rothschild, thanks for making this much smoother than it could have been." The two of them were actually on a first-name basis. But when working on a case, Macy kept to protocol and never called her colleague in law enforcement by his name, "Marvin."

Yet, it never once occurred to either of them that meanwhile, "Gaylord" was collecting intel on them—although thankfully, as it so happened, he would never have the opportunity to use what he had observed for any nefarious purpose.

Macy paused for a moment before leaving the mansion. She knew the news reporters would be waiting for her and "Gaylord" on the doorstep waving their microphones with their cameras rolling and flashing. To herself she thought, *Where's Missy when you need her*? But just as a house servant held the front door open for her, she heard Priscilla's unmistakable voice.

"OK, guys," Priscilla was saying, "by now, you all know what Attorney Macy Stoner's client, Gaylord Millsap Omiros, has just learned. So give her a break. And give that client of hers, too, some time to sort through all this. I'm certain he'll make a statement. But I gotta tell you, the man inside this lovely home hasn't the foggiest idea what to make of what he's just learned." Then she gave them all a curt nod of dismissal.

But one persistent reporter could not resist a follow-up question. "Do you know whether Gaylord will join his mother and her husband in Greece?" Then, as he realized how awkward his question was, he answered it for himself, "Later, maybe, but, considering… not just yet."

Before Macy knew anything else, she sounded like her friend Priscilla when she said, with a sort of smile, "Sure, when we know more, so, too, will you."

But then she beamed at her girlfriend, who had just rescued her from the press mob, and all was forgiven, well, pretty much all.

Three days after the FBI and the international intelligence officials finished their analyses of the data that they had collected and essentially, although prematurely, cleared Gaylord Millsap Omiros of any "intentional" wrongdoing in the case involving "the mysterious affair at the

Met," FBI Agent Rothschild delivered the good news to "Gaylord" at the Sutton Place mansion. Meanwhile, Priscilla had made her way to the same place, where she discretely pulled the FBI Agent aside and brought him into the loop with the information that CF Agent Macon had shared with her about how to tell these twins apart.

Then, as Agent Rothschild was about to tell "Gaylord" that he was free to leave the country for what he had said was "a much-needed vacation," "Gaylord" held out his right hand to shake the other man's hand.

Agent Rothschild held his gaze steady. There was no pink birthmark on the inside of this man's right wrist. And although the FBI agent did not move to apprehend the man, he winked at Priscilla in acknowledgment that this man was, in fact, the other twin, Artemis Thibaut.

Priscilla gave the FBI agent the very briefest nod. The two of them had also worked together before, and so without saying a word, they both understood that they needed to dispense with their original scheme of things. So, they both gave Artemis Thibaut even more rope.

After bringing her FBI colleague up to speed about how to discern the difference between the twin brothers, Priscilla made her way out of the Millsap Manhattan mansion, but she would soon return.

Later that same day, Defense Attorney Macy Stoner was on her way again to see her client on Sutton Place. But to her surprise, just as she was about to enter the front door of the mansion, Priscilla got out of a taxi and joined her.

"Funny seeing you here again," Macy said, with much sarcasm, "'*after* the mysterious affair at the Met' has been solved, at least the part that concerns my client." Macy still had a bit of an attitude concerning Priscilla. It was nice that she had handled the news reporters as she had done earlier, but Macy still did not know what Priscilla had told FBI Agent Rothschild about the distinguishing birthmarks. Moreover, she had lingering resentment from her earlier encounter with Priscilla at the hot dog stand.

Nevertheless, Priscilla had already pushed past all of that.

"I told you that your Gaylord would be all right. Sorry for the prolonged agony. But now, we need to go over one more thing." To Priscilla's knowledge, Macy did not know that the man who she thought was Gaylord was, in fact, his twin brother Artemis Thibaut. It was time that Macy knew what was what and who was who.

Macy's eyebrows arched. "Now what?"

"Now we need to make sure that Artemis Thibaut *and* Ignatius Devoe get wind of the fact that we're onto something else that those disreputable creatures have done."

"Iggy, too?" Macy frowned. "Now, what're you going on about?"

Priscilla sat down on the doorstep entrance to the mansion and lightly patted the cement next to her. After a second's hesitation, Macy sat down beside her.

The two of them had their heads together as Priscilla told her the whole truth, or a big chunk of it anyway. By then, the entire New York City press corps knew that the Millsaps were fine art collectors. But what virtually no one but Priscilla and her intelligence associates knew was that Artemis Millsap III had held the authentic Chagall *Soleil dans le Ciel de Saint-Paul* in his possession for nearly forty-two years. But the next revelation had come from FBI Agent Rothschild and his international intelligence colleagues during their interrogation of Ignatius Devoe. He'd apparently been sufficiently terrified that he had talked and talked and talked, eventually confiding where to find the authentic Monet *La Promenade* and Bordone's *Diane and the Two Nymphs*.

Priscilla said that "as this whole mess unravels, many people the world over will learn of the treachery of both Thibaut Francois and his son Artemis Thibaut."

As it turned out, Iggy had kept his secrets for so many years so that he would have an ace in the hole as leverage if ever his day of reckoning came. But it was yet to be determined how much weight his leverage actually carried.

At that revelation, the lawyer whistled. "Well, damn." Actually, she used stronger language.

As for how all this impacted not just Iggy but also Shane, the executive director at the Met had problems of his own with the feds and the international intelligence officials; by taking Shane into his confidence, Iggy had made him an accessory after the fact and had used him in much the same way as Thibaut Francois had used him long ago in Paris. But by the time the authorities had finished interrogating and running background checks on Shane, it was clear that Shane had only known whatever it was that Iggy had wanted him to know—which, as it turned out, was not much. Even so, as the investigation had lingered much longer than he had ever anticipated, Shane had grown increasingly despondent. Mostly though, after having been Iggy's colleague *and* lover for some dozen or more years, he suddenly realized that he had never known the real Ignatius Devoe, a.k.a. Ignatius Devonshire, after all.

18

Shopping in Gay Paree & Raid at New Rochelle

Priscilla's direct line at her Midtown Manhattan PR office was ringing off the hook. She snatched it.

"PJ here."

"Hi there, famous one."

Priscilla whooped. "Girlfriend! What's happening?"

Julia grinned, newly aware of how much she missed her longtime friend and confidante. Columbus was different, and definitely lesser, without her. "*What's happening* is that you're happening. So many calls, so many offers."

It was true. P.J. Austin and Associates, Incorporated was growing, primarily due to Priscilla's increasing notoriety as a *PR consultant extraordinaire*, not to mention public perception about her handling of the scandal at The Metropolitan Museum of Art.

"Anything I need to know or would really want to do?" Sometimes Priscilla thought that Julia knew her more than she knew herself.

"Some interesting speaking engagements. In particular, one from President Bernard W. Franklin at Livingstone College." She knew how much Priscilla loved her undergraduate alma mater, especially its new president and his wife.

"Depending on the date, that one's a definite 'yes,'" Priscilla said. "Details?"

Julia told her it was for Founders Day 1991 and identified a February date. Then she read aloud the invitation: "Many of our students will benefit from the wisdom of someone of your prominence, someone who once walked 'beneath thy maples and thy oaks.'"

Julia laughed aloud. "No mention of an honorarium, though. The president must be appealing to your better angels." Julia kept laughing.

Even as Priscilla agreed, she was remembering her hallowed time "beneath thy maples and thy oaks" and deciding that the theme of her speech would be "Taking Ownership of One's Own Life."

"Is this one a go?"

"Yes, Julia. 'This one is a go.'" Priscilla hardly ever passed up a chance to return to her alma mater.

"What else you got?" she asked as she eagerly listened to an array of additional requests to speak at other colleges and schools, and organizations such as the American Association of University Women, the National Association of Professional Women, the Public Relations Society of America, and the NAACP. Some came with hefty offers of honoraria for keynote speaking, whereas others were pro bono and began with buzz words and phrases such as "the joy of giving back to…."

After Priscilla had heard enough, she ended that part of the conversation. "Say, Julia, let's talk about something else."

The two friends caught up with the minutiae of their everyday lives. Priscilla shared how thankful she was that she and Carlton could not be happier, and for a while, she talked about fixtures and hardwood floors for her Harlem brownstone.

"And my work on the Met case is going great," she said. "Investigating a mystery at the Met is the likes of which I never before imagined would have crossed my desk. Eat your heart out, Nick and Nora Charles!" She almost mentioned Sherlock Holmes but reconsidered since this, after all, was the late twentieth century.

But she did tell Julia her exciting news that, as part of her Met case, she was planning two European jaunts, one to Paris and another to the Greek island of Mykonos.

"Wow," Julia exclaimed. "You go, girl!"

But that same morning that she had been on Memory Lane with Julia, Priscilla received a letter from Arvana, who was still incarcerated at the New Hampshire Correctional Facility for Women in Goffstown. She recognized the letter immediately because of all the numbers and the seemingly encrypted data on the envelope's return address section. Priscilla's eyes welled with tears as she read that Arvana had already recruited three fellow inmates to work with her in establishing her program to help women who had suffered abusive relationships or who themselves were narcotics addicts. Arvana had been pampered all her life, had been an international jet-setter, and had rarely risen from her bed at Bow Lake before noon. Yet she had adjusted to prison life remarkably well. More importantly, since Arvana finally sounded happy, so, Priscilla was happy for her, too.

Yet, when she finished reading Arvana's letter, Priscilla's reflective mood continued. Not everyone in her world—and especially her family—was as happy as she wished they were. Not Carlton's mother and not her own mother, either.

Although Lady Chelsea was pleased that Priscilla and Carlton had taken up residence closer to Bow Lake—New York is closer than Columbus. But she had made no effort to hide her disappointment that Priscilla had purchased a Harlem brownstone, where she and Carlton planned to reside eventually. She had dreamed, when Priscilla announced that she was opening a branch office in "the City," that the couple would live with her and Father at Bow Lake, from where she maintained they could "easily commute to the City."

But Priscilla had frankly wanted some space between her and her in-laws, not to mention the opportunity to begin anew in their own place in Harlem. "And that," Priscilla had told Lady Chelsea and Father, "does not include residing at the Waldorf Astoria forever, either." Although she loved the lavish hotel, it was not exactly an ideal place for her to live and make a go of her new life. Happily for Priscilla, Carlton had agreed with his bride and supported buying the Harlem brownstone.

In a way, Liza also had issues with Priscilla's lifestyle choices. Over time she had grown weary over her daughter's moving about so much. She had mainly been very cool when Priscilla had phoned her with news about a trip to Paris and the Greek islands. For Liza, Priscilla's quarterly trips to Zimbabwe and South Africa as part of the Bernhardt Foundation work involved more than enough traveling. Priscilla had tried to be patient. She knew how hard it had been for Liza when she herself had been so at risk during Priscilla's first time in southern Africa. Liza and her grandson Germane, too, had been in fear for their lives as part of all that. She supposed, however, that Liza might be trying in her own way to overcome her fear for her daughter's safety. But still, Priscilla had continued with her plans for this next European trip. In time, she hoped her mother would come to accept that she loved traveling for practically any reason.

Priscilla wished that both Lady Chelsea and Liza would come around and accept her as she was. She remembered what her former boss and mentor, the late Senator Callahan, used to tell her all the time: *Sometimes ya gotta do what ya gotta do to get what ya want*. But at that memory, Priscilla's mood darkened, for she still mourned him. He had died not so long ago during her special envoy mission. But Priscilla realized, and not for the first time, that her life had taken a completely different course than any of her friends and colleagues back in Ohio could ever have imagined.

Macy was at Priscilla's office very late that afternoon, in fact, just before six o'clock. She had come at Priscilla's invitation. Later they were going out to dinner.

But first Priscilla needed to come clean about Gaylord and Artemis Thibaut. She had tried to do this on the front steps of the Sutton Place mansion. But with all the comings and goings of the FBI agents and those nosey New York news reporters, she had kept being interrupted.

Finally, there in Priscilla's Midtown Manhattan office, Macy frowned as she listened hard to the tangled tale. When Priscilla told her that the man who she recently thought was her client Gaylord was actually his twin brother Artemis Thibaut and that the real Gaylord still did not know that not only Priscilla but the American and the international intelligence authorities were onto him, Macy felt faint, then furious. Mostly though, she felt deceived. Then she recalled her uneasy feelings about "Gaylord." *Should have listened to my gut.*

While Priscilla finished her story, Macy collected herself and then asked about something else Priscilla had recently said, and that was still on her mind.

"Okay, Missy, I understand about the switcheroo. But what's all this stuff you were saying about going to Paris? And are you also telling me that you're planning on going to Mykonos, too? That this case now stretches to France and Greece?"

"Yes, and yes. And I'd like you to come along with me."

"Me, in France?" Macy leaned forward in excitement. "*And* the Greek Isles?"

"Work," Priscilla said with a shrug. "What can I say? Sometimes ya gotta do what ya gotta do." She laughed.

Then, more seriously, she said, "But really, I'm asking if you're up for a shopping spree in Gay Paree? And Mykonos?

"Paris, I get that. From what you say, it all started in Paris. But what's the Greek connection? I understand that the mother of the twins lives there, but what has she to do with any of this?"

"In due time, Girlfriend. But I still have two questions for you. Is your passport up to date, and where do you want to go to dinner tonight?"

Macy laughed and held out her right hand in the shape of a fist. They fist-bumped and then high-fived. "You're on," she said. "And let's do steak tonight. I'm in a red-meat kind of mood."

In the middle of the following night, television news hawks eagerly watched as the story about "the mysterious affair at the Met" crossed the Atlantic.

International intelligence officers, including the American CIA— and, some said, even an FBI agent or two—converged on the lavish Moreaux property in Paris and, later, inside the gates of the stately country chateau, which Thibaut Francois once owned, and now by his twin sons Artemis Thibaut and Gaylord.

Throughout Priscilla's look-alike, Laverne Macon—who was already in Paris working as the CIA agent—kept Priscilla briefed about the investigations at each property. Just as she had successfully played her part as Priscilla in New York City, she was about to do the same in Gay Paree and later in Mykonos. The paparazzi who captured her with their long camera' lenses were none the wiser on the Continent than they had been in New York City. They thought that Priscilla was in France long before she had ever even crossed the Atlantic with Macy.

Meanwhile, Priscilla and Macy were finally in Gay Paree, shopping at an haute couture boutique on *La Rive Droite*, "the Right Bank." But occasionally, at regular intervals, when Priscilla was a safe distance away from Macy, she would intercept and read another handwritten note from Agent Macon that somehow had ended up in her possession.

"You might find some amusing entertainment under wraps at the Moreaux estate," one note had read. "We're confiscating it as I write this note. BURN!" But in a postscript, she had written: "Incidentally, how do you do what you do in these darn high heels? They're killing me! Ta ta!" Priscilla had laughed when she read that one, and then, as she walked outside the high-fashion boutique, she had flamed her cigarette lighter to the note and burned it. But when she looked up, Macy had been staring at her through the boutique window with a puzzled expression on her face.

Nonchalantly Priscilla tossed the burning note to the sidewalk and stomped on it before waltzing back inside the shop. "Just getting rid of some incriminating evidence," she said in an exaggerated hush-hush tone, as though that possibility were hilarious.

"You sure are a strange one," Macy said, telling herself that, of course, Priscilla could not possibly be some sort of intelligence agent. "But look here, Missy. These dresses are to die for."

Clever as she was, Priscilla did not know everything that was going on.

Mostly, she was unaware that "the boys," who had begun to call themselves "and Associates, Incorporated," had, in fact, been CIA plants for the entire time that her new business venture had been operating.

CIA Deputy Director James Froley and FBI Agent Rothschild, who often worked together, knew Priscilla well. It had been clear to both of them that Priscilla would never have passed up some kind of ongoing work with "the boys," with whom she shared natural history. For example, they had looked out for her during her recent special envoy mission to the Middle East. So, of course, they had infiltrated P. J. Austin and Associates, Inc.

But these seasoned FBI and CIA officers also assumed that "the boys" had accomplished this infiltration with the highest motives and positive operational methods. Both agencies still had functional relationships with Laverne Macon as a CIA special op, and they counted on her to make sure nothing "the boys" did would get out of hand. Priscilla, too, was still on board as a CIA intelligence agent. Only this time, in this mission concerning the Met, if she had thought about this at all, they thought she would probably not have maintained that she was operating as an intelligence agent either on her own or "in service to our country."

There were other rather technical facets as well. None of them, not "the boys," Laverne, or Priscilla, had given much thought to the Executive Order that prohibited active duty by special operatives on American soil. But at least Priscilla had covered her tracks by keeping FBI Agent Rothschild apprised of her movements.

As things stood, no one, except FBI Agent Rothschild and CF Agent Macon, knew what Priscilla, and now Macy, knew—that the twins had swapped places.

While Priscilla, Macy, and Laverne were in Paris, back in America, slightly north of New York City, in the community of New Rochelle, the real Gaylord Millsap Omiros had not the slightest idea that he had been shadowed since his visit to the Ignatius Devoe Art Gallery.

He and Adrienne Hopkins, Artemis Thibaut's girlfriend, and the woman who had accompanied the real Artemis Thibaut to the Met on the day of the howling gales and torrential rains in May, were simply enjoying a moment of calm now that they believed they were out of the fray. Like many others, they had watched Ruth conduct her latest, perhaps last, press conference at the Met. So that evening, they were just enjoying what they thought was a quiet time at this stately Victorian home they had rented.

But something unexpected happened.

First, the doorbell rang, which was peculiar because no one knew they were even there. *Who could that be*? they both must have wondered.

Then they heard the voice of a young man shouting, "Pizza delivery!"

Unthinkingly, Gaylord made for the door. "I didn't know you ordered pizza," he said to Adrienne as he opened the door.

Then, before Gaylord and Adrienne knew it, they watched as a battery of men wearing riot gear with big block letters FBI printed on their bulletproof vests and carrying heavy weaponry—raised to the ready—rushed across the threshold. At lightning speed, more men wearing riot gear were pouring in from the rear of the house. Even more frightening, they were pointing their heavy weaponry at Gaylord and Adrienne.

"Nah, this cannot be happening," said Gaylord. "We're not drug dealers or anything of the sort. Why're you people here? Surely," he declared matter-of-factly, "you have the wrong house."

The FBI had the right house, all right.

But did they have the right man?

FBI Agent Rothschild stood in front of Gaylord Millsap Omiros, who, like his twin brother Artemis Thibaut, bore the blonde hair of his mother Miriam Millsap Omiros and the blue eyes of his father Thibaut Francois. He was trim, tall, and handsome, too.

Then, FBI Agent Rothschild read the man his constitutional rights:

"Artemis Thibaut Millsap Moreaux, you're under arrest for the theft of Marc Chagall's *Soleil dans le Ciel de Saint-Paul*, Oscar-Claude Monet's *La Promenade*, and Paris Bordone's *Diana and the Two Nymphs*, three highly-valued portraits from The Metropolitan Museum of Art. You are also charged with forging Pablo Picasso's *Nude: Green Leaves and Bust*, *Bullfight: The Death of Toreador*, and *The Death of Casagemas*. For extortion, too, here in New York, in Paris, and Mykonos. You have the right to an attorney. Anything you say can and will be used against you in a court of law.'"

Gaylord Millsap Omiros stared at the FBI agent in utter disbelief. "No, no, officer," his eyes blinked. "You've got the wrong man. You're looking for my twin brother Artemis Thibaut."

"Sure," said FBI Agent Rothschild. "Tell it to the judge."

Gaylord was in shock and, for once, turned silent. But his thoughts raced: *Can't they see I'm not my twin brother? And my brother would never have done those awful things.* After nearly forty-two years of limited acquaintance with his twin, Gaylord still had no idea that his brother had stolen or even forged art masterpieces, not to mention extorted money from some of his, Gaylord's, that is, Met board associates.

But the FBI agent was handing him a paper. "This is a warrant to search the premises." As Gaylord took hold of the warrant with his right hand, Agent Rothschild caught a glimpse of the pink birthmark on the inside of his wrist. He knew he had the right twin brother this time, despite the fact he had called him by the other twin brother's name. But the FBI agent knew precisely what he was doing.

He turned his attention to Adrienne. He said he was arresting her because of what he termed her "association with a known felon, someone who has forged, not to mention stolen, highly-valued works of art here in America, in Paris, and Mykonos." Then Agent Rothschild read Adrienne, too, her constitutional rights.

After that, he turned his attention to another officer and said, "Cuff 'em and take 'em away."

FBI agents handcuffed the pair and then escorted the couple outside and put them in the backseat of an unmarked vehicle. Moments later, a fleet of those vans pulled off, their engines roaring.

They were followed immediately by another vehicle driven by CF Commander Tommy Wozniah, who all this time had been waiting in an unmarked SUV on the street across from the house. He was fully aware that a CIA operative like himself was prohibited from active duty here in the homeland. Still, he had hoped to have somehow been able to participate in the apprehension.

It would take a little while before the CF commander would be brought into the loop about the arrest of the man who he, too, thought was Artemis Thibaut Millsap Moreaux but who was, in fact, his twin brother Gaylord Millsap Omiros. After all, Tommy was not supposed to be there in the first place, anyway.

19

Under Wraps

Priscilla's and her friend Macy's time together in Paris was not all fun, games, and shopping.

The two of them were unusually quiet and sober-faced in the taxi as they rode to the Moreaux family homestead—which both twins had supposedly inherited—in the nearby countryside but not so far from Paris. The two women had caught the news about the New Rochelle raid on CNN earlier, which was when Priscilla had finally sat down with Macy and clued her in on the real reason for their shopping spree in Gay Paree, and on to Mykonos later.

They both leaned forward as the taxi driver drew near a cluster of blinding lights of government-issued vehicles parked behind high but open, ornately designed gates on the perimeter of the chateau.

"*Entrée*," Priscilla called out to the taxi driver. Her French was poor, but as usual, her confidence was high. The driver sped inside the gates. Outside on the immaculate grounds of the impressive entrance of the chateau, Priscilla and Macy counted six, then seven, then a total of eight uniformed government agents—who knew from which agencies and countries? —carrying wooden crates and boxes to unmarked vans. Other agents paced about the grounds and ducked in and out of the mansion. There was also the ever-presence of news reporters and the paparazzi with their cameras all set up and taping, but they were cordoned off on the periphery of the estate.

"Follow me," Priscilla told Macy as the taxi slowed. Then she threw a wad of francs on the front seat and rummaged in her shoulder bag before triumphantly brandishing whatever it was she had been looking for. As the taxi skidded to a stop, Priscilla threw open the door and called out: "Move it, Macy!" The women leaped out and made for the front door of the chateau, ignoring the cluster of shouting reporters.

In the lead, Priscilla coursed inside, flashing her government-issued identification badge to every uniformed agent that she and Macy passed. One of the first was Agent Laverne Macon, but neither Laverne nor Priscilla seemed to have seen the other. Macy, well, she was so out of breath that the remarkable resemblance between Priscilla and that other agent did not even register on her.

While Priscilla paused, looking around that magnificent inner foyer, Macy asked the obvious: "What's with that badge?"

Priscilla shrugged. "Just my ID. You can't just stroll into an active investigation of this magnitude. But I'm sure you get that, being an attorney."

Macy nodded and frowned, yet chose not to pursue the matter here and now. She was beginning to have more suspicions about her girlfriend. *What was up? Is Missy some kind of "secret" government agent of sorts*? "Nah," she said to herself. *But why's she showing her ID? Nobody's asking to see mine.*

Back outside, some of the news reporters and the paparazzi had their own mounting suspicions as well as growing confusion.

"Well," one reporter who had recently transferred from New York to Paris whispered to another, "that one, who just pushed her way in there, sure looked to me like P. J. Austin-Bernhardt. You know, the one always in the news. She's involved with that art scandal at the Metropolitan Museum of Art in New York. I can't place the other one, though. But I've seen her on the news before, too. Who is she?" The other reporter, who had picked up some mannerisms since he had been assigned to France, lifted his shoulders in a credible Gallic shrug.

Back inside the chateau, Priscilla noticed another familiar face coming her way. One of the uniformed agents must have notified the American intelligence officers about the two American women's presence.

CIA Deputy Director Froley greeted Priscilla. "Well, well, well, if it isn't P. J. Austin-Bernhardt in the flesh! No need asking why you're here."

"Jim Froley," Priscilla said in her customary breezy way. She picked up his clue to act like they were mere acquaintances when, in reality, he was her CIA supervisor. "Looks like you've got 'some amusing entertainment under wraps.'"

Then, "Pardon my manners." She smiled and pulled Macy closer to her. "But I believe you've already met Defense Attorney Macy Stoner."

"We are previously acquainted," said the CIA deputy director stiffly, as his mind raced back to the time when she lambasted him in court during Arvana Bernhardt's trial.

"Charmed," Macy said with sarcasm, matching his disdain. Her suspicions about Priscilla's association with all these intelligence agents peaked. But now she realized that now, she, too, must have crossed some invisible line and was herself, somehow in the mix. Whatever it was, the CIA had obviously authorized Priscilla to see and even to participate in here, she herself would have to keep "under wraps." But she would have a peck of new questions for her girlfriend as soon as the two of them were in a secure place.

Then the CIA deputy director made the situation even more explicit: "Ms. Stoner, I'm not here, and neither are either of you. Are we *all* clear on the situation?"

While Priscilla did not react, Macy nodded. She understood, at least enough to keep her mouth shut.

"This way, ladies," the CIA executive said, pointing straight ahead.

As Priscilla followed her supervisor, she understood that one major consequence of being on foreign soil was that the CIA had jurisdiction, not the FBI, as it did at home. Anyone who had ever read a spy novel or watched an espionage drama on television knew that. She also reasoned that the longstanding working relationship between CIA Deputy Director Froley and FBI Agent Rothschild had made this particular investigation all the smoother.

The CIA deputy director escorted Priscilla and Macy to a private sector of the chateau. En route, several uniformed agents occasionally brushed up against them. "Pardon me." "Sorry for bumping into you, ladies." "*Pardonnez-moi.*"

Because the intelligence agents wore civilian clothing, Priscilla had no clue which was CIA or Interpol, much less MI5, DGSE, EYP, or only God knew what other international law enforcement or intelligence agents were. Only select staff wore uniforms with the big block letters signifying their respective agencies. But Priscilla and Macy did notice that some of them, working in pairs, struggled carrying wooden crates of different sizes—portraits perhaps, and cardboard boxes of artifacts and reliefs and file folders.

Deputy Director Froley occasionally pointed at some of the heftier items. "Those sculptures were taken from the garden out back," he said, "but it'll all be returned, pending completion of this investigation." Then, the CIA deputy director stopped talking.

He halted suddenly at a wall near the end of a corridor, off from the kitchen. When he pressed his hand flat against the wall, a way opened up. At that, Priscilla remembered her first time in southern Africa. Onslow, one of the CF agents, had needed to solve the riddles on three engraved wooden statues that led them through three secret passageways into the dungeon under the Anglican Cathedral of Harare. But this time, she was not on the run with her life in danger; this time, she was above ground, and she had two others with her, too.

"Some folks can afford all sorts of stuff—elaborate keys, hidden doors, the works," the deputy director said as he shook his head and walked through the opening in the wall. Then he beckoned to Priscilla and Macy to follow him into an enclosure with floor-to-ceiling shelving, rather like a well-stocked food pantry. But instead of boxes and cans, the shelves were stocked with dazzling *objects-d'arte*—ceramics of different colors, sizes, and shapes; miniature music boxes; some golden-clad crowns and tiaras adorned with huge diamonds and jades and rubies; jeweled-porcelain eggs; Egyptian artifacts and reliefs; even beaded and feathered American Indian artwork; and an array of other artifacts from all over the world.

Then the deputy director pressed the palm of his left hand against another wall, and another room was disclosed. This one featured valuable-looking paintings, each erected on an easel. Both Priscilla and Macy gasped when before them they saw a painting they recognized from the scandal at the Metropolitan Museum of Art—Marc Chagall's *Soleil dans le Ciel Saint-Paul.*

Priscilla asked the deputy director: "The original?"

"You got it," he answered. As the two women continued gazing in awe at the painting, he elaborated: "According to Ignatius Devoe's deposition, Thibaut Francois stashed this one here for future insurance purposes."

Priscilla asked for clarification: "Are we talking about leverage in some kind of blackmail or extortion racket? Or its financial value?"

"*Leverage*," CIA Deputy Director Froley answered. "Just in case his father—yes, I said, his father, Monsieur Moreaux, the grandfather of Artemis and Gaylord—ever considered informing the authorities about any of this, his son Thibaut Francois was prepared to frame his own father for the theft of this Chagall. But we think the old man was never aware that this authentic painting was even on his property."

Priscilla was so disgusted that she blurted out, "One can't sink much lower than a rat."

"His *own* father, too," Macy said emphatically.

Priscilla's forehead wrinkled as she asked about the Chagall that hung on the wall at the Met.

"Just an 'excellent reproduction,'" said the CIA deputy director. "It's been hanging there for so long that it's a miracle someone only just noticed something *peculiar* about it." Sheepishly he laughed. "For years and years, the world's top curators have looked at this painting, but it took a volunteer docent to spot what turned out to be a fake."

"God bless volunteers," Macy said as she thought about how proud she was that her own mother had once been a museum docent.

Priscilla grinned. Then she mentioned something neither the deputy director nor the attorney had anticipated. "You know, I think there's a hefty finder's fee connected to this Chagall."

"If you're thinking what I'm thinking," Macy said, "seems to me that that docent is the one who'll be getting that big fat check for seeing whatever nobody else could see in this painting about 'the sun in the sky in

Saint Paul,' or whatever the heck this painting signifies." Even though she had stepped down temporarily from the Met board while she represented Gaylord, Macy seemed to have overlooked the ethical standard prohibiting museum staff, volunteers, and board members from benefiting financially, or in any other way, from their affiliation with the Met. But all was not lost for the volunteer docent.

"Maybe yes, maybe no." Priscilla had another idea where that money could go. For the time being, she did not yet know how she could channel that fee to Arvana's new narcotics recovery program. But she did know that she would do her best to accomplish precisely that. Still, it was best to leave all that to another time.

For now, she asked another question: "Jim, what's next in all this?"

"Whoever gets the finder's fee is of no concern to the CIA or any of the other intelligence agencies."

"But *I'm* the board's attorney," Macy reminded them. "I may have something to say about this to the insurance agency." Again, Macy was being presumptuous.

Priscilla looked at her friend and smiled as she steered the conversation in another direction. "I'd just like to pick up this painting, gift wrap it, and courier it back to the Met in New York. I'd suggest, Jim, that you have one of your most trusted agents do exactly that. I'm partial to female agents." She and Deputy Director Froley exchanged knowing smiles, aware that she was obliquely referring to CF Agent Macon. But of course, Priscilla had just been joshing him. The CIA deputy director would be bound to keep the protocols for the return of the stolen property. But Priscilla also knew that now Jim Froley owed her big time. He had benefitted from the tapes she had shared with him about Iggy and Shane, which had led to Iggy's subsequent interrogation. Priscilla was aware, too, that Iggy had played his ace-in-the-hole well and that probably he would succeed in leveraging whatever additional information he had supplied to eventually reduce sentencing for himself. She antici-pated, further, that Iggy would become a witness for the prosecution in the case against Artemis Thibaut.

But then, Priscilla casually passed on some more stellar intel that she had gleaned from communiques from Agent Macon.

"Ah, Jim," she said. "This must have slipped my mind. But I think you'd be interested in knowing that the man FBI Agent Rothschild charged in that New Rochelle raid was the wrong brother. He arrested Gaylord Millsap Omiros, not his twin Artemis Thibaut Millsap Mo-reaux."

Then she shared even more sensational information on exactly how to tell the difference between the two men. "Artemis Thibaut stutters and wears a pink birthmark approximately two inches in diameter on the nape of his neck," she said. "But Gaylord blinks and wears a pink birthmark of the same dimensions on the inside of his right wrist." And then she shared credit where credit was due: "Agent Macon found doc-umentation about the birthmarks in the family papers seized from the family's Sutton Place mansion." Finally, she added, "Even Iggy never knew how to tell the brothers apart; at least, as far as I know, he didn't."

While Priscilla briefed her supervisor about the twins' differences, the deputy director reflected on how far and rapidly Priscilla advanced as an intelligence agent. He recalled how he'd first perceived her when, nearly four years ago, he and FBI Agent Rothschild first visited her Co-lumbus home office. To Jim Froley, at the time, Priscilla seemed so young, innocent, and carefree.

He stared at her, and then, before he knew it, "Good job, A—" he almost called Priscilla by her professional intelligence title, "Agent Aus-tin-Bernhardt." But he caught himself. "I mean, Ms. *Austin*-Bernhardt."

Meanwhile, he continued reflecting on how well his recruit had fit-ted into the intelligence realm, not to mention the circle of high society types. Then, he thought about how well she seemed to have adjusted from her horrible experiences with those mean-spirited Arab Islamic terrorists during her recent mission in the Middle East. And he had to admit to himself that he had grown fond of Priscilla J. "PJ" Austin-Bernhardt; she had become one of his stellar agents. Mostly though, like so many other people who knew her, CIA Deputy Director Froley had come to admire Priscilla because of her unassuming nature, someone who still did not see herself the way other people saw her.

As he reflected, he did not realize that he was staring at the two women, especially Priscilla, nor that he had ceased talking.

At that, Priscilla and Macy both wore expressions of curiosity. *Was Jim Froley having second thoughts about sharing such vital information with them*? But that thought never even entered his mind.

As the deputy director caught himself, he proceeded as if he had not been caught staring at Priscilla. Quickly, he removed some cloth covers from a pile of paintings. Each was a study of a naked woman. He lined them all up so that they were leaning against a nearby wall.

"Behold!" he exclaimed. "The source of decades of blackmail."

He pointed to the pile of paintings and continued. "All the dirty work of Thibaut Francois and his son Artemis Thibaut over many years. You see here the source of much anguish for many affluent American women who had the misfortune of encountering those two scoundrels."

So this *is why he paused and stared at us, especially at Priscilla*, they both thought. The two friends believed that Jim had not wanted to show them what he perceived as "dirty pictures." They both knew Jim Froley was old-school.

"Wow!" Priscilla and Macy kept saying. "Wow!" Their eyes opened wider, and their jaws dropped, too.

Then Priscilla asked, "Including the nude portraits of the women from the Met board?"

"The very same." The deputy director nodded. "Among so many others."

"Holy cow!" Macy knew some of these women through their membership on the Met board or their marriage to the board members. But she had never before seen any of them like this.

Priscilla blurted out: "Man alive, did Thibaut Francois and his son Artemis have the goods on a lot of women!"

"Now, ladies," said the CIA deputy director, "kindly wait here while I attend to something else."

The CIA deputy director stepped a safe distance away from Priscilla and Macy and placed a call to his people back at Langley. First, he instructed them to share the intel that he had just learned about from Priscilla with the FBI. He also urged his colleagues to "discretely coordinate the apprehension of the real Artemis Thibaut with the FBI *before* he slips out of the country using his twin's, Gaylord's, passport." Then he listened for a while longer before returning to Priscilla and Macy.

"News from home," he began. "One of our teams found some more nude portraits under the floorboards in the old man's bedchamber on Sutton Place. It's my guess that the Millsaps never even knew they were there, either. Or surely they would've destroyed them."

"So, Thibaut Francois, and later his son, must have bled those women for all they could get and for a very long time," Priscilla surmised.

She thought about it: "Wait a minute. That dirty scoundrel and his son were also setting up old man Millsap—the twins' other grandfather! And to think I didn't think either of them could sink any lower?"

"You'd be surprised, PJ," Deputy Director Froley insisted. Then he repeated himself, "You'd be surprised."

As she watched Priscilla and the CIA deputy director talking and moving about so casually and comfortably with each other, Macy finally understood that both Priscilla and the CIA deputy director had wanted her to know for sure what so plainly her eyes and ears had discerned. Mostly though, Macy now understood that Priscilla and the CIA deputy director trusted her to hold their confidence close.

Back in the States, where he had watched a CNN report on the arrest of his twin brother and his girlfriend in New Rochelle, Artemis Thibaut continued to enjoy the comforts of the Millsap mansion on Sutton Place. He liked pretending to be the master of this house. He enjoyed experiencing the extraordinary lifestyle of his brother.

Artemis Thibaut lifted his martini and toasted his brother. Hopefully, Gaylord—and Artemis Thibaut's own girlfriend Adrienne—would learn to thrive in their jail cells, too.

Artemis Thibaut drained his drink and hailed the house manager for another. He yawned. He supposed he should grab a taxi to the John F. Kennedy Airport, be up and away to some nice hole someplace where they had no extradition treaty with the United States. But it was so comfortable here. Again he yawned.

"One more day won't matter," he said aloud as one of the household servants brought him another martini. Then he smirked to himself. Just like his father, he was more intelligent than all the rest.

Meanwhile, the real Gaylord Millsap Omiros sat sweating in an interrogation room at the FBI headquarters in New York City, where he'd resumed pretending to be his twin. Still, he was beginning to wonder if he would do that forever. He had trusted Artemis Thibaut. They were brothers—identical twins. For forty-two years, he never once imagined that his own flesh and blood would deceive him. But Gaylord had grown up mainly in Greece. Suddenly it hit him that his life, and his very presence in this interrogation room, was the stuff of Greek tragedies.

20

Seafarers in Mykonos

Priscilla and Macy gazed out of their window onboard their Aegean Airlines flight. The mountainous terrain below encompassed a multitude of islands of different shapes and sizes scattered throughout the Aegean and the Ionian Seas.

"Absolutely magnificent," Priscilla said.

"I can't believe it," Macy breathed. "Greece! I've always wanted to see it."

"And I've always told you, 'stick with me,'" Priscilla grinned.

The two of them had flown over twelve hundred miles from the City of Light to the cradle of democracy. They had left in the wee hours of the Parisian morning because Priscilla had intended to arrive in Greece before the American and the other international intelligence officials were expected to meet with the Omiros family tomorrow. Priscilla hoped that

Agent Macon had had her dates right. It would be close, too close. She did want to get to the family first.

Then, they disembarked in Athens, where, after clearing customs, a limousine took them to another gate, where they caught a commuter flight to the island of Mykonos.

They were up and down in a matter of minutes. Then they taxied to a hotel, which had been booked by Macy's travel agent back in New York. Their room overlooked the Aegean. The water was the most beautiful shade of blue that either of them had ever seen.

They changed into bathing suits in what seemed like seconds and ran out and jumped in the infinity pool. They swam and splashed like children and sunbathed for nearly an hour.

"Greece," Macy kept yelling. "I'm really in Greece!"

But then someone from the concierge desk brought a message. Priscilla read it and told the waiting staffer to send their unexpected guest to their suite.

"Trouble?" Macy asked.

"I hope not. But maybe you should wait here." Priscilla wrapped a towel around her wet body, returned to the suite, and threw on a caftan. Shortly she heard someone knocking ever so gently.

An elegant woman of indeterminate age was in the doorway, wearing stylish high heels and a colorful, flowing silk top over white slacks. Long blond hair bounced on her shoulders underneath a big, wide-brimmed, floppy straw hat. She wore what Priscilla called "Jackie O sunglasses," much like the ones Priscilla donned back in New York when she wanted to go incognito or slip away from lurking reporters and paparazzi. The woman was tall—maybe five feet nine—and towered over the petite Priscilla.

"Good day, Ms. Austin-Bernhardt," said the woman who seemed not only glamorous but also to possess remarkable aplomb. "I am Miriam Millsap Omiros. Pardon my intrusion."

Priscilla covered her mouth with her hand, a mannerism like her mother's that she reverted to when she was not entirely comfortable in a social situation. She did her best to maintain a calm composure but instantly had known from photographs in one of the case dossiers that this was the woman she had come to see. But what was this unexpected visit to her hotel suite all about? Like her twin sons, Miriam was "a person of interest" in the investigation into the possible tampering with, or maybe even theft of three highly-valued works of art from the Met. Later she would have to contact CF Agent Macon and let her know whatever transpired with this Miriam, and then she supposed Laverne would pass on any intel to the FBI and the CIA, respectively.

But here and now, she would have to concentrate on her guest. "Good day to you, too, Madame Millsap Omiros."

"Miriam. Call me, Miriam."

Priscilla was hearing a trace of New York City in her accent. She remembered that her unexpected guest was a native New Yorker who had long since resided in Greece—and by reputation was a wealthy jet setter who traveled extensively.

"Call me, PJ. And do come inside." She was ever-so-grateful that at least she was not stuttering. But she was surprised that she was so nervous. Usually she sailed through social situations. She supposed the family she had married into—the Bernhardts of Bow Lake—were of comparable net worth to Miriam's family, but there comes the point when the amount of one's wealth is inconsequential compared to one's social station. And even though Priscilla had come to accept that she herself had a reputation as a heroine of sorts and was regarded as a celebrity, she sure did not live the high life of the seafaring Greeks. Mostly though, the unassuming Priscilla still had no idea how other people saw her. But she would feel so much better—more secure, she supposed—having Macy here. Priscilla collected herself and offered her guest "a cool drink or another refreshment," which Miriam declined.

Then she said, "Please make yourself comfortable while I ask my associate to join us." While Miriam settled in one of the high-back chairs clustered around a glass-topped cocktail table in the suite's salon, Priscilla returned to the pool and whispered with some urgency to Macy.

"Girlfriend, you're not going to believe this, but the woman we've come here to see is sitting in our suite. C'mon inside, Macy. I need you."

"No lie!" Macy exclaimed.

In a flash, the two American women joined their visitor inside. But before Priscilla introduced Macy, Miriam immediately smiled and spoke up. "I suppose you're wondering why I'm here. Well, the hotel concierge, who is a friend—I have many friends! —told me that the illustrious American, P. J. Austin-Bernhardt, and a friend were vacationing here on the island. We like to keep abreast, you know, of who's here and who could be good fun." She laughed a trilling little sound and then made an airy gesture with her bejeweled hand.

"And, well, since my husband and I are hosting a dinner party for a small group of close friends … we thought you might—"

"I'm Macy." She smiled in anticipation of being included in the invite.

"Ah, yes," Miriam said. "The friend. We'd love to have you too, of course. The more, the merrier."

By this point in the conversation, Priscilla had regained her poise and dared to laugh like Elly May Clampett: "Heck, yeah. We'd love to join you."

Macy chimed back in, "Me, too."

One would never have guessed that Priscilla and Macy were the illustrious women they were. Both had long been accustomed, each in her own way, to being commanding presences at home, not just in business but in social situations. But there was something about Miriam Millsap Omiros that made them feel, by comparison, like teenagers around a *grande dame*. They could not help behaving as though an Oscar-winning movie star had just offered them a juicy plum.

"Then it is settled," said Miriam as she gracefully rose to leave. "I'll send my man to pick you girls up around six. First, we'll have cocktails. On the yacht, of course. That's the *Piraeus*."

The two American friends nodded, trying to look like a dinner invitation to a yacht in the seas of Greece was an everyday occurrence. At least they already knew that since few, if any, private cars were allowed on the island, most visitors rode busses, taxis, and small passenger boats. So having a chauffeured car would at least make getting to the boat, or rather the *yacht*, a little easier.

"Dinner is at eight," Miriam said and smiled again. "Attire is casual. Throw on any old thing. This is Greece, after all! We're all on eternal vacation!" She laughed, and so, too, did the Americans, as the visitor let herself out.

As soon as the door closed behind her, Priscilla and Macy jumped up and down like high school teenagers. Then, as one, they sank down on the suite's sofa, shrugged off their sandals, and put their bare feet on the cocktail table.

"Wait 'til my folks get a load of this!" Priscilla felt ecstatic. She would have liked to ring up her mom and share all this. *Later*, she thought.

"*Your* folks! What am *I*? Chopped liver?" But Macy laughed. "It's about time hanging out with the likes of you paid off."

Both women laughed.

But then Priscilla sat straight up in alarm. *Wear any old thing?*

"Huh? What's up, Missy? I thought we were going to relax."

Priscilla shook her head. "No, we're going out. I, for one, need to find the perfect 'any-old thing' to wear tonight!"

Before long, basking in the warm summer morning sun, they shopped their way through the trendy boutiques spread along the narrow but hilly cobblestone streets. They snapped pictures of the white-washed houses with colorful doors and window frames and admired the vivid pods of red geraniums that flourished everywhere. They walked the length of the famous Matoyánni Street—where tourists enjoyed high-end shopping, cafés, and five-star restaurants. They mostly bought stuff, wonderful things, fabulous gauzy dresses, colorful sandals, and an assortment of big, floppy hats in vivid colors.

"Don't you just love these?" Macy had on not only a magnificent red hat with an extraordinarily wide brim but a colossal pair of sunglasses. Priscilla could barely see her friend's face.

"A perfect disguise," Priscilla noted. She selected four hats like that in yellow, black, white, and a vivid blue that seemed the exact color of the glorious Aegean.

But the two of them spent the most time choosing something spectacular to wear for the party on the yacht. They had both correctly understood that "any old thing" was a woman's code for knockout outfits. After trying on many dresses and such, Priscilla settled on a glamorous silky gold number laced with Lurex that glittered in the morning light. Macy chose sophisticated black, telling Priscilla—and assuring herself, too—that a woman never went wrong with black. The gauzy, low-cut jumpsuit accented her curves.

Finally, although exhausted, they made their way down to the harbor and searched for the yacht. When they could not find it, they questioned a grizzled elderly fellow selling tickets for a tourist excursion boat.

He simply pointed over the waters, where a giant white yacht bobbed in the waves.

"Holy cow!" Macy said as she took off her sunglasses and shaded her eyes to get a better look. She whistled. "What? Will we have to take a *boat* to get to the yacht?"

Then the two of them rushed back to the hotel. They spent the remainder of the afternoon at the poolside, aware that they needed to rest up for their big night on the yacht. But when Macy was napping, Priscilla managed to call Agent Macon to clue her in as to what was happening work-wise on Mykonos. She then instructed Laverne to share this intel with both the CIA and the FBI.

But little did Priscilla know that both of the American intelligence agencies, the CIA and the FBI, were already one step ahead of her game and were, in fact, most grateful that she would, so conveniently, be a guest on the *Piraeus* that evening.

On and around the Mykonos dock, enterprising paparazzi used long camera lenses to take pictures of the beautiful people climbing into the launches for the trip out to the big white yacht. It was summer, and the seafaring Greeks hosted international guests who excelled at party-going the world over. Demetrios Omiros II and his wife, Miriam Millsap Omiros, were apparently among everyone's favorite hosts and hostesses.

The paparazzi, most of them entertainment and society hawks, kept close tabs on spectacular event gatherings like tonight's soirée on the Omiros yacht. They were aware of the twenty-seven on the guest list and that many of them were already onboard. That mainly included middle-aged and older individuals who sported quite an assortment of outfits, some in scantily clad bathing suits and sandals or even bare feet. Some wore cotton, linen, or silk pants, while others wore shorts, skirts, or sundresses. But the faces of nearly all the women were hidden by those trendy Jackie O-style sunglasses. Although the sun had already set, many guests even wore baseball caps or huge floppy hats. To Priscilla, it looked like many of them were going incognito.

But the paparazzi's attention was caught by the glamour of Priscilla's gold gown and Macy in her black jumpsuit, as the pair succeeded in gracefully moving from the pier to the launch for the trip to the *Piraeus*.

"Get a load of those dames," said one photographer.

"I like movie-star glam," said another. "I hate it when these people dress like they're going to a baseball game. There are no standards anymore." He himself was wearing shorts, and a too-tight tee-shirt stretched over his protruding paunch.

But another had been staring at the shorter one in the gold gown. "Isn't that P. J. Austin-Bernhardt?" The cameraman pointed at Priscilla. "You know, the PR consultant who married that rich fellow who had those designer gowns made *exclusively* for her?"

"Nah," said another. "Can't be. I just saw her in the feed about an hour ago, back in Paris, at that chateau. Interpol was all over it. Art forgery case, I think."

The pack of paparazzi continued staring at and taking photographs of Priscilla as the engine of the launch revved up. "Hmmm," agreed another reporter. "I think you're right. But if the woman we just saw boarding the launch *is* the illustrious P. J. Austin-Bernhardt, then *who* was that woman back at the French chateau?"

Yet another photographer said, "Wow! She sure gets around."

But stubbornly, the cameraman persisted.

"Man, do you hear yourself? That woman *cannot* be in two places at the same time. So what gives?

Aboard the *Piraeus*, already the atmosphere was festive when Priscilla and Macy joined the throng. At first they were confused. They had been expecting an intimate evening, but they guessed there must be thirty or so people on deck. Someone crooned songs made famous by Shirley Bassey and Johnny Mathis, while on the far end of the yacht, a small band played music by Miles Davis and then, in marked contrast, Davie Bowie. Some guests were playing poker, but in another alcove, another pair played chess. Everyone was drinking. Many were toasting with fluted champagne glasses. Servants moved about with overflowing trays with hors d'oeuvres. And although Priscilla nor Macy knew it, the paparazzi were taping all the festivities from small boats nearby.

Despite their earlier trepidation, both Priscilla and Macy easily fit in with the other guests. Man alive, did they fit in! Both were soon dancing with some of the most handsome men they had ever laid eyes on. "Like matinee idols in the movies," Macy was later to describe them to Priscilla.

"And I had to keep reminding myself that I'm a married woman," Priscilla admitted. But she had also told herself that she never really felt concerned about being out of place, or in danger, for that matter, because her dance partner barely spoke English.

And to think both women had only moments earlier felt too exhausted to move their tormented bodies.

Soon the music stopped; it was time to dine.

Everyone flocked to the far deck, where a long table was exquisitely set in shades of sparkling gold, illuminated by small dancing lights.

Miriam and Demetrios, who had been absent earlier, greeted all the guests before taking their seats. When it was Priscilla's and Macy's turn, they asked them to come with them to the head of the table.

"Ladies and Gentlemen," Miriam said, "allow me to introduce our special guests, PJ Austin-Bernhardt, and—" Miriam paused for an awkward moment. She looked at Priscilla with an unspoken plea for help.

"Macy Stoner," Priscilla said when she realized that Miriam had forgotten her friend's name.

"And Ms. Macy Stoner," Miriam said. Priscilla and Macy stood and waved. A ripple of applause came from the table, and then their hostess clapped her hands. "Now, everyone, enjoy!"

Immediately, however, all the guests raised their glasses and shouted. "Hip, hip, hoorah!" Then they saluted her again and drained their glasses.

Priscilla flushed, suddenly aware that she was the one who all these strangers had just saluted.

Miriam took Priscilla's arm. She escorted her new friend to sit beside her at one end of the long table, with Macy at her side. Demetrios walked to the other end of the long table and sat at its head.

Priscilla was not aware of eating much and could not even remember what had been served afterward. Mostly she listened as Miriam and her friends peppered her with questions about her first time in Africa and what she had thought, really, of Zimbabwe and South Africa. They also wanted to know about her work on the Hollingsworth Presidential Election Campaign. Then—with intense interest—they asked about the fabulous gowns that Carlton had had made exclusively for her by Oscar de la Renta, especially those she wore to the Hollingsworth Presidential Inauguration. They asked her, too, about how the Bernhardts of Bow Lake were doing, particularly Arvana, whom many knew well.

Priscilla was frustrated. She felt used. She felt like she was the entertainment. She even thought: *There really aren't any free meals. Eh?*

But she soon recovered after her thoughtful hostess noticed her changed demeanor.

"Oh, PJ, I am so sorry," Miriam said. "We're imposing." Then she turned to her other guests and said, "Enough with the questions. We're making our guest a tad uncomfortable."

However, Miriam did not understand that part of the reason that some of her guests had been unable to resist questioning Priscilla was that they noticed the scars on her neck and right shoulder that she had sustained from the attempted assassination of her life in September 1987. This was one of those times that Priscilla had not concealed her neck and right shoulder. Usually she covered the scars, but today she had fallen in love with that fabulous gold gown. Reminded of her wounds, she became self-conscious of her scars again.

She gave Miriam a thankful look. "Glad you called off the hounds." She lowered her voice. "I *was* feeling a little put on."

Apologetically, "It's my fault, PJ," Miriam said. "I guess I was so excited having you with us that I forgot what it's like to have people probing into the intimate details of one's life. My apology."

Priscilla gave her a sharp look, aware of how close Miriam's comment was to the actual, although still hidden, reason for her coming to Mykonos in the first place. But the socialite's face seemed without guile.

Finally comfortable with each other, the two talked about shopping in New York, Gay Paree, Milan, Mykonos, and even Dubai. When Priscilla mentioned Dubai, she got Miriam's attention even more.

Lulled by their small talk, not to mention some of the chatter among the other guests, Priscilla and Miriam did not hear some of the whooshes and thumps. Nor did they even notice the sudden silence that permeated the once-festive atmosphere. The deck was suddenly bathed in bright light, and dark figures arrayed behind some of the guests' chairs, including the host's and hostess'.

But over the stillness of the wine-dark sea, others were paying keen attention as they kept snapping their cameras and rolling their tapes.

"Nice of them to light it up for us," said one photographer.

Then another of the paparazzi exclaimed, "Not *her* again!" But he continued to take pictures of one woman in a kind of cat burglar outfit, near that other one in a black jumpsuit. She looked just like that other woman in gold that he had photographed earlier. That P. J. Austin-Bernhardt. "What's happening? Am I seeing things? I'd swear I just saw this woman in a gold-color floor-length gown, dancing on deck. And now she looks more like a cat burglar." He paused and considered. "Or a government agent." But he narrowed his eyes as he continued taking photos of a woman who sure looked to him like P. J. Austin-Bernhardt. "Didn't we just see her boarding and then dancing on the deck a couple of hours ago? And wasn't she dressed like a dinner guest? But she now seems to have some kind of ID badge clipped to her belt. Look hard. You can see it. There, at the waistband of her pants."

"Man alive," another photographer said as he zoomed in his camera's lens for a better look. "You're right."

"I'd swear there are two of them, right before our eyes." The other reporter laughed and then said, "Will the *real* P. J. Austin-Bernhardt, please stand up?"

21

Just One More Day

———————⌄———————

Television viewing audiences all over the world hunkered closer to their screens, watching live streaming of the latest installment of what everyone was calling "the mysterious affair at the Met."

Television viewers wondered what was happening. For, they watched as law enforcement and international intelligence officers cordoned off lavish estates, confiscated artwork, and arrested suspects in this case involving a vast international art scandal.

Now the action was at sea, just off the coast of the Greek isle of Mykonos.

"Ah, crap!" Priscilla blurted out as soon as she recognized her intelligence colleagues' unexpected presence, whom she did not expect until the next day. She continued grousing to herself: *But I was just beginning to enjoy myself!* And then, *I'm still hungry, too!*

CIA Deputy Director Froley stood directly behind her, his eyes boring into the back of her head. As his eyebrows raised at her words, he uttered, "We're here to clean up this 'crap,' young lady." But then he went silent, not wanting to implicate or to involve his own agency in any way more than it already was; Priscilla was, after all, one of their own. Instead, he focused on his Greek counterpart in the EYP, explaining to the mostly English-speaking guests why his agents were on the yacht of Demetrios Omiros.

Priscilla still sulked and was still hungry. She regarded her Greek dish called "kopanistí" still on her plate and took a tentative forkful. *Tasty*, she thought—g*oat cheese and peppers.* Even as the Greek agent continued trying to explain himself, first in Greek and then in nearly perfect English, she proceeded to devour her food. Finally, she looked up when she heard him asking to speak to Demetrios and Miriam in private. She watched her hosts following a whole pack of what appeared to be intelligence agents or law enforcement officers inside the cabin.

Delicately she patted her lips with a fine linen napkin. Her eyes met Macy's, and Priscilla shook her head. Macy nodded, having gotten the message. She stayed put when Priscilla rose swiftly and followed the others into the cabin. Priscilla smiled along the way when the band struck up again just before she shut the cabin door. If she knew this lot, in a moment, they would be dancing again. *These folks certainly know how to enjoy themselves.*

She could see the other intelligence agents tramping down metal stairs, so she followed. She saw CF Agent Macon, among others inside the cabin doors, searching intensely. *Looking for more stolen artworks,* Priscilla correctly surmised.

By the time she caught up with the pack, the agents had already begun interrogating Demetrios and Miriam, who sat close together on a sofa while the agents ranged around the room. But none of the intelligence agents asked Priscilla for her credentials. Evidently Jim Froley had already tipped them off to leave her alone. She stood off to the side.

But Demetrios could not stop staring at her, and then loudly, he whispered to his wife: "I told you, Miriam, that something was not right. I saw this PJ on live television in Paris not long ago. And now she's *here*, too." He pointed an accusing finger at Priscilla. "It's no secret that you represent The Metropolitan Museum of Art. But what puzzles me is your presence *here* and at *this* time."

But then an unnamed agent—Priscilla learned later he was a higher-up official from Interpol—asked her to use whatever influence she had to get Demetrios and Miriam to explain their relationship with the notorious Thibaut Francois. "So far," he said, taking care not to call her by her name or her title, "she's not talking. How about explaining to your newfound friend the *gravity* of the situation before her?" He then beckoned her to join the couple on the long leather sofa.

Priscilla motioned for Demetrios and Miriam to make room for her. With her back to Demetrios, she faced Miriam. When she dared to take her hand, she felt it trembling. She thought she saw fear in her eyes. Or was that something about her past that was about to come to light?

"Miriam," she began, "something tells me that your darling husband is *not* as oblivious to your past as he might let on." Demetrios started mumbling something, but everyone else in the room ignored him. They only had eyes for Priscilla and Miriam. "So, please, Miriam," Priscilla begged, "tell us whatever you know. And then I think you'll be able to shut the door on what I'm thinking was the worst thing that has ever happened in your life."

Miriam's eyes pooled with tears. She stretched her neck and stared into the loving eyes of her husband. When she saw consent, tears slid down her cheeks. Then she turned back to Priscilla and nodded: "OK."

She took a deep breath, wiped away her tears, and said: "It all began back in Paris, long ago…."

What followed kept all the agents on the edge of their seats.

Miriam related how Thibaut Francois had extorted an enormous sum of money from her father, how he had taken Artemis Thibaut back with him to Paris, and how he had taught Artemis Thibaut how to create "excellent reproductions," and how to steal highly-valued works of art.

"And how do you know that Thibaut Francois taught your son how to forge and steal highly-valued works of art?" asked the Interpol agent of her.

"Why, Gaylord, told me," she said matter-of-factly. At that, every one of the intelligence officers snapped to attention.

"Gaylord," she said, "tells me everything. The twins have interacted throughout much of their lives." Her eyes filled with tears again, and she turned again to her husband. "I guess it was my secret, how they knew each other. I'm sorry, but I just couldn't tell you." She tore her gaze away from her husband and seemed to be pleading with the intelligence officers as she looked from one to another. "My boys are just like other children, other siblings. And don't forget, they're *twins*. They're close. They've always exchanged information about how they were raised. They talk about their hobbies, their friends, their businesses …."

Grimly, some of the agents nodded.

Miriam had just confirmed that Gaylord had, in fact, known that he had a twin brother and that he'd known of his father's criminal past, well, or at least about some of it. But that was a rub. The agents still did not know how much Gaylord had actually known, either about his father or his twin.

As he interrogated the couple for more factual information, the unnamed Interpol agent turned his attention to Demetrios. "And how 'bout you, Mr. Omiros? When did you first suspect your wife's relationship with Thibaut Francois? And that he was Gaylord's father?"

Miriam's head was still bowed, but she suddenly lifted it when she heard her husband saying, "From the very beginning." He smiled at his wife. "Yes, I've known from the very first day when your father brought you and the child to my father's home, and I've loved you ever since."

The Interpol agent insisted. "But *how* exactly was that?"

Demetrios responded matter-of-factly. "Even a fool can sense a mother's love, and my wife talked in her sleep." He looked from the officers to Miriam. "You wouldn't know this, but you used to cry out to Thibaut Francois by name, and you begged him to bring Artemis Thibaut back to you. Sometimes I would even cry along with you. But you'd been through so much. I knew you'd be crushed if you knew that I knew about your… youthful indiscretion. So I kept it to myself."

"Oh, Demetri," Miriam cried out as she broke out in fresh tears. And so it was that after nearly forty-two years, her long-held secret had not been so secret, after all.

Demetrios elaborated. "And remember, I, too, am adopted. So who was I to deny an innocent child the chance to be raised by his own mother? So I acquiesced and played along." He smiled at her. "Besides, I knew the day would come when you'd confide the truth. And here we are." He smiled at her and then shrugged his shoulders as if making light of the matter.

Now that's true love, thought Priscilla. Even she, who shied away from sentiment, was moved.

Then Demetrios turned to Priscilla. "PJ, I want to thank you. You've made all this much easier than it could have been. Bless you." He patted her right shoulder, the one that bore the scars.

CIA Deputy Director Froley stepped in. "I hate to break up this little cum baya. But we still need to know, Mr. and Mrs. Omiros, what you know about the missing paintings. What's still unaccounted for is Monet's *La Promenade* and Bordone's *Diana and the Two Nymphs*."

"*What* missing paintings?" Demetrios frowned.

"I believe we're about to find out," answered the Interpol agent, as CF Agent Macon came into the room carrying a painting. Then he said, "Is that one of them?"

The CF agent nodded in response to the Interpol agent. "The missing Monet."

But the painting was not the only remarkable thing that the Interpol agent and the others in the room noticed. Everyone in that room looked from CF Agent Macon to Priscilla, then back again. Why, even Agent Froley did a double-take. But no one dared to ask any more questions.

The CF agent broke the silence. "This painting—Claude Monet's *La Promenade*," said she, "was hidden in the yacht's office behind a portrait of the *Piraeus*, which—in his deposition—was precisely where Ignatius Devoe said that it would be. But, he also said that neither Mr. nor Mrs. Omiros was aware of this."

"And that's the truth," said Demetrios, as he and Miriam looked at each other, shrugged their shoulders, and then shook their heads, as if to say that they had had no idea the Monet painting had been hidden on their yacht, and, well, they had not.

Later that evening, when the intelligence officers dusted the Monet painting for fingerprints, the only ones they found had matched Thibaut Francois's. Demetrios and Miriam were cleared of having tampered with, much less from having stolen, that painting.

Meanwhile, the CIA deputy director also shared with the couple that Ignatius Devoe had told them that Thibaut Francois had passed on the cache of his extortion racket to his son Artemis Thibaut. "His eventual plan was to extort another vast sum of money from the two of you."

"No!" Miriam shrieked. "Oh, no!" Oddly, she shed no more tears.

Priscilla was surprised. She half-expected Miriam to be devastated to hear that her own son had been plotting to extort her—his own mother. *Could a mother's love run that deep*? Priscilla reflected that she had no clue, primarily because she had no children.

Before Priscilla knew it, she spoke candidly but with compassion, "Oh, Miriam. Artemis Thibaut will surely be prosecuted. Beyond that, I honestly do not know about any legal consequences."

While Priscilla spoke to Miriam, the CIA deputy director, the CF agent, and the other intelligence officers present suddenly realized that the two women had already somehow bonded. They watched as Priscilla stood up, and then as Miriam and Demetrios scooted back closer together on the sofa and while he reassured his wife, "Don't worry, my darling. I'll get him the best darn legal counsel possible." Miriam clung to her husband and continued weeping.

As she gave Miriam's hand a supportive and final little squeeze, Priscilla bade the couple farewell. Then she took a moment to speak to CIA Deputy Director Froley and CF Agent Macon, who were examining the portrait of *La Promenade*.

Then, ultimately, she rejoined Macy and the continuing party back up on deck. But she continued to consider the unpredictable power of a mother's love. Despite everything that had happened, Priscilla thought about how Miriam still loved her son, Artemis Thibaut, "the bad seed."

What happened next would have been no surprise to Carlton and "the boys" or Liza and others who knew her well.

Priscilla signaled to a waiter and said, "Please bring me a hot meal, maybe some lamb chops, you know, the works."

But Macy, too, was no stranger to her friend's prodigious appetite. She sat down beside Priscilla and poured them both fresh flutes of champagne. When the waiter soon returned with a laden tray, Macy watched Priscilla stuffing her food into her mouth.

Yet the other dinner guests stared in disbelief that a woman so small could eat so much as she seemed to be devouring everything on her plate.

Then Macy leaned over to her and said in a near whisper, "Okay, Missy, after you finish feeding your greedy face, I want to hear it all, and I do mean *all* of it."

Priscilla looked up at Macy, and with a mouth full of food, she said, "Well, Girlfriend, looks like we've got ourselves another finder's fee. And, oh yeah, think you can represent Gaylord's twin brother? You know, 'the bad seed?'"

The expression on Macy's face was priceless. But Priscilla pretended not to notice it as she continued cleaning her plate as if she had not eaten in days.

That night, shortly after Priscilla and Macy returned to their hotel suite on Mykonos, she pretty much pleaded with Macy to spend an extra day on the island. "Ah, come on, Mace. One more day, just one more day." Priscilla wanted to get a suntan, something to boast about upon returning to the States. "It's not every day that one can brag about a suntan from the Greek Isles."

"*Absolutely not!*" Macy turned a stone face to her friend. But then she laughed. "I'd like to stay a *couple* more days myself."

"Really!" Priscilla's eyes were alight. "Three, maybe?"

Macy raised her hand, and they gave each other an exuberant high-five.

But, the next day, Priscilla's first hour or so sunbathing had not been altogether pleasant. Macy had been beyond herself, and she had let Priscilla know it, too.

During the night, Macy had considered Priscilla's request to represent Artemis Thibaut if, and when asked to do so by his father, she decided to decline. "My God, PJ, you all but served me up as legal counsel to an art forger. And, he's a thief, too!"

"Mace, please," Priscilla had said. "You know this sort of case is right up your alley. Since when do you say 'no' to representing, shall we say, a client of questionable character?"

"Now you're being insulting."

"Ah, come on, Mace."

"And stop calling me *Mace*, you twit. My name is *Macy*."

"Okay, *Macy*. You know full well that I would never mention your name to a prospective client without first asking you. But Demetrios said he's going to get the *best darn* attorney he can find to represent Artemis Thibaut, and my guess is that's you. And besides, the whole wide world already knows the work you did for Arvana in those conspiracy trials that came out of my troubled time in southern Africa." Priscilla smiled at her recollection. Everything, really, had begun back then. "Anyway, to my way of thinking, everybody deserves the best legal counsel, even shrewd and disreputable folks the likes of Artemis Thibaut Millsap Moreaux. After all, Macy, you *are* the best!"

"Don't patronize me." Macy fumed, although the angry lines on her face softened. But she wasn't about to give in, not yet. "Hell no! I will not take that case. Make that a double, 'hell no!'"

Then Priscilla proceeded to really grate on Macy's nerves. "I'll bet Ron would take the case." Ron Chester was the prosecutor for Merrimack County, New Hampshire, where he and Macy were often courtroom adversaries. But Priscilla and most people who knew them believed not only that Ron and Macy carried a torch for each other but that the couple had recently taken their relationship a few steps further.

But Macy flared again at what she perceived as Priscilla having added a personal insinuation as part of her argument. "I cannot *believe* what you just did! You have some nerve, bringing Ronnie into this."

"Ah, Macy, lighten up. I was just teasing you." Actually, Priscilla admitted to herself; she had been dead serious. But perhaps now was not the time to admit that. "I just think you'd be the best attorney for this case. Who other than you can sort through all this? You know the board of the trustees' members, and you know the board's policies. Why, you even know some of the key players: Iggy and Shane and Gaylord. As for Artemis Thibaut, well, you're about to get to know him, too. So stop acting like you can't weave your way through this tangled web."

Priscilla closed in, much as Macy does in the courtroom.

"Ah, c'mon, Macy, listen to me—dust off those international law books and journals. And consider bringing in a couple of bigwigs from Paris and Mykonos to help with the particulars on their end. Go for it, Girlfriend. Try this out: *The son who so desired his father's affection that he adopted his criminal practices, anything to get his father's love and affection.*" There now, Priscilla had concluded her argument on behalf of Artemis Thibaut. "I rest my case."

Priscilla wore a smirk on her face, but Macy roared, "And stop calling me 'Girlfriend,' too."

On a roll, Priscilla risked more. "So when Demetrios, or one of his people, calls, the only thing you say is, 'When do I start?' Got that?" Priscilla had reverted to the language of the den of the politicians that she'd once associated with during her time in the Ohio Senate. Though she did not care for Artemis Thibaut—or Iggy or Shane, either, for that matter—she wanted to appease Miriam Millsap Omiros.

So while Priscilla had sunbathed to a bronze crisp the next afternoon, Macy had stretched out on the chaise next to her, wrecking her brain and tearing at her conscience about not so much whether, but *how* she would represent the man she had begun to think of as "the bad seed."

As it turned out, it was good that Priscilla had already given Macy a formidable heads-up. She'd been half-asleep in the sun when the concierge delivered an urgent message for Macy to call Demetrios Omiros. *How*, Macy had wondered, *does Missy know these things*? When she rang Demetrios back, he did ask her to represent his entire family.

Macy had taken careful notes of his words. He had not asked her to represent Artemis or Gaylord or, for that matter, Miriam or himself. No, he had asked her "to serve as legal counsel for the Omiros family."

As she'd listened to the Greek tycoon ramble on, she'd already calculated her fee in her head. *Two sons, the parents, and only God knows who else is involved.*

Thanks to Priscilla's groundwork, Macy had agreed to take on this case, after all.

For the rest of that afternoon, Macy had forgotten all about the hot Greek sun. She'd sat in their hotel suite and begun making notes on a yellow legal pad, which she always carried in her luggage. It was a complicated case. But she had already vowed to give it her utmost.

22

Raid at the Manhattan Mansion,
and Then

The next day, in New York City, Artemis Thibaut was still at the Millsap Manhattan mansion on Sutton Place, sipping a fresh martini as, with amusement, he continued watching on television what seemed to be a continuous feed from the French family chateau that his paternal grandparents had bequeathed to him and his brother Gaylord.

He laughed as he watched the international intelligence authorities scurry about the grounds, carrying wooden crates of artwork, boxes of artifacts, and file folders from the impressive chateau.

"That's not it, either, you stupid fools," he chortled, unaware that CF Agent Macon had already discovered and retrieved the authentic Chagall that his father had concealed behind the wall in that secret space near the kitchen so many years ago. For Artemis Thibaut and his father had taken such glee about their private stash and had been ever so sure that no one would ever find it. But they had not reckoned with Iggy's perfidy, as he revealed all that he knew or even suspected to the international intelligence authorities.

Artemis Thibaut then set down his martini and fiddled with the television remote until he was playing back the tape he had previously recorded of the arrest of his twin—and his own girlfriend, too—at that other raid in New Rochelle.

But he frowned as again he watched the feds handcuff Adrienne, frog-march her outside, and secure her in a big black government SUV. She had been faithful to him, and they had shared good times together.

But for sure, she never suspected he would mistreat her. *Not like this*, she must have thought at the time.

Momentarily he wondered if he himself were in any danger. Then he shook his head. He was too smart for the police and the international intelligence authorities. His father had seen to that. He entertained himself a little longer, watching the agents searching the New Rochelle premises. *No paintings there, for sure*! Again he laughed out loud.

Next, he reran the footage of the international intelligence agents boarding the yacht *Piraeus* in the seas off Mykonos, and then apparently scouring the vessel for more lost paintings. As he later watched the agents leaving the yacht, he had no idea that they had successfully retrieved another masterpiece—this one, Monet's *La Promenade*—which he and his father had hidden on that fabulous yacht so many years ago.

So absorbed was he that he let down his usual vigilant guard. He had no idea that five FBI agents and four of their colleagues from the DGSE, MI5, the EYP, and Interpol were approaching the mansion's front door. Nor did he notice the multitude of federal law enforcement agents wearing riot gear with big block letters FBI printed on their bulletproof vests and carrying heavy weaponry—raised to the ready—surrounding the mansion, awaiting orders to advance. Indeed he had no notion of the squadrons of New York City Police officers who had cordoned off the Upper East Side area where the mansion was situated.

Perhaps most significantly of all, Artemis Thibaut continued to be blithely unaware that a trusted member of the household staff—the British house manager named "Rupert," who had been with the Millsap family shortly after World War II—not only knew about the distinguishing birthmarks between the twins but was also unquestionably familiar with Gaylord's ways. Rupert knew Gaylord did not drink much and that he was seldom demanding. So it was that he had been suspecting for some time that the man slurping martinis in the family room had to be the other twin, Artemis Thibaut, not his beloved Gaylord.

Yet Rupert was trained in discretion and loyalty to this family. He could not decide what he was called on to do concerning the identity of the drunkard on the couch in the other room. Why, even house managers are up on current events. For, Rupert had seen the same televised news about the raid at the Moreaux mansion in Paris and the New Rochelle Victorian house as had other television viewers.

But this mansion was Rupert's world, and he had already keenly noticed the activity outside. So when he happened past one of the tall windows and glimpsed the agents secreted near the front door, this time, he hesitated one more minute but then did his duty.

First, he glided to the family room door to assure himself that Artemis Thibaut was still nearly lethargically inert after consuming one too many martinis. Then he stood in the window and simply crooked his finger at an agent who bore big block letters FBI on the back of his jacket. A second later, Rupert slipped outside, intentionally leaving the front door unlocked, as he huddled with that intelligence agent.

"I can assure you," Rupert told him, "that man inside is *not* Gaylord Millsap Omiros. He's his twin Artemis Thibaut, 'the bad seed.'" No sooner than that FBI agent was on his radio, relaying what the house manager had just told him than another agent escorted Rupert away to a safe place.

Whichever of the twins was inside; neither was known to be violent. Yet, the FBI and the international intelligence authorities were hardly going to take any chances. They had come ready for all possibilities.

As it so happened, across the way in an undisclosed location in the City, CIA Deputy Director Froley and CF Agent Macon waited for word from their friend and colleague FBI Agent Rothschild about his apprehension of the real Artemis Thibaut Millsap Moreaux and for word that he'd also discovered and retrieved the third missing painting.

As for CF Commander Wozniah and "the boys," they all sat in Jordy's office at P. J. Austin and Associates, Inc. several blocks away, where they also watched live streaming of the episode on their television and awaited word from their friend and colleague FBI Agent Rothschild.

FBI Agent Rothschild finally received the "all clear" signal that the premises had been secured. It was time for him to wrap up this part of the case. He and his team—four more from the FBI along with the four international intelligence agents representing the DGSE, MI5, the EYP, and Interpol—walked up the sidewalk and strode to the front door of the Millsap Manhattan mansion. Agent Rothschild rang the doorbell, and then he banged the big brass knocker. He waited and then repeated that sequence.

Artemis Thibaut thought that he had heard the doorbell ringing and then someone knocking on the door a couple of times, but each time that he had listened to the doorbell ringing and someone knocking on the door, he had also assumed that Rupert or one of the other household staff was going to answer it. Of course, he himself never once considered getting up from his comfortable seat to see who was at the door.

But then, a third time, the doorbell sounded, and the brass knocker knocked.

This time, however, Artemis Thibaut thought he heard the front door actually opening. And he surely heard someone—Agent Rothschild—crying out: "We're coming in. This is the FBI, and we are coming in."

Finally—but too late—Artemis Thibaut sprang from his seat. His first thought was that he had no weapon, specifically, a gun. He had always lived by his wits. But now he wished he had possessed a weapon.

Before he realized anything else, agents swarmed through the front door and into the family room where he had been streaming live scenes of "the mysterious affair at the Met."

He took in the sight of the big block letters FBI printed on the agents' bulletproof vests—all those men and women carrying heavy weaponry, raised to the ready. Then, he whirled around and saw more men and women wearing riot gear rushing down the corridor and into the family room, where he stood startled. Then, some of the men and women wearing riot gear opened up a way. FBI Agent Rothschild, the four other FBI agents, and the four agents representing the DGSE, MI5, the EYP, and Interpol walked through it.

The once-inebriated Artemis Thibaut stumbled about, raising his arms as high as they could go, then mumbling—stuttering was more like it—unintelligible words. "Surely, fellows, this is some kind of a mistake. Who're you looking for?" Then, miraculously, he declared quite emphatically, "I'm no *criminal*. Don't you know who I am? Why… why this is unheard of. You'll hear from my lawyers about this."

The FBI was in charge, for they were on American soil.

All the while, Agent Rothschild pretended that Artemis Thibaut had not even spoken. Then, after Artemis Thibaut declared who he was not, the FBI agent introduced himself and read Artemis Thibaut his constitutional rights:

"Artemis Thibaut Millsap Moreaux, I'm FBI Agent Marvin Rothschild. It is my duty to inform you that you are under arrest for art forgery, tampering with and stealing highly-valued works of art, *and* for extortion."

Two FBI agents stepped forward and possessively held Artemis Thibaut's arms.

Then Agent Rothschild introduced the four international intelligence agents from France, Britain, Greece, and Interpol. So Artemis Thibaut was made aware that he might face extradition to those other countries that had been part of his international criminal enterprise.

Artemis Thibaut concentrated on two tasks throughout his momentary detention, both controlling his own face and features. He wrinkled his forehead to look puzzled, even dumbfounded. And he did, for a second, let his eyes stray to the painting above the fireplace.

Agent Rothschild then read from a printed list the proper titles of the artwork that Artemis Thibaut was accused of having forged, tampered with, and stolen. But he did not read the names of the parties from whom he had extorted vast sums of money, especially not the seven confederates affiliated with the Met's board of trustees who were portrayed in that cache of nude portraits that had been "unwrapped," as it were, at the Moreaux chateau outside of Paris.

"Cuff 'im," said Agent Rothschild. The startled Artemis Thibaut did not resist when the two FBI officers pulled back his arms and fastened the handcuffs. Besides, how could he not see all those big repeating rifles raised at the ready?

But before they took Artemis Thibaut outside and whisked him away, the agents made him wait and watch as they purposefully began going about the rest of their business. Artemis Thibaut knew very well what that must be. He steeled himself for what surely would be a long search for the original painting or paintings stashed on the premises. Of course he well remembered what his father had told him had happened back in 1947 when he, that is, Artemis Thibaut, was a mere baby boy. Thibaut Francois had given Miriam's father what he had described as an "excellent reproduction" of Paris Bordone's *Diana and the Two Nymphs*. But, in fact, that had been the *authentic* masterpiece. And so it was that, for almost forty years of his life, the magnate who had been Miriam's father and the twins' maternal grandfather had loved having this "excellent reproduction" hanging above the mantle in his family room.

But to Artemis Thibaut's shock, two agents immediately went to the fireplace and pointed to the painting on the wall. He watched as they called out to Agent Rothschild: "This one?"

"Yes," Agent Rothschild answered emphatically as he studied Artemis Thibaut's face. Ignatius Devoe had been definite that the painting above the fireplace was, in fact, the missing masterpiece. But Agent Rothschild noted that Artemis Thibaut's face was blank. He nodded at this master criminal. "Game, match, set," he said.

But Artemis Thibaut retorted: "No, that's an 'excellent *reproduction*.' The original Bordone *Diana* is in the Met."

But when his plea was ignored, he shifted his tack. "Ah, come on, gentlemen, you've got this all wrong. I'm not Artemis Thibaut. I'm his twin brother, Gaylord."

"Save it for the judge, Bro'," said the FBI agent as he ordered his men to take Artemis Thibaut away.

Then he cautioned the other men who were reaching for the painting. "Careful with that. It's worth more than any of us will earn in our lifetimes." Appreciatively he regarded this masterpiece, which had been hidden in plain sight for so many years. "We've got wrappings in the lead SUV. Cover it up and keep it safe, yet inconspicuous, as we take it to headquarters."

Then Agent Rothschild turned his back to them all and turned on his walkie-talkie. He contacted CIA Deputy Director Froley and CF Agent Macon and the "boys," who had been waiting for word about Artemis Thibaut's arrest and the retrieval of the third original painting involved in the Met art scandal.

Later, too, when Agent Macon called her at her Mykonos hotel, Priscilla was not only elated at that outcome but also had another thought: *A third finder's fee! On behalf of her PR consultancy, she herself was going to lay claim to all of that.* She had a hunch that Arvana would be thanking her for years to come.

The fairly uneventful raid at Sutton Place, which included the arrest and the asset seizure, was later cited as a textbook example of how to carry off an operation like this. It was also perhaps a perfectly publicized one.

The local law enforcement and the international intelligence authorities had tipped off the New York City press corps about what was unfolding in the Met case. Before the raid had begun, red plastic cones and waist-high barricades had already held back and corralled the news reporters on the adjoining sidewalks and streets. A host of international entertainment and news reporters, including the paparazzi, had also been tipped off about the operation and had turned out in full force as well.

Cameras rolled, and photographs were snapped as the authorities closed in on the unsuspecting Artemis Thibaut. Television networks had begun streaming live feeds of the action, including anyone coming and going in its vicinity. The bulletin at the bottom of TV screens all over the world headlined: "Breaking News: American and International Intelligence Authorities Corner the Culprit in the Mysterious Affair at the Met."

All over the world, interested parties, including jet setters and prominent socialites, were enthralled as the episode played out live on their televisions. They watched Artemis Thibaut Millsap Moreaux being escorted in handcuffs from the lavish Millsap mansion in Manhattan, New York!

Many television viewers were confused, though. Had they just seen this same man being arrested a few days ago in New Rochelle? Others sagely clued them in that twin brothers were, in fact, the perpetrators.

Some said, "Wow, identical twins!"

Others mused. "You just can't make this stuff up."

But there was yet another kink to this mystery.

What really stumped observers of the international entertainment and news shows was another confusing resemblance. No one in the know could fathom the double sightings of P. J. Austin-Bernhardt at both the Paris and the Mykonos sites at virtually the same time.

Some even said, "Two P. J. Austin-Bernhardts? That's crazy. Why can't the media get their stories straight?"

But for once, the media representatives did not put their two cents into this double identity question. Although some were still puzzled at Priscilla's evidently being at two places simultaneously, at least none of them had captured images of Agent Macon during the Sutton Place operation.

And actually, at that time—although Agent Macon was, in fact, part of the Sutton Place raid—the real Priscilla was still enjoying "just one more day on Mykonos!"

Onboard their yacht *Piraeus* in Mykonos, Demetrios and Miriam watched the same televised entertainment and news stories about Artemis Thibaut's apprehension at the Millsap Manhattan mansion in New York.

"Oh, my God!" Miriam clung to Demetrios.

He had to ask her. "Is that really Artemis?"

"I think so," she said, frowning. "They already arrested Gaylord."

But he could see that she, too, was not sure. However, he was glad that he had already secured the services of the American attorney, that Macy who palled around with P. J. Austin-Bernhardt. And from what he had heard, if anyone could get to the bottom of this—and keep them all out of jail, or, at the least reduced, sentencing—she was the one.

As for which twin was which, Demetrios was aware that both he and his wife, along with a select group of American and international intelligence agents—still believed that Gaylord, not Artemis Thibaut, had been arrested in New Rochelle—which would logically mean that indeed Artemis Thibaut had just been the one handcuffed in New York City.

There was one final event that night back in New York City.

FBI Agent Rothschild held a news conference outside the Sutton Place mansion. He began with a brief statement:

> Ladies and Gentlemen of the press, the FBI has just arrested one Artemis Thibaut Millsap Moreaux—one of the twin sons of the notorious Thibaut Francois Moreaux—on suspicion of forging, tampering with, and stealing three highly-valued works of art from The Metropolitan Museum of Art.

The agent paused. He was well aware that attorneys for the U.S. Department of Justice had already deposed some of Artemis Thibaut's extortion racket victims, including, but not confined to the seven confederates who served on the Met's board of trustees. But the Justice Department had also already agreed to lessen any further harm done to those board members and the other victims of the father's and son's extortion racket. So the FBI did not release their names or any explanation about how they had been subjected to Thibaut Francois's and his son Artemis Thibaut's elaborate extortion racket for decades—ergo, Agent Rothschild having omitted their names in his otherwise detailed statement to the press.

But an art reporter asked the obvious: "For clarification, did you say 'from the *Met*?'"

At that, FBI Agent Rothschild realized that he had been the first American law enforcement officer—intelligence agent was more accurate—to publicly acknowledge that some paintings had, in fact, been forged, tampered with, and stolen, not to mention directly connecting the crimes to "the mysterious affair at the Met."

Agent Rothschild nodded. "To be clear, yes, I said, 'from The Metropolitan Museum of Art.' That's the Met. Here in New York City."

Immediately the reporters began screaming questions:

"What *exactly* did Artemis Thibaut do?"

"What artwork was involved?"

"Did he forge, tamper with, or steal some of the masterpieces?"

But Agent Rothschild nodded again, this time in finality. "Now, if you will excuse me, I have no further comment."

"Stop! You can't just leave us hanging!"

As the FBI agent walked away, the news reporters, and the paparazzi, too, continued shouting questions and even comments at him:

"More arrests coming?"

"How is this linked to the arrest four days ago in New Rochelle?"

"Exactly what was stolen, and when, from the Met?"

Agent Rothschild ignored the questions and comments. He had said all that he intended to say. He knew the agency's public information officer would eventually issue their own statement and probably everyone else involved in all this.

Even after he reached his car and quickly sped away, the reporters kept talking to one another, trying to make sense of this muddle.

"I think this is a scandal of epic proportions," someone said.

"But what's with this theft from the Met?" Another reporter shook his head. "This is my beat, and this is the first we've heard about any big art theft. A possible breach of ethical standards, but not this. Not art forgery, tampering, and *theft, too.*"

The next day—her final one on Mykonos—a satisfyingly suntanned Priscilla was sitting in a seaside *taverne* sipping ouzo and nibbling bite-sized chunks of salty fish. *I could get used to a life like this.*

Beside her, Macy was dreamily watching a beautiful Greek sunset. "I hate to go back to New York," she murmured. She was oh-too-aware of the mountain of work that awaited her, not just with this crazy Met case but with other work as well.

"Me, too," Priscilla agreed. But she supposed in a way that the time she had spent on the phone this afternoon with Agent Macon, Ruth, and "the boys"—and Darling Carlton—had left her feeling that already she was halfway home. She loved to work, and a case like this one, so tangled, so confounding, was as close to something "earthy" as it could get.

She stared into the dying sunset, thinking hard. But what was her next step? Ruth had told her that one of the reporters had called the office, asking why there had been no definitive public statements about the forgery or theft of any highly-valued works of art from the Met. She reconsidered. Had there been footage live-streamed on television of those paintings recovered in France and Greece? She was not sure. Possibly there had been some shots of what could have been paintings, but if so, they would have been wrapped or even packed. Maybe it had not even been possible to be certain that there were paintings among all the stuff carted away from New Rochelle, Paris, or Sutton Place. She eventually decided that the reporter who had called Ruth had been on a fishing expedition.

But Priscilla did know that in New York, the media representatives had been focused on the possible violation of the Met board's code of ethics by Gaylord Millsap Omiros. To herself she sighed. Would that only that *that* had been the case! But the FBI statement on the scene at Sutton Place had escalated suspicions. No wonder they were still calling it: "the mysterious affair at the Met." The arrest of both twins had raised more public scrutiny than it had solved. Now observers wanted to know what had led to the mystery in the first place.

She reflected that none of them knew which masterpieces were involved—the Chagall, the Bordone, and the Monet—much less that the Met had been defrauded and had been hanging forgeries rather than authentic masterpieces for decades. She wondered how to play this. How to let this information go public in the best possible way for her client, the museum? To herself she added: *And of course to the public.*

Priscilla came to a preliminary conclusion: It was best not to rush this. All would come out right in the end, and she would do her best to ensure that it did. But it would take some time for all of it to play out.

She popped a curl of fried calamari in her mouth and drained her ouzo to the dredges. As she signaled to the waiter for another round of ouzo, Priscilla considered that maybe this case was winding down. *Both twins were locked up. The three paintings have been retrieved. What else could happen*? But a shiver went through her. *A premonition? You never know*, she thought. *Could be more surprises*! But if she were right, soon, this little adventure would be at an end. *Careful*, she cautioned herself. She always risked making mistakes when she was getting bored at a time like this. Yet, she must not jump in and hurry everything along. Impatience was one of her challenges. What she should do instead was find some other diversion to fill the gap. Maybe something that would please her darling Carlton, whom she had not given much attention to lately. *What else can I sink my teeth into*? She snapped her fingers.

As she clinked her tiny fresh glass of ouzo with Macy's, she declared, "Life is good!"

23

The Fashionista &
You've Got That Wrong

The two American women took turns admiring themselves in the full-length mirror at their Mykonos hotel suite.

Priscilla had just wrapped a long bright blue silk scarf around the crown of the white straw hat she had bought in an island boutique and tied it so the ends trailed to her shoulders. "What do you think, Mace?" But before her friend could answer, she threw off the blue scarf and instead used a gauzy white scarf the same way. "Or white on white, *très chic*, no?"

"No," Macy said firmly. "The blue's better. Looks good with that blue and white silk top." She nodded approvingly at the look her friend had copied from the fashionista Miriam Millsap Omiros: the straw hat, the scarf, the tunic, the white linen slacks, the stylish high-heel sandals, and, of course, the gigantic Jackie O sunglasses.

"Imitation is the most sincere form of flattery," Priscilla said. "Thank you, Miriam!"

"Actually, she's the one who's been thanking you," Macy said. "Demetrios, too."

The two of them had been out on the yacht *Piraeus* every day of their stay. Yesterday, Demetrios even let Macy pilot it. She thought, *A bonus for agreeing to take on the twins' legal defense, Gaylord Millsap Omiros and Artemis Thibaut Millsap Moreaux, yeah, the whole Omiros family.* But she went back to gazing in the mirror.

"My goodness, Missy, you look like a movie star."

"You're not looking bad either, Girlfriend," Priscilla said of Macy's similar attire. As usual, Macy favored black: her big black straw hat, tunic and linen pants, and high heels, all set off with clunky gold-toned Greek jewelry.

Macy continued staring at herself in the mirror. "You know, Missy, I'm beginning to like this look." Left unsaid was the necessity of traveling incognito to put off the international entertainment and news reporters, especially the paparazzi, who were on the hunt for the real P. J. Austin-Bernhardt on the docks and at the airports in Mykonos and Athens. But they would be outmaneuvered again because Priscilla had deepened her naturally tan complexion to a bronze crisp from having sunbathed beside the infinity pool so long. Macy reflected that although she was a prominent attorney back home, she had not understood what it meant to be a celebrity like Priscilla until they made this trip together. "But do you think this is over the top for just flying home? I mean, the hats and glasses, not to mention the rest of it."

"Not if we carry it off, Girlfriend." Priscilla grinned and then looked at the two of them one last time in the mirror. After she looked herself and Macy over one last time, she said, "Oh well, here goes nothing."

They caught a commuter flight from Mykonos Island National Airport to Athens, where no one at that airport even bothered to ask them to remove their sunglasses and floppy hats before boarding the flight. As they settled into the first-class compartment, they wondered, in whispers, whether they were getting special treatment or whether the staff was simply accustomed to prominent citizens and superstar tourists demanding to be permitted to hide their true identities.

But they were glad to take off those big floppy hats.

"Love this hat," Priscilla said, but she felt a tremendous weight lifted off her when she removed it. "But, you know, my head is scorching. Man alive does taking it off feel good."

"You bet." When Macy removed her hat, she fluffed up her hair. "It was itchy, too."

They laughed and ordered champagne for the long flight home.

When Priscilla's and Macy's flight landed at John F. Kennedy Airport, the customs agents curtly ordered them to lose the floppy hats and sunglasses. They obliged but donned them again before heading out of the terminal. The international entertainment and news reporters, and the paparazzi, too, were on the prowl by the taxi stands and even lurking in the parking lots, ready to snap photographs of anyone famous or notorious. Priscilla and Macy grabbed hold of the handles on their luggage-on-wheels, put on their New York attitude, and prepared to push and shove their way through the crowd toward an exit to stand in a taxi line.

But as soon as they emerged through the door, Priscilla heard a familiar voice: "Missy, over here!"

She looked up and scanned the sidewalk and street. Then she heard the familiar voice ring out once more.

"Missy, over here!"

"There he is!" Carlton was easy to spot because he was so much taller than most of those waiting for their loved ones to appear. Although he sported his trademark ponytail, he, too, had donned a simple disguise: a baseball cap turned backward, a fake moustache, and a big but masculine pair of sunglasses. He waved, aware that his Miss Prissy had finally seen him.

"Uh oh!" She was a little taken aback that her husband had so readily recognized her, even with what she had hoped was such an excellent disguise. She had forgotten, too, all about the tracking device implanted in her lower back and that Carlton would have access to that intel as well. She grinned. What was she thinking? Carlton had been an intelligence agent a lot longer than she had. A master of disguise, he had trained the decoys that the agency had used during that southern African mission. Mostly, Carlton was Priscilla's husband. He knew everything about her: her idiosyncrasies, the way she walked and talked, stood and sat, her every gesture, such as what she called her "New York attitude" when she threw her head back, raised her arms, and pumped her elbows as she moved about the hustle and bustle of the city streets. Carlton knew his woman.

"Welcome home," he said when he caught up with her and Macy. He swept his wife in his arms, kissed her hard, and then, as he looked her over, tried not to laugh at her crisp bronze suntan. "What were you trying to do, make out like a chocolate Easter bunny?"

As Priscilla laughed, Carlton turned and kissed Macy on her cheek. "Thank goodness you were with her. As I'm sure you are aware, Missy tends to get into a spot of trouble."

Macy smiled. "Only a *spot!*"

Carlton took hold of the two women's luggage handles and led them away from the ever-growing taxi line. Then, without incident, they arrived where his Land Rover SUV was parked. He put their luggage inside, held the doors for the two women, and then drove the two friends away from the JFK Airport.

At one point during their ride into the City, Priscilla heard what she thought was someone snickering behind her. "What's so funny? Let us in on whatever it is."

"'What's so funny' is *you*, Miss Prissy," Macy said. "To think you thought your hat and sunglasses would fool even your husband. But he sure had no problem picking *you* out." Then Macy intentionally tried to get on Priscilla's nerves—payback for manipulating her into representing "the bad seed." She said, "Say, Carlton, did you check us out on the deck dancing on that fabulous yacht *Piraeus*? All those handsome men!"

Carlton laughed a hearty laugh, which Macy joined in with gusto.

Priscilla's crispy bronze suntan darkened with a flush. "Ah, come on, guys. It's wasn't *that* funny."

After dropping Macy off at her Manhattan apartment, and since their Harlem brownstone was still not quite move-in ready, Carlton and Priscilla continued on their way to the Waldorf Astoria. When they walked into the grand hotel lobby, Carlton told Priscilla that he wanted "to pop by the front desk for something."

When the couple reached the front desk, the receptionist greeted him. "Ah, Mr. Bernhardt. And who might this lovely lady be?"

Still in a cheerful mood, Carlton removed Priscilla's big floppy hat and sunglasses.

The receptionist's mouth opened wide. She blurted out: "No! Not Madame PJ!" But she got flustered at her own familiarity. "Oh, Madame, I do apologize. Honestly, I do."

"No problem," Carlton said as he plopped the big floppy hat back on his wife's head and handed her Jackie O sunglasses back to her. Priscilla removed her hat and swatted Carlton with it. Then she continued playfully hitting him with her hat all the way to the elevators. Carlton grabbed her and planted a warm kiss on her lips; all was forgiven.

But when the elevator door opened on their floor, he said, "By golly, Tommy *was* right."

"'Tommy *was* right' about what?"

"I knew who and what you were when I married you. And I still say, 'Each day is like a day with Lucille Ball.' You never cease to amaze me, woman." Then Carlton laughed that hearty laugh of his again, and Priscilla hit him with her hat again, too.

No one could have prepared Priscilla for what lay ahead. Just two days after returning from Europe and the scintillating homecoming she had spent behind closed doors at the Waldorf Astoria with her Darling Carlton, everything unexpectedly fell apart.

It started when she was sitting in her office, listening as Ruth began telling her what had happened while she had been in Paris and Mykonos.

Ruth started with a summary of the mountain of mail and messages that had piled up. One stack consisted of requests for employment and internships, with impressive résumés. Another was keynote speaking requests. Finally, there were messages from the booking agents of news broadcasts and television shows; they all wanted Priscilla to appear on their news and talk shows.

"The price of fame," Ruth said. "You're back to being an A-list celebrity again."

"Ah, crap!" Priscilla said as she tossed most of it aside.

Ruth teased her. "Is the illustrious P. J. Austin-Bernhardt not comfortable in her own crisp-fried skin?"

"Not you, *too*?" Priscilla was getting tired of being teased about her bronze suntan. "What's wrong with a little color?"

But just as Ruth finished with the mail, the intercom sounded. It was Alfrieda. "There's a call waiting. A personal one for Ms. PJ. She says she's her sister Helen. And that it's important."

"Put it through." Priscilla glanced at Ruth, who stood up to leave so that Priscilla could have some privacy. "No, stay. This probably won't take long. There're some updates about the Met case I need to share. Nothing urgent, though. Mostly just legal stuff and media outreach. Questioning of the twins. But nothing public yet. Nothing that we'll have to face the media about. But I like to make sure you're in the loop."

Then another voice came over the intercom, apparently Priscilla's personal call.

"Priscilla? Is that you?"

Priscilla was quite surprised to hear her sister's voice. Why she called her at her office—instead, as was her family's custom of calling one another in the evenings at home—was most unexpected. "My goodness, Helen. Everything all right?"

Helen hesitated, then: "Priscilla, there's no easy way for me to tell you this, but Ellen, well, she *died*."

Priscilla blinked. She must not have heard her sister correctly. "Excuse me? What did you just say?"

"Priscilla, I said, 'Ellen died.' She had a heart attack in the night."

"No, Helen. You've got that wrong. Ellen can't be…. No, I tell you. I just saw her a few weeks ago, and she was fine."

"I know, Priscilla, and I'm sorry to bring you such sad news." Then, Helen asked, without waiting for any reaction, "How soon do you think you can get to San Francisco?"

Priscilla blanked out and was silent for a long moment. Then she said, "Today, sometime today. I'll let you know." She hung up without as much as a goodbye. Then she just sat there, staring into space in her executive swivel chair.

"Priscilla?"

Priscilla did not respond.

Ruth got up and disappeared when Priscilla did not seem to hear her. Moments later, she returned with Jordy and Alfrieda. But still, Priscilla did not respond to their anxious efforts to get through to her. The three of them looked at one another.

Finally, Priscilla broke her silence. "I can't believe this, really. It's so strange! So terrible!" She took a deep breath. "Ellen is…was…our big sister. The oldest of the girls. The one who lives in San Francisco." She blinked at the sudden tears in her eyes. "Helen said that Ellen *died* of a heart attack last night."

Ruth remembered her saying that she had visited Ellen in San Francisco when she went off on that "personal business" of hers. Just now, she asked, "You're flying out?"

But Priscilla did not answer. She had never imagined one of her siblings would die before she even reached middle age. And Ellen! Ellen, gone! Her favorite sister had…died.

Ruth and Jordy exchanged worried looks of concern. Although they suspected that Priscilla was far less indomitable than she mostly appeared to be, they had never seen her like this. But her brother and sisters could have told Priscilla's friends that it had taken ten years of denial before she had gradually begun to accept her father Nelson's death.

Unsure what to do, Jordy quietly ducked away to track down and alert Carlton, who happened to be at the United Nations for a high-level appointment.

Alfrieda looked at Ruth. "Let me know how you want me to handle her calls and appointments. Or book her flight." Then she, too, scuttled away.

But again, Priscilla had gone silent.

Ruth said softly: "I'll be in my office. You let me know what you want me to do."

But before she could leave, Laverne, as though somehow she had sensed that Priscilla was in need, rushed straight in from the elevator. "Something's happening! What's happened?"

When briefly, Ruth told her, instantly she leaned over and took Priscilla in her arms. She cooed and stroked her back. Ruth watched in wonder as Priscilla's arms closed around Laverne's shoulders. She would never have guessed that Priscilla would have been so responsive to Laverne's physical comfort. Everyone knew how Priscilla shied away from being touched. But not now, Ruth reflected, as she left the two women alone.

Laverne kept cradling Priscilla. Only the two of them knew how, back in southern Africa, the agent had held her just like this when Priscilla had been in shock from the violent end of her mortal enemy in that platinum mine. This, for a certainty, was the source of their bond. Laverne's innate warmth had once more cut through Priscilla's reserve.

Priscilla pulled away and, as the tears streamed down her cheeks, sobbed, "Can you believe this? I can't." Then she clung to Laverne again, who continued gently embracing her and rubbing her shoulders. And so, she was able to relieve some of Priscilla's pain.

Only a little while later, Carlton arrived. He embraced her and held her tight.

Finally, Priscilla seemed aware of whose arms now held her. She opened her teary eyes and looked blankly into the face of her husband.

Carlton stroked her hair. "It's me, Missy; it's me."

Priscilla seemed to come to. "Oh, Carlton, my darling Carlton!"

Then she fainted in his arms.

He picked her up and tenderly put her down on the leather sofa at the far end of her office. Then, totally forgetting about the intercom, he raised his voice. Shouted, really:

"Alfrieda, call Bow Lake. Get that jet of ours down here and ready to take us to San Francisco. And Laverne, go pack our bags at the Waldorf. Black clothes! The ones she really likes! Enough for a week." He looked down at his wife, who was still out cold. "No, better make that two weeks." Again he glanced at Priscilla. "Just pack anything she could possibly want."

But Priscilla had begun to stir. He pulled her back into his arms.

"I'm here, Missy, I'm here." As he serenaded, Priscilla nestled in her husband's arms.

24

A Celebration of Life

Hours later, Priscilla stared out the window of the Bernhardt private jet somewhere over the Midwest, Carlton at her side. Laverne leafed through a magazine as she sat across from the couple. Then, as she felt eyes upon her, she looked up and returned Priscilla's smiling at her.

"Missy's back with us," Laverne said. "Good afternoon."

"That's debatable." Priscilla's smile died on her lips.

Carlton caught the flight attendant's eye and ordered coffee for all of them. As they were sipping and nibbling on some pastries he had brought, they small-talked awhile.

Then Carlton took a chance and prompted Priscilla to talk about her sister Ellen. He had, of course, met all her siblings. He remembered that her eldest sister Ellen and the only and eldest brother Nelson, Jr., had been the ones Priscilla had spoken of most favorably and often. But the other siblings, he quietly recalled, had always been cool to him.

"I remember Ellen and how special she always was to you," he began. "But I'm wondering why you were so close?"

"Oh, Carlton, my darling," she said with a big grin, "I'm so glad you asked. I guess it was the little things I remember most. But I guess it's always the little things that you can't ever forget." Then Priscilla talked and talked.

She told Carlton and Laverne about how Ellen used to take her along with her to the movies when she was a teenager. She shared some of her favorites: "You know," *Doctor Zhivago* and *Valley of the Dolls*. Back then, I was only a girl, although I believed I was altogether grown up. I really had no idea what was happening in those grown-up movies." She let out a little laugh. "But I felt so big and smart and important as I sat beside my *big* sister Ellen."

Then Priscilla told them about how her parents had forced Ellen to give up her child for adoption. She had given birth to the baby out of wedlock. She especially recalled how Ellen had suffered over that. "Oh, the pain in her face," Priscilla said as she dropped her head in her hands. "Such pain." Then she raised her head and threw it back, in her customary way of pretending to be in control of her feelings. "Then Ellen showed all of us how strong and resilient she was. She went out West and worked as an accountant for a major architectural firm. Then she married a realtor. They had a happy marriage." She sighed. "But he died. He died, too. But Ellen helped his uncle manage a group home. I remember how she described the men she helped there. For her, they were always 'clients,' as she always said." Priscilla paused as she recalled what Ellen had made her say about that. "'My clients are developmentally disabled high-achieving autistic men.'" Priscilla's eyes were ashine, and this time not with tears. "Ellen made a real success of that group home. The rest, as we say, is history."

Both Carlton and Laverne sensed the tremendous pride she carried for Ellen. They were also conscious of how intimate and trusting Priscilla was with the two of them, as she would start weeping again from time to time. Usually, Priscilla would not break down in front of anyone but family and very close friends. But the two of them, for a certainty, had won a place in that firmament. They took turns handing Priscilla the box of Kleenex. Then Priscilla would blow her nose and then resumed telling her stories.

At one point, when she took a break from telling her stories about how much fun she and Ellen once shared, Carlton openly reflected on the situation in his youth.

"You know something, Missy," he said, "at least you and Ellen hung out and had fun together. I don't have a single story like yours to share." But before Priscilla could comment, Laverne concurred.

"Yes, PJ. Carlton is right," she asserted. "I'm the youngest of a house once full of children, and I never spent time hanging out with any of my siblings. And no one ever *asked* me to hang out with them either."

As if she did not believe them, Priscilla said, "Ah, stop it. You guys are just trying to make me feel better." But when she saw the serious expressions on both of their faces, she knew they had spoken truthfully.

Yet, she picked up where she had left off as if neither Carlton nor Laverne had said a single word.

"You know something else?" she confided. "Whenever we visited Ellen, she'd pull out all the stops. She took us to great seafood restaurants. She knew how much I loved seafood! We would walk along the beach, too. Ellen lived right near the bay. We would climb the stairway onto the cliffs. Or see whatever there was to see in Haight-Asbury. And more than once, we caught a ferry or some other kind of boat and sailed past Alcatraz en route to Sausalito."

Priscilla munched on some snacks that the flight attendant had thoughtfully given her and continued.

"And Reno! How could I forget Reno! Man alive, Ellen always had tickets for overnight trips to Reno, where she'd plant herself on a stool in front of one of those old slot machines. Then she'd fill up a plastic container with the coins from her winnings, after which she'd head over to the card tables. As for me, well, I always hunkered down at one of the slot machines and pulled that same lever all night long.

Priscilla laughed but yawned. *Why am I so tired*?

Still, she mustered up some strength and continued: "Sometimes we'd go to pawn shops that were everywhere. We'd watch the people coming in with fur coats and diamond rings and their family's silver service. Remembering how it had been in Reno, I just knew those people were avid gamblers wanting to hock their valuables in return for cash to play the slot machines and the card tables with the hopes of replenishing their losses."

Then Priscilla could share no more. She pressed the button on her armrest, leaned back, and closed her eyes. Moments later, she fell asleep. And yes, she snored.

After arriving in San Francisco, the threesome checked into a hotel and headed over to Ellen's stately Victorian home just off the bay on West Forty-Seventh Street.

From the point of their arrival, they were all taken aback at the hustle and bustle and much else that they encountered.

Priscilla's youngest sister Camille and her next-to-the-oldest sister Harriet moved about carrying artifacts, paintings, jewelry and packed boxes of different sizes and shapes. Priscilla later learned they had shipped those items to their homes.

Helen, meanwhile, rummaged through many file folders. She told Priscilla that she was searching for Ellen's last will and testament, which Priscilla suspected did not exist. She remembered Ellen having once told her, from frustration, because she could not get one of her family members to help her out when she needed them, "Well, when I'm gone, they can just fight over everything." Ellen had implied that she intended not to draw up a will, which was probably exactly what she had done.

Finally, Priscilla spotted her mom. Liza was sitting alone at the kitchen table, sipping coffee and fidgeting with her hands. She shook her head. Her family could be great, or her family could be terrible—there was no question which behavior was happening now.

Priscilla set aside her grief and rose to the occasion. She stood by the stairwell and bellowed: "OK! Everybody!" She waited until she seemed to have caught the attention of at least some of them. "What's going on?"

Harriet was the first to sound off in response. "Everybody! Priscilla and her *rich* husband are here." She ignored the presence of Laverne.

Priscilla bit her lip hard. Was that what they all thought of Carlton and her marriage?

Harriet continued. "And get a load of Miss Prissy! That *must* have been her in the news again, on that fancy Greek yacht. She's burnt to a crisp."

Priscilla supposed she should not be astonished at Harriet's cruelty. The two of them had never been particularly close. Harriet had always been so jealous of everyone and everything. Still, to be so mean at a time like this seemed…awful. She looked over at Carlton. He had told her before that he had never felt accepted, much less loved, by most of her family. But now she knew he had been right. As for Laverne, she felt a new wave of sympathy for her friend. *No wonder Priscilla never says much about her family, except for her father, who she still apparently misses very much.* Something else occurred to her: *No wonder Missy behaves as though she were an only child.* She looked the sisters over. Except for the slight resemblance with the two younger ones, one would never have guessed they were all related.

But then everyone heard a more welcoming voice: "Aunt Priscilla!" Germane ran down the stairs to the main floor to greet her. "So you *did* come. You made it!"

Priscilla's spirit soared. As her favorite nephew ran to her, she held her arms open wide for an exuberant embrace. "Oh, Germane."

Then Carlton wrapped his loving arms around the two of them and introduced Laverne.

The teenager looked from his aunt to the newcomer. "If I didn't know any better, I'd swear I had *two* Aunt Priscillas! From a distance," he said to Laverne, "I'd swear *you* were Aunt Priscilla."

Then he gave his actual aunt a more intensive scrutiny. "Wow! Aunt Priscilla! I don't think I've ever seen you so *dark*. Are you working on a special project? Or, did you just *feel* like getting a deep suntan?" Then he laughed, and Laverne joined him, and the two of them began talking about Priscilla as if she were not even in their midst. Then the three of them laughed some more.

Carlton had joined his mother-in-law in the kitchen. He leaned down and kissed her on her cheek. "Hello, Miss Liza. It's me, Carlton. Missy's husband."

Liza looked up at the tall man with that thick, long, wavy black ponytail he still had. *Except for that ponytail, he is so handsome!* She met his gentle eyes. *Kind, too,* she thought, *like my Nelson.* Wanly she smiled and reached up to touch his cheek. "Oh, Son, it's so very good to see you. Where's Missy?"

Priscilla heard her mom's meek voice calling out to her. So she stepped away from Germane and Laverne and went into the kitchen.

Liza was still sitting at the table. As she looked at her mom, she was struck by the thought that her mother reminded her a lot of her own mother, Grandma Lilly, for the first time ever. It was more than Liza's crouched posture of despair, Priscilla thought. Of course, her mother and grandmother had always shared the same petite frame. Their feet never touched the floor. The two of them had never weighed more than one hundred twenty pounds, and both had high cheekbones and long wavy salt-n-pepper hair that they parted down the middle and wore in two long braids that drooped down their shoulders. But now Liza looked sad. Nelson had always called her his "angel," but he might not call her that now. She was shrouded in such immense sadness.

As Priscilla hugged her mom, ever so gently, she felt her sorrow and her anguish.

"Oh, Momma, I am so sorry. I know how much you loved Ellen. I did, too." She sat down beside her mom and Carlton at the kitchen table and poured herself a cup of coffee from the carafe but realized upon her first sip that it was cold. As she got up from her seat, Germane happened into the kitchen with Laverne.

Introductions ensued, with Priscilla making a fresh pot of coffee and Germane helping Laverne find a soft drink in the fridge. Then they all looked at one another. Nobody was sure what to say.

Priscilla simply regarded her mom, noting the evidence of her pain. Liza's face seemed to have suddenly acquired deep new furrows, and her hands trembled while she held her cold mug of coffee. Priscilla disengaged her mother's hold on the cup and held those hands in hers. She tried to imagine how her mother must feel. Ellen was her firstborn. Priscilla had not seen that much sadness in her mom's face since the night she told her and her other siblings about Ellen's pregnancy and that Nelson had arranged for the adoption of Ellen's first and only child.

Then Priscilla remembered again how Ellen had once declared that her sisters could fight over her estate. Ellen had been so disillusioned that none of them had answered her one desperate plea to help her with the group home. That had been such a dark time for Ellen, whose husband Nathaniel had died unexpectedly around then. Ellen had been despondent, and she had said she was going to leave her estate intestate. Priscilla sighed. Camille, Helen, and Harriet were about to find that out for themselves.

On their second day in San Francisco, Priscilla joined her sisters at a meeting at the Duggan Funeral Home. Almost immediately, she was appalled as they argued about everything from who would read a poem to the inscription on the tombstone to the garments in which to bury Ellen. Priscilla reminded her sisters that Ellen and Nathaniel had already taken care of their final rites and paid for their burial services. "That included a headstone," she told them, so all they had to do was to add the date of Ellen's death. Even so, Harriet and Camille fought about purchasing a separate headstone for Ellen. They also insisted on buying a new outfit in which to bury her.

"Wow!" Priscilla said. "This is terrible. Are you guys losing your minds or something?" She also noticed that Helen sat quietly and still while the others argued. *Grief*, Priscilla thought. *This is all about their different ways of grieving.* Yet as they kept up the conflict, Priscilla could not at one point stop saying to herself, "Surely, this isn't happening."

Then Harriet rounded on her: "And Missy, you can keep your *rich* man's money in your wallet. His money's no good here."

Priscilla took a deep breath and tried not to snap back. But she was hurt enough to flinch at each hostile word they spoke. She had always suspected these sisters harbored envy and perhaps even animosity toward her, but now it was apparent how deeply their differences divided them.

When she could take no more, she made for the door. "Let me know when you've worked everything out. I'm headed back to the hotel." Priscilla left her sisters squabbling over the minutiae.

The next day the memorial service took place in the small chapel at the Duggan Funeral Home. Liza sat motionless on the front pew, her four surviving daughters surrounding her. Liza kept fretting. "Why'd she have to die before me?" No one knew what to say to her. Priscilla suddenly realized how hard it must be for parents to fathom their children, predeceasing them.

Just before the service began, Nelson, Jr., walked down the aisle. He had flown in just in time.

When Priscilla noticed her brother, she rushed down the aisle, embraced him, and whispered in his ear that he was lucky to have missed being with the family the day before.

"*Lucky*?" he frowned.

"Well, ole buddy, ole pal," she said, "if only you could have seen *your* sisters squabbling over minor details about this service, you might not wish to claim any of us." Then she smiled at her brother, with whom, apart from Ellen, she always felt close.

"Oh, little Sis, everything'll be all right. It'll all be over soon. Let's just concentrate on how well a life Ellen led and how much joy she brought into our lives."

"The one who can always spot a silver lining," she said. But she was glad he was there.

Then Carlton and Laverne, who were seated in the middle of the chapel, watched as the five Austin siblings closed ranks and arrayed themselves all around Liza in that front pew. Although Camille's husband and Nelson, Jr.'s wife were not there, none of the other in-laws infiltrated that front pew.

Germane whispered to Carlton and Laverne, "Sorry folks, but they've got their ways."

The service moved along fairly quickly: a song, a poem, and a few statements of fond memories from some guests. Then there was the eulogy, another song, and then a prayer.

But it was the statements of fond memories—the celebration of Ellen's life—that captured Priscilla's and her family's attention the most. Ellen's able assistant, Jason Garner, shared words of comfort and fond memories of his relationship with her. Then representatives from the California Department of Health and Human Services, Ellen's and Nathaniel's close friends and colleagues, and Ellen's neighbors spoke.

But when one of the "high-achieving autistic men" stepped behind the microphone and began speaking, everyone, especially Priscilla, sat amazed. The man stood proudly and said in a slight stutter, "My name is Wyndham Whynot, and I speak for all of Ellen's clients. Ellen tried hard not to be our friend because she used to say, 'Business is business,' but she was our best friend." He paused, looked at the Austin family, and continued. "She made sure we all had good jobs, good-paying jobs. She cared for us better 'an our own families did. When she remodeled her part of the house, she remodeled our living quarters, too. Ellen trusted us, and even though we were supposed to live separately, sometimes she did not fuss at us when we showed up in her part of the house. Ellen was good to us." When Wyndham finished his remarks, he asked the other clients to stand and be recognized, and they all stood. Then Wyndham nodded at the Austin clan and returned to his seat.

Priscilla stood, walked down the aisle, shook hands, and greeted as many guests as possible at the end of the service. But she felt somewhat guilty that she had never known any of Ellen's circle of friends, colleagues, and acquaintances.

As they milled about the chapel, Germane stuck with Carlton and Laverne. Then he caught the eye of Nelson, Jr., who was coming to greet Carlton and meet Laverne.

"Sorry for your loss," Carlton and Laverne both said as Carlton shook Nelson, Jr.'s hand. "Ellen was a wonderful person to all these people."

Then Laverne extended her hand and said, "It's good to meet you."

But just as Carlton was about to formally introduce Laverne and Nelson, Jr., to each other, Germane interrupted: "What do you think of her, Uncle Nelson?"

As he gave Laverne the once-over, Nelson, Jr., laughed out loud and then said, "My, my, you could easily be taken as my little sister's double." Then all of them—Germane, Carlton, and Laverne, too—shared that hearty laugh, unaware of the significance of their observation and words.

The Austin family and Ellen's friends and business acquaintances soon reassembled at the burial site. As Priscilla watched the casket being lowered into the Earth, she cringed at the finality. Carlton held her steady, and she looked gratefully up at him.

After the interring, the Austin sisters finally consented to Carlton's umpteenth offer to treat the family to a meal before he and Priscilla, and Laverne departed. They rode in two separate limousines to a restaurant on the Bay. The atmosphere was friendlier and more relaxed than before—mainly because Germane entertained them with stories about his time visiting Bow Lake. He talked about the times that he and Carlton swam nude in Bow Lake, about the magnificent horses they rode, about the enormous, impressive mansion in which the Bernhardts lived, and about the particulars of the Bernhardt lifestyle. But when he noticed his aunts wearying of his stories, he cut them short. Then, one by one, each of his aunts gave updates about their families.

As she made the occasional comments—"So very good to hear," or "You must be so proud of him"—it never once occurred to Priscilla that part of the reason her sisters did not want to hear details about her new life was that they could not fathom it. Priscilla played in much higher cotton than they ever imagined possible, save for her father Nelson and Ellen—and both of them were gone now. Just as Priscilla had realized her life had progressed far beyond that of her friends Amber and Cathy, she now realized the same had held for her own family. But she took solace in knowing that her father Nelson and her sister Ellen had appreciated her growth and development, and now, so, too, did Nelson, Jr., and Germane.

Finally, it was time for everyone to say farewell.

Then Priscilla, Carlton, and Laverne headed back to the hangar, where they boarded the Bernhardt private jet. Priscilla had thought that they would be heading back to New York City. But Lady Chelsea had insisted: "Carlton, after the funeral, bring PJ back home to Bow Lake."

25

A Bernhardt Welcoming

It was dusk when Priscilla, Carlton, and Laverne stepped off the Bernhardt private jet into the Merrimack Airport's inviting atmosphere.

Then, much to Carlton's delight, Priscilla said, "Gee-whiz, it sure feels good to be home."

And it did, to her, feel like a real homecoming.

When Priscilla saw Shelton, the Bernhardt chauffeur, she ran to him and embraced him. Shelton felt the genuine warmth of her embrace and held her for a long time. Then Priscilla rode shotgun next to him in the Bentley, and Carlton and Laverne sat behind them, where they both noted her heretofore uncharacteristic affectionate behavior. Priscilla laughed and talked a lot and occasionally hit Shelton on his shoulder—

one of her gestures of goodwill. At long last, Priscilla was showing significant signs of accepting her new family and circle of friends.

As they drove through the grape vineyards, Priscilla told Shelton what she had previously confided to Carlton and Laverne about her sister Ellen. Shelton felt Priscilla's love and pride for her eldest sister. Then he told her some family news. "The Bernhardts," he said, "have received some good news from Arvana."

"Oh?" Priscilla smiled. "And what, pray tell, is Arvana up to these days?"

"She's excited about starting a program for abused women and for women who are narcotics addicts."

Priscilla pretended that everything he said was new to her. "I am so happy for Arvana. I can't wait until she's released. There's so much I want to do with my new big sister."

At that, Carlton and Laverne looked at each other and smiled. Then Carlton tickled Priscilla behind her ears. "It's so good to have you back home again."

Then he went silent as she continued chattering in the front seat. He reflected that Priscilla, in general, had been warming up not just to Shelton but to Laverne and Arvana. *Good news*, he thought. *The best news, really.* He could hardly wait to share all this with Lady Chelsea and Father and Ramses. But he would have to wait his turn because Shelton could hardly wait to blabber.

Even so, when the love of his life was happy, Carlton was happy, too.

As the Bentley coursed through the impressive, ornately designed, cast-iron gates and drew up at the English-style manor, tears pooled in Priscilla's eyes.

She breathed. "Oh, it feels so good to be home again!"

The Bernhardt family and staff were lined up to greet her, for the flight attendant had called ahead to inform them of their arrival.

Priscilla could hardly wait for Shelton to stop the car before she ran from person to person and greeted everyone: Poppa and Marlena, Ramses, Father and Lady Chelsea, Jamison, Harry, Melissa, and the other household servants.

After she greeted everyone in the customary Bernhardt way, she ran under the portico inside the foyer, stood still, and repeated, "Oh, it feels so good to be home again." And although everyone recognized the unmistakable resemblance between Priscilla and Laverne, for whatever reason, no one broached the subject. No one. Priscilla's happiness was all that mattered to everyone in the Bernhardt household.

Priscilla's display of such delight was music to Lady Chelsea's ears. "My dear, oh, my dear," she said as she embraced her. "Oh, PJ, my darling child, it's so good to have you back home again, where you belong."

Priscilla spent three days at Bow Lake. Carlton stayed for the first day, but duty called him back to urgent work in the nation's capital. But Priscilla was acutely aware of his work's endless demands and how insistent Carlton's superiors could be.

Besides, she wanted to spend some quality time with Lady Chelsea and Father and Ramses. She updated them on the renovations to her Harlem brownstone, which Lady Chelsea only tolerated because she still resisted "the children" planning to live anywhere other than Bow Lake. However, Priscilla's account of her experiences in Paris and Mykonos, especially about that fabulous Greek yacht with the beautiful people, was more to her delight. She even told them about her speaking engagement for the Founders Day Program at Livingstone.

But when Lady Chelsea told Priscilla her news, Priscilla could not believe her ears. "A masquerade ball! Here! At Bow Lake! Wow!"

"PJ, my darling child, have you ever worked—or gone to—a masquerade ball?"

"Actually, no." Priscilla laughed. "But I have a funny feeling that is all about to change."

Then Lady Chelsea explained to Priscilla some of what lay ahead.

"We Bernhardts," she said, "host a masquerade ball every two years, always in December. And although it is a fundraiser for the local children's hospital, it has become a coming-out event for debutantes and new family additions. And you, P. J. *Austin*-Bernhardt, are a new family addition."

"Wow!" was all an elated Priscilla could say. "Wow!"

Laverne prepared the next day to return to the City. She was satisfied with how well Priscilla was handling grief at her sister's death and heartened how well she was taking such noticeable comfort with her in-laws of Bow Lake.

"Time for me to go," she had told Priscilla. "Lots of stuff still to do on this case at the museum. Besides, it's time for me to find my own way and my own place, too."

"I'll be down soon," Priscilla said. "But thanks so very much for all your help. And we'll rev up the family jet. No need for you to fly commercial."

Luxuriating in the comfort of that flight, Laverne vowed to herself that she would do all that she could to continue being a very good friend to Priscilla. She resembled her from a distance and had grown to admire her even more, up close and personal.

Then, back in "the City," Laverne's first stop was Priscilla's office to complete paperwork on the mission that even "the boys" were calling "the mysterious affair at the Met."

There, she took care to paint a rosy, upbeat picture of her encounters with Priscilla's family in San Francisco. *No need for everyone to know how it really had been with most of the Austin clan.* But she added more truthfully: "Her nephew Germane is so absolutely handsome and fun-loving!" Some of "the boys" remembered the young man from previous encounters, mainly how well he had danced with his aunt on her wedding day, so Laverne's comment gave her report an aura of authenticity. Then she was off to look for an apartment in the City. She had enjoyed living with Priscilla and Carlton in the lap of luxury at the Waldorf, but she thought it was time that the couple, still considered newlyweds, had their privacy back.

Back at Bow Lake, Priscilla started by spending quality time with Lady Chelsea. One morning, over coffee, the two discussed Arvana's plans to establish the program for abused women and narcotics addicts.

Lady Chelsea was ecstatic at her daughter's development.

"Why, I never imagined her having a care in the world for anybody but herself," she said. "Father and I are so pleased. We couldn't be happier for Arvana." Lady Chelsea added what a joy it was that Arvana had finally begun thinking about using the "Bernhardt brand" to help others.

Priscilla relished the happiness of her mother-in-law.

Another morning, as the women had settled down in the parlor for another long chat, Father and Ramses decided to join them.

"So-o," Father began, "I think it's about time that we two had a chance to spend some quality time with my favorite daughter-in-law, not to mention my *only* daughter-in-law."

"Of course," Lady Chelsea said. "You've always been welcome to join us."

Father nodded to his wife and then turned to Priscilla. "Well, PJ, my darling child," he began, "Ramses and I were wondering if you've given any thought to your costume?" He spoke to her as if the masquerade ball must have been the topic of her and Lady Chelsea's conversation.

Priscilla asked, "My costume?"

Ramses answered. "You can't come to a masquerade ball without a mask and a costume. I was hoping to convince you to come as Cleopatra, especially if you keep this lovely bronze suntan."

Priscilla gave Ramses a wide smile. He was the only one—not just at Bow Lake but also at her Midtown Manhattan office and, more recently, among her family in California—who seemed to approve of her crisp bronze suntan wholeheartedly.

But then, Father chimed back in: "Oh, no! I was hoping she'd come as one of my favorite entertainers. You know, Dorothy Dandridge, Shirley Bassey, Lena Horne, heck, Tina Turner!"

Priscilla laughed as she always felt comfortable enough to tease the two of them. "You two 'ole geezers' are off your rockers." Then, she was pleasantly surprised to see Lady Chelsea laughing, too.

At that, however, Lady Chelsea raised her eyebrows and asked her, "Well, PJ, who do *you* want to come as?"

Priscilla shrugged her shoulders. With everything else on her plate—her grief for Ellen, not to mention the complications of this case with the Met—her costume for this masquerade ball had not been on her mind: "I guess I haven't thought that far ahead. Besides, what's wrong with coming as myself and just wearing one of those gorgeous Venetian masks? You know, maybe one of those on a holder, the kind I can hold up to my face and then take away?" She mimed holding up a mask and then whisking it away to reveal her face.

"Coming as you are is unacceptable," Ramses said with unusual severity.

"Oh?" Priscilla turned from one to the other. "I didn't know that."

"Ramses, of course, is right," Father said. "You must choose a famous character. Someone notable." He knew that many people were not familiar with the particular protocols of masquerade balls as the Bernhardts and many other New England upper crux families. And of course, he was astute enough not to put this awareness into actual words. But he so wanted his "favorite daughter-in-law" to agree to join in the festivities. And so, too, did Ramses.

"As I said," Ramses repeated. "Someone…such as Cleopatra. You were born to play her."

Priscilla took in the insistent expression on Ramses' face. She considered that neither he nor Father realized how deeply she still grieved the loss of her sister Ellen and that the last thing on her mind was a costume for some social event at Bow Lake. But the two of them were so very kind to her, and they seemed so eager that every detail of this party be precisely right. She would do her best to please them.

"Then Cleopatra it is," she said, unaware that Ramses, in particular, would continue to attach such importance to this commitment. Eventually, though, she forgot all about this the second after she had said it.

Their mission accomplished, Father and Ramses both stood up in finality.

"Done," Ramses said and swiped his hands.

As the men left the parlor, Priscilla asked Lady Chelsea, "What was that all about?"

"Oh, PJ, my darling child, you could not have made their day any better. Now those two 'ole geezers,' as you call them, are going to instruct the household servants to pull out the decorations from storage and commence with the transformation of our little abode. As we roll into December, you're going to think you're living in an Egyptian palace. Trust me; you're about to experience the gala of your life."

Uncertainly, Priscilla nodded, but then she told her mother-in-law that she had minimal experience with significant social events like this masquerade ball, other than receptions and banquets for political fundraisers. As for high society social events, she elaborated:

"The only balls I know about are those little coming-out events we used to attend in my youth, back in Prendergast. But I didn't understand what was going on back then, either. Just looked like lots of teenage girls dressed to the hilt being escorted about by young men who seemed uncomfortable in their suits. Or were those tuxedos? Then again," she said, quite matter-of-factly, "the only masquerade ball that I've seen as an adult was Andrew Lloyd Webber's version of *The Phantom of the Opera*, which I absolutely loved." Then she asked somewhat meekly, "Do your guests dress as lavishly as the characters in that movie?"

"And then some. You see, PJ, once you get to my age, you find yourself wanting to do things you never before dared to do. So dressing up and pretending to be characters of our childhood fantasies is what we do." Then Lady Chelsea giggled.

"Okay," Priscilla said. "I give. What's so funny?"

"Wait 'til you see Father's and Ramses' costumes!"

"I can hardly wait." Then Priscilla took Lady Chelsea's hands and kissed them ever so gently. "And God bless you for your kindness during what has been a most difficult time for me."

Lady Chelsea smiled at her daughter-in-law, noting with pleasure how affectionate Priscilla had become. She was so different from the standoffish, aloof young woman she had first met back in the summer of 1987.

Lady Chelsea welled up and returned the compliment. "Oh, my dear sweet child! God bless you for all the love and cheer you bring to our family."

Then the two women hugged and shed tears of happiness.

26

The Invitation

The next day Priscilla returned unannounced to her office in the City.

Alfrieda greeted her warmly when the elevator opened, and Priscilla breezed inside. "Welcome back, PJ. I trust you'll find everything in order. Do let me know what you need, even if it's only a Nathan's hot dog with sauerkraut." She grinned. She, along with the others, had learned about Priscilla's preferences.

Then Ruth rushed to greet her. She spoke from the heart. "Oh, PJ, I want to say again how sorry I was to hear about your sister, Ellen. But my mom wanted me to pass on some advice. 'Keep busy,' she said, 'and try to remember the good times with your sister.'"

"Wise words," Priscilla said with a sigh. Then, as she made for her office, she said, "Give me a few moments, Ruth, and then let's catch up."

Priscilla pulled out her executive swivel chair and sat down. She reached for a big stack of mail and messages and began leafing through some of them. But there were so many, and a quick glance indicated that most were inconsequential. So she set all the mail aside, buzzed Ruth, and asked her to join her.

A moment later, her branch manager—and second-in-charge—was sitting across from Priscilla's desk, with her notepad and pen at the ready.

"I hope you don't mind, PJ, but I put everybody and everything on hold. I told everyone that you were dealing with a personal emergency and that it would be a good week or so before you would be available."

Priscilla nodded. As usual, Ruth had done exactly the right thing without having to be told. "And the Met case?"

"Iggy and Shane are at their wits' end, PJ. Nervous, really nervous. Do you think you can see them later today, or maybe first thing in the morning?"

"Pencil the twerps in for tomorrow morning," Priscilla said, without even looking up.

"Consider it done." Ruth was aware that Priscilla meant the two "twerps" no ill will. But what she did not know was that Priscilla had already gone out of her way to "save their bacon," as it were, with the law enforcement, international intelligence, and legal authorities. But at Ruth's words, Priscilla raised her head and stared at her as if she had been insulted.

Taken aback by Priscilla's expression, Ruth wanted to know, "What's wrong? Was it something I said?"

Priscilla shook her head. "No, just a ghost. I once knew someone whose favorite words were those: 'Consider it done.' That was my former boss, the esteemed Ohio state Senator Daniel P. Callahan."

"Ah, from back then. I know very little, actually, about your work in the Ohio Senate."

"How could you? That was long ago and far away. But I learned a lot, especially from that master politician. And to think I never even thanked him before he was gone." She sighed but then, with an effort, returned to the here and now. "What else have you got for me?"

"Well, PJ," Ruth began, a little doubtfully, unsure how Priscilla would cotton to this, "there's the New York Fashion Show. It's quite an extravaganza. It starts in two weeks. And this year, they've added something that sounds pretty cool. A boat ride here on the river with the crème de la crème of persons of color in the world of fashion. You might like to be part of it."

Priscilla managed a grin. Between her grief and the Met case, something new and fun—the masquerade ball and now this fashion show *and* a boat ride—could be precisely what she needed. "Tell me more."

Ruth did not have to be asked twice. She handed Priscilla the envelope she had been holding nervously.

"What's this?" Puzzled, Priscilla stared at its logo, which was one she did not recognize. She hoped it wasn't one more offshoot of this case at the Met, which was turning out to have too many "legs."

"An invitation to the boat ride," she said. "I was sort of hoping that you'd agree to attend. It's an effort to connect with people of color. And those who want to influence the who's who in that world."

"I didn't know you were a fashionista," Priscilla said. "And what makes you think that I am, either?" Then she remembered that Ruth's family was in the garment business. Steiner Clothiers had long been a leader in that field. Clearly, this fashion thing meant something to her assistant. She liked Ruth, and she wanted to continue to build their relationship. "But, on the other hand," she said eventually, "even though fashion isn't my thing, I could use a little diversion from this art fraud case. If *you* think I should go, then sure, I'm game."

"Great, PJ! And besides, you're all the rage in the fashion world since we all saw you hobnobbing with the beautiful people on that yacht in Greece."

Priscilla wrinkled her forehead. "You have got to be kidding me!"

"I'm quite serious," Ruth said. "You're becoming quite the fashionista! Not just because of the Greek trip. Or that Miriam, who is part of the Met case. Maybe you're the last to see yourself as others do. Consider this: I think you've been known for your understated elegance for some time. Plus, you're married to a *Bernhardt*. Don't forget how Carlton got all that good press when he had those designer gowns—Oscar de la Renta, no less—made exclusively for you by the very designers who are displaying their garments at the show. So you hardly need to *copy* anyone else who happens to be rich and famous. You're rich and famous yourself. And besides, you've got your *own* style."

"Get out a' here!" Priscilla did not believe she could ever be as elegant as Miriam Millsap Omiros. "You're just blowing smoke up my skirt."

"Like hell, I am! PJ, you're your own fashionista. And I repeat: You don't need to *copy* anyone else's style. If only you knew how many women copy *your* style! And listen, I know you think of me as an art expert, and that's why you hired me. And I may not be a fashion plate myself, but I grew up in the rag biz. I know that world. Your style is simple, understated elegance, not flash and bling, like the ladies I saw on that yacht in Mykonos. It was all on TV, you remember."

"OK. OK, Ruth, you win. This round anyway." Priscilla grinned. "I *said* 'I'd go.'"

Ruth nodded. "We'll need to carve out at least a half-day. Or more. Then there are the private parties that last well into the night."

But as she listened to Ruth listing all that was entailed in this new commitment, Priscilla thought, *Surely she doesn't expect me to spend a whole day and night frolicking with folks in the fashion industry?* Then she thought about her new obligations at the Bow Lake masquerade ball. This rich and famous stuff was a lot more time-consuming than it maybe deserved to be.

Yet Priscilla was, in fact, warming up to the fashion showboat ride. "Any chance I'll meet your folks?" Then she remembered another aspect of the Met case. "And let's not forget Gaylord Millsap Omiros. He's a fashion designer, and doesn't he have a fashion house of his own?"

Again Ruth nodded. *Leave it to PJ to sniff out that connection.* "Sure thing. Gaylord always has a spot in the show." But she was ever so grateful to learn that Priscilla was interested in meeting her family as they were eager to make her acquaintance as well. "And yes, my family would love to meet the illustrious P. J. Austin-Bernhardt."

Priscilla was not so grief-stricken that she had forgotten about her primary PR account. It could not hurt to learn more about the so-called "good seed," Gaylord. In the back of her mind, a question had been building: *Was Gaylord as innocent as he seemed to be?*

27

And Associates, Incorporated

The only not-so-pleasant experience of Priscilla's first day back at the office happened in a meeting with Laverne and "the boys," all of whom—except for Carlton, who was in the nation's capital—assembled late that morning in the conference room of their seventh-floor office suite. So Priscilla prepared to host her first official meeting with Laverne and "the boys" altogether.

When she walked in, she was met with warm greetings:

"Sorry for your loss, Missy."

"I hope you're OK."

"Let me know what I can do if anything."

But only moments later, "the boys," especially Tommy, took off their gloves.

Tommy led the charge as he expressed his "disappointment in your seemingly *loose cannon* behavior."

Her temper flared. "*Loose cannon*?"

Tommy did not back down. "Yes," he snapped. "You heard me. I said, 'loose cannon.' My God, PJ, every time we turned around, there you were, or one of your surrogates from the feds and the international intelligence community. On TV, even. We're *your* security guys, but we felt sabotaged, and by *you*! What were you *thinking*?"

Her temper cooled. She should have realized they might feel like this. "Oh," she said, "*that*."

But Tommy was not done. "Why hire us to solve a case that you're using the FBI, the CIA," he ranted, "and every government agency in the world to do the exact same thing?"

"Oh-h, now I see, for sure," she said. "Well, if—"

But Tommy cut her off again. He was hardly finished expressing his fury about what he considered was her "poorly contrived plan of action," especially the parts designed to reel in Artemis Thibaut Millsap Moreaux.

"Every time we showed up, either the feds or the international intelligence boys met us coming in or going out of each stakeout. And they seemed to get a kick out of telling us that we didn't have jurisdiction. This is *not* the way we operate. It's either them or us. Your call, Missy."

Priscilla had never seen Tommy so angry.

She supposed the others—Angel, Jordy, Onslow, and Laverne, too—had previously been observers and maybe even objects of Tommy's wrath, although it had never been directed at Priscilla. Not like this. The other male agents surreptitiously looked from Tommy to Priscilla. But they did not pile on.

Laverne kept her head down and did not utter a single word during the entire meeting. She had worked with "the boys" before, and she knew how closely knit they were. Moreover, she knew "the boys" were old school, which included being unaccustomed to female authority figures. Tommy, in particular, was used to doing pretty much as he pleased, and now he found himself taking orders from a woman—and one he had once rescued back in southern Africa, let alone the several other missions that he and "the other boys" had been commissioned to protect her.

Priscilla kept silent while Tommy fumed. She noted that Laverne was keeping out of it, as were "the other boys." None of them looked comfortable, but no one dared intervene. She bit her lip. She supposed some of this was her fault. She had long since identified a potential problem in unresolved issues as to what if any, role "the boys" were to have in her new firm. Yet she knew—except for Jordy, who she had retained to help collect intel, analyze the few frames of footage from the Met, install listening devices at the Met offices, and then monitor the tapes—she had never actually hired the rest of "the boys" to participate in *solving* the Met case in the first place. So she instinctively supposed that Tommy—and maybe even Carlton, Angel, and Onslow, too—had *assumed* that she had wanted them to help solve her case.

But by the time that Priscilla could get in another word edgewise, Tommy had apparently come to the same realization that she just had.

For the first time, he met her eyes. His voice lowered. "But you didn't exactly *hire* us for this particular case in the first place. Or did you?" The silence in the conference room was penetrating. One could actually have heard an ant sneeze.

"There's the rub," she said ruefully. "Tommy, ole buddy, ole pal, as I tried to say, I 'hired' a couple of staffers to have a presence at the Met and to conduct research on specific highly-valued works of art. And I hired Ruth and Laverne to aid my efforts here at this office. I also notified the folks at the FBI and later—after learning of the international components—the folks at Langley. Then Langley brought in the fellows from the international intelligence community. As for Jordy, well, since he was the only one among you here when the assignment first came across my desk, I brought him on as an intelligence expert.

Priscilla took a deep breath. "But to answer your big question, given prohibitions against such activity on American soil and all, 'no,' I never hired or retained the services of the 'and Associates, Incorporated' in the first place."

At that, each of "the boys" pursed their lips. Onslow flushed. Otherwise, they all remained silent.

On a roll, now, Priscilla continued:

"However, since you've done such an excellent job, and since the folks at Langley agree with me on that assessment, as far as I'm concerned, you're to be adequately compensated for services rendered as local 'security experts.'"

She added, "Towards that end, I have some papers for you to complete from Jim Froley. This will make your work legit as subcontractors to P. J. Austin *and Associates, Incorporated.*" She dared a conciliatory smile. "From now on, however, how 'bout we all come together and formally decide, on a case-by-case basis, which ones will contractually involve the 'And Associates, Incorporated.' Deal?"

Quite soberly, Tommy and "the other boys," all said in near unison, "Deal."

There was relieved laughter then, and their erect postures softened to slumps. They had finally gotten past a significant misunderstanding.

Then Priscilla broached something else.

"By the way, I wanted you all to know that Macy Stoner—you all know my friend Macy—has agreed to represent the 'bad seed,' one Artemis Thibaut Millsap Moreaux."

Leave it to Tommy to express his discontent. "You have got to be kidding me."

But Priscilla was not up for going another round with him, at least not just now.

Instead, Priscilla, who had learned about commanding respect from her time in the Ohio Senate, rose to her feet and declared: "We'll reconvene after lunch to complete our discussion about your roles as subcontractors. I'll bring the papers Jim sent for your signatures at that time."

She left her file folder open on the conference table, leaving "the boys" with their mouths gaping wide open.

Only Laverne smiled at her retreating back. She had noted Priscilla's growth and development from when she had been on the run from those South African terrorists back in 1986. *Priscilla*, she thought, *has learned how to command respect*. It was something she later would confide in her newfound friend, confidante, and, it seemed, private-sector employer.

Priscilla ate lunch at her desk, wolfing down the two hot dogs and sauerkraut that Alfrieda had fetched from Nathan's kiosk. She thought, all things considered, that things with "the boys" had gone pretty well, at least so far. Again, she reproached herself for not having prepared for the confusion that had just developed because she had not taken this ongoing relationship with "the boys" in hand.

But at least this relationship was well on the way to being settled. Now she had to seal the deal about which she and "the boys" had just reached an agreement.

She gathered the papers that CIA Deputy Director Froley had sent and that Alfrieda had already slipped into folders marked with each agent's name.

Then she returned to the conference room, where Laverne and "the boys" were already waiting.

"As I began to say this morning, the folks at Langley have provided us with a way to ease you into private, domestic practice. One way—and I believe the best way—is for the agency—that is, the CIA—to *subcontract* certain jobs for detective/intelligence gathering/security services to P. J. Austin and Associates, Incorporated." Perhaps most noteworthy was the ease to which Priscilla spoke, and so openly for the first time about "the boys'" affiliation with the CIA. Never before had she done so. But because she spoke so casually, and quickly, none of "the boys," including Laverne, said a word.

"So, from this point forward," Priscilla continued, as Alfrieda passed around the individualized folders with the forms that Jim Froley had provided, "we're off and running."

At this point, Alfrieda's suspicions about "the boys'" "other jobs" were confirmed. But Alfrieda, and Ruth, too, had been sworn to secrecy during their final interview with Julia and Priscilla, not to mention at their signing off on their employment contracts, which contained a nondisclosure clause.

Meanwhile, Angel, just to be sure, asked for clarification. "So the folks at Langley *will* authorize our services on American soil, but as subcontractors to P. J. Austin and Associates, Incorporated?"

"Yes," she said. "You got it."

Onslow had a comment: "So we really are 'And Associates, Incorporated.' But I'm hoping that maybe, you'll give us a wee bit more challenging work than bugging offices as we did at the Met or eavesdropping and stakeouts at apartments and posh resorts. Any low-level detective could do that."

There were murmurs of accord up and down the table.

"Yeah," Angel shook his head and elaborated. "Never felt so underutilized in all my life. Was worse than babysitting. Reminded me of that job we did reeling Senator Madison back into the fold in Ohio some time ago."

"The boys" all laughed.

"Alright, fellows," Priscilla said. "I get it. And even though we got our wires crossed on this one, and the job wasn't exactly what you're used to doing, at some point, you need to learn that not all jobs involve the type of action and heavy weaponry you're used to." Belatedly, however, Priscilla realized she ought not to have said that. But before they could react, she soldiered on, "But gear up, fellows, because I suspect you'll soon get what you're yearning for, and sooner than you might expect."

As she finally dared to pause, she observed their expressions perking up. Yet, she was unaware that the CIA was hardly releasing "the boys" from their official roles with the clandestine CF unit. Instead, apart from their work as high-powered Ohio lobbyists, the folks at Langley had found yet another way to give them acceptable work on the home front through her new detective/intelligence/security agency. The implication in these papers they were signing was that their "unauthorized" missions would continue.

On that note, "the boys" were more than one step ahead of her. Poor Priscilla. If only she had known that that large architectural rendering that "the boys" had been leaning over in Jordy's office not so many days ago was, in fact, an aerial image of their next mission. So, at this very moment, they were already gearing up for yet another "unauthorized" secret mission.

Back to the here and now, Jordy asked another meaningful question. "This is good for us, but what's in it for you? Surely, if we're subs, that means we're pretty much in control of what we do."

"That much I'm clear on," Priscilla said. "I just wanted to set up an entity that allows you all—and especially Carlton—to ease out the grips of your 'other jobs.'" She smiled. "And, I need to remind you guys maybe, that my firm gets the standard twenty-percent markup fee on all subcontracts. So to answer your question about 'What's in it for me,' is that it's a hefty fee, Bro'."

They all nodded. That was business. "The boys" all got that.

But each of them groaned when Priscilla said, "Now, there's one more item to settle."

She summarized administrative details: Someone would need to manage all the paperwork, keep track of accounts payable and receivables, and file many reports to Langley.

All eyes fell on Jordy, who nodded, "I know my role." Then, he looked across the conference table at Onslow and noted, "But *you're* my backup."

Onslow nodded in agreement. "As usual."

Priscilla watched contently as they completed the CIA paperwork. When they seemed finished, she said, "One last thing."

At that, "the boys" all frowned.

"Now what?" Jordy asked.

"I need you," she said, "to clear your calendars for the second weekend in December." She could not resist a laugh. "Now, don't go crazy. This one *can* be, no, *will* be fun."

"*Fun?*" Tommy said the word like it was a curse.

"Well, boys, and Laverne, too," she began. "Lady Chelsea, my mother-in-law, is hosting a fundraiser for the Children's Hospital in Merrimack." Her voice became hopefully seductive. "It's a masquerade ball, Venetian masks, Harlequin outfits, the works. And you *must* wear a costume."

Tommy's voice was once again rising. In a moment he might be shouting. "*Masquerade ball!* You have got to be kidding me. I'm not putting on some stupid costume."

But this time, "the other boys" were not on his side.

"Ah, Tommy, man, come on," Angel said. "When was the last time we had a little fun?"

"You could be a pirate, Tommy," Onslow observed. "You'd like that."

Their guffaw seemed to shake the very walls of the conference room. But then, to everyone's surprise, Jordy said, "Besides, I finally have a *date!*"

"The boys" laughed and hollered even more vigorously, Laverne, too. Some of them gestured high-fives and fist bumps across the conference table with their comrade. After all, Jordy was the only one among them who had never introduced a woman he was dating to the others. So if for no other reason than to take a look at Jordy's girlfriend, "the other boys" and Laverne all cleared their calendars for that weekend to attend the masquerade ball at Bow Lake. But another reason for the trek to New Hampshire was to stay in the good graces of Lady Chelsea. For they all fully understood that this gracious society lady was to be crossed at their peril from previous encounters.

So it was that just after the meeting finally adjourned, Tommy was on the phone with his wife Christina, Angel called his girlfriend Anita, and Onslow called his wife Laura. As for Jordy, he was not quite ready to reveal the woman in his life's name.

And Laverne would think of something or someone.

When Priscilla returned to her office, she was pleasantly surprised to see her friend Macy staring out the window. When Macy turned around and saw Priscilla, she quickly moved to embrace her.

"Oh, Missy, I felt so bad when I heard about Ellen. Why didn't you call me? I would've come with you to your sister's funeral. I am so sorry. From your descriptions of her and especially about how she taught you self-reliance, I so admired her. But I only just learned about Ellen's death."

"Oh, Mace, you needn't apologize. I'm the one who failed to call you. But I was so distraught. I just wasn't thinking straight."

In another attempt to mend what she felt was an unforgivable mistake, Macy asked, "Feel up to a hot dog and sauerkraut?" But that was hardly the way Priscilla saw the matter.

"Thanks, Girlfriend, but I just had two of them." Priscilla laughed. "I'll come with you, though. A walk would be nice just now."

What Macy had wanted was an excuse to go someplace private to talk, anyway. Instead of the hot dog stand, they headed to a nearby diner, drank coffee, caught up on the Omiros twins' cases, and talked about the celebration of life service for Ellen.

Macy told Priscilla, "Gaylord has been released on his own recognizance, along with a hefty bond, of course." She chuckled, looked away from Priscilla, and then added, "But nothing doing for the 'bad seed.'

"Even the mediators," she continued, "realized that Gaylord had been primed by his own twin brother to be duped over all those years."

At that, Priscilla found herself repeating an earlier observation: "Just when I thought Artemis Thibaut and his father couldn't stoop lower than a rat."

Nevertheless, Priscilla was so glad to see Macy. Her friend had developed into someone she admired and was comfortable discussing business with to a greater degree than she was with the other women in her life—with the exception, of course, of Julia. Her feelings about Macy seemed to be mutual. Priscilla had a habit of calling females she liked "Girlfriend." But in the case of Macy, that word carried special intimacy. As she talked and laughed with Macy, Priscilla could almost feel her grief at the loss of Ellen begin to heal. Her sister had been a gift from God to her.

And so, too, was Macy Stoner.

28

A PR Charade

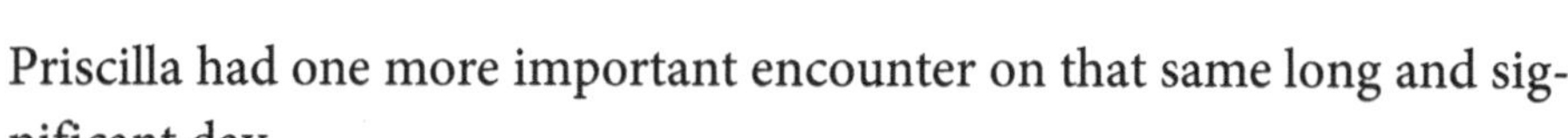

Priscilla had one more important encounter on that same long and significant day.

She and Ruth met to focus on their next public relations steps in their most important case.

They agreed that regarding "the mysterious affair at the Met," Priscilla, in particular, needed to step up to the plate, be more visible, and put out any brushfires that may have sprung up.

Priscilla also said, "The situation has escalated to the point that press conferences are out of the question. To control the story, we need to be selective about which media outlets and aspects of the various incidents we will discuss. At the same time, however, we will refer everyone to Macy Stoner when other facets, such as legal issues, spring up. And although she has long since been the legal counsel for the Met, she's now the defense attorney for both of the twins." Priscilla frowned. "Is that a conflict? Does she have to recuse herself from her duties with the board?" But since Macy had already stepped down from her position on the Met board, that was a moot point.

Still, Ruth said, "Why not ask her, anyway? Especially since the law is her purview."

"Good point. OK, so that takes care of the legal issues." Priscilla took a deep breath. "Now, back to what I was saying about being selective about our media outreach." She added that they needed more media coverage and that these days, the most magnetic media was television. "And at the top of the heap," she said, "are the morning news shows."

She gave Ruth a laser look. "So we gotta do it."

"*We?*" Ruth blanched.

"Yes, Ruth. The two of us will have to go on camera. But don't worry, I'll do most of the talking." Priscilla was adamant that Ruth shared some of this. "There is no way that I can cover all of it myself. And believe me, we have to work together to control it all."

So the plan was hatched: The two of them would accept three prime network morning news slots, during which they would provide updates on the case involving "the mysterious affair at the Met."

Uncertainly, Ruth nodded. But then she asked, "Exactly how and when did you learn how to orchestrate something like this?" Then she listened, wide-eyed, as Priscilla shared that, back in the Ohio Senate, when she had worked as a legislative aide to Senator Callahan, part of her job had been to schedule interviews for him with news anchors, reporters, and editors of various media.

"But I could never get over how masterful he was at this," Priscilla said, "how he was able to bring the interviews around to whatever it was that he had wanted to convey to them in the first place. He called the process 'PR charades' because he would spin his version of specific issues."

Ruth asked, "So he taught you how to do it?"

"Nah." Priscilla shook her head. "I just watched and learned. Before long," she said, "I had even come to understand how he'd examine the ratings of certain media outlets for the demographics of their audiences—and then, accordingly, decide who to talk to about what."

"My goodness," Ruth said. She was fascinated as she listened to how Priscilla intended to use her political background to plot how the two would use the network morning news shows to publicize what they wanted the viewers to know about the Met art scandal's recent developments. She chose which anchors and stations to go after and explained why certain ones would probably be friendlier to a case like theirs.

A few mornings later, Priscilla and Ruth found themselves rushing to and from the green rooms and the sets of three different mainstream media studios—ABC, CBS, and CNN. Priscilla had been grateful to God that she managed to book her first three choices. One by one, the staff of the two networks and the cable news show applied makeup and conducted rehearsals checking sound and lighting to stage their interviews.

Then it was airtime.

The anchors introduced Priscilla as "the illustrious P. J. Austin-Bernhardt, *PR consultant extraordinaire* for the Metropolitan Museum of Art" and "her second-in-charge, Ruth Steiner, an expert on the billion-dollar-art world."

Priscilla and Ruth stuck to the highlights they had prepared—not scripts, exactly, more like talking points. But Priscilla—and Ruth, too, who had been publicizing art for years—had long ago mastered the art of chatty television interviews: how to get their message across exactly as

they had previously decided, but also how to do that with the air of having just-that-second thought of a fresh insight that would easily yield
sound bites and headlines for the next news cycle.

Priscilla was especially good at this. For the first interview at CBS,
she began:

> As it turns out, Gaylord Millsap Omiros *is* related to
> someone who has forged, tampered with, even stolen,
> highly-valued works of art. So, if he wants to return to
> the board of trustees at the Met, it falls to his attorney,
> Macy Stoner, to represent him in that endeavor.

"So tell us," asked the first host, "who *is* he related to?"

"That's the crazy part," Priscilla said. She had begun and continued
to do most of the talking, which meant the camera lingered on her pho-
togenic face.

> Gaylord is the twin brother to Artemis Thibaut
> Millsap Moreaux, a shrewd and disreputable art forger
> and thief of highly-valued artworks. And, as we're sure
> your viewers are also aware, the FBI, along with the
> international intelligence authorities, have already ap-
> prehended Artemis Thibaut, who many call the 'bad
> seed.' Apparently, Artemis Thibaut acquired or inher-
> ited the bad habits of his notorious father, Thibaut
> Francois Moreaux.

"Hard to keep them all straight," murmured the interviewer.

"Indeed." Sagely Priscilla nodded. But then, she continued:

And then there's the mother. That Miriam Millsap Omiros—one of the most beautiful women, a New York socialite and the wife to Greek shipping magnate Demetrios Omiros II. [Priscilla leans forward and lowers her voice confidentially.] Miriam loves both her sons and wants them to be well-represented in the American criminal court system *and* the international criminal court system. So her family has retained the illustrious Defense Attorney Macy Stoner to represent *both* of her sons.

"Macy Stoner," said the interviewer. "I've heard that name before."

"For-mid-able." As Priscilla stressed Macy's legal prowess, she arched her eyebrows into the camera's lenses and smoothly went on:

But The Metropolitan Museum of Art retains its own legal counsel, for whom I do not speak. When the Met has something to say about the impending legal proceedings, their legal counsel will talk to you directly. My firm, P. J. Austin and Associates, Incorporated, is a public relations consultant to the Met. I'm not their legal counsel, which accounts for my guarded comments.

But the interviewer was interested in that mother and son angle. She asked, "Can you tell us a little more about the relationship between this Miriam and her son Artemis Thibaut, the so-called 'bad seed?'"

At that point, Priscilla pretended she did not hear that question, partly because she already knew that most television viewers were up-to-date on the relationship between Miriam Millsap Omiros and her twin sons. That much Ruth had shared in an earlier press conference.

As Priscilla continued her PR charade, she turned to Ruth, sitting next to her, and said, "But I'm sure your viewing audience wants to hear our good news. Ruth, you tell them."

Before the interviewer could retake control, Ruth spoke up:

> We are so pleased to report that the three price-less works of art—Marc Chagall's *Soleil dans le Ciel de Saint-Paul*, Oscar-Claude Monet's *La Promenade,* and Paris Bordone's *Diana and the Two Nymphs*—have all been recovered.

And so it was that, apart from the first public statement by FBI Agent Rothschild about stolen artwork from the Met, Ruth had just cor-roborated his account by identifying the masterpieces in question.

Then, instead of allowing the television host to follow up, Priscilla asked Ruth, "Are they OK? I mean, any damage?"

"Each of the three masterpieces is intact," Ruth said. "None of them has been tampered with. And they *will* be returned to the Met after au-thentication by the respective accrediting agencies." Ruth beamed.

But the television anchor managed to take charge again. She dog-gedly asked again about the mother and son aspect. "Will Miriam Millsap Omiros return to the States to participate in the trial of her son Artemis Thibaut?"

Blandly, Priscilla smiled. Then she responded:

> As I mentioned a moment ago, answers to all questions about the legal proceedings, as well as about the next steps for The Metropolitan Museum of Art,

can only be addressed by the Met's legal counsel and, of course, 'the best gosh darn defense attorney this side of the Granite State.' That's one, Macy Stoner. She represents the Omiros twins.

It was the same story, with only minor variations, in the ABC and CNN interviews. The anchors who interviewed Priscilla seemed frustrated at times, even irritated. Priscilla was even more elusive than they had expected. But none of the interviewers seemed to have known about Priscilla's background in the political arena, a place where politicians almost always manage to get their message out, no matter the question or the nature of the interview. As Priscilla "absolutely" refused further comments, the television viewing audiences, switching from one channel to another, all got the same story. But television viewers got more: they all saw expressions of disappointment on each of the three network news anchors' faces at the ease with which Priscilla masterfully maneuvered their interview.

But each of the three anchors finished strong.

"There you have it, folks," said the *CNN* anchor. "Ms. Austin-Bernhardt and her second-in-charge, Ruth Steiner, have said all that they *intend* to say.

The *ABC* anchor concluded, "So now we must wait and see what else unravels—or shall we say, comes to the light of day. It's clear that there is more to this story. So stay tuned right here on *ABC* for the continuing saga of "the mysterious affair at the Met."

However, after the interview, there was irony in the fact that what grated the anchors and their station managers the most was how masterfully Priscilla had gotten in her plug not only about her own PR firm but also about Macy Stoner, legal counsel for the Omiros twins. Nonetheless, the stations, for the next twenty-four hours, kept repeating the headlines from "Our exclusive interview with PJ Austin-Bernhardt, providing the inside scoop on the art scandal of the century."

But it was the select group of New York City art media reporters who had attended Ruth's two press conferences in the Met's boardroom and called this story their own who were the most frustrated and disappointed. Priscilla spinning her story on major television networks, as she had this morning, had left them aware that there probably would not be any more breaking news for them. Now, the New York art media would have to wait for television news bulletins to follow the case as it continued unfolding.

29

Finders' Fees

Back at their Midtown Manhattan office, after completing their "PR charades" on network television, Priscilla and Ruth heaved sighs of relief and then made a round of mutual congratulations.

The two of them were in Priscilla's office, glorying in their success. They had told the network anchors and a sizeable portion of the American viewing public precisely what they wanted them to know.

Then Priscilla said, "There's something else."

Ruth groaned inwardly and braced herself. But all she said was, "Sure."

"Relax, Ruth. This one's easy." Priscilla laughed. "I was wondering how I could get my hands on an extra ticket for Macy to attend the New York Fashion extravaganza. Even though she's representing Gaylord—

the one with the fashion house—*and* his twin brother Artemis Thibaut, I want her to be seen associating mostly with Gaylord."

"No problem," Ruth said. "I'll contact Gaylord and get him to *offer* a ticket to Macy—of course, not even mentioning your name. Then he can request that Macy joins the two of us because he knows 'PJ is coming with Ruth.' How's that?"

"Perfect. Nice and roundabout. And thanks again, Ruth, for all that you do."

Ruth laughed. "You don't ever need to thank me for doing my job. Just keep those hefty checks coming." But just as she mentioned "those hefty checks," she remembered something more important than the New York Fashion Show.

"My God, PJ. I almost forgot." Ruth headed into her office. Priscilla followed her. Ruth opened her desk drawer and handed Priscilla a handful of envelopes that had come in the mail.

Priscilla raised her eyebrows. She immediately noticed three of the envelopes bore the logo of insurance companies that represented the Met. As she opened each of them, she waved the checks that were inside and read each aloud:

"Payable to P. J. Austin-Bernhardt $315,000.00." The memo read: "Finder's fee–Chagall's *Soleil dans le Ciel de Saint-Paul*." She opened the second envelope and took out a check that read: "… $227,750.00: Finder's fee–Claude-Monet's *La Promenade*." The third check read: "$229,750.00: Finder's fee–Bordone's *Diana and the Two Nymphs*.

"Holy macaroni!" Priscilla exclaimed. "The finders' fees for the recovered paintings! I can't believe I almost forgot about them! She made a silent prayer of appreciation for Jim Froley, who she just knew had worked all this in her favor and who she also knew that she was hardly going to keep the money, at least not all of it. Then she did a rapid calculation in her head. "That's almost three-quarters of a million dollars!"

"Not chump change," Ruth said. But she called Priscilla's attention to the rest of the envelopes that her boss had dumped on the desk. She knew what was in each of those envelopes. "But wait, there's more. Seven, I think."

Like a child on Christmas morning, Priscilla tore them all open. Each contained a check, which she handed to Ruth.

Ruth read one aloud: "Payable: P. J. Austin-Bernhardt, $100,000.00 for services rendered." She riffed through the other checks. All were signed by different women but for the same amount, $100,000.00. "PJ, these checks come to a total of $700,000.00!"

Surprised. "You have got to be kidding me!" Priscilla said. "I understand the first three finders' fees from the insurance companies, but not these other seven checks."

Ruth enlightened her. "One-hundred-K from each of those seven board members who had been blackmailed for so many years."

When Priscilla still frowned, Ruth added: "You know, the victims of that nude extortion racket."

"Ah, yes! The women in those nude portraits!" Priscilla had not expected these generous checks from those seven members of the Met board. She remembered those nude portraits that she and Macy had glimpsed inside that hideaway at the Moreaux chateau outside Paris. But she never once thought that she would receive financial compensation for the good deed she had done, that is, for having asked the FBI and the CIA not to publicize the nude portraits.

But Ruth said in a near whisper, "PJ, if you hadn't insisted on recovering those portraits, it is highly likely that Artemis Thibaut would have tried to continue extorting money from those women, indefinitely. Besides," she explained, "now that their portraits are state's evidence and will *not* be publicized, not ever, I bet those women *insisted* that you be compensated for handling their involvement in what could easily have been the scandal of the decade, yea, even of the century, and so *discreetly*, at that."

Then Ruth recited verbatim what each of the women had said to her. For, each of them had called the office and asked where they should send the checks. Priscilla, at the time, had been at her sister's memorial service in San Francisco.

"'It's only fair,' one of them told me," Ruth said, "'that PJ Austin-Bernhardt deserves every penny of this, and we'll speak nothing more of it.' The others said pretty much the same thing."

And they had all added that they also realized that they would have to relinquish their seats on the board at the Met. But they'd all declared further that "service on the Met board is of secondary concern" to them. What mattered most were their reputations.

Perhaps it was something that Ruth said about those seven women's appreciation for what Priscilla had done because Priscilla confided: "You know something, Ruth. There was a time when I might not have been so kind, especially to people I didn't know."

Ruth did not comment.

But Priscilla's next musings made Ruth laugh again. Even as she had commented about how she must have changed, Priscilla made a rough calculation of the numbers in her head.

"Ruth, are you aware that we just raked in a whopping $1.4 million *on top of* our two-million-dollar retainer for this case?"

"You go, girl!" But Ruth had already done her own calculations and had come up with a slight correction. "But the *exact* figure is $1,472,500.00."

"Bank it," said Priscilla. "Some of that'll come in handy during the dry seasons, 'cause Lord knows, we can't be on top forever."

"Maybe not 'forever,'" Ruth said, "But with fees like these, who needs to work 'forever?'"

Priscilla had yet to tell Ruth that she was donating most of her retainer, not to mention her finders' fees, to Arvana's new program for abused women and narcotics addicts. But now that she knew the exact amount of her finder's fees and what she called "gratitude" from the seven confederates on the Met's board of trustees, she knew that her firm would keep a small portion "for services rendered."

But Priscilla would also share her firm's bounty with the volunteer docent who had first brought everyone's attention to the Chagall. She would later instruct Ruth to set up an art fellowship, anonymously, of course, with a hefty allowance.

Notwithstanding, she already knew that CIA Deputy Director Froley understood that she never intended to keep all that money, anyway. But unlike when she'd first set out as a PR consultant, Priscilla no longer gave much thought to the financial rewards of her work, so she shrugged off Ruth's comments.

As she returned to her office and settled back at her desk, she put aside that whole matter of the finders' fees and the gratitude checks.

That was when it occurred to her that she had not told Julia about Ellen's death.

Only a few moments later, Priscilla took care of that lapse.

Julia answered on the first ring. She told Priscilla how diligent Ruth and Alfrieda had been in keeping her up to date on all the news, including the sad tidings about Ellen.

"Still," Julia said, "I wish I could have joined you and your family at the memorial service." Then she asked about each of the Austin siblings by name and, of course, about Liza and Germane. They reminisced for a while about memories of happier times with Ellen and her family. There would always be a special place in Priscilla's heart for Julia. They might not be related by blood, but for certainty, they were closer than most sisters.

Then Priscilla laughed as she had an inspiration.

"Julia, old buddy, ole pal, how would you like to attend a masquerade ball? Better still, how would you like to come with me to Bow Lake in early December? You could help me help Lady Chelsea decorate our little house and make final preparations for the event?"

"Sounds like fun. But are you sure, Missy, that my presence is necessary? I mean, Lady Chelsea has been hosting that event for years. And even though I suspect she's enjoying teaching *you* how to conduct such an event, my presence might be 'too many cooks spoiling the broth.'"

"Come on, Julia. Lady Chelsea *likes* you, and besides, I'm tired of making excuses for your absence. Why, every time we talk, she asks when last I talked to or saw you. And, oh yeah, you'll never guess who else thinks of you often?"

"Oh? Who might that be?"

"*Arvana*, Julia, my friend. Arvana is hoping to discuss something she wants you to work on with her." *There now*, Priscilla thought. *I've finally cracked that egg!* She was sure that Arvana had longed for her to do exactly that on her behalf. Now, it was left to Julia to follow through.

"Oh, all right, you win." But Julia so wanted to participate in the masquerade ball and, her curiosity ripened with Priscilla's mentioning of Arvana's interest in talking to her.

Mentally, Priscilla crossed Julia off her to-do list.

Then she headed down the corridor to find Laverne. When she saw her in her office, she stepped across the threshold and said, "Do you have a minute?"

"Sure, PJ, anytime and anything for the boss lady."

"How are you with masquerade balls?"

"The one you mentioned earlier in our meeting?" Laverne almost screamed with delight. "My life here just keeps getting better and better!"

"Well, newest girlfriend in my life, we're *all* invited to the fund-raiser. It's a good cause, don't forget. To benefit the Children's Hospital in Merrimack."

She assured Laverne that she would arrange for Ruth to take the two of them shopping for costumes. Even though she had the vaguest of memories, Lady Chelsea, Ramses, and Father seemed to think she would be coming as Cleopatra.

"Oh, PJ," Laverne said. By this time, she had mastered the art of sounding nearly exactly like Priscilla did, thereby making their resemblance all the more remarkable. "Wait," she said, "until my folks get a load of this!"

Priscilla grinned. She was beginning to understand that whenever she brought joy to someone else, much of their joy rubbed off on her, as well. Besides, this time, Priscilla asked Laverne for a personal favor, not part of their work together. That felt good, very good.

Then, as Priscilla was about to return to her office, Laverne pulled out some brochures and printouts from her desk drawer and showed them to Priscilla.

"What do you think?" she asked, pointing at this and that apartment and sharing her thoughts about those she was considering.

"Each of these suits you perfectly," Priscilla said.

Laverne returned to a printout of an East Side studio. "It's an elevator building with a doorman," she said. "And right off the subway and on the major bus routes, too. Perfect."

Priscilla was pleased that Laverne was settling in as a New Yorker.

30

Put a Sock in It, Iggy

As she turned into her office, Priscilla was surprised to see Ignatius Devoe and Shane Carpenter sitting—red-faced and perspiring, in the matching striped-silk upholstered high-back chairs in front of her desk. "Ah, crap," she said underneath her breath. For a microsecond, she wondered how they had apparently gotten past Alfrieda. But then, considering Iggy's criminal actions, she supposed slinking in here was easy.

She gave them a terse hello and took her seat. The two of them were highly stressed. She could swear Iggy was actually trembling. Priscilla already knew that Iggy had some idea about the gravity of his charges and that he was in her office to give his best performance at pleading for more relief. *Anything*, she read in his desperate eyes.

Iggy wasted no time.

"PJ!" he pleaded. "You have *got* to help us! Especially me. I know I should've *come clean* earlier, but that wretched Artemis Thibaut had me over a barrel. But I'll do any—" He stopped, aware that what he had obviously started to say was not true and that she would know that, too.

Priscilla's mouth had narrowed into a hard line.

"Oh-h, put a sock in it, Iggy."

Then, without even looking at Shane, she pointed and said to him, "Close my frigging door."

While Shane got up from his seat and did as Priscilla had instructed him to do, she walked to the window behind her desk and stood there with her back to the two men. As she stared out of the window, she fought to contain her lingering anger from when she first learned that Iggy and Shane had deceived her. Then she threw her head back, squared her shoulders, and sat down in her executive swivel chair.

"What we resolve to do here," she said, "must never leave this room." She clasped her hands together and gave the two men an intense look. What was the most effective way to get across at least some of what Macy had told her the other day during their coffee confab? She nodded to herself and said, "Here's the deal, fellows."

For the first time, she looked at Shane. "If you want to keep your job at the Met, then you need to take a little hiatus, say, something like two weeks to thirty days. Is there someone who can manage the museum in your stead?"

Shane's solemn expression quickly turned into eagerness. His natural skin tone was restored. His tear-filled eyes glistened.

"Yes, PJ. Yes!"

"Then instruct that person on exactly everything to do in your absence. Give that person a contact number in the event they require your guidance. But that is all. Hear me clearly, Shane: you must not be accessible to the media, not to any board members, not even to Iggy." Then she looked into his eyes more intensely. "Is that clear, Shane? And now, do you have any questions? Now is the time to ask."

"Oh, PJ. My God, thank you for 'saving my bacon' again. But what happens *after* my 'hiatus?'" Shane knew his situation was still precarious.

"There *is* one more thing," she said. Then she elaborated:

"Contact an attorney and fill them in on everything that you know for a certainty, especially about your interrogation by the feds and the international intelligence authorities. Your attorney will take it from there *and* prepare you for the impending court proceedings, mediations, whatever course the Met board pursues."

"*Court proceedings?*"

Those two words were all that Shane had heard. He shrieked. "Oh, no!" Shane's face turned an ugly red color.

Priscilla snapped.

"Shane, don't make me curse. You're the doggone *executive director* for *the* Metropolitan Museum of Art. Surely, you know the court will be interested in your take on this so-called 'mysterious affair.' Along those lines, your attorney will drill you on what to say and how to say it. Other than that, I have nothing more for you. You're free to go."

"*That's it*? I mean, don't you want to know what I know and how I know—?" Suddenly, he looked like his handsome self again.

"Shane, I manage the *PR* for the Met. I'm not an attorney. I just told you to get your own attorney and that, according to my sources, you need not worry about criminal prosecution or anything of the sort. You speak exclusively on behalf of what you know about the goings-on at the Met. Period. Got that? Damn it. Now you've gone and made me curse. Good day to you, Shane Carpenter."

Priscilla stood up and waved her hand toward the door.

"Shut it tight."

But before he did as Priscilla had instructed, Shane stood up, ran around her desk, grabbed hold of her, and hugged her. Then he even dared a peck on her cheek. Tears flowed freely from his puffy red eyes, and he wiped his runny nose with the back arm sleeve of his tailor-made blazer—a behavior most unbecoming of a New York City socialite like himself. Social status aside, Shane wanted Priscilla to know how grateful he was for her support, for someone who had deceived her from the start, at that. Unlike Iggy, Shane had a contrite heart. Instinctively he now understood why others spoke of her as "discreet." He just knew that somehow she knew something, if not everything, about his and Iggy's past. But he also sensed something about this woman that suggested she could care less about his lifestyle; it was saving his humanity that mattered. Then he rushed out of Priscilla's office without even a backward glance or a goodbye, either to Priscilla or to the one he had already begun thinking of as his *former* lover. Shane had also surmised that Iggy was facing a far more devastating fate than even he could imagine.

As Shane slammed the door shut and bolted down the corridor toward the elevator, Alfrieda happened past Priscilla's door and peeped inside the glass. She caught Priscilla's eye and raised her eyebrows.

Priscilla frowned and waved her off. Later she would have to ask Alfrieda about how the twerps had gotten past reception and had been waiting in her office in the first place. *Maybe we need tighter security in our own offices.* She almost smiled as she also thought, *At least that's something else for "the boys."*

Then Priscilla walked around to the front of her desk and perched on its edge in front of Iggy. He was guilty of so much more than Shane, yet her voice lost its edge and its contempt as she began with him. "I'm sorry, Iggy, but even you know your situation is far more complicated than Shane's. But you didn't need me to tell you what you already know."

Iggy wailed, "But PJ, I—"

As she cut him off, she could not recall last when she had needed to have such an unpleasant conversation with anyone, not a college student, not a client, not a family member, not anyone.

She cut to the chase:

"Iggy, to some extent, you're at the mercy of the international intelligence authorities. Interpol, to be exact. And since I have minimal knowledge about those guys…." She shrugged. "Oh, hell, Iggy, I don't know beans about Interpol. I can only pray for you." At that point, she could see the fear mounting in his face.

He flushed and popped beads of sweat, and seemed for a moment to hang his head.

Regardless, Priscilla continued with her not-so-good news:

"Iggy, if you do not already have an attorney, first, I advise you to retain one *immediately*. In case you haven't been following the news, even Artemis Thibaut has an attorney. So lawyer-up. Protect your assets. And yourself."

When he did not respond, Priscilla continued:

"Second, I'm not a lawyer, so I can't give you legal advice. But let's just say that it's obvious to me that if you haven't already turned what is commonly referred to as 'state's witness,' 'witness for the prosecution,' whatever the bloody phrase…. I'm pretty sure that's the first thing your lawyer will recommend." Priscilla already knew that Iggy had been the sole source for the successful retrieval of the three highly-valued works of art that Thibaut Francois had hidden away some time ago in Paris, Mykonos, and Manhattan.

She paused, hopeful that he would say something, anything, to indicate that he understood what she was suggesting.

But, as the tension mounted, and before Priscilla told him the actual bad news, weakly, he pleaded with her again.

"Oh, PJ," he cried. "You helped Shane. Isn't there *something* you can do to help me, too?"

She shook her head. "Iggy, the most I can do is appeal to our law enforcement, particularly the FBI, to exercise leniency. Then again, I have no official role in the impending legal proceedings, criminal trials, mediations, or whatever comes next. I'm the *PR* person for the Met, and so it is the *Met* board of trustees and attorneys with whom you must contend. And as I'm sure you are aware, they have a battery of attorneys. So, again, I say, you need to lawyer up, Iggy. *Comprenez-vous?*

Again, she paused, and again, he pleaded with his eyes.

"Iggy, only a good attorney can 'save *your* bacon,' which reminds me: you're no longer chairman of the board of trustees at the Met. According to the bylaws, the vice-chair, Aryeh Asher, is in charge now. That information will be released in a PR statement by me in about one week to ten days."

As Iggy began to cry real tears, he continued with his pleading.

"Please, PJ, you've got to help me, too."

Priscilla simply continued with what she had to say.

"Once I receive confirmation about how your situation and those other cases will be pursued or prosecuted—if you still happen to be a free man—I *might* be able to help secure work for you elsewhere. But not in America or Western Europe. That's just not going to happen." She did not tell him about her efforts to aid him.

Iggy dropped his head in his hands and sobbed aloud.

Priscilla hid a sigh. This briefing was no fun for her, either. Yet she continued:

"But Iggy, I *cannot* get ahead of the impending legal proceedings. And if it's any consolation, I do have it on good authority that no one is interested in seeing you fry for the horrible part you played under the influence of Thibaut Francois. Or his son, Artemis Thibaut, for that matter," at least so far as Priscilla knew at the time. But the case against Ignatius Devoe had yet to begin.

Hopefully, he raised his head.

But she was not about to delude him. "Iggy, don't forget way back when you were party to the grand scheme of things. Remember? *You* sketched all those portraits that Thibaut Francois and later Artemis Thibaut painted. And by the way, your seven confederates are no longer on the board, either. At the behest of the vice-chair, as we speak, something to that effect will soon be released to the public, as well."

"Oh, no! But how'd you know about what you called "my seven confederates?' And those paintings?"

Poor Iggy. He still had no notion that Priscilla had used her intelligence-gathering prowess to eavesdrop on him and Shane.

Priscilla nodded. "I'm not the only one who knows about all of that, either."

She left it to him to figure out who else she meant and how all of that would impact his future.

Then she enlightened him. "Don't forget, this is the later part of the twentieth century. Advances in technology make it increasingly difficult for you *and me* to shield anything from law enforcement. What you and I say, others might hear and read."

She stood in dismissal.

"Now go to your office at the Met, clean out your desk, say farewell to everyone. But be careful what you say. What I recommend is that you get one of the clerical staff to take down a statement. Say something like: 'Under the apparent circumstances, and since this debacle happened on my watch, I'm tendering my resignation, effective immediately.' And then sign it, and don't say another word before you leave. And Iggy, please, contact an attorney *immediately*."

Something else belatedly occurred to her.

"One more thing. And this is important. If and when the illustrious Macy Stoner calls you, do not talk to her *until* you retain your own legal counsel. And then, simply refer her to your attorney. Got that?"

But Iggy didn't even nod his head. His sobbing had grown louder. Priscilla moved toward the door and opened it for him.

"Iggy, pull yourself together. What you have to do now is try to restore the good name of The Metropolitan Museum of Art."

Priscilla beckoned with a wave of her hand for Iggy to leave her office. "Now disappear from my sight."

When Iggy left, still sobbing, Priscilla tried to take comfort from the fact that, whether he understood this or not, to some extent, she had gone out of her way to "save his bacon," too. Priscilla harbored no ill will for him or Shane, the "two twerps" who had first set out to deceive her.

Yet she sighed. One can never do enough to please some people, and Iggy was one of those people for whom no one could ever do enough to satisfy. After all, he had "dug his own grave, anyway."

31

No! You Can't Be ...

The file folder had been on Priscilla's desk since she received the news about her sister's death. And there it had remained. Even Ruth knew not to tamper with files that bore the imprint of either Laverne or "the boys."

Now, more than a week later, Priscilla opened the folder and saw a report from Laverne about the seven Met board members who had met with Iggy and Shane at the Highland-on-the-Hudson near Poughkeepsie. Five board members were married men; the other two were women: David Abercrombie, Woody Beranger, Vincent Broadnax, Raymon Kehlmeier, Henri Yancey, Pauletta Christenbury, and Annette Faulkner. The five male board members were married to the women who had long ago posed nude in Paris.

Laverne's report indicated that Iggy knew his board members not just well but better than anyone would have expected. He knew about their financial circumstance, lineage, and lifestyles, especially their travel preferences for holidays in Paris. More importantly, Iggy had been the common denominator between each of the seven board members and Thibaut Francois and, later, between them (or their respective spouses) and Artemis Thibaut.

It turned out that Iggy's relationship with Artemis Thibaut had caused him tremendous grief. Artemis Thibaut had tracked Iggy's movements from when he'd left Paris and settled in New York until he'd obtained his cherished seat on the Met board and then had ascended to the board's chairmanship. Most disturbingly, for well over twenty-odd years, Artemis Thibaut had also extorted huge sums of money from Iggy in exchange for his silence about his disreputable past as a sketch artist—which is to say, *forger*—of highly-valued works of art.

Laverne's report also documented that for more than twenty years, Artemis Thibaut had familiarized himself with the lifestyles and the travel preferences of the seven board members as they frequented Paris, particularly at Montmartre, where at some time he'd snared each of the seven unsuspecting women. First, as they strolled along the Boulevard de Rochechouart or nearby the Eiffel Tower or the Champs Elysees, he might offer to sketch them. Then he would lure them to his art studio, where he charmed them into allowing him to paint them in the nude. Then, just as his father Thibaut Francois had done before him, so, too, had Artemis Thibaut extorted vast sums of money from each of the seven unsuspecting women: "If you pay me my asking price, I will not display your nude portraits for sale."

Priscilla nodded at Laverne's report, nearly identical to what Ignatius Devoe told the feds and the international intelligence authorities about Thibaut Francois and his son Artemis Thibaut. That meant that the international intelligence, federal, and police authorities had all the corroboration they needed, that—along with the confessions of the seven women themselves—to seal the case against Artemis Thibaut for at least seven counts of extortion. He had, of course, also extorted money from the squiggly Iggy himself.

Priscilla closed the folder. So her admonitions and advice to Iggy had been apropos, after all. For starters, she knew he needed high-quality legal counsel. As she reviewed her conversation with Iggy, she put that folder in a bin to be filed and prayed that she herself would not get caught up even as an eyewitness in any of the impending legal proceedings. Not that the thought brought her any comfort, but she was fully aware that she was not the only one praying. She knew that the seven confederates on the Met board had already been deposed and informed that no further testimony was required. That left Shane and Iggy, not to mention the Omiros twins and Artemis Thibaut's girlfriend, Arianna's real name, but Priscilla was least concerned with the twins. She also knew that more than herself, both Shane and Iggy dreaded the thought of the forthcoming legal proceedings, regardless of how they would be conducted.

She shifted from thinking to being constructive and drafted three press releases. One noted personal time off for Shane Carpenter, the Met's executive director. Another announced Ignatius Devoe's resignation as board chairman and introduced his replacement, Vice-Chairman Aryeh Asher. The third announced the seven board members' resignations "because they felt that they had not performed due diligence to avert the incidents in the first place."

Priscilla gave the draft press releases to Ruth to edit and to prepare for release. She told her to send out Shane's at once and the others in a week to ten days. No reason to link Shane's time off to the other more serious announcements.

As the day wore on, the office telephones at Priscilla's New York City branch PR office rang continuously. Calls came in from the New York City press corps, the mainstream and cable news reporters, the international entertainment and news reporters, and the paparazzi. They had all seen the three "exclusive interviews" of Priscilla and Ruth on the three different television networks earlier that morning. But although Priscilla and Ruth had stated previously that they had said all she intended to say about the matter, the other media representatives wanted to follow up. Some begged for "More insight," but others showed their desperation by asking for "Something," or even "Anything."

Priscilla referred reporters she did not know to Ruth, whom she had instructed to turn them all down with a terse "No further comment," or maybe a casual, "Nothing doing."

Those she knew, she talked to herself. To some, she said, 'I have no further comment" or "Wait to see what steps the Met takes," or "That's a matter for the lawyers."

When Priscilla decided she had had her fill, she put on her New York attitude and commenced her power walk from her office back to her and Carlton's suite at the Waldorf Astoria. Then she changed into her work clothes—a plaid shirt, jeans, and sneakers—and headed to her Harlem brownstone. There she intended to take solace in getting her hands dirty renovating her new home. And she hoped to get better acquainted with her newfound friend, "Jules, Ma'am."

Somewhat surprised, Priscilla looked at the piles of building materials spread out across the small front lawn and up against the exterior of her Harlem brownstone. She had only been away for a few days. But now there was so much more stuff: crates of hardwood flooring to replace some of the wood damaged by years of neglect and low maintenance, and three sets of wooden French doors had been left leaning against the side of the house near stacked boxes of various sizes and shapes containing *who knows what.* She also saw buckets of paint, sacks of plaster, and replacement mirrors for the broken ones on the dining room wall. *My goodness,* she thought; *I had no idea this place needed this much work.*

But, as she stepped across the threshold of the open front door, she could not believe her eyes. The living room had been a shambles the last she saw it, with remnants of wallpaper hanging from the walls, a darkened and scuffed hardwood floor, and broken windowpanes covered with plywood. Now it looked like a move-in-ready living space. Mr. Hunter and his men had replaced the broken window panes, nearly completed refinishing the hardwood living room floor, and removed all the damaged wallpaper. And they had cleaned, sanded, and painted the walls a beautiful Tuscany color that Priscilla had selected from a picture in a magazine.

"Wow!" she kept saying as she stood still in her tracks. Then she heard someone calling her name. Mr. Hunter was yelling from the top of the stairs.

"Missus Austin-Bernhardt? Is that you?"

"Oh, Mr. Hunter!" she exclaimed. "I can't believe my eyes!"

He descended the staircase and spoke cheerfully. "Well, the fellows and I decided to cease our work upstairs and do something to make you feel good upon your return. We were so sorry to hear about the death of your sister."

"Oh, Mr. Hunter, thank you. Thank you. And thank you again."

"No problem," he said. But as he turned to go back up the stairs, he said, "Oh, that little rascal from up the street has come-a-calling every day since you've been away. It's my guess he already knows you're back now."

Then, just as he was about to say more, "Jules, Ma'am" darted through the front door.

"Well, Beautiful Lady," he said, "it's about time you came home." Jules had already taken to calling Priscilla "Beautiful Lady," both because that was what he thought of her and because he did not like the formality of calling her "Mrs. Austin-Bernhardt."

Then, like ole buddies and pals, Priscilla and Jules walked into her kitchen and sat down at the table.

"Jules, my newfound friend, want to fill me in on your life in my absence?"

The two unlikely friends talked and talked and talked. However, when Priscilla realized that her newfound friend might be hungry, she thought about feeding him. She already knew there was no food in her refrigerator, so she suggested they either "order delivery or walk around the corner to a neighborhood restaurant."

But the young man stared at her curiously.

"Oh, Beautiful Lady, you really are new to the neighborhood. No *delivery trucks* come to our neighborhood, 'specially no food services."

"Okay, then," she said. "Up for a short walk?"

"Heck, yeah, lady."

Although Priscilla thought Jules McCorkle could be no more than seven or eight years old, he grabbed her hand and walked his "girlfriend" proudly up the street. Along the way, he pointed out who lived in which houses and what some of the inhabitants did for a living. More than once, however, Priscilla noticed that he skipped some of the houses, and when she asked him who resided in those houses, the young man grew silent. But Priscilla noticed, too, that he avoided walking toward his own home. Yet, she decided to give their relationship some time to develop before insisting on going to his house and meeting his folks, especially his mother.

Priscilla also soon learned that Jules did not share similar eating habits as hers. He kept stopping and gazing at fast food establishments, where the vendors sold hamburgers and tacos and burritos—what Priscilla called "junk food." He paid no attention to full-service restaurants. When she insisted that they go inside a restaurant and sit down and eat, she noticed how hesitant he became.

Then she remembered a well-known, nearby soul food establishment. "How 'bout Sylvia's?"

"Nah, that's for rich folks."

But Priscilla had eaten there before. Sylvia's was a family-friendly establishment where many couples and ordinary people had a good meal. Maybe rich and famous people dined there, too, but it was not known as a dining establishment for "rich folks."

Then something told her to ask, "Jules, when was the last time your mom took you to a restaurant or cooked a hot meal for you?"

"Oh, we eat out all the time."

"Really? Show me where you 'eat out all the time.'"

When Jules pointed to a McDonald's Restaurant, Priscilla realized that her definition of a restaurant and Jules's definition of a restaurant was entirely different.

Shortly after her first experience eating out with Jules, Priscilla began stocking her refrigerator with food to cook for her unlikely acquaintance. It took some doing, but after a few tries, she started preparing dishes such as chicken and lamb chops and even T-bone steaks, along with baked potatoes with sour crème and other side dishes like corn on the cob and Bush's Baked Beans. Before long, Jules was asking her to prepare the meals that he especially liked.

Jules, Priscilla also observed, was a neglected child. He often wore mismatched clothing, and sometimes, he might even come visiting in woolens during the heat of the summer; and his shoes were too big for his little feet. He also lacked good hygiene.

Considering all this, Priscilla—who, after all, did not have any children—was about to venture into risky territory. She did not stop to think, or even to remember, what happened once before when she had not obtained parental consent before buying an expensive present for her favorite nephew, Germane. The year before her father died, Priscilla ignored her mother's advice and bought Germane an elaborate electric train set, tracks, and all. But her sister Helen had complained, telling their mother that Priscilla had no right to buy "such an expensive gift for my child *and* without my permission." So, once again, it did not even occur to Priscilla to ask Jules's mother's permission before buying him some new clothes and some toiletries.

Priscilla then decided to surprise Jules with her gifts and meet his mother at the same time. Since she already knew where Jules lived, she lugged her presents down the street in two large, overly-stuffed tote bags. When she reached the top of the front steps, she put down the tote bags and knocked on the door. Although she thought she heard someone talking and music playing inside, she knocked on the door again, and louder.

But she caught her breath when a brawny black man dressed in a dingy T-shirt and tight-fitting briefs finally answered the door. A cigarette hung from his mouth. What should have been the whites of his eyes were brown. He reminded Priscilla of an unsavory character in the British television series *Keeping Up Appearances*.

Insolently he looked Priscilla over and asked, "Who the— are you, bitch?"

"Well, I, uh … I'm PJ Austin-Bernhardt, your neighbor." She spoke as cheerfully as she could. "And I, well, I brought some gifts for Jules. Is he in?"

The burly man snapped. "Some *gifts*? For *who*?"

Priscilla trembled in her tracks as she watched the repellant man snatch the tote bags and then toss them inside on the floor. From where she stood, the dimly lit front room appeared to be somewhat untidy.

Then the man yelled over his shoulders. "Mamie! Woman. Get out here! This here woman claims to be bringing that youngling of yours some gifts."

Then he turned back to Priscilla and laughed at her. "Ha! Ha! Ha! Lady, you must not be from 'round these parts. Nobody of good intentions brings no gifts to nobody in this neighborhood. Sure you ain't from Children's Services, checking up on Mamie and that little snot?"

Priscilla barely understood whatever he was saying because he slurred his words so much. But she heard the words "Children's Services." Her anger was rising, and she had stopped trembling. Now she wanted to slap the man. Blood rushed to her head. But when she saw Mamie, the woman who had to be Jules's mother, she wanted to cry.

Mamie looked to be maybe twenty-five years old. She wore a drab and tattered sleeveless dress and a full head of thick, long, but unkempt hair. She was not just skinny but looked undernourished. And Priscilla guessed, from the vacant look in her eyes and the way she shivered, that Mamie was high on something. Jules's mother was a narcotics addict.

Priscilla blurted out: "No! You can't be … Jules's mother?" She wished she could call back the words.

She changed her tacks.

"Why, he speaks so admirably of you." Although Priscilla was already stunned, she was wholly unprepared for what came next.

Mamie's eyes came to life and flashed to her. "So you're the *bitch* my boy's been going on about. For a while there, I thought he was make-believing."

But before she could say more, Jules suddenly appeared. He ran between the two women and grabbed his mother's hand. "Mother, *please*, come back inside with me. I'll take care of you, just like I always do."

Priscilla watched in disbelief as the burly man slapped Jules hard on the back of his head. But the child did not even recoil.

"Sorry, Beautiful Lady," Jules said to Priscilla. "I am so sorry." He hung his head low as he walked back inside the house, still holding his mother's hand.

For a moment, Priscilla stood in the doorway, wondering why the child had apologized to her. It was not his fault that his mother looked to be a drug addict and that she kept house with the likes of that mean brawny man. But she noticed something even more revealing and troubling: Jules had been looking after his mother—at such a young age—not the other way around, as it should have been.

Thoughtfully, she ambled back down the street to her home, unaware that many of her neighbors were watching her. They could pretty much read the shock and disappointment on her face, too, as the earlier excitement manifested in her face, and her strut was noticeably gone. So now her neighbors knew that she knew so much more about Jules and that none of it was good.

But, short of kidnapping the youngster, there was almost nothing that Priscilla could do to intervene. If she called Children's Services, before long, they would remove Jules from his home, and probably, if she were right about the drugs, they would recommend his mother undergo treatment for narcotics abuse. They might even incarcerate her for child neglect. Moreover, if Priscilla returned to the McCorkle residence, no telling what that brawny man might do to her. So, once again, she faced one of those seemingly unbearable circumstances of life, rather, in a small way, compared to Jules.

What Priscilla did not know, however, was that she was surrounded by people—her contractor, Onslow's men, and virtually all of her neighbors—who had already known about the situation at the McCorkle residence. But tacitly, they had all concluded that Priscilla would have to experience the situation for herself, even though they somehow knew it would be a rude awakening for her.

The next time Priscilla saw Jules, he crept into her kitchen ever so slowly, head bowed, with shame written all over his face.

"Oh, Jules," Priscilla cried at the sight of the young man. Then she reached for him. "I am so sorry. I didn't mean any harm. I just wanted to surprise you and, of course, to meet your mom. But I had no idea."

As he welcomed her open arms and warm embrace, Jules began to weep, and so did Priscilla.

"No problem, Beautiful Lady," he finally managed to say. "You meant well. But I just couldn't let you see my mom the way she is." Then he cried some more. "But my mom's a good woman." He pulled away from Priscilla and looked into her reddened, watery eyes: "It's just that, well, she can't seem to leave those drugs and those bad men alone." Again he paused and wept.

Priscilla was overcome with compassion for this child who was caught up in a life of such pain and misery.

Jules wiped his eyes on the sleeve of his shirt. "But my mom really *is* a good woman. Please believe me."

Priscilla nodded in encouragement. She so wanted to believe that Mamie was "a good woman," and she was so moved by Jules's steadfast love for his mother, too. But Priscilla wished that she knew more about the effect of narcotics on a person. She recalled that other people had previously criticized her for not only having a skewed perspective—or maybe even erroneous—but also for looking at the world through her rose-colored prism. For now, however, she knew she did not have the background she needed to make more informed decisions about what to do to help Mamie and Jules. But she supposed that one day, maybe when Arvana's program would be up and running, she might know more and be in a position to do more in a situation like this.

For the moment, though, she and Jules simply took mutual comfort in crying together a while longer. Then, suddenly, they heard a deep masculine voice and looked around.

Mr. Hunter stood in the doorway. "Sorry to intrude, folks," the contractor said as he realized that he must have interrupted a private moment. "But I was wondering if you'd like to take a stroll upstairs. Check out some of our work."

"Let's do this thing!" said the tearful Priscilla, as she noticed that sometimes when she was surprised or embarrassed, she sounded more like "the boys" than herself.

They both staggered up the stairs behind Mr. Hunter and wiped their eyes and runny noses along the way.

Upstairs they wandered here and there, taking in the many repairs and renovations. Mr. Hunter, they agreed, had done a fantastic job. Jules could not contain himself as he kept jumping up and down and hollering: "Wow! Look at this place!"

What really captured Priscilla's attention was when she heard the youngster saying, "I've never seen anything like this before. Nobody on this street lives in a house all done up like this. On TV, maybe, but not in real life."

But when Jules was out of earshot, the contractor lowered his voice. "Not so sure if you know this," he said, "but Children's Services has been on the prowl for this young man. It's only a matter of time before they intervene and take custody of the kid. Sorry to break it to you like this." Mr. Hunter knew that there would never have been a good time to share that information with Priscilla. But he thought it was important to deliver an early warning so she would not be caught entirely unawares.

"Oh, no!" Priscilla fretted. "That can't be."

"Sorry, Missus Austin-Bernhardt, but that's pretty much the way of life in these parts. Drugs. Prostitution. Children's Services. Incarceration."

Priscilla stared at her trusted contractor in confusion. She was unfamiliar with child neglect or narcotics addiction, not to mention prostitution and incarceration. She did not even know what kinds of questions to ask him. But she did know about Arvana's plans for when she was released from prison. Maybe someday, she would even be able to secure a place for Mamie in Arvana's new drug rehabilitation program. As for Jules, well, she sighed. She would have to put his precarious predicament out of her mind, at least for now.

As things stood, she was grateful that she could so easily compartmentalize issues that could not be solved just yet. She would deal with that problem later, tomorrow maybe. Otherwise, she simply could not fathom what Mr. Hunter had just told her.

32

The Special Edition

It seemed as if August went by ever so quickly. Priscilla spent nearly as much time hanging out at her Harlem brownstone as she did at her Fifth Avenue office. Then, as September rolled in, she surprised herself by looking forward to the New York Fashion Show, which, she was about to learn, was New York Fashion *Week*!

Three days shy of NYFW, Ruth handed Priscilla an impressive-looking envelope bearing the White House seal! "I had to sign three different forms before they gave me this. Next, I had to attest to my identity *and* acknowledge that I did not open the envelope *and* that I subsequently confirm its delivery to you." She handed Priscilla another document. "And here's the form that *you* need to sign attesting to *your* receipt of the delivery *untampered*. Such is the stuff of spy movies and novels, eh?" Then she laughed, unaware of how much truth there was in her words.

Priscilla's invitation to what was called the "Special Edition," the kickoff to the NYFW, spanned over *nine* days.

However, she was puzzled for a moment as she regarded the fancy invitation printed in gold ink with a silk ribbon wrapped around it. Then her face cleared.

"Ruth," she asked, "is this very big deal what I thought was that nice little boat ride you talked me into going to before?"

"Yes, PJ." Ruth's smile had never been wider. She then gave Priscilla a brochure detailing what to expect in the "Special Edition."

Priscilla poured over it. The "Special Edition" was an unpublicized White House-sponsored event with an African American culture emphasis. It started at Battery Park, proceeded with a boat ride to Ellis Island, and ended up in Harlem for a reception at the Schomburg Center for Research in Black Culture. Finally, participants headed over to the newly renovated Apollo Theater with an homage to black artists, entertainers, and writers the likes of Phillis Wheatley, James Baldwin, Josephine Baker, Dorothy Dandridge, Sammy Davis, Jr., Etta James, Billie Holiday, Paul Robeson, Langston Hughes, Zora Neale Hurston, Nancy Wilson, Richard Wright, Ethel Waters, and Eartha Kitt. Originality was the theme. Priscilla smiled and thought: *Perhaps knowing the first black president does have its privileges, after all.* This particular "Special Edition" to NYFW was the unofficial start of the season's most prominent social event. It signaled the first of several such events and programs that the Hollingsworth Administration had begun offering to orient high-level government officials to the changing demographics of the U.S. population, such as the growing presence of descendants of African, Hispanic, Asian, Eastern European, Middle Eastern, and, multicultural and other ethnicities and nationalities.

The "Special Edition" began late on Wednesday morning of Fashion Week, when Priscilla and nearly three hundred other special guests boarded a private cruise ship at Battery Park. As they sailed along the Hudson River en route to Ellis Island, guests enjoyed cocktails and hors d'oeuvres while admiring an Ebony Fashion Fair Show on deck. Priscilla was spellbound as black men and women—all tall, slender, shapely, and gorgeous—strolled and strutted and whirled about the deck modeling stunning garments, from bathing suits to evening attire.

Then a cultured masculine voice sounded over the loudspeaker:

"Ladies and Gentlemen, we are about to disembark at the site that epitomizes the American Dream." There was a dramatic pause, then: "Welcome to Ellis Island!"

Priscilla and the others disembarked and headed to a shelter in front of the welcoming Statue of Liberty, where the voice on the loudspeaker read aloud the famous inscription added to the base of the statue in 1903:

"The New Colossus"
Give me your tired, your poor,
Your huddled masses yearning to breathe free,
The wretched refuse of your teeming shore.
Send these, the homeless, tempest-tossed, to me:
I lift my lamp beside the golden door.

At those stirring words, Priscilla and the other guests applauded and took their seats. More inspirational information about the Statue of Liberty followed: "German-born poet Emma Lazarus wrote that stirring inscription in 1883. The statue—then called 'Liberty Enlightening the World'—was a gift to the United States from France in 1886. Designed and sculpted by Frederic Auguste Bartholdi, the statue's framework was constructed by Gustave Eiffel, who later built the Eiffel Tower."

"I didn't know all that," Priscilla heard someone say, and neither did she, until now.

"As for the actual property," the voiceover said, "the federal government purchased this land, which had originally been a fortification site, from the State of New York. It is most famous as an immigration station. It is estimated that this was the first stop on American soil for eight million immigrants—mainly from Western and Northern Europe—from the mid-1800s to the early twentieth century. Over the next half-century, another four million immigrants were processed here, totaling more than twelve million immigrants on Ellis Island. In 1965, the site was declared the Statue of Liberty National Monument. Later, after the historic restoration, it was opened to the public on a limited basis."

As she continued listening to the history of the impressive and welcoming statue, Priscilla reflected on the irony of her lineage. *Although my family's African side may not have come here as willing immigrants, we're here. And how*! Priscilla smiled to herself and then was warmed by the thought: *It's good to be American.*

Her thoughts returned to the moment. She scanned the crowd of special guests when she spotted Vice President JK McDougal seated regally amid what appeared to have been some other important people. She caught his eye, and the vice president smiled at her. Then she caught sight of Deputy Director of State Harry Middleton. "Ah, crap," she said to herself. Seeing Harry reminded Priscilla that she was a special agent of sorts. *I sure hope those bloody bastards aren't up to their old tricks again and call me out on another mission just now*. Then she turned her attention back to the moment and pretended not to have seen any of the familiar faces, although she was aware that many of them had now seen hers.

Priscilla leaned back in her seat and continued listening to the voice-over. "The restoration of the monument cost over $160 million, and in1990 was reopened to the public as the Ellis Island National Museum of Immigration." Two million tourists were expected to visit the site annually.

Then there were another twenty minutes of the Ebony Fashion Fair Show. This time they saw models sporting ready-to-wear outfits and more bathing suits. They watched as the models—with the Atlantic Ocean as a backdrop—flaunted haute couture for the finale. All around her, Priscilla heard exclamations from the crowd. "What a way to end the show! *Bravo! Bravo! Bravo!*" Priscilla especially liked the fashion show because she identified with the race and ethnicity of many of its models. She also liked that they had "meat on their bones," something she would soon learn was not the norm with the mostly Caucasian models at the other NYFW events.

But the "Special Edition" extravaganza was just getting started.

As Priscilla and the others ascended the plank and were back on board, she was surprised to hear and see a young up-an-coming Wynton Marsalis and his orchestra performing many jazz and rhythm and blues hits by Count Basie, who died in 1984. She continued enjoying the music and wondered what other delights she could expect as they cruised in the waters around New York City.

While she continued listening to this music she had always loved, she remembered the summer she had gone home to Prendergast from graduate school at The Ohio State University. She and Amber had attended a performance by the Count Basie Orchestra at the Chautauqua Institute. The two of them had gone backstage and met "The Incomparable Count," who encouraged the two friends to "stay in school" and "follow your dreams." Priscilla regretted that she had lost the autographed playbill that the Count had given her.

Then a woman sitting at the same table as Priscilla whispered to her. "Did you hear? Lena—"

Before the woman completed her sentence, the stunning diva appeared before them. Priscilla and the other guests leaped to their feet as one: "Lena Horne!" they cried out. "Lena!"

The star of the show waved her long slender hands and arms. She bowed low, almost touching her hands to the floor of the deck. As she lifted her head back up, she nearly took Priscilla's breath away. The diva threw her head back and began singing the first line of "Stormy Weather" at the top of her lungs. At seventy-six years of age, Lena Horne was still attractive, youthful, and wholesome and even had a striking figure. She reminded Priscilla how the president's wife, Selena, might look at her age. Lena's robust and vibrant voice burst through the air as she sang, "Stormy Weather."

The song was so easy on the ear and yet somehow so sad. Priscilla had been married for less than a year and was madly in love with her husband. Her parents had been happy together, too. Thoughtfully she asked herself what this "stormy" reference in relationships was all about. Smart and intuitive as she was, Priscilla could not yet relate to the anguish that some people felt at the loss of love or their lovers, or maybe other loved ones. But she absolutely loved Lena Horne's singing!

As the cruise ship neared Battery Park, someone handed Priscilla an itinerary for the remainder of the events. A private reception was scheduled at the Schomburg Center for Research in Black Culture, where she would stand on a colorful globe of inlaid marble that highlighted the world's major tributaries. At the same time, someone recited Langston Hughes' "The Negro Speaks of Rivers." The executive director would then lead a facility tour while sharing amusing stories about famous black authors and playwrights. That evening there would be a star-studded event at the Apollo Theater featuring pop artists rendering their versions of the music of black entertainers and musicians who had paved the way for their success.

Priscilla was enchanted. She thought *I must have died and gone to heaven!*

And so it was that Priscilla warmed up to the NYFW, after all. Or at least she did while she was attending its "Special Edition." It never occurred to her, that wonderful day on the river, to wish she had a friend by her side. But she had long since learned to step out on her own. She especially enjoyed that no one—and by this, she mainly meant the international entertainment and news reporters and the paparazzi—bothered her by snapping their endless photographs and asking their endless questions. Most of the other guests, including some famous people, also seemed to appreciate private time away from the demands of celebrity. Priscilla was to discover later, however, that this was the only day of the NYFW that she would not be bothered by the news media or, for that matter, anyone else.

33

And Who're *You* Wearing?

Eventually, Priscilla, Macy, and Ruth did get together to attend the dizzy whirl of the first public event of the New York Fashion Week.

The opening fashion show spotlighted designs by some of the biggest stars in the world of fashion: Sergeenko, Versace, Ferretti, Herpen, Scognamiglio, Dior, Schiaparelli, Pei, Mabille, Deacon, Mendel, Vauthier, Margiela, Aouadi, Saab, Gaultier, Viktor & Rolf, Valentino, Murad, van der Kemp, Givenchy, and Fendi. So many models!

At first, "Spectacular!" was all that Priscilla could say, but her attitude would shift considerably and fast.

At one point, she felt like she had turned into an automatic electric fan, turning her head to the right, then to the left, and then to the right again. No sooner had she seen one garment than another model appeared wearing something equally impressive. So Priscilla was uncertain whether her vertigo had set in or all that head-turning had simulated her discomfort. But that was also around the time when Ruth told her that NYFW was scheduled at different sites throughout the City and around the globe over the next *nine* days.

Yikes! she thought. *Nine days?* She supposed she must have been told that before, but now that she was in the thick of it, the prospect was not pleasing. Yet, she rather liked hearing that similar shows were happening simultaneously in other major cities such as Milan, London, Kyiv, Tokyo, Seoul, Paris, and Copenhagen.

Then they were off to the next event, which Vogue hosted. Priscilla learned the names of even more designers and what they were famous for, too. Thom Browne and Kate and Laura Mulleavy's "Rodarte Collection" were lacy and delicate with flashes of red lame. Jack McCollough and Lazaro Hernandez presented their "Proenza Schouler Collection," which was colorful and voluminous.

"Finally," Priscilla blurted out when she heard the name "Gaylord's Fashion House." As the handsome man promenaded down the runway and bowed, Priscilla, Macy, and Ruth were caught unawares as most of the other guests stood to their feet and applauded determinedly.

The three friends now understood how Gaylord had fitted into the fashion world. His colleagues and friends were mainly displaying their support for him as he and his family endured the ongoing investigations and criminal prosecutions regarding his twin brother's involvement in the theft, tampering, and forging of masterpieces, not to mention the allegations about all that extortion he and his father had committed, and over so many years, at that.

As it so happened, Macy remained standing and clapping her hands not only because she was pleased with Gaylord's collection but because she had wanted him to see she was there. Then, before she knew it, she shouted, "Bravo, Gaylord! Bravo!" But this time, although Gaylord did see Macy and even waved at her, Priscilla and Ruth stared at the once somewhat sedate Macy.

Then, Jonathan Saunders' classic updated wrap dresses showcased Diane von Furstenberg's approach, which apparently surprised onlookers at their "affordability." Priscilla smirked to herself. There was a word she had not heard much at these fashion shows.

Then came the Chanel models, whose designs Priscilla absolutely adored. "Bravo!" was all she said as she stood up and clapped for the first and last time that week.

By the final event on the ninth day of New York Fashion Week, Priscilla had had her fill of all of it. Her patience thinned; she grumbled at this and that, including the "bony" models. "My goodness," she kept saying, "Aren't they hungry? They're so skinny. Besides, who can fit into those doll clothes?" She was bored and restless, and she did not like being closed in and forced to sit for long periods. She longed for the work that remained to be done at her brownstone. She yearned to be back at her office, even doing paperwork. Oh, how she complained!

"How much more of this," she groused, "can one person take?" She did not care that she might be perceived as uncouth or even patronized as unaccustomed to such highbrow experiences. *Enough already.*

Macy and Ruth mostly kept quiet as they concentrated on soothing Priscilla. At one point, however, Ruth whispered to her, "All right, PJ. Here's how this works: it's not so much the *model's size*, all of whom are tall and 'bony,' as you put it, that matters. Instead, the focus is on the *garment* she wears. The models are chosen to embellish; no, really, it's to *spotlight* the garments. So try to see yourself in the garments. Forget about the models."

"I hear you, Ruth," Priscilla said, although the set of her jaw belied that she agreed with what Ruth had just said.

Then she said, "But when do we eat? I'm starving."

"This show ends in about fifteen minutes," Ruth said. "Can you hold on until then? And don't forget, we're dining with my folks at Per Se. It's a three-star Michelin restaurant. You'll love it! But remember, it's in the 100 block of Columbus Circle." Ruth mentioned the location to remind Priscilla that it would take a while to maneuver the traffic to get there.

Priscilla was not appeased. *Three Michelin stars*? What mattered to her was having to wait longer than she had expected to eat. It would take forever to get to Columbus Circle. She pouted: "'Per Se!' A restaurant? I thought we were heading to your parents' home." Then she muttered, "Ah, crap!" Although she had looked forward to meeting Ruth's parents, she had forgotten that that was *today*. She would have to try to be more gracious. She did not want to offend Ruth.

Unhappily, then, she noted the growing presence of those dreaded arts, entertainment, and fashion news reporters, all swarming around her. She hissed to Ruth and Macy, "Will this media frenzy ever end?" She remembered how much more she had enjoyed that "Special Edition" happening the previous week. Despite the presence of so many high-level dignitaries—including the vice president and First Lady Selena Hollingsworth—no media had been allowed. She reflected that, even though she had not been aware of the first lady's presence at the time, she supposed she should have guessed something to that effect because of the presence of so many Secret Service agents.

But Priscilla sighed. By way of contrast, the whole media mob was here today for the fashion extravaganza's closing events. Present was an entirely different group of celebrities, entertainers, artists, editors, and fashion designers. Nor did this group command the intense security that the vice president, the first lady, and the other high-ranking federal government officials of the previous week.

Macy grinned at Priscilla. Then she joked, "Well, PJ, that's the price of celebrity."

Ruth and Macy could not resist laughing out loud. They both were well aware that Priscilla did not appreciate the reporters following her. More often than not, she just wanted to enjoy herself like any other ordinary person. But Priscilla had long since been anything but ordinary.

As soon as the last models and designers had bowed, the audience rose to its feet and applauded, signaling the barrage of arts, entertainment, and fashion news reporters to surge toward celebrities.

They repeatedly tried but failed to ambush Priscilla. They waved microphones in her face as their cameras flashed and rolled.

"You have got to be kidding me," she said more than once as she kept eluding them. Priscilla had taken for granted how CF Agent Laverne Macon mainly had shielded her from the media during her time in Paris and Mykonos, especially onboard the yacht *Piraeus*. But Laverne was not at the NYFW event. So, Priscilla was on her own, dodging the arts, entertainment, and fashion industry media.

But then, one of the reporters called her out, "Not the illustrious P. J. *Austin*-Bernhardt! Surely you know *you're* newsworthy."

Priscilla did not respond. She just kept trying to weave away from the reporters. But then one of them stopped her in her tracks when he called out to her, "And who're *you* wearing?"

"*Me*?" Priscilla's eyebrows rose. "'Who am *I* wearing?' Well, my own clothes, that's 'who?'"

All around her, people laughed.

As the same reporter repeated his question, Ruth nudged her. "The designer, PJ. Tell him the name of the *designer* of your lovely pantsuit."

Priscilla gave in. She was tired, hungry, and fed up with fashion, but she resigned herself to an impromptu interview in front of the cameras. She would speak her truth, even if it shocked everyone, not just those around her but everyone watching the news feed on their televisions at home and elsewhere.

"Oh, this," She touched a lapel on her three-quarter-length, colorful, striped silk jacket. She was aware, too, that her tan high-waist pipe pants made her appear taller than her mere five-foot-five inches. She also wore tan leather high heel boots and carried a small matching handbag, not her overly-stuffed leather shoulder bag. This event was, after all, a fashion show. So she had dressed for it more carefully than was her habit. "Let's just call this a P.J. Austin original." Her smile widened.

But then she shocked the onlookers when she said, "I made it myself."

There were murmurs from the crowd.

One comment rose above the others: "Did you hear that? PJ said she made her own outfit."

Then Ruth, who had grown up in the rag trade, could not resist getting into the act. "PJ, let me see this jacket."

Priscilla obliged. When she removed her jacket, she revealed a simple high-collar, long-sleeve, crème-colored silk blouse that concealed the scars on her neck and right shoulder, which were hardly a secret to anyone who knew her well.

In an amazed tone of voice, Ruth said as she examined the jacket, "Look at all this detail … topstitching, slip stitching! And these sleeves are virtually seamless! And these buttonholes! And look at this, folks. The lining is as good quality as the outer fabric!" The cameras' lenses captured every detail as Ruth pointed out how well Priscilla's jacket had been made.

Priscilla said, "Well, what do you expect of people who can't afford to buy haute couture and high-end clothing?"

But many onlookers who knew the name "*Austin*-Bernhardt" were surprised that this newest member of New England aristocracy spoke so openly about her humble beginnings, at least by comparison to the Bernhardt billionaires. But Priscilla had been born and bred an *Austin*, which was still her foremost identity. She knew who and whose she was, and there was no shame in any of it, either. She let these fashionistas extoll her understated elegance, simplicity, and eye for good quality.

And, darn it, she was proud of how her mom had taught her how to sew. She said, "Pop by my place in Columbus, and I'll gladly show you my $100 Sears sewing machine and the Vogue pattern that I altered to make this outfit." Then she ran her hands across and up and down her sleek pipe pants to illustrate her point. She smiled in the cameras' lenses and posed like some of the models who placed their left hand on one hip while putting their right foot forward, and then she periodically shifted her weight, as she had watched the models do all week long.

Onlookers observed Priscilla's aura of confidence as she casually slid part of her left hand inside the corresponding hidden pants pocket, carefully gestured with her right hand, and continued expounding: "For the record, when I was young, my mom used to cut out patterns for my sisters and me from brown paper bags and newspapers. Then she'd lay the patterns on top of the fabric and cut to size each of our particular outfits. Then, she'd roll out her old Singer Sewing Machine, you know, the one with the foot pedal." Priscilla smiled, looked down, and tapped the floor with one of her stylish, fine-leather boots. "Momma also taught my sisters and me how to sew. As for this pantsuit, it took me a good three months to make it. Well, it would have taken less time, but we working girls do have our day jobs."

Then, when she said, "So, I take it you like what you see?" She tugged at the high collar on her crème-colored silk blouse, the only part of her outfit that was store-bought. But she was surprised at the onlookers' appreciation for what she had just described as "Oh, this."

After she had had fun surprising the onlookers and the viewers of the televised NYFW event with her acknowledgment that she'd made her outfit, she concluded with her customary, "Ta ta."

As the international arts, entertainment, and fashion news reporters all yelled more questions at her, Priscilla commenced her power walk—leaving Ruth and Macy behind—Ruth still holding her jacket.

Astounded, Ruth and Macy stood still, their mouths gaped open until they realized that Priscilla had already exited the scene. They hastened to catch up.

Priscilla was already outside, hailing a taxi to Per Se. Was she Elly May Clampett? PJ Austin? PJ *Austin*-Bernhardt? It really did not matter to her. Jacketless, she stood on the edge of the sidewalk and waited for her two friends to catch up with her. Nor did she fully realize that television viewers the world over had just learned something more about the already illustrious PJ *Austin*-Bernhardt.

Back inside the fashion extravaganza, fashion folks and other media representatives were still talking about her making her own clothes. "My God," many were saying, "PJ even makes her own clothes. Who would've thought?"

While Macy and Ruth elbowed their way toward the exit, they, too, were wondering what Priscilla would pull out of her rabbit's hat next. Neither still had any idea of Priscilla's extended résumé. Well, Macy had some idea.

Finally, the three women reunited on the sidewalk, where Ruth helped Priscilla once again don her now-famous and fabulous, home-sewn striped silk jacket. For, even though it was a mild, mid-September day, it was windy and a little chilly in New York City.

Meantime in the Midwest, Liza sat in the dining room of her modest dwelling in Sills Creek, watching the live streaming of the NYFW event on her small television. Priscilla's mother was sitting with Cousin Myrtle and some of their other relatives and friends. They laughed as Priscilla explained how she had made her outfit and how her mom had taught her and her siblings how to sew. Liza and Cousin Myrtle and some of their other relatives and friends especially liked Ruth's illustration of Priscilla's sewing finesse, as she showed onlookers the intricate details of the jacket and its lining.

Cousin Myrt said, "Seamstresses, fashion editors, and designers, eat your hearts out."

"That's right," Liza said. "Child, you keep telling the truth. Tell those highbrow rascals about how you learned to sew and to make whatever the rich and famous wear."

"And don't forget," chimed back in Cousin Myrt, "they pay plenty more money for their clothes than we pay." She smiled at Liza. "You sure raised Miss Prissy well. She's so proud of her humble roots and wants everybody to know it, too. I'm so happy our girl is still herself, you know, surrounded by all that wealth and all." Then as Cousin Myrtle hugged Liza, she watched her well up with tears and cover her mouth with her hands, as she always did to conceal her emotions.

Cathy sat on the sofa in her living room at her home in Cheyenne and laughed and cried tears of joy as she watched the same NYFW show on her television.

"That'll show 'em, Priscilla. But *why* is it so hard for some people to believe that not everybody changes their stripes when they come into money?" Then Cathy sighed in relief that her former college classmate was still "the same ole Priscilla."

When her husband Sleeter came into the room, he asked her what the matter was. He had heard her talking to someone or something that he now knew was the television.

"Oh, nothing, Sleeter," Cathy said. "Just watching Priscilla raise the eyebrows of some highbrows at that NYFW show in New York. That's all." Then she laughed again.

At Priscilla's home office in Columbus, Julia went into the dining room and uncovered the very Sears sewing machine that Priscilla had just referenced in her impromptu interview on television. The small, tabletop sewing machine sat on a small wooden rollout table in a corner, covered with a big, colorful beach towel. Julia had seen Priscilla sewing on the machine, so she knew her friend spoke the truth.

Julia also knew that Priscilla made some of her clothes, especially during her years in the Ohio Senate. Priscilla, she recalled, hated buying clothes that were poorly sewn. So whenever she saw an outfit that she liked in a store but that she thought was poorly made, she headed to the nearest Jo Ann Fabric Shop. There she would purchase a similar pattern, fabric, and notions to recreate the outfit herself.

Later that same day, when Julia received a call from Cheryl Tupper of the local CBS affiliate, she gladly allowed her to film the Sears sewing machine and some of Priscilla's patterns, too. Cheryl knew Priscilla well from her earlier interviews, including a "watch party" that Priscilla had hosted during the Democratic presidential primary, which Fleetwood Marshall Hollingsworth had eventually won.

At the afternoon interview, Julia told Cheryl that she remembered how Priscilla thought much like her mom, Liza, who once said, "Why pay full price for something that's poorly made?"

When the reporter left, Julia thanked God for keeping Priscilla so grounded. *Same ole Priscilla,* she said to herself with a smile.

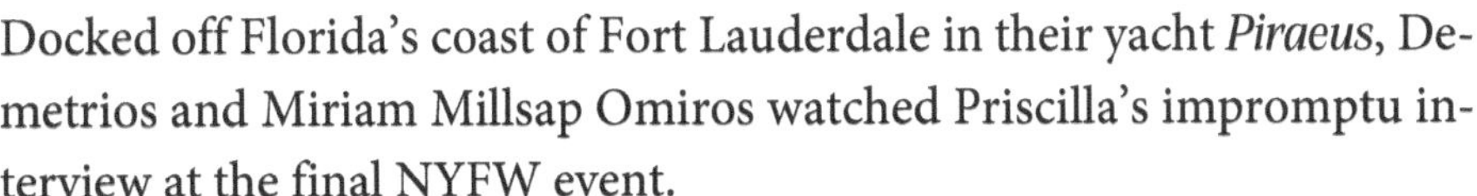

Docked off Florida's coast of Fort Lauderdale in their yacht *Piraeus*, Demetrios and Miriam Millsap Omiros watched Priscilla's impromptu interview at the final NYFW event.

"My, my," said Miriam. "I had no idea of that young woman's background. One would never know she comes from humble beginnings. But that outfit she has on is simply exquisite. I'm sure it puts some of those designers to shame. I wonder whose she is wearing today." Miriam assumed that some well-known designer must have altered what Priscilla was wearing during the interview.

Then Miriam paused and considered before she said, "Where's Gaylord? I wonder whether he even knows about PJ's skills as a seamstress. Ah heck! As a designer!"

Then, Demetrios stood between the television screen and his wife and said, "Now, Miriam, what, pray tell, are you up to?"

At their home in Bow Lake, Lady Chelsea, Father, Ramses, and Jamison watched Priscilla's impromptu interview at the fashion show. But it was Lady Chelsea who had the most to say.

"That young woman never ceases to amaze. I'm not surprised that she knew something about sewing, but I had no idea how talented she was. Can you believe this? And to think she's sharing that information on television and at the New York Fashion Week! Why, that's just not done. Does she have any idea about the impact of her words? Oh my!"

"Our favorite daughter-in-law," said Father, "just can't help it; she's so talented! From what she just said, some of the world's greatest designers are learning firsthand that an ordinary person alters their designs to suit her style. Surely she's not the only one doing it. How on Earth do you think poor and middle-class people do what they do, anyway? They copy the wealthy. It's been going on since the beginning of time. And, sometimes, the wealthy copy the poor and the middle-class folks, too. We all do it."

For whatever reason, Ramses changed that subject to another topic that was, in fact, weighing on his mind. "About her Cleopatra outfit." He paused, aware that sometimes even Father suggested that he was a tad obsessed with the Cleopatra costume and all things Egyptian at the masquerade ball. "I suggest we may have to rethink her Cleopatra costume."

"What's that you say, Ramses?" Father asked, somewhat perplexed by the sudden change in the conversation.

"We need to use the bigger, wider necklace and bodice."

"Why?" Lady Chelsea and Father both asked.

He hesitated a fraction of a second and then said, "You know, the scars on her neck and shoulder."

Father nodded. "Good thinking." Then they all stared from one to the other.

Nonchalantly, Lady Chelsea said, "Well, maybe we can improvise."

"Yeah, maybe," Father said in a similar nonchalant voice.

But as one, they frowned. They were all familiar with the alternate necklace and bodice that Ramses had suggested. It was lovely but would be too heavy for Priscilla, or anybody else, to wear for any length of time.

Then Ramses surprised them with what else was on his mind. "I think PJ has just landed herself another income stream. Her own fashion brand." Animated, he declared: "Someone is going to ask her to create a PJ Austin-Bernhardt brand. Soon, her clothes will be all the rage. They'll be seen on the same runways that she experienced for the first time these past nine days. Money-on-it."

As the others gradually caught the same wave that Ramses rode, Lady Chelsea and Father, and Jamison too, all looked at him and nodded in agreement.

"My goodness, Ramses," Lady Chelsea eventually said. "I think you're onto something."

So it was that Priscilla as if P. J. Austin-Bernhardt were not already a household name, was once again all the rage and about to face yet more media and public attention. If she thought she was sick and tired of all the media attention she was getting, she had no idea what was forthcoming. Poor Priscilla. So unassuming. She still did not see herself the way that so many other people saw her.

34

Oh, But You Really Should

Back on the curb outside the finale of the NYFW, three attractive and illustrious women piled into the backseat of the taxi and told the driver, in near unison, "Step on it!"

Ruth proceeded to give him directions and then added, "We've got reservations at Per Se, and they're not exactly waiting for us."

So the taxi driver—a real New Yorker—swung his left arm out of the window and signaled to oncoming traffic to yield and allow his entry. Rhythmically, he honked his horn in gratitude for the way that was made for him as he swerved his taxi into a momentary stream opening. In seconds, he was in the thick of the fast-moving, horn-honking, bumper-to-bumper New York City traffic.

Priscilla watched in fascination as the taxi driver leaned his head out his window and shouted what sounded like obscenities to some pedestrians who haphazardly wandered in front of his vehicle. Periodically, he took his hands off the steering wheel and made unpleasant gestures. He kept up his performance as rhetorically he asked, and then answered his own questions, defining the role of pedestrians, as well as the purpose of the streets:

"Where're you people from?"

"Ah, come on, folks, this is New York, not Disneyland!"

"Get-a-move-on-it!

"Streets are for vehicles, not *people*!"

"Get on the frigging crosswalks, you stupid idiots!"

And he kept honking his horn as the startled pedestrians moved away from the front of his vehicle.

Priscilla was so preoccupied with the taxi driver that she hardly listened to Ruth and Macy. But then she thought she overheard Ruth talking about something or someone.

"PJ, you know, you threw us for a loop when you told us that you made your own outfit. I had no idea you even knew how to sew."

"Yeah, well, whatever." Priscilla kept her attention fixed on the taxi driver.

Then, "PJ?" Ruth yelled, "Are you even listening to me?"

"Sort of. You see, Ruth, you, too, Mace." Priscilla did not even look at either of her friends when she said, "I'm thinking about hiring our driver, 'cause this is far more fun than a rollercoaster ride or even those fashion shows we just saw."

"PJ!" Macy exclaimed. "I've always known you to be a little weird, but joy-riding in a New York City taxi is *not* exactly something I find amusing. Are you *sure* you're okay?"

"Just hungry, ole buddy, ole pal. Just hungry," she said, and she said no more until the taxi driver stopped at 10 Columbus Circle.

A short time later, as the taxi pulled up to their stop, Priscilla wiggled to the edge of her seat to pay the taxi driver. But Macy pulled her back, as emphatically she declared: "Nothing doing, kiddo. I got this one. You may get your jollies off in taxi rides, but this is the cheapest date I'll ever have. This one's on me."

All three of the women roared in laughter.

The last one to get out, Priscilla slammed shut the taxi door and looked up and around. Taking in the impressive Time Warner Center, she decided that this would *be one delightful evening.*

But this rendezvous was to meet Ruth's parents, so she took the lead as the threesome walked inside the stately building and followed her to the elevator. "This way, ladies," Ruth said. "Per Se is on the top floor." Then she turned to Macy and asked, "Been here before?"

"Once," Macy said. Then, with a big grin, she said, "Ruth, your folks sure know how to enjoy themselves." With three Michelin stars, Per Se ranked as one of the City's finest dining establishments.

Priscilla smiled because she now knew for a certainty—or so she thought—that she would enjoy her night out. But Priscilla was also about to experience a significant bonus that would link her even closer to Ruth. She already knew that she and Macy were both daughters who had been raised like sons and who had both been closely bound to their father and at the end of this evening, she would understand that Ruth was cut from the same cloth.

As the elevator opened, Jacob Steiner, a handsome man of medium height and build with a full head of neatly trimmed black hair, stood a comfortable distance from the elevators, eagerly waiting for his daughter and her two new friends to appear. When the three women stepped out of their elevator, Priscilla and Macy watched as Ruth ran to her father's waiting embrace.

Then, Jacob turned to Priscilla and Macy and gave each of them a warm cheek-to-cheek. He looked the two women over and smiled at both as if he were pleased with what he saw. "Welcome, young ladies," he said. "Thank you for all the joy you bring to my beloved Ruth."

Before Priscilla and Macy could react to Jacob's warm welcome, the maître d' led Jacob and Ruth—who were arm in arm—along with Priscilla and Macy, to the Steiner's table.

He seated the three friends on one side of the table, facing what appeared to be most, or maybe all, of the multigenerational Steiner family. Ruth started introducing her two friends, but her mother interrupted her when she said, "Oh, Ruth, the illustrious PJ *Austin*-Bernhardt needs no introduction. Ms. Austin-Bernhardt, I'm Eloise, Ruth's mother." Eloise Steiner wore little makeup, just enough to highlight an already attractive face, and her blond-colored hair was long, neatly curled at its end. She nodded in the direction of her family, beginning with her husband, who Priscilla and Macy had already met. Then, "To my right is our eldest, Joseph," who strongly resembled his father, though noticeably taller. Cheerfully, he nodded at the two women. "To his right, our youngest, Mary Steiner Rosenberg," who wore her makeup and colored hair like her mother, "and her husband, Benjamin," who stood out with his naturally blond hair and bore the resemblance of the staunch Wall Street broker that he was; stiffly, Mary and Benjamin both nodded as one at Priscilla and Macy as well. So, like Priscilla, Ruth was also a middle child.

"And?" Eloise Steiner paused significantly.

"I'm Macy." She smiled. "Macy Stoner."

"Ah, yes, Ms. Stoner," said Eloise Steiner as she seemed to emit a sour taste while simultaneously squinting her nose with an uppity air.

"You're that defense attorney everyone's going on about, representing those twin scoundrels who stole art from the Jew—"

Jacob cut his wife off before she finished her sentence. "Eloise, darling. You promised. No politics tonight."

Almost immediately, Priscilla jumped to a conclusion. *So that's why we're not dining at The Modern.* Also, Michelin-starred, The Modern was located at the Metropolitan Museum of Modern Art. *The ole bat has a burr up her—.*

After that not-so-subtle reminder from her husband, Mrs. Steiner refocused her attention on Priscilla. "So-o, Ms. Austin-Bernhardt—"

Immediately, and without apology, Priscilla corrected her.

"PJ, please. Call me, 'PJ.' And would it be inappropriate of me to ask that we dispense with formalities?" She said that because she sensed the Steiners were a family that projected greater social status than they actually possessed, especially the matriarch. But imagine her surprise when Mrs. Steiner accepted her request to tap down the formalities.

"Then, 'PJ,' it is."

The drinks waiter, it seemed to Priscilla, timed his appearance just right. She thought that everyone at the dinner table, except for Mrs. Steiner, already wanted to change the subject to something more pleasant, even this early in the evening.

Priscilla ordered a Tanqueray and tonic water with a twist of lime, but then she amended her order. "Make that a double. I'm going to need it." She felt Macy kicking her ankle. But Priscilla first looked into Mrs. Steiner's cold eyes and noticed what appeared to be a fake smile on her face. Then she thought, *Why the hell invite us to dinner in the first place?*

Then Ruth's brother Joseph, whose wife was noticeably absent, asked Priscilla what she thought about the NYFW, adding that he had seen her television interview. "You seemed so annoyed with the media and the cameras," he said, "except during your stellar performance about how you made your outfit. But I have to say, and you looked darn good in it. My wife even said it was 'to die for.'"

Priscilla was not the only one at the dinner table to notice his mother's disapproval for complimenting her on her outfit. But she, for one, was not about to ignore the developing dynamic.

"For starters, Joseph," she began, "I was a wee bit undone because your darling sister Ruth had led me to believe that NYFW was a *one*-day event. Then again, I might have misunderstood from the start."

Priscilla sat back and observed the astonished expressions at the dinner table, except for Ruth and Macy. But then all the Steiners, except for their matriarch, laughed mildly, as they seemed to understand what a dry sense of humor Priscilla had. Why, even Mary and Benjamin relaxed a tad more.

Then Priscilla continued: "Why, I had no idea how elaborate and extensive the NYFW was. But, overall," she said with a big grin on her face, "I have to admit, I absolutely loved it.'"

But Joseph asked her again, "And the media frenzy?"

"As for that lot," Priscilla said, again with a big grin, "even a PR girl sometimes tires of cameras and reporters." She smiled at Joseph, who laughed aloud.

His sister Mary picked up where her brother left off. "PJ, about your open admission to altering designer patterns?"

In her response, Priscilla reverted to what might aptly be called "playing the dozens."

"Sue me," she snapped, and in a sharp tone of voice, at that. Then she quickly realized that the Steiners were hardly familiar with her personality. So she said, "Or not." She smiled at Mary to take some of the sting away by letting her know that she was joshing her.

Just then, two waiters appeared. Once again, Priscilla and some of the others seated at the dinner table felt rescued. One waiter began his spiel while the other one passed out menus.

While everyone studied their menus, Priscilla felt Macy nudging her arm. As she leaned over, Macy said in a near whisper, "Brace yourself, kiddo; we're in for a bumpy ride."

Priscilla smiled and pretended to wipe her mouth with her cloth napkin. Then she ordered a house specialty called "Rib-eye of Elysian Fields Farm's Lamb," which came with fancy fixings. She enjoyed her meal, which was comparable to the cuisine she had eaten onboard the yacht *Piraeus*.

However, as the evening progressed, it became ever so clear to her that Mrs. Steiner was none too pleased with Ruth's employment at P. J. Austin and Associates, Incorporated. At one point, she said, "Why, my Ruth, well, she can handle that incompetent Shane Carpenter's job in her sleep." Then, she further unleashed her disapproval when she said, "All those years of studying and training in art and archeology, and my daughter is working in a *PR* firm, of all places."

But Priscilla did not leap back into the fray. She'd already surmised that her profession, and perhaps her lifestyle, too, were hardly on Eloise Steiner's A-list. So Priscilla had resolved to enjoy this delicious meal, to ignore her hostess, and to confine her comments to the occasional, "Oh, this lamb is so tasty." However, she noted that her bland reaction seemed to infuriate the already disgruntled Eloise Steiner even more.

Eventually, when he had had his fill of his wife's rudeness to the very guests whom she herself had asked Ruth to invite, Jacob intervened. He said to their two guests, "You see, PJ and Macy, my wife is of the tradition that children should follow in the footsteps of their parents, in our case, the garment business. She can't seem to accept the fact that some things in this world have changed." Then, he paused and asked Priscilla, "So, young lady, how do *your* parents feel about your career?"

Before Priscilla answered, she caught the attention again of the passing drinks waiter by lightly tapping her cocktail glass. Then she said, "Unlike Ruth, I got a different kind of pressure from my folks. My mom wanted me to go into business, but Momma never specified what *kind* of business. So, when I started my PR firm, she didn't criticize me. But I think she was, and remains, baffled over what I actually do. As for Daddy, well, he always spoke of 'the noble profession of teaching.' Then, shortly before he died, he openly pleaded with me, 'Be happy, child. It would please both your mom and me if you started living your life to please yourself.'"

Priscilla looked around the table. She could not help noticing a certain calmness had set in—much calmer than the first half-hour or so of the dinner. Then she held her gaze steady on the hostess. "You know something, Mrs. Steiner? For a very long time, all I ever did was whatever I *thought* pleased my parents. That was because of the way they had raised me. Then, shortly before Daddy died, he changed what I called 'the dialogue,' so I was at a loss. But I eventually found my way."

Her voice rose as she spoke with more resolve.

"Mrs. Steiner, I am so sorry that you disapprove of Ruth's working with me at my PR firm. But if only you could see her there—not just the high quality of her work but how she seems to enjoy it."

This time it was Ruth who kicked Priscilla's other ankle. But given Ruth's utter silence as the evening unfolded, Priscilla suddenly had an important insight: Ruth's closeness to her father disheartened her mother, and her own apparent distance from Ruth, and maybe Mrs. Steiner also regretted that she herself did not possess the depth of influence that her husband had on their daughter. So perhaps Ruth's silence throughout much of the evening had been a sign of respect for her mom, not disapproval. Social etiquette aside, Priscilla threw her head back and pretty much poured the fresh gin and tonic that the waiter had just brought her into her mouth. It seemed to her, too, that maybe at the heart of this, Ruth's mother resented the fact that her daughter loved her father more than she loved her. It was not so hard, after all, for Priscilla to come to that conclusion. For, both she and Macy had once loved their fathers more than they had loved their mothers. Priscilla felt an actual pang of sympathy for Eloise Steiner.

But to Priscilla's surprise, what appeared to be a genuine smile softened Mrs. Steiner's face. *Apparently, she's accepted my olive branch.*

Just as quickly, she noticed things turned sour again, as Mrs. Steiner turned on Macy and once again questioned her role in the Met's art forgery case.

Oh, no!

But Priscilla also noticed that this time, Macy was ready for her adversary.

Macy cleared her throat.

"Mrs. Steiner," she began, "I'll be blunt. Unlike Girlfriend, here," she pointed to Priscilla, "I don't have the liberty to even comment on cases in litigation. But I do empathize with your disdain for anyone who has stolen artwork from Jews, especially those of you who suffered the ravages of World War II. But this is America, where *everyone* is entitled to equal protection of the law and due process. So, please, Mrs. Steiner, I don't want to spoil the evening quibbling over politics, PR, or law, for that matter." Then, deftly, she changed the subject and caught Mrs. Steiner completely unaware when she said, "Incidentally, Mrs. Steiner, I was so looking forward to you telling us about *your* work with some of the designers at the NYFW."

But Macy's gambit may have been too little, too late. At that point, the dinner party had been dying for over an hour and a half.

But just then, another waiter rolled in a tall cart filled with eye-catching scrumptious desserts.

Right on time, they all must have thought.

That Priscilla no longer cared what Mrs. Steiner or anyone else thought about her was most evident when finally she said, "Oh, but I really shouldn't."

But she had no idea how refreshing the others found her, especially when, in near unison, they all said, "Oh, but you really should."

So it was, despite Priscilla and Macy's best efforts to salvage the night, in the end, it was the scrumptious desserts that left a sweet taste to the dinner party.

A day or so later, Priscilla met Macy for breakfast at the diner near her Fifth Avenue office. The two friends laughed as they chewed over their time with the Steiners at Per Se.

"My goodness," Macy said, "How on Earth does Ruth put up with her awful mother? She's such a bitter woman."

"Yes, I know, but Mace, has it occurred to you that her mom is expressing frustration over Ruth's apparent closeness to her father?"

"What do you mean?"

"Well, didn't you notice how close Ruth and her father were? And there's certainly not a lot of affection between mother and daughter, at least, none that I could see."

Macy met Priscilla's eyes. "Maybe. Now that you mention it."

"Besides, Girlfriend," Priscilla explained, "Ruth is already doing what pleases her in life, and I think that's what has her mom so riled. It has nothing to do with her work at my firm; Mrs. Steiner wants Ruth at Steiner Clothiers, where she can wield her influence on her daughter. That's the crux of *her* problem."

As Macy thought about what Priscilla had just said, she nodded: "Yes, now I get it." Macy had taken her own taut bond with her father for granted, which was what Priscilla had spent most of her life doing, until the other night at Per Se when she noticed the implications of Ruth's similar bond with her father, Jacob.

The friends shared a look.

Then Macy said out loud what they both were thinking, "We have more in common with Ruth than I thought."

35

Another of Life's Seemingly Unbearable Circumstances

It seemed to Priscilla that the last two weeks in September passed just as quickly as the first two weeks had raced by. But September would end dramatically different than what she had anticipated. What was remarkable about this particular day was that Carlton had popped by the Harlem brownstone, which was the first time Priscilla had seen him there since she had signed the papers to buy the property.

Priscilla was pleasantly surprised when she looked up and saw that handsome husband of hers standing on the threshold of the living room in their Harlem brownstone dining room. Carlton had been socked in for some time working on high-level crisis after crisis at his desk in Washington, D.C. Yet here he was! What was especially telling, he showed up in ready-to-work attire: a tattered old Harvard College sweatshirt and blue jeans and sneakers.

"All right, Missy, Carlton Elliott reporting to duty." That, he said, as he raised his right hand to his forehead as if saluting her.

In marked contrast to her customary black pantsuits or that striking striped silk jacket that she'd worn to the finale of the NYFW, she wore a favorite gray sweatshirt that bore an image of ivy encircling the seal of her beloved Livingstone College; its sleeves cut off above her elbows. Her bleached denim blue jeans had holes long ago cut out to resemble age. Brown leather sandals covered her feet. Priscilla felt comfortable sporting such attire. She had been leaning over a box of sconces when, at the sight of her darling Carlton, she'd stopped unpacking, ran to him, and hugged him ever so tightly.

Carlton could not recall when last he had seen Priscilla so happy. Moved by her display of emotion, "Say, what gives?" he asked, aware that she was also not known for public displays of her affection, at least not as freely as she had just done.

She grinned. "You'd think I'd be used to our time apart from each other. But for some reason, this time, I really missed you."

"Me, too, Missy." But just after he planted a warm wet kiss on her lips, they both heard someone, or something, moving about and somewhere close.

"Uh, oh!" Priscilla said, aware of who that might be. "I suppose I need to introduce you to the new love in my life." She loosened herself from Carlton's embrace.

"Hey, there," she called out loud enough for her young friend to hear her in the kitchen or somewhere else close, probably playing with his toys. She waited for a moment.

Sure enough, Jules sauntered in from the kitchen. He was dragging his big Snoopy stuffed animal that Priscilla had given him but had left his trains and trucks on the kitchen floor.

"Carlton Elliott, meet Jules McCorkle. Jules, this is Carlton."

Jules stared at the tall, handsome man wearing his long, wavy black hair in a ponytail.

Then, to Priscilla, Jules turned and said, "Ah, come on, Beautiful Lady. You told me I was your 'main man.' Who's *he*?"

Priscilla smiled, conscious that she did not want to hurt this young man whose life had left him so vulnerable.

"Why, Jules, you're still my 'main man.' But Carlton Elliott…. Well, he's my husband."

Jules considered, sighed, but then tried to match her smile. "All right, then," he said. "I suppose I can try to live with that."

Then he addressed Carlton: "But do you *treat* her good?"

"Oh, Son, I sure do. I do indeed, and thanks for asking." Formally he extended his hand. "Pleased to meet you, too, 'main man.'" Carlton had always been good with kids and knew enough to keep this first encounter light. And he noticed immediately why Priscilla had been so drawn to this lad. Jules was well-behaved and smart. He possessed street-savvy, too. But, maybe, most of all, he reminded Carlton of a younger version of Priscilla's favorite nephew, Germane. No wonder his wife had taken to him. A shiver of pain coursed through him. What was going to happen today would hurt her so much. The boy, too. Carlton had tried hard to avert it, but he had failed. As a man, as a husband, this would be one of those rare, if not first, times that he would be unable to protect her.

"All right, then," Jules said. But uncertainly, he looked into Carlton's troubled eyes and then quickly withdrew his hand.

Carlton was perceptive enough to guess that, for whatever reasons and circumstances of his life, Jules seemed at this moment to be feeling jealous and maybe even possessive of Priscilla. So he prepared to head upstairs on the pretense of helping Mr. Hunter and his crew. He thought that his wife and Jules could use some time to sort all this out. And to be honest, he could use that time as well.

But before he left, he told Jules, "Let me know when you two are ready for a bite to eat."

As Carlton went upstairs, Jules retreated to the kitchen. With a small sigh, Priscilla resumed unpacking her household treasures. She had hoped that Jules might want to talk to her more, but she respected his apparent need to be alone with his Snoopy and toy trains and trucks. Without the two of them even talking about this, she had understood that he could not take his toys home for fear that his mom and her boy-friend would sell the toys for cash to buy drugs. Yet Priscilla had taken solace in the fact that Jules had trusted her enough to tell her at least the truth about his mother. Yet he still always defended her, "My mom's a *good* woman," he would say: "Honest, she is."

An hour or so passed before Carlton came back downstairs and told Priscilla that he was intending to treat her and Jules to "a real home-cooked meal." Then he looked at Jules and added, "But no McDonalds' today, 'main man.' Today, I'm taking you and Beautiful Lady to a res-taurant that I like called 'Sylvia's.' Got that?"

Jules quickly consented. "Got it?" He had heard talk about how good and how expensive this Sylvia's was, and, now, he would have brag-ging rights with most of the other youngsters in the neighborhood, not to mention some of the adults who had never before dined at the restau-rant, or so he thought.

And so it was that Carlton took Priscilla and Jules to Sylvia's, where they actually enjoyed themselves. Priscilla liked the food, and Carlton liked the camaraderie of the restaurant's warm and inviting ambiance.

As for Jules, well, Priscilla had never before seen him smile as much as he did this day. She noticed him staring primarily at black men and women, coming and going and treating one another with kindness. She doubted he had seen much of that from the men in his mother's life.

"I like it here," he said more than once to Priscilla.

Carlton, meantime, wrestled with himself, even as he played the generous and fatherly host. Was now the time to prepare Priscilla for what was about to happen? But the child was here, listening.

So it was that Carlton missed what he had thought of as his opportunity to prepare his wife for impending heartbreak. In growing anguish, he saw what Onslow and Mr. Hunter had told him about the close bond that Priscilla and the youngster had developed. But time was passing, and when he kept checking his watch, Priscilla became annoyed.

"All right, Carlton, I should have known. We're imposing. Listen, if you've got something else to do, or someplace else to go—"

"Oh, Missy, no. I'm so sorry to have annoyed you. And you are not, nor will you ever be, an 'imposition' in my life. But I do need to step out a minute if you don't mind."

After Carlton "stepped out" of the restaurant, he punched in the telephone number on his cellular phone to someone who he did not want Priscilla or Jules to know about just yet. A moment later, he said, "Still at Sylvia's. But it might take another fifteen minutes before we return to our brownstone." Then, he seemed to plead with this person on the other end of the line: "We agreed, not in the restaurant. Back at the house." For confirmation, he asked, "That's not going to be a problem, is it?"

The woman on the other end answered, "Fifteen minutes, max. I've already violated one too many protocols, especially since you're not even a legal custodian of the child."

Carlton nodded and felt a minuscule measure of relief. "Great."

But then the woman continued: "Fifteen minutes, Mr. Bernhardt. Our men and the NYPD are already on the street, so I guess I need to alert them. Fifteen minutes and counting."

"Thank you for understanding," Carlton said before disconnecting the call.

Back inside the restaurant, Priscilla said to him, "Well, that didn't take long. Hope everything's all right."

"Yeah, Bro'," Jules echoed. "'Hope everything's all right.'"

Priscilla beamed at the child. The thought struck her that he sounded like a young Germane. That was her first conscious thought of that comparison.

"We're cool," Carlton said, forcing a smile he almost choked over his lie. But then he considered that actually, he had not lied. He had done the best that he could. The child would be safe. And who knows? Maybe eventually, Jules could somehow be a permanent part of his and Priscilla's lives. So he said, "You two twerps good to go?"

"*Twerps*? Who you calling a 'twerp?'" Yet Jules was grinning. "Besides, I'm the 'main man.'"

"Alright, 'main man,'" Carlton said. Then, he nearly welled up with tears. This was a friendly kid. No wonder Priscilla loved him.

The three of them headed back to the brownstone where, just as they were about to walk up the steps to the front door, a dull gray sedan with New York state-issued license tags pulled up to the curb. Carlton was ever so conscious of what was about to happen. He watched some of the neighbors peering out their windows and others pausing and staring as they walked down the street, many of whom were all so familiar with the vehicles driven by the borough's agency for children's services. But not Priscilla, nor Jules, either.

Oblivious to what was about to happen, Priscilla unlocked the front door, and Jules scampered inside the brownstone ahead of her.

Like clockwork, a black woman and two white men dressed in professional attire emerged from the dull gray sedan and waited on the sidewalk until two NYPD officers joined them.

And, still standing on the stoop outside the brownstone's front door, Carlton raised his right hand in what looked like a pleading gesture. He wanted a moment to tell Priscilla and Jules what to expect. But nothing doing.

The Harlem Division of the Borough of Manhattan's Children's Protective Services official shook her head, which indicated "no." She was the one who Carlton had spoken to on his cell phone outside Sylvia's Restaurant, and she'd already cautioned him that she had breached one too many protocols. At that, and with so many other officers present, she had no choice but to approach the front door and demand custody of the child.

While she, her two department officers, and the two policemen advanced up the steps, Carlton ducked inside and ran into the dining room.

Jules had already returned to the kitchen, picked up his Snoopy, and was framed in the dining-room door.

Priscilla, meanwhile, was bent over a crate about to continue unpacking her sconces. But something in the air caused the hairs on the back of her neck to stand up.

Almost simultaneously, Priscilla and Jules both looked up and stared at Carlton, who had turned ashen. Then she and Jules both looked in alarm at each other. At that very moment, it was clear to both of them that what they had both feared most, down deep inside—but had never broached—was just about to happen.

Priscilla flushed. Her gorge rose; she swallowed hard to keep it down.

Jules squeezed one of Snoopy's overstuffed arms. The youngster's face seemed to swell, even as his own little eyes squinted shut as if he did not want to see what he knew was coming. Then his mouth gaped open, but no sound came out.

Priscilla straightened up and stepped across the threshold to her newly renovated living room. She saw strangers and police officers entering her home.

Jules ran to her. He grabbed her hand, and with his free hand, he clutched Snoopy to his chest. His eyes bulged.

Neither he nor Priscilla could find their voice. Their dread rose and rose.

Vaguely they heard Carlton pleading: "Oh, Missy, Son, I just didn't have the heart to tell you. I'm so sorry. I tried—"

But neither Priscilla nor Jules could tear their eyes away from the professionally-attired black woman and the uniformed police officers.

Then one of the policemen asked, "Are you Mrs. Priscilla Austin-Bernhardt?"

"Yes," she managed to say.

The officer handed her some papers and said, "Since you're not the legal custodian of young Jules McCorkle, and since his mother is no longer in her home, and also no longer his legal guardian pending further court action…. By the powers invested in me, by the State of New York and the Borough of Harlem in Manhattan, I declare that you must surrender one Jules McCorkle or face—"

"*Hold it*," ordered the woman from the children's services agency. So far as she knew, Priscilla was wholly unaware that Jules' mother had not been home for the past three days and that that fact had been reported to her agency. According to affidavits from neighbors on the street, she also knew that Priscilla had shown only love and support for young Jules. She indeed showed no indication of kidnapping the child or doing anything else that might be construed as criminal. Oh, but she knew more.

Like anyone who followed the news, the woman from the children's services agency was familiar with one P. J. Austin-Bernhardt's high profile. Like most people who knew of her, she also knew that Priscilla was a woman of understated elegance, someone who was formidable, too. But the woman before her was anything but any of that. For, the woman before her appeared to be just like any ordinary woman, casually dressed, even getting her hands dirty, as it were, renovating a fixer-upper. Mostly though, the woman before her seemed undone, hurt, bewildered, and at a loss for words.

At that revelation, the woman from the children's services agency said, "Officer, I suggest that we desist from the formalities."

The policeman locked his eyes with hers and emitted what could only be described as a growl. But then he nodded, took a step back, and said no more.

The woman from the children's service agency was a licensed social worker and had a kind heart. She spoke gently: "Ms. Austin-Bernhardt, I realize all this must come as a shock to you. But our agency is responsible for the general welfare of children, and since you're *not* Jules's legal custodian, he cannot stay here with you. Do you understand me so far?"

Still utterly perplexed, Priscilla did not utter a word. But as she tightened her steady grip on Jules' trembling hand, she did manage to nod her head.

"OK then," said the woman from the agency. "Now, may I ask you to release your hold of the child's hand so that we might take custody of him? I promise you; he'll be all right." She exuded genuine compassion for what was ostensibly a most troubling situation for Priscilla, who held the child's hand so tightly.

But when Priscilla did not budge, the woman shared more than she had intended to convey. "We have found a perfect, temporary foster home for Jules, and I can assure you that you and your husband *will* have visiting privileges. *Now*, do you understand why we're here and what's going to happen?"

The two women stared at each other for a terrible, long while.

What Priscilla did not know was that today's authorities' visit resulted from Mamie McCorkle's disappearance and CF Agent Onslow's ongoing protective surveillance of Priscilla's safety and—in the last week or so—of Jules's safety as well. Onslow had called Carlton in Washington to tell him that Mamie McCorkle had disappeared several days earlier and that Jules had been on his own in that house. Carlton, after intense soul-searching, had informed the Children's Protective Services Agency of the situation at the McCorkle residence. At that point, the agency had decided to take custody of Jules and place him into at least temporary foster care. And although Carlton had tried hard to arrange for him and Priscilla to assume custody of the child, the agency had refused: the Bernhardt couple had not been authorized in the system as potential foster parents, and, all of the money in the world, and all of that Bernhardt prominence, had not been enough to cut through all of that New York State red tape—at least not on such short notice. The most that Carlton had been able to accomplish was visiting privileges for the couple with the foster parents. So it was that his reason for showing up at the Harlem brownstone that morning had been to warn Priscilla, to soften the blow, as it were, and to comfort her. Yet, despite his best intentions, he had been unable to lessen her heartbreak with a last-minute warning. Nevertheless, he told himself, at least he had succeeded in being there. But in the end, he had been helpless to do anything to make it all the better for his Miss Prissy.

Finally, Priscilla looked away. When she found her voice a few moments later, it cracked. "I un- understand." She leaned down to Jules, who continued standing there trembling but still speechless. Priscilla had managed to balance herself, so she was as close as she could be to him. Tears that had pooled in her eyes poured down her cheeks. She tried to reassure him, and maybe herself as well.

"Jules. Oh, Jules, my friend. God is with you as He is always with me. As soon as you get settled into your new place, I mean, your new home, I'm coming to see you. I'll even beg your foster parents for weekend and holiday privileges."

At that, Carlton, the woman from the agency, and the policemen, too, all looked from one to the other. This weeping woman obviously had not heard a word the woman from the agency had just said to her about visiting privileges. She was too upset and in too much pain.

As was Jules.

All the while his Beautiful Lady had been talking to him, Jules's small body trembled as he continued staring at her in apparent shock.

As for Carlton, he stood by seemingly helpless and praying to God to give him the wherewithal to heal his darling Miss Prissy's broken heart and maybe their own relationship.

Then, one of the men from the Children's Services Agency picked Jules up. The child's lanky little legs kicked and kicked.

His powerful voice wailed and wailed at the top of his lungs. "No-o-o-o-o!" But he would not let loose Snoopy.

Nor did he lose eye contact with Priscilla as she walked behind him and the policeman who carried him outside and down the steps to the dull gray sedan. Even though Priscilla had tried to reach out and touch the wailing child, the policeman carrying him moved too fast for her to catch up.

Her cracked voice continued: "Think of me, Jules, when you kiss Snoopy 'good-night.' And Jules, I'll look in on your mom and keep you informed of her progress."

Again, the others looked at one another. In this, too, Priscilla clearly did not understand what had happened. She thought Mamie must still be at home, but Mamie had already been taken into custody for child neglect.

The more Carlton witnessed Priscilla's and Jules's parting, the more he realized how closely the two had bonded. Yet, at that very moment, he was reminded of one of the opening songs in *The Phantom of the Opera* when Christina sang, "Think of me." He felt an unswallowable lump in his throat.

At that point, Mr. Hunter and Onslow watched as Carlton suddenly stood still. He seemed to them to be in a trance. Carlton felt the hairs standing up on the back of his neck and down his spine. He envisioned the Earth crumbling under his feet, swallowing him up, or someone close to him. But he could not make out the other person's face. All he knew was that he was helpless, more so than now. He shuddered. When he came back to himself, he sensed someone staring—not at Miss Prissy and Jules—but rather at him.

"Carlton, man," said Onslow, "you look like you saw a ghost."

"I believe I did." But somehow, Carlton knew that whoever that "ghost" was was not present among them now. Then, just as quickly, those morbid thoughts disappeared, down deep into the recesses of his mind, for some time to come.

And so it was that Carlton experienced his own reckoning about how powerless he truly was in this situation—and one yet to come. He was a member of an elite military intelligence cadre that helped put down terrorists and narcotics dealers around the globe. But with something seemingly as simple as obtaining custody of this vulnerable child, he suddenly confronted his own helplessness. This instance, too, was the first time that he had been unable to give his wife her heart's desire; and this was also one of the first times since her father had died that Priscilla had no one, absolutely no one, to give her what she thought she had wanted most in the world. And even though Carlton loved Priscilla with all his heart, he knew her faults as well as her strengths. Some might still call her spoiled and maybe even self-centered, although she was perhaps just still accustomed to having things her way. Yet, even with all that Bernhardt wealth and all those prominent people that he and Priscilla both knew, it seemed that nobody could have intervened and stopped what had just happened. In his anguish, he thought: *My poor Miss Prissy!* She was only maybe beginning to realize that there were some things that money, prominence, and popularity could not buy. Oh, how Carlton's heart ached for his Miss Prissy.

With tenderness, he felt his wife's pain. With love, he distressed over her puffy, red, weeping eyes. Carlton was most of all so very sorry that even he was unable to rescue the young man whose little hands and little arms—and Snoopy's, too—stretched as far as they could, in a vain effort to reach his Beautiful Lady.

He watched as, inside that dull gray sedan, Jules wailed, "Beautiful Lady, help me! Please, don't let them take me!"

He turned his attention back to Priscilla.

Mutely, Priscilla stood on the sidewalk outside her front door. All she could think was: *A nightmare.* Then, *Surely, this is the Twilight Zone.* Waves of guilt swept through her. She felt so despondent, so dejected. If this indeed were another of life's seemingly unbearable circumstances, then this one for sure she did not wish to bear.

Meanwhile, Carlton kept trying to reach out to Priscilla, but something kept telling him, *Don't you dare*. In fact, something in the air was telling everyone else not to touch her, either. So no one dared touch her, not the woman from the children's services agency nor the police officers, not even Onslow or Mr. Hunter.

As that dull gray sedan drove away—Jules wailing inside—the sound of Jules's wailing trailed off. Priscilla grew dizzier and dizzier. The Earth seemed to open up beneath her. She wanted to cry, but no tears came out of her now bone-dry eyes. She tried to scream, but her vocal cords were clogged. She tried praying out loud, "God help me!" Yet, at that very moment, it seemed to Priscilla as if God were telling her that this was one thing she could not have. *But why, God? Why are You doing this to me?* That scream was silent because she had lost her voice. Then, in one last feeble attempt, she stretched her hands towards the heavens and tried to get God's attention again; but nothing doing, or so she thought.

The next thing she knew, she was looking up from the sidewalk on which she lay prone. Although everything was blurry, she did not see the dull gray sedan anymore; it was gone. She did, however, see people standing around her, staring down at her, and talking about her in the third person:

"There, now, she's back with us."

"I thought she'd had a heart attack or something."

"Man alive, I didn't think she'd take it so hard."

As slowly she revived, Priscilla vaguely recognized the faces she knew: Carlton, Onslow, Mr. Hunter, and some of her neighbors who she would soon learn had made favorable reports to the children's protective services agency workers about her relationship with Jules McCorkle. For a few moments more, she would, however, remain entirely oblivious as to why she had fainted in the first place.

Although she would eventually recover from the trauma of watching this child, who she had grown to love, being taken away by the Harlem Division of the Borough of Manhattan's Children's Protective Services Agency, for now, the pain was unbearable. But there was one silver lining. Some of Priscilla's and Carlton's neighbors had never before experienced a situation where someone from outside had come into their neighborhood and done something for the good of those who lived there. As a result, some of these same neighbors had already warmed to her, as evidenced in their affidavits to the Borough of Manhattan's Children's Protective Services Agency.

But for the time being, all was most certainly not well. Carlton—and the neighbors, too—rightly understood that now was not the time to try to talk Priscilla into accepting this situation, if only temporarily. So they—all of them, Carlton, too—let her sulk and fume and suffer, which she did for a very long time.

36

Ship My Belongings, Such as They Are

Priscilla's heart hardened, something that had not happened in years. She lost herself in minutia and also lost her dry sense of humor. She rarely smiled or talked about pleasant things to her family and friends, including Julia, Ruth, Macy, Laverne, Alfrieda, and "the boys."

Mainly, her changed demeanor impacted her relationship with Carlton. Where once they enjoyed lots of merriment and passionate lovemaking, Priscilla grew cold and indifferent. Making matters worse, she would not even talk to him about what had happened with Jules; and it would be sometime later before she'd learn about how hard Carlton had tried to avert the hurt that he had feared would devastate his Miss Prissy, which eventually was what happened.

In the middle of October, Priscilla and Carlton prepared to attend another regularly scheduled meeting of the Bernhardt Foundation for Boarding Schools for Zimbabwean and South African Girls.

But before the couple departed, Carlton placed separate calls to Liza, Julia, and Lady Chelsea. He wanted to talk about what he had come to characterize as "a most disturbing situation with Miss Prissy and me."

Carlton reflected on that traumatic day when Priscilla had lost Jules, seemingly forever, and wondered if he had had a premonition of the effect this would have on his marriage. He recalled his assumption that Priscilla would take this loss badly—and the reasons why.

As far back in their relationship as he could remember—from the time that he first met her during her tenure in the Ohio Senate in the early 1980s—there were some things about Miss Prissy that Carlton had overlooked: how accustomed she was to having her way, how she had never quite gotten over being spoiled by her father, and how she still merely assumed that if there were something that she wanted, someone special in her life would get it for her. And lest one forgets how Senator Callahan used to provide for her every need, or if he even thought there was something that she wanted, he would "Make it so," and miraculously, it would come to pass.

But Carlton feared that Priscilla would never get authorization to adopt or obtain custody of Jules McCorkle. And his corollary fear was that she would never forgive him for what she perceived as his role in the whole tragic affair.

Yet he'd hoped that, just maybe, those who loved her the most and the longest could help him find the key to unlocking her heart.

As he made his first call to Liza, he reckoned, *Everyone always says that the mother knows her child the best.*

Afterward, Carlton needed a sedative. He told himself that he should have taken a couple of Alka-Seltzer tablets—or maybe even a couple of Priscilla's meclizine tablets before he'd called Liza.

He'd first felt sick when Liza started with an astounding comment:

"For some time, I've suspected," she said, "that Priscilla couldn't have children."

Carlton had blanched. *What? Couldn't have children?*

Not sure that he had heard her correctly, he asked, "What was that? Liza, what'd you just say?"

"I'm so sorry, Carlton," his mother-in-law said tartly. She almost sounded defensive, "but I learned a long time ago not to put my two cents into other people's marriages, especially my children's. So if you and Missy 'are going at it,' as you young people say, then only the two of you can work it out."

Carlton had wondered why, as usual, she'd sounded so insensitive to him. He had tried so hard to be kind and attentive to her. But Liza had never quite warmed up to him. Carlton did not, and could not have known, that she'd preferred Sedgewick, an earlier boyfriend of Priscilla's, and that she had also been more compassionate and under-standing with that other suitor.

But Carlton had been desperate to solve the situation that had developed between him and his wife. He had even pleaded with Liza.

"Liza, please! I'm at my wit's end about what to do about this. Surely, there's something you can tell me."

As she sensed her son-in-law's sadness and his undeniable plea, Liza had then shared some of what she and Nelson had once discussed about their daughter.

"Son," she said, "all I know is that Nelson and I never thought Missy ever even *wanted* to have children, anyway. It just wasn't something she ever talked about, at least, not like the other girls did."

"But she's so close to Germane, and now, Jules."

"Carlton, listen to me," Liza seemed to struggle to help him understand the contradiction in what seemed to him to have been, in his words, "a most disturbing situation."

She talked as if she knew that Carlton already knew something about women. She said that Priscilla did love Germane, and now, apparently, this young Jules.

"And I agree," she stressed, "that Priscilla, like most women, *does* possess *some* maternal instincts. But that does not equate to a *desire* to give birth, and certainly not a desire to raise children."

As he had held the telephone to his ear, Carlton got a first-hand example of how blunt Liza could be. Yet, his perception had been somewhat contrary to her assumption that she was kind and forthcoming to her son-in-law, especially since he hardly ever called her, anyway.

But all Carlton could say had been, "Oh, no, Liza, you can't mean what you say."

When Carlton called Julia, she had told him something similar to what Liza had said, although Julia had been less impersonal and blunt.

"Oh, Carlton," she had begun, "let's just say that Priscilla tends not to manifest maternal instincts, and those she does have are, at best, pretty much superficial and transient."

Later, she added, "I'd say Missy has always viewed parenting as off-limits. In fact, I think she's always seen herself as 'the favorite aunt.'"

At that, Carlton had begun to grasp some of what Liza had tried to tell him earlier.

But then Julia surprised him by turning the tables on him. "Well, Carlton," she had asked, "when last did you and Priscilla discuss having children?"

His heart sank, for he had always *assumed* that having children had been part of their marriage package. But they had never talked it through—neither of them, he as much as she.

At that point in the conversation, he suddenly recalled their pre-marriage counseling session with Father Absalom Lansberry and Reverend John W. Simms. Over breakfast one morning, both clerics had broached the subject of children, about which Carlton now remembered that neither he nor Priscilla had said much. His memory had served him correctly because both he and Priscilla had kept saying, "We'll cross that bridge when we get there."

Finally, Carlton had asked Julia what had weighed heaviest on his mind: "But why is she so distraught over the situation with Jules?"

"Oh, Carlton, I'm sorry to be the one to tell you this. But Jules—well, like Germane—is Priscilla's 'play child.' You know, make-believe. But if she ever had to take care of either one of those boys, I think that—knowing our girl—that would drive her mad. Unless, of course, she's changed."

Carlton had cringed at those words. He had learned another side of his beloved Miss Prissy, and he had not been so sure that he liked what he had been hearing.

But then Julia had amped up the conversation. "And remember, Miss Prissy's passion is politics. She's just on a little odyssey of sorts right now. Trust me. She's going to tire of what appears to be fun doing PR for the Met, and man alive will she come out swinging again. And how!"

At that, he had blurted out, "As Missy would say, 'Ah, crap!'"

"Exactly. 'Ah, crap' is what Priscilla gets her jollies off of. Come on, Carlton," Julia had insisted, "you knew she was a political animal when you met her." It had seemed to Carlton that he had heard those words before, and by someone else, at that. Then he recalled that both his long-time friend and CF associate Tommy Wozniah and, more recently, Dr.

Chisholm—Priscilla's PTSD psychiatrist—had mentioned those very words to him.

Then he had even wondered whether he had ever indeed known the real Priscilla.

After she heard the sadness in her son's voice, Lady Chelsea had tried to address his troubles as delicately as she could.

She had begun, "Son, your father, Ramses, even Jamison and I, have all talked about this topic. And, well, Carlton, I'm so sorry to tell you this, but we all see the situation similar to Julia's take on it. In fact, we believe Julia has put it rather mildly."

"Oh, Mother, no!"

"Carlton, my dear one, I am so sorry."

At that point, Carlton had had enough of "I'm sorry to tell you this, but …" and "I thought you knew …." But most of all, there was the reminder that had pierced his heart: "You knew Miss Prissy was a political animal when you met her."

Of the three women, Lady Chelsea drilled the deepest. "Carlton, do not forget or doubt that, above all else, PJ loves you. She can't help the grip politics has on her. But I've got to hand it to her; PJ has expended a tremendous amount of time, energy, money, and other resources trying to temper her true passion. She's been trying so very hard to please you, starting back when you contracted amnesia. It was as if she thought she'd lost you. Then, after you regained consciousness, we all noticed how she seemed to try to be less formidable and began doing the kinds of things she *thought* pleased you."

Carlton could not believe his ears. So he had asked his mother, "Are you saying Missy's doing all this to please me?"

"Yes." Lady Chelsea had been quite emphatic: "And although the situation with Jules has broken her heart, just let someone from the Hollingsworth administration call, and she'll be off without a moment's notice. Why, Carlton, my darling son, she knows her heart's desire just as you know yours. Neither of you is about to give up the passions of your life. And frankly, why should you? Why should either of you?"

And when she had gotten no response, she had then changed the subject entirely: "And, Son, I'm almost certain she's bored stiff with that PR account at the Met. Why else do you think she spends so much time away, especially working on her new house in Harlem?"

His mother had ended the conversation with a challenge:

"Son, I've said more than I ought to have said. It's up to you to work things out with your wife. Meanwhile, Missy needs your love and support just like you needed hers back when you were out of yourself with amnesia." Lady Chelsea had hidden her sigh. She knew that everybody who knew Priscilla understood that she was a political animal *and* an independent woman. Moreover, Lady Chelsea knew that anyone who had any sense of perception and knew Priscilla could see that she had been raised to think and behave like a man.

So it was that all three of the principal women in his wife's life had understood and done their best to help Carlton understand that he not only had his work cut out for him but that the survival of his marriage had depended on how he set about resolving the matter.

Consequently, it had been up to Carlton, all along, to find a solution to this first significant issue that had threatened their young marriage.

Carlton and Priscilla sat together physically but remained distant in all other ways on their flights, first to London and then to Harare. He kept turning over again in his mind the phone conversations he had had with

Liza, Julia, and Lady Chelsea. Then he remembered how long it had taken Priscilla to accept his umpteenth marriage proposal.

Meanwhile, Priscilla shrank away from him, leaning against the window and staring out at the clouds. She was glad Carlton was leaving her alone. She could not imagine what she would have said to him.

Every few hours or so, they exchanged words when one of them had something to say about the upcoming board meeting at the Bernhardt Foundation for Boarding Schools for Zimbabwean and South African Girls.

Earlier, in January, Priscilla had just convened her regularly scheduled board meeting when the SANM PG had raided the Rainbow Towers Hotel and Conference Center in downtown Harare. In so doing, the South African terrorists had seriously damaged the conference room, especially the ceiling. But, in short order, the conference room had been restored to its well-known luster. Also, since that time, Priscilla had met with the board at least twice. But for this particular meeting, Carlton had decided it best to accompany her because he did not think Priscilla was up to conducting the meeting, and for sure, she was not up to interacting with the one hundred children who awaited her, or so he had thought.

One of the original twelve board members had been removed because of her revolting role in Priscilla's special-envoy mission last winter. The other eleven still served. Even before the meeting began, the dynamic seemed strained. Board members wondered why Priscilla, who was usually so gregarious, hardly said a word to anyone. But wisely, they kept their questions to themselves. Then Carlton, too, seemed out of sorts. He surprised everyone by raising trivial objections to any number of minor issues. The other board members looked from one to the other and shrugged. This man was not the Carlton that they all knew and admired. What was happening with Priscilla and Carlton? They were acting like their honeymoon was over already.

But, of course, the board members had no clue about the personal issues that had developed between the newlyweds. They could not have guessed how frustrated Carlton was, not just from what he had only recently learned about Priscilla from Liza, Julia, and Lady Chelsea, but also because of the lull in their love life. And when the other board members mumbled among themselves and looked to Priscilla for her reaction, she stared straight ahead, not even listening to the discussion about the finance report.

As an uneasy silence fell over the gathering, Carlton suddenly snapped to attention. His nitpicking, coupled with Priscilla's acting as she would rather be elsewhere, was unquestionably impacting the board meeting. He cleared his throat and looked expectantly at his wife.

When she did not even notice him, again, he cleared his throat. Then all the other board members looked from him to Priscilla, who was simply staring at the agenda in her hands.

Finally, Joseph Sabato, the board member sitting to Priscilla's right, nudged her.

Priscilla looked up. "Oh, I am so sorry. Is it time for my report?"

Joseph lowered his usually commanding voice: "PJ, what's the matter? We can see you're worlds away from here. Do you want to take a moment?"

Joseph then looked across the conference table at Hugh Makakela, asking for permission to excuse the two of them, and he nodded in agreement.

Even though Carlton had prepared to chair the meeting, it did not take long for the ever-vigilant Hugh, the vice-chair, to assume this role.

"This board," Hugh said, "is in recess, ten-to-fifteen minutes or so."

While the board members stood, milled about, and then dispersed outside the conference room, Carlton approached Hugh and apologized for his uncharacteristic behavior.

"Sorry, Hugh. I guess it's pretty obvious that something's out of kilter between Miss Prissy and me."

But Hugh surprised Carlton with his response.

"No problem, young man," said the vice-chairman. "But try to remember that *all* couples experience a little turbulence during the first year or so of their marriage." Hugh smiled faintly. "That's when each one *really* discovers who the other one is." Hugh chuckled. "That's what happened with my wife and me, and we almost split up. Thank God, we finally realized that we *both* had to keep putting our best foot forward and that maybe we hadn't shown our true selves during our engagement, in a misguided effort just to keep the other one happy."

Again Hugh smiled, but then he commented on something that Carlton and so many other people took for granted when he said, "But Carlton, don't forget, you married a young woman who the whole world regards with the greatest admiration. Have you ever given any thought to how she even feels being *perceived* as 'America's little sweetheart?'"

As the recess stretched to nearly one-half an hour, Carlton went to an adjoining terrace to mull over what Hugh said. He realized that this was the first time he had given any thought to how Priscilla had even felt about her high-profile persona. Then he recalled her saying once how she hated what she called "this image stuff." She had added that it reminded her of what she had tried to escape when she'd first left Prendergast, only to find herself in a series of far more magnified situations. Carlton took a deep breath, glad that finally, he was becoming aware of another aspect of what made his complex wife really tick. Could it be that Priscilla felt that she had graduated from "Daddy's little girl" only to become "America's little sweetheart?" The truth was that she no more desired the later image and role than she had the former. Carlton smiled to himself. A highly recognized profile does have its downside.

As it turned out, the board members had no way of knowing that Carlton had no notion about what had happened a little over a year ago in that very conference room. As things stood, Hugh and the other board members merely assumed that he knew. But since neither Carlton nor Priscilla had said a word about the incident—the SANM PG's raid of the conference center last winter—none of the other board members mentioned it. Yet, they all wondered whether Priscilla's distant attitude was in reflection of it. And even though that incident had already been covered in at least two previous board meetings, the trauma of it all remained fresh in everybody's minds, well, except for Carlton's and Priscilla's. Priscilla's mind was on young Jules McCorkle and Carlton's on her.

The board reconvened.

Hugh consulted his agenda and called for the CEO's report. No one had any idea how Priscilla would react or what she would say.

It was soon apparent that she was certainly not her usual feisty self. Instead, she was mechanical, terse, and unemotional. No fluff. No sidebars. No interesting anecdotes about any particular student, either. All cold, raw data with charts illustrating high enrollment retention levels, higher than normal aptitude levels, scholastic achievement, and early college placement.

As she finished her report, Priscilla looked around the conference table and asked, "Questions? Comments?" She did not wait for any responses and instead raced ahead. "There being none, Mr. Chairman," she said to Hugh, "Shall we call for a vote?"

As soon as Hugh asked for a vote to accept the CEO's report, one of the other board members interrupted the vote.

"But, PJ, did you forget to schedule a visit to the Anglican Cathedral Boarding School? We almost always pop in on them. They so love our visits and, the kids adore you."

Otherwise, no one else commented.

Masterfully stoic, Priscilla pretended not to have heard the question. But Carlton intuitively understood that the last thing she wanted was to be in the midst of maybe one hundred children. Of course, they would remind her of "Jules, Ma'am. I'm called Jules McCorkle."

Yet he intervened. "Why, yes. Great idea! My dearest *Dr. Ms.* Austin-Bernhardt. Shall we all head over to the Anglican cathedral boarding school?" At that point Carlton had just compromised on something that he himself had insisted never happen. He had objected to the title "Dr. Ms.," back when he had proposed marriage to her. Instead, he had insisted her title would be "Dr. Mrs." But now, at his wit's end, he would try anything to break through Priscilla's increasingly impervious heart.

Shocking everyone, especially her darling Carlton, Priscilla rose to the occasion and nodded at Carlton. "Sure. Why not?"

She glanced at the other board members' baffled faces and finally became aware of how distant she had been with them. She then spoke in a pleasant tone of voice, "Pardon that oversight on my part."

The Bernhardt Foundation board members arrived via shuttle at the Anglican Cathedral Boarding School a few minutes later. They all eagerly headed to the main building after they disembarked—well, Priscilla was hardly eager in her current mood. They chatted with some of the staff and toured the facility. Then Headmaster Warren Chambers led them up the cathedral's garden pathway, where one hundred young girls, ranging in age six to eighteen, waited but were less boisterous than usual. The headmaster had met with them earlier and told them, "Mrs. Austin-Bernhardt is a little under the weather today. Try not to holler and crowd her, as you often do, and keep your voices low. I'm sure she'll be fine. We all sometimes get a little under the weather."

So when Priscilla and the other board members walked inside the sanctuary, they watched as all the girls stood in respect and then chorused, "Good morning, Mrs. Austin-Bernhardt and others. Welcome back." Then the girls all sat back down in the pews.

Priscilla, who had not wanted to go there in the first place, exhaled.

Then she surprised the other board members by standing in front of the altar facing the girls. Soberly she shared the intimate story that accounted for the changed demeanor of both Carlton and herself:

"Girls, once I did not fully relate to or even understand some of what each of you has experienced in your precious childhood. But all that has changed. You see, I met a handsome seven-year-old young man named Jules...."

Not only the girls, but the board members, too, listened raptly to her story, until finally, she concluded: "So, you might ask, 'what to take away from all that?' Well, for one thing, none of us controls what or where we come from. But each of us has some control over the path forward. So I suggest that as you complete your education and begin your life's ambition, always reach back and bring someone else along the way. Always lend a helping hand to someone else. Remember, each one of us is where we are today because somebody else gave us a helping hand, not a handout, but a great big helping hand." By that point, she had become quite animated. Then, as she looked into the faces of the young girls, she asked, "Are we clear on the main point of the story?"

Priscilla herself nearly welled up when it sounded like each girl answered, "Yes, Mrs. Austin-Bernhardt, we're clear and, thank you for that lesson."

Priscilla was returning to her old self again.

As she took her seat on the front pew, she noticed hardly a dry eye in the sanctuary. Hugh, Joseph, Carlton, and a few other board members seated nearest Priscilla patted her shoulders and whispered affirmations like, "Good job, PJ," and "Excellent lesson."

But Priscilla looked in the direction of the chancel.

Sharp-eared board members and the students seated nearby heard her saying, "Suppose that was what *You* had in mind all along." Then she dropped her head in her hands. "Amen."

Carlton took advantage of the fact that Priscilla had already cracked the top layer of the defense of her impervious heart during her presentation at the Anglican Cathedral Boarding School. So that evening in their hotel suite, he told Priscilla that he needed to talk to her about something, and he consented when she stipulated, "Anything but Jules, all right?" Then he poured himself a scotch whiskey and offered her a drink, but she politely refused.

Carlton went for it.

"Missy, hasn't it occurred to you that we've had unprotected sex all these months since I recovered from my bout with amnesia, and I mean really good sex, too, but—"

Most unexpectedly, Priscilla interrupted her husband and talked as if she had prepared for this conversation all her life.

"Oh, Carlton, my love, I never knew how to tell you." She burst into tears.

When Carlton realized that she was not surprised about what he was about to discuss, the sadness on her face reminded him of the hurt he had seen there when she realized that the Borough of Manhattan's Children's Protective Services Agency was taking Jules away. Moreover, Carlton had always assumed that Priscilla was taking contraceptives, but boy, was he in for a shock.

Before he could comment any further, she continued. "After the rape, well, I don't know what came over me. But, as you and half the world already know, I didn't tell anybody at the time. I just couldn't. But what you *don't* know is what happened next. I made what I thought then was the most expedient decision. I made an appointment with a doctor, and, Carlton, well, I had an abortion." She stopped talking and then resolutely continued. "But Carlton," again she paused, but this time she looked intensely into his eyes, "I did much more than that. I was so angry, hurt, so humiliated. It was as if I wanted to remove all evidence of the horrible assault. So I told the doctor to do whatever was necessary to prevent another pregnancy."

Priscilla began crying hard, like a baby. After a while, she wiped her runny nose on the sleeve of her blouse. Finally, she found the courage to look into his reddened eyes and said, "I never imagined I'd meet someone like you *and* fall in love. I even remember asking Daddy if I was missing some genes or something because I never felt passion for any of the other men in my life … until I met you." She cried and cried and cried, and then called out, "Oh, dear God, what have I done?"

Carlton fought his rising desire to take her in his arms and comfort her, as he thought it vital she had the space to say what she needed to say. As for him, the importance of Priscilla's explanation about the aftermath of the sexual assault and the effect of the sexual assault centered on her finally daring to trust him with her deepest and most profound pain. That was a hell of a lot more than he had ever expected to get from her. Priscilla had always thrived on concealing her true feelings. Everyone who knew her understood that she could be as cold as ice and stoic and aloof, all at the same time. But not this time. This time Priscilla had shared the depths of her soul with the man she loved to no end. What she had just told him was all about love and less about the abortion and whatever else the doctor had done to her at her request.

Then Priscilla searched his face and said, "And now that I know for sure that having children is a deal-breaker for you," she bit her lip, "have the servants ship my belongings, such as they are, back to Columbus. I'll call Julia and tell her to expect my belongings, and me, too, shortly."

When he thought that his darling Miss Prissy had finished her take on what she truly believed was the end of their marriage, Carlton turned his back to her and, in a near whisper, asked, "You wouldn't happen to recall the name for that 'preventive procedure?'"

As he waited for her response, he gulped down his scotch whiskey to the dredges and, with his back still to her, fiddled with the ice and the bottle of whiskey. He was still intent on giving her time and space to tell her whole story, and he knew if he saw the pain on her face, he would be unable to stop taking her in his arms and holding her forever.

Priscilla shrugged.

"Oh, *that* procedure," she said in her customary matter-of-fact way. "I remember the discussion distinctly. First, the doctor tried to talk me out of any *permanent* preventive procedure because he said he didn't believe in permanent prevention. He said something about my young age and the likelihood of meeting what he called 'someone special.' Then, because he was so hell-bent on not performing any permanent preventive procedure, eventually, he recommended 'something less extreme,' his words, not mine."

Then she added, "Oh, Carlton, I was so distraught. I don't remember the exact name of the procedure. But I recall that he did say something about 'tying tubes.' And, to this day, I haven't inquired as to what the devil that even means. But why're you so interested? It's done now, and so, too, is my ability to conceive."

So Carlton got the answer that he had not anticipated. He had assumed from something she had once said that his wife had had a hysterectomy. But that had not been what had happened, after all. And so it was that for over fifteen years, Priscilla had continued *believing* that having had her tubes tied had *permanently* prevented her from childbearing.

Carlton then had the most wonderful premonition. He and Priscilla had just experienced something that he believed would carry them through whatever lay ahead. They had not only begun the process of crossing one of what would be many bridges in their marriage, but they had also just started talking to each other like husband and wife.

For the moment, however, he needed to dispose of that ridiculous notion of hers about packing up and returning to Ohio. But then he reconsidered. Perhaps that was not what he needed to say at this most precious moment.

With renewed hope in his heart, he turned back around and faced his wife.

Without saying anything more, he knelt in front of her, took her head in his hands, and, with a wide grin on his face, said, "Oh, Missy, you've got your sense of humor back! By the way, you're not going anywhere unless it's with me."

Her eyes widened and then once again filled with tears. "You mean, you still *love* me!"

"And how!"

Then one thing led to another, and before they knew it, they were making passionate love for the first time since the seemingly unbearable episode with young Jules.

37

Wrapping up Loose Ends

A week later, after Priscilla and Carlton had returned to New York, she and Macy were once again in the park on an unusually mild early November afternoon. Priscilla had almost finished devouring her hot dog with sauerkraut and rhapsodizing about how she and Carlton had worked their way through their marital problems while in Harare.

"You look so happy," Macy said. "I've never seen you look so happy. Married life is agreeing with you, for sure." She sighed. "Will it ever happen to me?"

Before thanking Macy for her compliments, Priscilla responded to her question first. "I'm sure it will." She expounded. "I had pretty much given up," grinned and said, "But then I met Carlton!"

She prayed a silent prayer that this would happen to Macy, too.

Finally, as if prophesying, "Maybe it's always like that. Just when you think it will never happen, there he is!"

The two friends laughed.

After much laughter, the conversation turned to the case at The Metropolitan Museum of Art.

Priscilla polished off the last of her hot dog, threw the wrapper in the trash, and said, "Say, Mace, how 'bout bringing me up to date?"

Macy nodded.

"As you wish. For starters, Iggy's definitely out at the Met. Although he's turned witness for the prosecution, he simply has too much excess baggage to remain on the board. So he'll never work in a reputable American *or* Western European museum again." She shook her head.

Then she looked at her friend as if she were trying to figure out how best to tell her the next part about Iggy. *Ah, what the hell,* she thought and then said, "Missy, the mediators are at a bit of a stalemate over how much time and where Iggy should serve out his sen—"

"Excuse me?"

Priscilla interrupted Macy and asked, "What do you mean by 'sentence?' Iggy turned state's evidence. He's a witness for the prosecution."

"Yeah, I know, but that pretty much only applies to law in American courts. The French authorities are demanding he serve some time on their soil. After all, he did sketch—or was that forge?—several masterpieces while associating with the ringleader at that studio in Montmartre. At first they were demanding a five-to-ten-year sentence, but the other mediators argued for less time and eventually got a reduced sentence to a minimum of six months in jail in France."

Macy concluded this part of her update as if it needed saying: "Iggy's a broken man. Then again, he did 'dig his own grave.'"

But Priscilla had already secretly inquired at a few lesser-known museums in Eastern Europe, where they would welcome someone of

Iggy's experience, with the caveat, of course, "He could never serve at the helm." Priscilla had understood. She was still grateful because she now knew that Iggy would forever be labeled "an ex-con." Even so, at least two museum executives would later reassure her that they would hire Iggy anyway because "Mr. Devoe's knowledge about the operations of a museum as renowned as *The Met* is priceless." At that, Priscilla had appreciated hearing that all was not lost for Iggy, after all.

After digesting Macy's unwelcome update on Iggy's situation and remembering what a couple of Eastern European museum executives had told her, she reluctantly asked about the twins.

"And the twins?"

It was then that Macy felt she was arguing the case for her clients again with the international intelligence agency officials and the independent mediators. She started with Gaylord, the easier of the twin brothers to discuss.

"Well, how 'bout I take them one at a time? Turns out that our boy Gaylord was, in fact, aware of at least some of the shady dealings of his twin brother. But what he never anticipated was his own flesh and blood using him in some of his criminal acts. Although Gaylord may not be legally culpable, for sure, he's off the board at the Met." Then she shook her head and said, "Sometimes one doesn't really know the very people one thinks one knows."

Since Priscilla herself was at a loss for words, she simply said, "Yeah, Girlfriend, I know what you mean."

When Priscilla did not seem surprised at that part of her update, Macy continued.

"As for his senten—"

Shocked, again. Priscilla cut her off again. "Wait a minute, Macy. Surely, Gaylord isn't serving jail time!"

"As I was about to say," Macy corrected her, "the consensus of all the mediators is that Gaylord's only crime, and I say that metaphorically, is being the twin brother to the nefarious Artemis Thibaut. On the other hand, since he *posed* as his brother at Iggy's art gallery and, later, at that New Rochelle residence—obstructions of justice—he received a sentence of six months of community service. Even I had no problem with that because I had already prepared him for some type of sentencing."

Then Macy took a deep breath, braced herself in anticipation of more interruptions from Priscilla, while Priscilla beckoned for her to continue, and said, "Alright, now, on to the 'bad seed.' So far, concerning Artemis Thibaut, we've got a portion of what could easily have amounted to three life terms *substantially* reduced. But it's yet to be determined to what extent. Remember, Artemis Thibaut left a trail of forgeries and stolen artwork all over the world: France, North America, Asia, Greece, South America, and maybe some other yet-to-be-identified places."

"But will the Met insist on a full-blown trial?" Priscilla was particularly concerned that she might have to produce a PR campaign to offset a major scandal if there were a trial. She just was not up to doing that now, or any other time, for that matter. She had already lost interest in the situation at the Met.

"Relax, PJ. The last thing those highbrows at the Met want is a criminal court proceeding. That would merely amplify what is already being billed as "the art scandal of the century." Then Macy smiled, aware she had just said what Priscilla had really wanted to hear.

"Artemis Thibaut," Macy exhaled and then continued, "is meanwhile getting accustomed to the less lavish accommodations of a federal prison. The FBI and the international intelligence authorities want him to have ample time to think about the harm he has done. So they're not yielding one bit to my request that he be detained for six to nine months, max. His detention amounts to that much, *plus* whatever the final recommendation from the mediators.”

“Wait a minute, Mace.” This time Priscilla asked for clarification.

“Are you saying that Artemis Thibaut *must* be detained for six to nine months in prison *in addition to* the mediators’ final recommendation for sentencing?”

“Yes. You heard me right the first time.”

Macy pulled some strains of hair that had fallen to her face and rolled on: “Added to that, similar to Iggy’s sentencing, the French and the Greek authorities are demanding he serves out part of his incarceration on their soil.”

“Gee–whiz, Mace, I always just assumed that bigwigs such as the Millsaps and the Moreauxes and the Omiroses got off much easier, and with lighter sentencing, ta boot. After all, this is a white-collar crime in the cotton patch of high art *and* his first offense. So far as I know, people like that are often released on their own recognizance with some sort of exorbitant bond.”

Macy nodded. “You got that right. That’s what *usually* happens. But it’s not happening this time, kiddo. Not happening. The crimes committed by Artemis Thibaut might be his first offenses, but they are *big* first offenses. So the feds and the international intelligence authorities are looking to make an example out of our boy Artemis Thibaut.”

“Then again,” Priscilla admitted, “I suppose he is getting off pretty light.” She gave a little shrug, and then she remembered the girlfriend.

“Oh, yeah. What of the girlfriend, Arianna? If I were her, I’d become a witness for the prosecution, too, especially since that rat threw her under the bus.”

“Well, PJ, that’s one way of looking at it. But Arianna held fast to her love for Artemis Thibaut. She’ll spend ten years in prison in France.” Then Macy concluded, “Love makes some people do strange things.”

"No!"

"Yes."

Next, she asked about her newest acquaintance: "And Miriam? How's she taking all this?" Priscilla was concerned about Miriam's coming to terms with the reality that her son Artemis Thibaut would be an old man after completing an untold number of years of incarceration.

Macy's eyebrows shot up.

"Ah, come on, Missy," she said with a smirk, "*you* should be briefing *me* on how Miriam's doing. I thought the two of you were kinda' tight."

She paused, but when Priscilla did not say anything, she continued.

"But since you asked, Miriam seems sad over the fact that her son is serving out mandatory detention for six to nine months *before* receiving his final sentencing. But of course, she is somewhat relieved that at least he's not going to be locked up for what could have amounted to over *three* life terms."

It was getting late, and Macy had to get back to her office. But the mischievous part of her could not resist bringing up one more subject.

She gave Priscilla an assessing look and then said, "Say, Miss Prissy, what're you going to call your new line?"

"My 'new line?'"

"Yeah, you know, that new designer label you're gonna' launch, the one everybody's going on about."

"Oh, Mace, get out a' here."

The two friends shared hearty laughter. And although Macy was quite serious, Priscilla was not in the least interested in the designer fashion business.

Priscilla took a circuitous route back to the office to give herself some time to process not only what Macy had told her but also what else had been happening in her Midtown Manhattan office while she had been away at her board meeting in Harare.

First, she smiled at that crazy bit that Macy had asked her about—a new designer fashion label. No way!

Her thoughts then centered on Macy's updates about the loose ends regarding "the mysterious affair at the Met." Funny how things turned out. For whatever reason, Priscilla had always believed that Macy would find a way to wiggle Artemis Thibaut out of an extended jail term. But in her thoughts, she had somehow forgotten—Or was that overlooked?—the fact that Artemis Thibaut had committed crimes in multiple provinces, ergo his extended sentencing. *Oh, well. He really was a "bad seed."*

But she was cheered by how wonderfully Ruth had kept the New York office humming along. She had kept on top of the Met case by issuing the series of press releases that Priscilla had written earlier—regarding Shane Carpenter's leave of absence, Ignatius Devoe's resignation from the Met board chairmanship, and the additional resignations of Iggy's seven confederates from the board. Ruth had also been thrilled to accept a new contract to work with the Met's communications staff in promoting two of its upcoming exhibitions—neither of which had interested Priscilla, but both of which had delighted Ruth.

Yet as she crossed the city streets and lingered in front of the tantalizing storefronts, she reflected that she was less optimistic about the news she had heard from "the boys." Another dangerous, secret mission was shaping up to take them far away to the war-torn former Yugoslavia. And apparently, the mission might soon expand north into Croatia.

Tommy, more than "the other boys," was beyond himself. "And to think," he kept laughing, "I thought we'd never enter the field again!" But the Hollingsworth administration had wanted to get an inside track on the goings-on in some of the former Eastern European nations, especially Bosnia and Herzegovina and Croatia.

Priscilla admitted to herself that she was wary about all this. She had been angling for some time to ease "the boys" into less life-threatening work. She supposed that the lion's share of her concern was that Carlton still was on-call "in service to his country." *But why?* she pondered, *does something always have to come along to interfere with my marriage?*

A few days later, satisfied that nothing in the New York office demanded her immediate attention, a wave of restlessness took hold of her. Carlton was once again socked-in working in the nation's capital, and "the boys" were still holding down the fort in the Midtown Manhattan office, where they had also hoped not to be dragged into the legal proceedings regarding the Met case. But they need not have worried because CIA Deputy Director Froley and FBI Agent Rothschild had already seen to that.

Off Priscilla went to Columbus.

She had so looked forward to returning to Columbus. She was uncertain about why, but something told her it was time to return there. Her only certainty was reuniting with Julia, her best friend and confidante in the whole wide world!

Yet, in a way, Priscilla had to admit that, compared to New York City's excitement, Columbus now seemed somewhat boxed-in: so orderly, so clean, and so serene and secure. *But maybe*, she thought, *too clean and serene and secure.* She considered but then was not quite ready to admit that she had acquired not only an appreciation but a preference for big-city cosmopolitan life on the East Coast. And although life in the Ohio capital had been good to her, at this time, she simply no longer saw any future for herself here.

With a growing sense of impending farewell, she drove her "little monster," her British racing green Mini Cooper, through the downtown and around the block toward the center of state government. But gone was the thrill and the sheer rush that she once felt at the sight of the Ohio Statehouse—of its massive dull gray stone structure and the imposing yet welcoming statue of Christopher Columbus. She drove past First Church but no longer felt the desire to enter and pray inside its impressive Gothic structure. Something was telling her: *Let go, let go of it all, and move forward.*

But before she left Ohio, she treated Julia and Willa Mae Robinson, a special ole friend from First Church, to Thanksgiving dinner at a fine Columbus restaurant.

It was a cold, overcast, dreary winter day. But the holiday meal was fine and lively, up to the point when Priscilla grew disappointed with Mrs. Robinson's growing interest, even fascination, with her high-profile persona instead of sharing fond memories of their years of friendship. *In some ways*, Priscilla thought, *this is like a celebrity interview with a society reporter*. Mrs. Robinson wanted to know about her work with The Metropolitan Museum of Art, her time on board the yacht *Piraeus* with the Omiroses, and her impromptu television interview at the New York Fashion Week. But out of courtesy, Priscilla continued smiling and saying, "Yes, yes," and "I know what you mean."

Afterward, she and Julia waved goodbye as Mrs. Robinson drove out of the restaurant parking lot and out of Priscilla's life for the last time.

Then Julia studied Priscilla's face before asking what seemed so obvious to her: "So, Missy, how soon before you shut down operations here?"

"Oh, Julia, I haven't thought through all that yet. I'm caught up between maintaining a shell of an operation and letting the two consultants continue managing whatever major projects happen our way. Or just dissolving the corporation here altogether. What sayeth you?"

Ever-attentive, Julia said, "This one's your call. But I think it's important that you make a decision soon." Julia had something else on her mind, but she did not think this was the time to bring it up.

But then, seemingly out of the blue, Priscilla grinned and said: "Up for a trip to the City? New York, New York!"

"Heck, yeah!" Julia exclaimed and repeated herself, "Heck, yeah!"

But first, the two of them spent most of the following week sorting through some of Priscilla's personal belongings, including clothing, artwork, and furniture. They donated much of it to the Goodwill and the Salvation Army or put it on the curb for interested passersby to take. They also packed treasured items, including family photographs, and tagged her piano—which had not fitted the décor in her New York City branch office—for delivery to the Harlem brownstone. By the time the two friends finished sorting through packing and categorizing everything, only a shell of a home office remained.

It was then that Julia told Priscilla what else was on her mind. She said, "I'm planning on moving from Ohio to New Hampshire and eventually working with Arvana on her new drug treatment proj—"

As she cut in on Julia's statement, Priscilla belted out: "You have got to be kidding me!" Gleefully, she did.

Then, "So when were you going to break all of *that* good news to me? And Arvana! For sure, I thought she would have said something by now. Just wait 'til I get my hands on my favorite sister-in-law!"

"Well, Missy, I'm telling you now. Anyway, you knew Arvana had sounded me out and that the two of us have been corresponding. Then again," Julia snickered and noted, "have you *any* idea how often you've dropped bombs on me?"

The two of them laughed.

Julia smiled gently as she looked into Priscilla's glistening eyes and said, "Missy, you know something? I've never known anyone who's led such an interesting and rewarding life. But now, I declare, it's high time you gave an equal amount of attention to your marriage."

Priscilla raised her eyebrows and ruefully nodded.

When Priscilla and Julia arrived in New York, Priscilla invited her friend to stay with her and Carlton at their Waldorf Astoria suite. "Besides," she said, fighting to hide her concern that he and "the boys" had been activated again, "Carlton will be away for a while." She shrugged and rolled her eyes. "He's off someplace. Who knows where?" Priscilla already knew that Julia knew that Carlton was a special agent of sorts, but she and Julia never openly discussed that part of her husband's life.

And even though Julia was somewhat concerned that Priscilla had seemed a little concerned that Carlton was "who knows where" again, she could not help noticing the posh dwelling.

But when Priscilla took her to Harlem to see the brownstone, Julia was nearly beyond herself. As luxurious as the renowned Waldorf was, Julia, like Priscilla, preferred the Harlem brownstone.

"All right, Missy," she said, "I get the five-star treatment at the Waldorf, but this place is to die for."

"There's just something so earthy, so *real*, about this place," Priscilla said.

"I know what you mean," Julia agreed.

As Priscilla toured Julia inside her "earthy" pride and joy, she heard her friend exclaiming, "Wow!" at her every turn.

Upstairs, Priscilla dramatically opened the door to one of the four bedrooms and said, "This one's reserved for you, Julia, whenever you want to visit."

At that, Julia was even more grateful. But then she surprised her friend even more when she said, "All right, Missy, when do we head off to Bow Lake?"

Priscilla shoved Julia lovingly. "Stop reading my mind."

"No problem there. I can read it all on your face." Then Julia snickered because she knew Priscilla knew that her statement about that way of hers was true.

"But you're right. We're off to Bow Lake this afternoon, Girlfriend, and I can hardly wait. But first, let's check in at my branch office. After all, you set it up, and you were the one who found Ruth and Alfrieda." Later, she would introduce Julia to Laverne, too, who had gone off with "the boys" on their secret mission infiltrating who-knows-which group in the war-torn territories of Bosnia and Herzegovina, and Croatia.

In early December, New York City experienced moderate snowfall and blistering cold. Bundled in their overcoats and boots, Priscilla and Julia walked through the revolving doors into the building, home to her New York branch PR office. Julia watched any number of people greeting Priscilla. Some even stood still in their tracks as if star-struck. But Julia also observed that Priscilla scarcely acknowledged any onlookers, not even the people who called her by her name.

On the ride in the elevator to the seventh-floor suite of P. J. Austin and Associates, Incorporated, Priscilla confirmed what Julia had already suspected: she had grown to resent her high-profile persona.

"It's like I can't even go to the powder room without someone following me." Then she said what Julia had sensed, "I've got to get out a' here, too."

But as the elevator doors opened, Priscilla put on a more cheerful face. She called out to a woman behind the reception desk. "Alfrieda, darling, how's it going with you?" But she did not lessen her stride.

Julia, however, stopped to greet Alfrieda. "How's it going?"

"Wonderful," Alfrieda answered. "Love it here."

"Glad to hear it," Julia said, but then she took off after Priscilla. "Gotta keep up with her."

Ahead, down the corridor, Julia glimpsed Priscilla disappearing into an office. Seconds later, she stood at Priscilla's office threshold, where beams of sunlight filled the room. Priscilla was already settled in her executive swivel chair, and across from her, Ruth sat in one of the attractive, striped-silk, upholstered high-back chairs facing the desk.

Priscilla watched as Julia and Ruth moved to shake hands, but Julia turned that into a fist bump, and Ruth happily obliged.

"I hear great things about you," Julia said.

"Glad to hear it!"

The two women beamed at each other.

But then Priscilla asked Ruth, "Any word from "the boys?"

When Ruth shook her head, Julia took the other seat facing Priscilla's desk and listened as Ruth updated Priscilla on office business.

But watching the signs of importance on Priscilla's unguarded face, Julia could see evidence that she had already lost some interest in her new PR venture in the City. As she glanced at Ruth, she guessed that she, too, understood that change in her boss's attitude. Julia wondered if Priscilla was on the way to shutting down both the Ohio and the New York offices. Was this the end of Priscilla's work in PR, or would she continue staffing the offices until some case or another piqued her interest again? Julia thought that Priscilla may not have decided yet what to do about any of that.

Priscilla stood.

"So! Off we go again." She gave Ruth a brilliant smile. "Julia and I are headed to Bow Lake earlier than previously planned."

She beckoned to Julia as she headed for the door. "See all of you guys at the masquerade ball!"

So she and Julia left her PR branch office as quickly as they had arrived. As soon as the doors to the elevator closed, they both laughed as if someone had told a hilarious joke.

38

Like A Page from *National Geographic*

Since the Bernhardt jet was otherwise engaged, the two friends taxied to LaGuardia Airport to catch a commuter flight to White Plains and then another to Merrimack Airport. And since Priscilla had already called ahead, Shelton was eagerly awaiting when she and Julia disembarked. Both women smiled when they caught sight of the chauffeur.

As they stomped the snow toward him, Julia said, "I still sometimes forget the privileged life you now live." She was so happy for her friend. She had known Priscilla for many years, but this, aside from her wedding day, was maybe one of the happiest times that she had ever seen her.

Spontaneously, the two old friends jumped up and down, stomping the snow-covered Earth.

"Isn't it simply gorgeous here?" Priscilla opened her arms wide as though embracing not only the snow-capped trees that bordered the small terminal but also the snow-covered airport itself, as well as the grounds, the garage, and the snow-covered wings of the airplanes.

Julia smiled at the glow of happiness on her friend's face.

Shelton, too, was jubilant as he watched the two women jumping up and down in the snow. "It's good you two like the snow because plenty of it will be with us in these parts until well after Easter." Then he giggled.

As he reached for their luggage-on-wheels, he grew a tad more formal and said, "Welcome back home Madame PJ, and you, also, Ms. Julia." Then he led them to the garage where he had parked the Bentley.

Upon sliding into the backseat, Priscilla told Julia the story about her first visit to the area. "Girl, you can't imagine how my heart nearly popped out of my chest when my eyes first gazed upon this big, beautiful car." Priscilla laughed. "And I remember exactly what I said: 'What an impressive vintage vehicle! Get a load of this fine horseless carriage!'"

"Oh, Miss Prissy," Julia said with tears of joy, "you are so blessed."

As Shelton drove the Bentley along the way to Bow Lake, Priscilla and Julia "oohed" and "aahed" as if this were their first visit here. At one point, Priscilla tapped Shelton's shoulder and said, "Are those chains on the tires I hear?"

"Why, yes, Madame PJ. How'd you know about chains?"

"Don't forget, Shelton. I grew up in the southern tier of the Snowbelt in western New York." Then she snickered.

"So you're used to chain-covered tires to maneuver the snow?"

"I sure am, and I absolutely love all this snow, too," she said as she wiggled back into the gulf of her seat beside Julia.

Ever-pensive, "I never tire of the beautiful landscape that surrounds this place," Priscilla said to Julia within Shelton's hearing. In early December in New Hampshire, most everything was covered with snow. "All these beautiful snow-capped vineyards and the woodlands, too.

Glorious." Priscilla's face was the picture of contentment. "Glorious, indeed."

"Oh, Missy, this was meant to be. You belong here." Then Julia added, "Now all you need are some cute little children romping about the snow." Plainly, neither of the two friends minded that Shelton could hear their conversation.

Although Shelton observed Priscilla's glee through the rearview mirror, he remained silent for the remainder of their ride home. Now, for sure, he had something exciting to blabber about to the Bernhardts of Bow Lake.

"Yeah, Girlfriend," Priscilla said somewhat soberly, "if only it were meant to be."

Julia did not comment. She had long since assumed that Priscilla did not desire any children. But she, like her friend, had also thought that Priscilla *could not* have children. But, oh, how she wished her best friend in the whole wide world would be so blessed!

Then they were inside the estate's ornately designed gates and could see ahead the whole family and staff had assembled to welcome them.

"Look, Missy, a full staff court!"

"Oh, my, they shouldn't have!" But Priscilla's face had lit up.

When Shelton stopped the Bentley in front of the portico, two eager servants ran to the car. One opened the door and helped them out while the other young man waited for Shelton to pop the trunk, and he retrieved the luggage and took it inside. He trekked through the foyer, without even stomping the snow off of his boots, and up the massive marble staircase, where he deposited each piece of luggage in the two friends' respective bedchambers.

Back outside, Priscilla and Julia shivered in the cold and snow as they hurriedly greeted the welcoming party, who were all bundled in coats, gloves, hats, and boots: Poppa, Marlena, and Ramses; and then

Father and Lady Chelsea; and finally Jamison, Harry, Melissa, and a host of other servants. They all performed the Bernhardt welcoming ritual of rubbing the two women's faces and their heads and warmly embracing them.

Then Priscilla and Julia dashed inside the foyer, where they abruptly stood still. As casually they stomped their snow-covered boots, they gaped in wonder.

Priscilla breathed, "Holy macaroni! Look at this place! I don't believe it." She gazed at the entry and then peeked into the drawing room. The country-style manor seemed to have been transformed into a shimmering Egyptian palace, complete with columns and statuary and tall vases stuffed with lotus blossoms and hieroglyphics painted in brilliant colors on papyrus—golden glory.

Julia chimed in: "My God, looks like a page from *National Geographic*! Everything's so Egyptian! Wow!"

While Priscilla and Julia stood mesmerized in the foyer, a female servant helped them out of their heavy winter coats and boots. Then the two friends spun round and round again, marveling at all that gold and glory they saw.

Lady Chelsea was beaming: "So, ladies, what do you think of our little decorations?"

"*Little*? They take my breath away!" Priscilla laughed out loud, joyfully beholding so much beauty and creativity.

"Julia's right," she noted. "This makeover, well, it's like walking through a spread in *National Geographic*, and then some." But then she almost ruined the compliment when she said, "You know, not long ago I read some interesting stories about Egypt by Elizabeth Peters. I'm sure she'd love these decorations." That, the insensitive Priscilla blurted out without nary a thought that Ramses was himself Egyptian. Indeed, he did not require affirmation about the artifacts' and other furnishings' authenticity from anybody else—novelist, archaeologist, or whatever she might be. Julia nudged Priscilla as if to remind her that hers was an unnecessary remark. But Julia, as did Lady Chelsea, both knew Priscilla often needed reminding that she, nor anybody else, for that matter, needed affirmation of who they were.

The ever-thoughtful Lady Chelsea kissed Priscilla on her cheek. "Nothing's too good for my favorite daughter-in-law." At that kind gesture, all was forgiven.

Belatedly, Father joined them. Because he had not heard her earlier remarks, he also asked Julia's thoughts on their transformed home. "So, best friend of my best daughter-in-law, in the whole wide world, what's your take on all this?"

"Magnificent!" Julia exclaimed. "I feel as if I'm in Egypt, and I've never even been there. But Missy has. And if she says you've captured it, then I agree."

"And how!" Priscilla likewise exclaimed. Then, under her breath, she repeated herself, "And how!"

Then, the others watched as Julia walked to Ramses II's tall golden statue, welcoming all just inside the drawing-room threshold. She dared to touch it. Then, without even looking at him, she said, "Oh, Ramses, you must feel right at home here."

And then, with amusement, they all watched as Ramses walked over, wrapped his arms around Julia, and said, "Did I ever tell you the story about how my people built the pyramids?" He knew that this was not Julia's first time visiting. Nor would it be her first time hearing one of his favorite stories. But while he spun that story again and then led Julia around the mansion and pointed out the decorations along the way, Father and Lady Chelsea led Priscilla on tour in another direction.

But both friends saw the same decorative highlights. Enormous, finely woven tapestries covered a single wall in each room on the first floor. One depicted a map of ancient Egypt during the time of Ramses II, another showed workers constructing the pyramids of Giza, and a third portrayed a pharaoh on his throne surrounded by servants carrying vases of wine and trays overflowing with fruits and nuts. What really captured Priscilla's attention were the tall, colorfully painted, hand-carved wooden statues of the different pharaohs situated in every room on the first floor. But the tall, golden image of Cleopatra, situated just where the grand marble staircase ascended to the second floor, was most impressive of all.

"Beautiful," she said. Priscilla had no idea that she was marveling at the very image that the Bernhardts were planning for her to portray at the masquerade ball. As she drew closer, she changed her description. "Stunning," she said, "absolutely stunning."

Everywhere she looked was a tasteful blending of evergreen plants and artifacts: succulents anchored the corners of each corridor alongside golden images of animals such as snakes, dogs, and birds.

Priscilla thought she saw gold everywhere, and she did. Golden tableware glowed at each place setting on the huge dining room table, set off by the highly polished sterling silver service on the buffet. Golden-laced throws and runners draped the tables, chairs, and settees, and golden-clad garlands streamed down the marble staircase banisters.

But the Bernhardts had not just arranged their decorations atop their usual furnishings. They had replaced most of the furniture. Gone were the traditional sofas and high-back upholstered chairs. In their place were settees upholstered in colorful silk and satin fabrics, along with intricately hand-carved, wooden sphinx benches and fluffy pillows for comfortable seating. There were even enormous floor pillows in the family room in bright decorative colors spread about the floors, which reminded Priscilla of Abdul-Hakim for the first time in a long time. It had not ended well between the two of them, yet she smiled as she remembered those more good times they had shared in Ras al-Khaimah.

Surrounded by so much beauty, Priscilla welled up and said, "So, you've made ready for an evening of festivity. What a masquerade ball this will be!"

39

Coming Out, Macy's Good News & "The Boys" in Croatia

Priscilla and Julia lent their helping hands to Lady Chelsea for two weeks or so, preparing to be the grand hostess at the Annual Charity Masquerade Ball. First, they helped with the kickoff event, the luncheon meeting for the Bernhardt Foundation board members, always held in the afternoon before the main event. Dutifully they prepared nameplates and designated seating arrangements.

"This is the business part," Lady Chelsea explained to the two friends. "We report on fundraising at the luncheon meeting, and then we all have fun at the masquerade ball."

After approving the work that she and Julia had completed, Lady Chelsea reached for her daughter-in-law's hand. "PJ," she said, "I suppose there *is* one aspect of the event that I have yet to share with you."

"Oh?" Priscilla braced herself.

"My dear, over the years, the masquerade ball has come to be regarded as a setting for, well, a coming-out affair." Before continuing, she paused again. "And I have a feeling that you're not all that keen on society events. But it would mean so much to Father and me if you would allow us to *introduce* you to our friends."

At that point, Julia had to cover her face to conceal her smirk. Even though she *suspected* that such events were not Priscilla's favorite, she herself knew that that was true. But she also knew that Priscilla would do just about anything to please Carlton. So she waited with bated breath for Priscilla's response to Lady Chelsea's special request.

For a moment, Priscilla resembled her mother. Just like Liza, she covered her mouth with both her hands when she was moved or perturbed. Then she collected herself, and after another short silence, she finally asked, "And what exactly does being *introduced* entail? Will I have to speak?"

"Oh, PJ, my child, no. You do not need 'to speak.' All *you* need to do is *show up* and, of course, be escorted down the staircase by your darling husband, Carlton."

Priscilla brightened. "You mean Carlton will be *with me*! So I won't have to stroll down those humungous marble stairs all by my lonesome!"

"Why, yes, PJ. You make such a handsome couple. Everyone will love you, that's for sure."

But there was yet more to come: the matter of Priscilla's costume for the masquerade ball.

Lady Chelsea contemplated broaching the subject at that moment, for she'd never quite gotten around to confirming with Priscilla the exact details of the outfit that the family had wanted her to wear. She must have had an inkling, though—in addition to shying away from being presented as a debutante—that her daughter-in-law might not be too thrilled about being decked out as Cleopatra. But Priscilla had, in fact, told Ramses some time ago that she would come as the fabled Egyptian queen. *Let him deal with this.* Finally, Lady Chelsea determined. She would inform Ramses of her new plan later.

As things stood, she just gave Priscilla a radiant smile and cooed, "You and Carlton will be such a beautiful couple coming down those stairs."

Priscilla sighed with relief. "Deal! That is, if you're sure, that's *all* I need to do?"

"Indeed," said a gleeful Lady Chelsea. Everything was falling into place, just as she had planned. But she had a momentary qualm. Was all this too easy? Were she and Priscilla really on the same wavelength?

However, Lady Chelsea was unaware that Priscilla had pretty much forgotten about her commitment to Ramses and that she had already purchased a Sherlock Holmes outfit: a coat, a hat, and a pipe.

As she listened in on the conversation, Julia was well aware of Priscilla's plans to come as Sherlock Holmes but said nothing because she had no idea about the Cleopatra costume.

"Missy, as I've said before, you're so blessed, so very blessed, indeed." Julia might have had more to say if she had known what Ramses had in store for her, too, for the masquerade ball.

Just then, amid all the preparations for the grand ball, the one Priscilla enjoyed introducing as "the best gosh-darn defense attorney this side of the Empire State" made a surprise visit to Bow Lake.

She had the best of reasons, but this time, none of what she had to say had anything to do with the Omiros twins or anything else remotely connected to "the mysterious affair at the Met." Instead, it was personal. Very personal and excellent news, too.

"Missy," she said, as soon as she sat down on one of the elaborate Egyptian settees in one of the parlors, "Ron and I are married."

"What was that you just said?" Priscilla had been asking one of the servants to bring refreshments, but she could have sworn that Macy had just told her that she and Ron were "married," or something to that effect, which was crazy. So far as she knew, Macy and Ron had been rivals in the relatively small world of New England lawyers. But then she remembered the rumors of not so long ago, which she had dismissed, that the two of them were more than rivals.

Macy laughed. "You heard me right the first time. 'Ron and I are married.' We eloped!"

Priscilla jumped up and hugged Macy. Again Macy laughed, but this time in surprise at this open display of Priscilla's affection. Then Priscilla lightly slapped Macy's face, as girlfriends might do.

"Wow! This is excellent news." Priscilla wanted all the details. "When, where, how, and who else was there?"

But before Macy could answer, Julia interrupted her.

"What wonderful news, Macy! Our Missy can use all the good news life can bring." That she said because she, as was Carlton, was fully aware that Priscilla still felt somewhat distraught over what had happened with Jules McCorkle. Then Julia dared to rub Macy's shoulders when she said, "It could not have happened to a better person. Besides, Missy really likes you."

"Oh, Julia," Macy said as she cheeked-to-cheek her, "I'm so *thrilled* you approve. You know, everybody envies your relationship with Miss Prissy."

"No-o," Julia said, a little embarrassed. It had never occurred to her that Priscilla's other friends and acquaintances might be envious of their long and close friendship.

"Hell, yeah," Macy corrected her with much animation. Macy had long since known about the close ties between Priscilla and Julia. The last thing she wanted to do was to come between them. So she was elated when Julia had reached out and maybe opened up to her.

Even so, she still did not provide any more details about her marriage to Ron Chester, save for the fact that they would take "a much-needed vacation and honeymoon, the latter part of December."

"Well, now," Priscilla said. "So we'll miss the two of you at the masquerade ball?"

"No." Again, Macy corrected her. "We wouldn't miss *your* coming out for anything."

While the three women continued laughing, talking, and drinking cocktails and hearing details about Macy's and Ron's elopement, from time to time, Father, Ramses, and Lady Chelsea looked in on them, behaving so at home in the family room of the mansion. They were delighted that Priscilla was finally settling into her life as a Bernhardt, and using their estate as her new home, at that.

As the day for the masquerade ball drew near, Priscilla became increasingly concerned because she had not heard a word from Carlton, nor were her contacts at Langley talking when she had tried delicately probing about her husband's whereabouts. She held her breath every evening as she watched the televised news about the mounting death tolls and the carnage in the Balkans. She studied longer accounts of the situation in newspapers and magazines about some of the disparate groups in the region where Carlton and "the other boys" were deployed. It wasn't easy to discern the differences among the groups, such as the

Christian and the Muslim Bosnians and the Christian and the Muslim Herzegovinians. Whether watching the televised news or reading about the war, Priscilla often emitted susurrations as if she herself were on the battlefield. Of course, she was unaware of her murmuring.

Meanwhile, Father and Lady Chelsea, Ramses, and Jamison pretended to be unaware of Priscilla's anguish. But they, too, feared the worst and prayed for the best. Who was fighting whom, and over what issues? Making all this much harder was Priscilla's awareness that even if something tragic had happened or was happening with "the boys," none of it would be reported in the news, anyway. "The boys" were CF special ops on a secret "unauthorized" CIA mission.

Priscilla had no way of knowing it, but the CF unit had completed its mission. Yet "the boys" were experiencing difficulty departing the war-torn territory. Although Tommy and "the other boys" had been separated, they had eventually reunited at an abandoned farmhouse near Croatia, where, finally, to the man, they all used different words to make the same declaration: This was it for them—no more missions in the world's hotspots. Then Tommy led his longtime friends and CF associates in a prayer of thanksgiving. Even he believed that this would be their last such mission if they survived this particular assignment.

But "the boys" had felt that way before.

Meanwhile, the thought of something terrible happening to Laverne had never crossed Priscilla's mind. Priscilla felt this way because Laverne had emerged from their one-time southern African mission unscathed. So to Priscilla, her friend seemed invincible. She had no way of knowing that, when "the boys" had all gathered at that abandoned old Croatian farmhouse, they had no clue about the whereabouts—or the ultimate fate—of Laverne. So as they waited to be airlifted to safety, they all continued praying that none of them leave war-torn Eastern Europe without her, the woman whom Priscilla now treated as a sister.

The day finally came when this brave woman and the men, who had taken an oath "in service to their country," came face to face with what felt like their last hurrah.

Inside that abandoned old farmhouse—surrounded by enemy troops bearing down on them with high-powered repeating rifles—finally, "the boys" heard the clattering sound of their rescue helicopter hovering overhead. Through a crack in one of the filth-covered windows, they could see the long-awaited chopper nearly touching down to the ground. But just as quickly, some of the enemy soldiers shooting at them turned their rifles on the helicopter as well. So Tommy and "the other boys" prayed hard and then discussed whether they should make a run for it or remain inside.

They decided to make a run for it.

As each team member ran, turning from side to side, towards the whirlybird, their weapons pointed and shooting rapidly at the enemy, amid continuous returning rounds of gunfire, they chorused: "It's now or never," as they ran for their lives with the blessing of God Almighty.

Carlton had chosen to be their backup because, up to that point, he had been the only one who had not sustained any significant injury. So he was the last one to reach the helicopter. Meanwhile, Angel had already positioned himself to help him on board, and Jordy and Onslow were covering for him, so they did not hear or see what eventually ensued when Carlton reached the aircraft.

As Carlton shouldered his heavy rifle and began pulling himself upon the shaky aircraft, he felt something pierce his left shoulder blade. But for some crazy reason, he did not think that it was a bullet.

So when Angel tried to pull him up—unaware that Carlton had been hit—he sensed that Carlton was not carrying his own weight.

"Come on, man. Why aren't you moving?"

Somewhat dazed, Carlton felt the floating movement of the helicopter and his legs wagging. He also felt the warm blood spilling down his cold back and chest. Wearily, he stared into the eyes of his friend.

"I've been hit," he said calmly and matter-of-factly.

For a moment, though, he wondered whether this could be it for him. But that thought quickly dissipated when he heard Angel screaming, and to him, it sounded like the voice of hope.

"Carlton's hit! Help me get him on board!"

At first, none of the others had heard Angel's cry for help. But then they noticed that it was taking longer than usual for their comrade to get on board. So, they stopped shooting at the enemy one by one and began helping Angel pull Carlton onboard the shaky, bullet-ridden aircraft.

Shortly after they succeeded in pulling him onboard, unbeknownst to Carlton, the others saw the blood streaming down the back of his camouflage jacket. Again it was Angel who spoke, "Damn it, man, that's blood coming out your jacket."

Although exhausted and in much pain, Carlton managed a smile at Angel and spoke as if he prayed to God, "Looks like I'm going home for Christmas after all."

Not only did he realize that he'd been shot, but that he had taken the bullet in the same shoulder as another gunshot wound he'd sustained back during Priscilla's first time in Africa. Then, amid the seemingly unrelenting sounds of the bullets ricocheting in and about the aircraft, he pouted, "Ah, not again! But I'm still going home for Christmas. Thank you, dear Lord."

As it turned out, Carlton was not the only wounded among the lot. Tommy suffered a severe injury to his right hand; it looked like gangrene, only it was not. Angel's right cheek was sliced through the flesh. Jordy limped from a bullet wound in his left leg's calf and, Onslow wore a raggedy tourniquet above his right knee.

Angel had managed to wind a makeshift tourniquet around Carlton's left arm and shoulder throughout the continuous gunfire when they were startled at the sound of the helicopter windshield shattering.

The pilot yelled, "Come on, fellows. We've gotta get a move on it!"

Even with escalating gunfire ricocheting about the whirlybird, "the boys" were all loathed to leave Laverne behind. They had never before left a comrade behind.

Then, Jordy caught sight of what appeared to be another comrade lying on a stretcher off to one side of the helicopter. "Who's on that stretcher?" He yelled out in anticipation that it just might be their colleague Laverne.

"Ready for takeoff?" the pilot kept yelling. "Fellows, we've got to get outa' here before there's nothing left of this bird." The pilot had grown desperate.

"Not yet," Tommy screamed back at him more than once.

Tommy held his wounded right hand with his good left hand and headed to the stretcher while the others limped and struggled behind him. They had to know the identity of their badly bruised and blood-stained comrade.

Upon close examination, they all saw the raggedy, soiled tourniquet that secured a gunshot wound in the soldier's left arm. But that was not the only wound the soldier sustained. "The boys" would learn about the soldier's other wound later, not just yet. For a few seconds, though, all they could see was ugly dried blood, dirt, and an unrecognizable face.

Carlton somehow managed to push himself up front. He leaned over the soldier and, using his cold right hand, wiped some of the smudges and the bloodstains from the soldier's face. The soldier winced.

"Sally!" Carlton shouted her agent name. "It *is* you!" So Laverne had already been on board the helicopter.

"The boys" all screamed, using her Christian name, "Laverne!"

She had already been rescued from somewhere else and had been waiting for "the boys" in this helicopter all the while.

Once known only as "Sally," CF Agent Laverne Macon opened her eyes and made a faint smile.

This time Tommy bellowed with all his might, yeah, even amid all the rapid gunfire ricocheting about what remained of the helicopter: "Let's get the hell outa' here!"

As the helicopter, or what was left of it, rose higher and higher into the Balkan sky, "the boys," which included Laverne, all chanted, "Thanks be to God."

40

The Masquerade Ball

Back at Bow Lake, it was the day before the masquerade ball.

As the family enjoyed breakfast, Ramses asked Priscilla and Julia to meet with him later.

Priscilla nodded and smiled, and while she wondered what was up, she asked the family what burned in her mind.

"Has anyone heard high or low of Carlton?"

The answer came from an unexpected quarter: Jamison, the house manager.

"Oh, Miss Prissy," he said, calling her by the name that Carlton used, "I'm guilty of a horrible oversight. Master Carlton called in the middle of the night."

Priscilla nearly rose from her seat at the table. Her eyes glistened. She took a deep breath. *He* is *alive*! Then, along with everyone else at the table, she leaned forward in anticipation of what she hoped would be more good news.

As he spoke, Jamison looked regretfully at Priscilla and the others:

"Master Carlton distinctly told me *not* to wake you, or anybody else, for that matter. He said that he and his friends—'the boys,' he called them—are back, that everyone's safe, and they plan on joining us sometime tomorrow, which is today. Probably late afternoon. But for sure, in time for the masquerade ball. I am so sorry for any anxiety my delayed message may have caused you." Jamison dropped his head in shame. Still, he need not have because everyone, including Priscilla, knew the situation, especially since his "master" had instructed him what to do.

Even so, everyone watched as Priscilla noticeably exhaled.

But before she could comment, Father spoke. "No problem, Jamison. Besides, that's the kind of news that is *definitely* better late than never."

Priscilla nodded at Father and smiled. But she reserved a unique smile for Jamison, who was relieved that she did not seem to harbor any anger for his delayed message.

"Indeed," Lady Chelsea chimed in.

She, too, had been anxious that none of them had gotten any word from her son. But now that they knew that Carlton and the others had survived and were still planning to come to the masquerade ball, her ever-pleasant composure came to the fore. She sat a little straighter in her chair and moved on.

"Now that that's taken care of," she said, looking meaningfully at Ramses, "Will you be requiring any assistance from me?"

No one but Father and Ramses had a clue about what Lady Chelsea had just alluded. But Priscilla and Julia were about to find out.

Ramses shook his head. "Oh, no, Lady Chelsea. I've got this." Ramses' chest seemed to swell with importance. A little later, when everyone had finished breakfast, he asked Priscilla and Julia to follow him.

The two young women did as he asked, assuming this must have been some last-minute arrangements for the masquerade ball. Their curiosity mounted as they walked with Ramses up the impressively decorated marble staircase and down the long upstairs corridor. Ramses rarely asked anything of either of them.

Melissa, the young servant who tended to Priscilla, joined them inside Priscilla's and Carlton's bedchamber, where, before all their eyes, an exquisite outfit was spread across the bed.

Priscilla gasped as she took it all in: an attractive array of gold necklaces and a golden bodice, a long-sleeved silk top, and a pair of golden-laced harem-style slacks with matching golden-clad jewel-laced leather sandals. Eye-catching. Priscilla could not help noticing the overall effect was a bit scanty, though. She reached down, dared to touch the gold necklaces, and then pulled back as if she had burnt herself. She felt the gold necklaces again, and then she stroked the golden bodice and the harem-style slacks. She picked up the gorgeous golden sandals inlaid with jewels, held them high, and then she jumped up and down like a teenager at Christmas.

"For me?" She sounded a little like Germane whenever he pretended to be humbled. But she was bedazzled. "Looks like something from a museum. You shouldn't have." Yet secretly, she thought, *I can be Sherlock Holmes next time.*

"Yes, PJ, exclusively for you."

But Ramses told himself that he must dare to be more forceful. For he had learned a long time ago that, if you want something, you have to go for it. And since he wished Priscilla to come to the masquerade ball as Cleopatra, that was what he went for. Or was that what he declared?

"Priscilla, you're coming as Cleopatra," he declared, as Ramses was among the few family and friends who occasionally called her by her real name, Priscilla.

"But Uncle Ramses…." Priscilla haltingly began. She had started calling Ramses "uncle," both because of his surrogate role in raising Carlton and because he reminded her so much of her Uncle Harold in Indianapolis. Finally, she said what she had been thinking, "Can I even fit into that skinny girl outfit?"

Smoothly, Melissa assured her. "I think you can. I've already compared its measurements to some of your other clothes. But why not try it on?"

Just as she started to undress, Ramses said, "Hold a while, PJ." Then he turned to Julia and said, "This way, please."

All three young women walked in lockstep behind Ramses down the corridor to Julia's bedchamber, where another exquisite garment awaited on her bed.

The women all leaned forward as one.

Ramses smiled.

"Miss Julia, you, young lady, are to be Nefertiti, the powerful wife of Amenhotep IV. She even wore the crown of a pharaoh—hence this headdress," he said, stroking the bejeweled headpiece.

Julia stood gaping—frozen in her tracks was more like it.

Then Ramses, exhibiting a hitherto unsuspected ability to sound like a fashion commentator, showered her with compliments:

"This statuesque headdress, along with this stunning floor-length gown, accentuates your alluring Nubian facial features, and your stunning shapely figure, and your height, too."

With every word that he spoke, Priscilla and Melissa nodded in agreement. Then they watched as he picked up the headdress and placed it on Julia's head.

"Perfect," he said.

"Wow! You do look like her!" Priscilla's eyes welled with tears of emotion. "Julia, Uncle Ramses, I could not have put it more precisely." She smiled at her friend. "Julia," she said, "you fit the image of an Egyptian queen far more accurately than I ever could."

Then she turned to Ramses. "Thank you, Uncle Ramses, for making my girlfriend's day," adding, "ah, heck, her life!" Then, just as she hugged Julia, that gorgeous headdress toppled. But Ramses caught it before it fell to the floor.

Julia wiped her eyes, saying, "Oh, Ramses, I would never have guessed you thought so highly of me. Never."

While Julia marveled at her outfit and continued thanking Ramses, Priscilla kept her arms around her best friend in the whole wide world. For, even she knew that Julia rarely, if ever, had been privy to such attention and so many affirmations. For, Julia had almost always been in the background for most of the events Priscilla had managed. In a way, she'd always been the bridesmaid, never the bride. But not this time.

Meanwhile, all three women watched as a jubilant Ramses rubbed his hands together in glee and finality. "Looks like my job here is done," he said. "Have at it, girlfriends." Then, regally, he strolled away.

As he descended the staircase, he saw Lady Chelsea, Father, and Jamison anxiously awaiting him in the foyer.

"Well, old man?" Father asked. "Don't keep us guessing. How'd it go?"

"Piece-of-cake," Ramses said and rubbed his hands again. He looked as sated as though he had just finished eating a delicious piece of cake. Then he left Father and Lady Chelsea and Jamison all spellbound at what he had accomplished with such evident ease. They had worried that Priscilla and Julia might not be so amenable, mostly because Melissa had blabbered to them about Priscilla's Sherlock Holmes outfit and Julia's Harlequin costume earlier.

Lady Chelsea smiled in satisfaction and thought: *Another catastrophe averted!* As she sailed toward the kitchen, intent on tackling another task, she reflected that there was nothing wrong with either of those other costumes. But the Bernhardts had agreed that her own plans were preeminent, and, like her daughter-in-law Priscilla, the lady of the house was always delighted when she got her own way.

Later that day, Priscilla and Julia talked about nothing but their exquisite Egyptian costumes. They talked so much that Father and Lady Chelsea and Ramses and Jamison, too, all felt as if they were listening to a broken record stuck on the same track that played over and over again:

Priscilla enthused, "And Girlfriend, all that gold!"

"And Girlfriend," Julia said, "that fabulous headdress!"

Then Priscilla laughed and patted her hair as she announced, "I'm ready for my close-up."

At one point, Father raised a balled fist in Ramses' direction and said jokingly, "Old man, you did this. You created *two* monsters!"

At that point, everyone, including Priscilla and Julia, shared hearty laughter.

For Priscilla, serving as Lady Chelsea's deputy, the day raced by ever so quickly. At some point, she thought she heard someone say that Carlton had arrived. But, busy putting out pre-ball "fires," she never even caught sight of him.

In the Bernhardt's dining room at midday, Priscilla was a guest of honor at the Children's Hospital luncheon for major donors. She took care to follow Lady Chelsea's instructions to be gracious and accessible. She sat for a few minutes, drank some tea, and chatted with some of the guests. Then, she politely excused herself:

"Oh, I really must check on my costume for the ball," she said, just as Lady Chelsea had instructed her to do.

Finally, in the early evening, it was time to get dressed for the ball. Melissa helped Priscilla and Julia put on their costumes. Then, when Priscilla was finally dressed, she heard a knock at her door. She looked at Melissa, who shrugged her shoulders, so Priscilla said, "Come in." She suspected that it was her impatient mother-in-law coming to sneak a peep at her in her Cleopatra outfit.

But to Priscilla's surprise, there stood a mysterious-looking man adorned in a handsome black woolen cape with striking white silk lining that covered his face. Priscilla knew her fabrics. Even from a distance, she could recognize good quality material. But she could not see the man's face. So she guessed who he might be.

"Oh, Father, stop teasing me."

Then she heard, "Try again, My Sweets," as the mystery man mimicked Father.

Priscilla still did not know who the man was. For whatever reason, she had dismissed the possibility that this could be Carlton. So she strutted over to the mystery man and pulled at the fabric covering his face.

He was still wearing a mask, but he was no longer a mystery.

She screamed at the top of her lungs, "Oh, Carlton, my love!" Then she laughed out loud. He was wearing a mask straight out of "The Phantom of the Opera." But she herself was disguised as Cleopatra, including a golden face mask. "So, how did you know it was I behind this mask?"

"Oh, Missy, I'd know you anywhere at any time!" Then he took his wife in his arms, lifted her mask, kissed her, and told her how stunning she looked, adding: "Pretty scanty, but all that gold! My golden girl!" He kissed her again.

But when she grabbed hold of his left arm, he flinched. Quickly, he said, "Just an old war wound."

Priscilla knew better. Under the circumstances, however, she left that particular matter alone. Her Darling Carlton had returned, safe and relatively unharmed as far as she could see, and she was hardly about to make an issue out of that.

"Oh, Missy, the whole family is right; you're a keeper." Then he kissed his wife again, held out his good arm, and said, "Cleopatra, your carriage awaits."

As Carlton and Priscilla headed up the corridor for the staircase, they saw Shelton—dressed as Amenhotep IV—escorting a radiant and oh-so-elegant Julia—dressed in Nefertiti—toward them. Julia's eyes sparkled with tears. She was so happy, and since Julia was happy, so, too, was Priscilla. It had been a very long time since Priscilla had seen her best friend so happy.

"We're Egyptian royalty, too!" Shelton exclaimed.

Lady Chelsea had matched Julia and Shelton together simply because neither one of them had had a date. And they had both eagerly consented to the arrangement. After all, who wants to attend a masquerade ball without a partner?

Downstairs, some three hundred guests milled about, shoulder-to-shoulder, packing the foyer, the parlor, the family room, the library, and even the corridors. They all could hardly wait to welcome the Bernhardt family's newest member, along with her best friend from back somewhere in the Midwest. At once, the two couples—Priscilla and Carlton and Julia and Shelton—heard a drumroll. Then everyone inside the Bernhardt mansion listened to a distinct and familiar masculine voice. No one was sure who was speaking—because he wore a mask and costume, too— although most knew it was neither Father nor Ramses.

"Ladies and Gentlemen," said the unidentified voice, "I present to you Ms. Julia Cahill of Columbus, Ohio, and—this is in the script, folks—'the best friend to PJ *Austin*-Bernhardt in the whole wide world.'"

Then he described Julia's outfit, just like the narrators did at the New York Fashion Week: "Ms. Cahill is wearing Egyptian Queen Nefertiti, and her escort, Mr. Shelton Ablewhite, is wearing Amenhotep IV." The guests all nudged one another with knowing smiles as if this were about clothes designed by Ralph Lauren or Chanel!

Then, amid much applause and laughter, the man with the unidentified voice said, "Are the Egyptians in the house tonight, or what?"

While Priscilla and Carlton stood at the top of the staircase and glorified Julia's and Shelton's introductions, she spotted a group waving their hands and arms in the downstairs crowd. She assumed they were trying to get her attention, and right she was. When one woman ripped off her Scarlet O'Hara mask, and the man beside her removed his Rhett Butler mask, Macy and Ron waved at Priscilla.

Then another man dressed as Zorro, bracing himself with a cane, pulled off his mask. *Jordy*! The woman who clung to him removed her Eléna Montero mask: *Ruth*! So Priscilla surmised that Jordy's mysterious date had been Ruth and that "the other boys" and their spouses and significant others surely must have made it to the ball as well. But she could not make out anyone who resembled Laverne. Carlton would tell her later that Laverne was still hospitalized. He assured her that Laverne was all right, but she was in no condition to attend the masquerade ball.

Then as Julia and Shelton began descending the staircase, they heard murmurs of "Stunning," "So beautiful," and "Absolutely gorgeous." Queen Nefertiti and Amenhotep IV stepped ever so gracefully down the stairs. *Just as well*, Julia thought, that no one knew that primarily they were so slow and so stately because she did not want her headdress to tumble off her head again.

After the couple descended the staircase and had begun mingling with the other guests, the announcer, with a distinct and familiar voice, said, "And now for the moment, we've long-awaited." He paused. Then, he asked and answered his own question: "When was it? Ah, yes, last January, they married."

The guests all laughed. Then, just as quickly, silence permeated the corridors, the parlor, the family room, the library, the foyer, every room in the mansion, every space in it, too.

"The Emerson C. Bernhardts II are pleased to introduce to you, Mr. and Mrs. Carlton Elliott Bernhardt!"

Carlton towered over Priscilla. He stood to her left, taking care to keep his wounded arm aside. He held her left hand and matched each of her steps down the impressive golden-garland-clad marble staircase. With every step, guests "oohed" and "aahed." However, the guests did not wait for the couple to reach the foot of the staircase to indicate their satisfaction. Instead, the closer the couple came to the foot of the stairs—where Father (The Count of Monte Cristo), Lady Chelsea (Queen Elizabeth I), and Ramses (Ramses II) awaited them—the guests applauded louder and louder and shouted cheers of adulation. Priscilla smiled and smiled, knowing with all her being that she really was at home.

Father, Lady Chelsea, and Ramses all welcomed her and Carlton. Then they escorted Priscilla a few steps away from the staircase base to meet the man with the distinct and familiar voice. As Priscilla's eyes fell upon him, she thought about how she had not felt this good since, just before her wedding, she had found herself consorting with all that royalty in Dubai, which included the emirs of the federation of the United Arab Emirates. *It doesn't get any better than this*, she thought, as she cheeked-to-cheek with Danny Thomas.

Danny Thomas and Carlton shook hands. Then Carlton stood beside his blushing bride and waved at the guests, who were still applauding.

Again, Danny Thomas spoke to the guests: "Don't they make a handsome couple?"

Priscilla's thudding heart almost popped out of her chest. Tears pooled in her eyes. She remembered how Liza and Nelson had so admired the man. She had no idea how happy she looked as she stood proudly beside her darling Carlton and one of her parents and America's favorite celebrities.

Priscilla already knew that the Bernhardt name was synonymous with "philanthropy" in New England. Still, everyone all over America knew the name "Danny Thomas" to be synonymous with St. Jude Children's Research Hospital. Later, she was to find out that the money raised from this year's fundraiser went directly to theSt. Jude Children's Research Hospital, not the local hospital in Merrimack as she had presumed. And since Danny Thomas and the Bernhardts were equally proud of their Lebanese lineage, he had been ever-so-pleased to lend his name to tonight's event.

And so it was that P. J. Austin-Bernhardt—along with Julia Cahill, her best friend in the whole wide world—was introduced as one of the newest members of New England's high society by the highly-esteemed television personality, producer, and philanthropist Danny Thomas.

All evening long, Priscilla kept thinking, *Gee! It doesn't get any better than this.*

41

Medical Appointments, Speaking Engagements ... *Oh, My!*

Priscilla hardly slept on the night of the masquerade ball. Neither did Carlton.

"Danny Thomas!" she kept saying. "Who would've thought?"

"Missy, go to *sleep,*" a thoroughly exhausted Carlton said more than once. Then, "It's nearly 3:00 in the morning, alright?"

Carlton was exhausted, not just from dancing with Priscilla and the many other women who wanted their picture taken with "The Phantom of the Opera," but he had not had a good night's sleep since he had gone away with "the other boys" to war-torn Eastern Europe. At one point, that sleepless night after the masquerade ball, he was so undone by

Priscilla's constant exclamations about Danny Thomas and her irrepressible singing of the theme song "Masquerade" that he covered his head with a pillow.

As it turned out, Priscilla had no idea that Lady Chelsea had taken a cue from their earlier conversation when she had mentioned the Andrew Lloyd Webber movie. Nor did she know that Lady Chelsea had passed that on to Carlton and how that had resulted in his wearing that dashing "Phantom of the Opera" costume. But as Priscilla kept telling him through that sleepless night, being part of those hundreds of guests dancing to the theme song from "Masquerade" had left her feeling like she had died and gone to heaven.

By the time his wife finally fell asleep, Carlton was already up, eating breakfast. Then he and "the other boys" headed back to Langley, recalled dealing with something related to their "unauthorized" Eastern European mission.

Hours later, when Priscilla finally awoke, she went into the bathroom and stood underneath the gushing showerheads, singing Andrew Lloyd Webber's version of "Masquerade" at the top of her lungs. Over and over, she belted out the song as she pretended to be one of the movie characters. Then, as she danced down the golden garland-clad marble staircase and pranced into the dining room, she sang the chorus as though she were on stage.

The family—Poppa and Marlena, Father and Lady Chelsea, Ramses, and Julia, too, who were all brunching—blinked at her over-the-top performance.

Julia, who was the most accustomed to her ways, called out: "Missy! Give it a rest. Please!"

"Ah, come on, folks," Priscilla sang another chorus and then said: "That was the gala of *forever*. And Danny Thomas, *too*!"

Father raised his eyebrows and looked at Lady Chelsea.

"And who was it that said, 'PJ would never consent to a *society event*, certainly not a masquerade ball?'"

"Oh, Father," Lady Chelsea demurely wiped her mouth with a linen napkin. "That young woman never ceases to amaze."

Priscilla danced toward the buffet as though oblivious to the killjoys at the table.

Jamison, at his post by the sideboard, executed a slight bow. "Let me guess; Madame PJ will get her own plate."

Priscilla, still grooving on the masquerade ball, called Jamison by the name of the Three Musketeer he had dressed to emulate. "And right you are, my dear Aramis."

She picked up a slice of bacon and turned back around, and waved it in Julia's face. Then she bowed and said, "And to Her Royal Highness, Queen Nefertiti! How is Her Highness this beautiful December morning? Ha! Ha! Ha!" Priscilla, in this particular mood, really enjoyed being herself.

Without waiting for any reaction from Julia, she returned to the buffet and commenced piling her plate with prodigious quantities of everything. "I'm starving."

Then she took her seat across from Ramses. "And, oh, to you, too, His Royal Highness! How are we on this glorious winter morning?" Ramses had worn the costume that depicted Ramses II, his namesake.

"My, my," Ramses said, "We really are feeling our oats."

Then, all of them, except Julia, who had seen her at the trough like this many times before, were transfixed. Poppa, Marlena, Father, Lady Chelsea, and Jamison watched Priscilla gobble down her overflowing plateful as if she had not eaten in days. Well, Lady Chelsea had seen Priscilla eat like this once before, the morning after Carlton's recovery from his bout with amnesia. Until this very moment, though, she had thought that a one-time thing.

But then Lady Chelsea and the others really got an eyeful when Priscilla ate everything on her plate, rose, and headed to the buffet for more. At least this time, she paused before she replenished her plate and asked, "By the way, where'd Carlton run off to so early?"

Julia answered.

"Well, Missy," as she fought hard not to laugh. "For one thing, it is *not* 'so early.' At half-past ten and counting, I'd say we're approaching midday."

Then, she added, "Carlton didn't have the heart to tell you that he had to return to his office. In Washington, I think. Something about some unfinished paperwork. He also said to tell you he'd be back in time for Christmas."

"Not until *Christmas*?" Priscilla pretended not to be disappointed. "He's probably peeved," she said, "because I talked his head off about Danny Thomas into the wee hours of the morning."

Father, unable to restrain himself, said, "You don't say. And when I saw him before he rushed off, I thought he made up all that story about 'a sleepless night.'"

Lady Chelsea gave her husband a disapproving look. She knew that he, too, had heard more than enough about Danny Thomas, as well as the lyrics of that overheated song, had meant no harm.

Of them all, however, Ramses was the most tolerant. He had long since surmised that Priscilla was at her best when she was happy. And man alive was Priscilla happy!

Over a week later, Carlton returned after completing his paperwork at Langley, and he and Priscilla were out horseback riding down to the lake. By then, finally, Priscilla had calmed down and stopped that exuberant singing and dancing that had so taxed everyone.

It was time, Carlton decided, to once again broach the subject that still weighed heavily on his mind.

"Say, Missy," he began, "seems to me that you and I are now pretty much situated in this part of the country. So how 'bout you and me signing up with the same medical doctor?"

When she did not answer, he continued, "We might also need to combine some of our possessions and transact some legal matters." He said that in the hope of taking the edge off what he suspected Priscilla might have felt having heard the words "medical doctor."

Then he quickly added, matter-of-factly, "I can take you for your first visit to whichever office you choose."

At this very moment, both the intelligence agent-husband and -wife compartmentalized that they both underwent routine physical and mental health examinations in the course of their unmentionable jobs. Yet, here they both were talking as if Priscilla had somehow been negligent. Talk about living double lives! Oh well, back to the moment.

"Gee, Carlton, I never even gave any of that a thought. Medical doctor, legal papers, even bank accounts."

She laughed out loud, adding whimsically, "Now we really *are* married. Ha! Ha! Ha!"

But, more thoughtfully, she nodded. "Maybe you're right. Ruth is handling things at the office, so I'm free for whichever and whenever."

Carlton smiled and concentrated, giving her the time and space to share her feelings and her thoughts. Benignly he looked out at the calm, still lake.

A moment later, she surprised her husband even more when she said, "Come to think of it; I haven't seen a medical doctor in ages, not even a gynecologist." She laughed again. "Well, I do see my shrink often enough, especially back during your bout with amnesia. Maybe too often." Then she laughed again.

Carlton kept smiling and listening. From what he had heard from Lady Chelsea after his recovery from that amnesia, he was aware of the healing role the psychiatrist had played when his wife was so traumatized by his long, drawn-out recovery. He was primarily aware of the advanced medical treatments that Priscilla had received after completing her secret missions as an intelligence agent. But she did not count any of that as medical care. Or was she just playing along with him? Carlton took a deep breath. He was oh-so-relieved that she had finally moved on from her high-spirited appreciation of the masquerade ball, not to mention Danny Thomas.

Later that morning, a secretary in the office of Martin Shoemaker, M.D., the Bernhardt family physician, told Carlton that he could squeeze them in the next afternoon, two days before Christmas.

"After that," the secretary said, "the good doctor is taking a much-needed vacation."

Mr. and Mrs. Carlton Elliott Bernhardt kept their appointment.

While sitting with Carlton in Dr. Shoemaker's office, Priscilla could not remember when she had been asked so many questions. Most of the doctor's queries were directed at her since he had been taking care of Carlton for most of his life. The doctor seemed to be asking a battery of questions from a chart on his clipboard, although he was also consulting the medical history forms that Priscilla had filled out in the waiting room.

He paused at one of her answers. "A smoker, I see." The doctor raised his eyebrows and stared at Priscilla. "We will be addressing that, I believe." He cracked a tiny smile. "Eventually."

Priscilla shrugged her shoulders and twisted her nose.

Then he moved on down his questionnaire. He paused at length, however, as he read her answers about her gynecological history.

Finally he nodded and said that he would schedule an appointment for Priscilla with a gynecologist and one for a mammogram. "Sooner rather than later," he added.

"Yuck," Priscilla said, at the mention of "mammogram." She whispered to Carlton, "I hate those archaic exams."

The doctor pretended he had not heard that. His focus was more on the gynecologist, anyway. Although he did not spell this out for the Bernhardt couple, his referral to the gynecologist was to determine whether Priscilla had actually had her tubes tied—as she had indicated on her medical history; and if so, whether the procedure could be safely reversed.

After a quiet Christmas in the bosom of the family—the masquerade ball had long been the holiday blowout, while Christmas was joyful and religious—Priscilla kept her scheduled December 29th appointment with the gynecologist. She insisted on going alone.

Priscilla took the position that all women knew in the examining room: knees propped up, the heels of the feet stuck inside cold metal stirrups. She distracted herself first by wondering why the room was so cold when she was covered only by a thin sheet, then by deciding that indeed this was the most vulnerable position she had ever been made to assume, and then by once again trying, but failing, to recall when she had last gone to a gynecologist.

But she certainly did not doubt that it had been a very long time since any doctor had asked her so many intimate questions. As the gynecologist pressed his hands on her abdomen and moved his fingers here and there, he asked for details about her sexual behavior.

Why, you nosey bloke, Priscilla thought. Then, the next thing she knew, aloud, she pled, "Enough already." And then, more assertively, "Besides, what're you looking for, anyway?"

But as she stared at the screen on a machine beside the high slab on which she lay, she saw a slight smile come across the gynecologist's face. Then she heard him saying, "Ah, yes, just as I suspected.

"Young lady, your tubes *have* been tied."

Priscilla had not been aware of holding her breath, but then she let it out in a sort of sigh that was not relieved but sounded just resigned. "I told you." She repeated herself. "I told you so."

She reached for the sheet that covered her and prepared to leave this office and the offices of all such doctors forever. "So I'm guessing we're done here?"

"Maybe not." The doctor's smile broadened. "If you like, I can try to reverse the procedure. And if the procedure works, as I believe it may, you might, and I repeat, you *might* very well be able to conceive." The gynecologist seemed pleased with his prognosis.

"Get out a' here," Priscilla said. She was wary. "Come on, Doc, I'm pushing thirty-seven or so. Kinda' old to start talking about children. Don't you think?"

"Young lady," the gynecologist said, "in your case, I suggest that age is not our primary concern. Now, tell me honestly," he said, peering deeply into her eyes, "what would you like to do?"

Priscilla considered deferring any decision until she had talked to Carlton. But then she recalled the gist of what the two of them had been discussing over the past couple of months. Carlton had always been more hopeful than she that at some point, and somehow, they might conceive with God's grace. She admitted, too, that maybe she knew Carlton better than she knew herself. She dared to smile at the doctor.

"Well, first, will untying my tubes hurt much? And second, let's see what Mother Nature has to say about all this."

"Okay." The doctor nodded. "But my question, young lady, still stands. If the procedure *is* successful, I need to know right now your desire to conceive. Otherwise, I really do like your prospects."

Then Priscilla surprised even herself when she said, "You know something, Doc, I've been blessed beyond measure. So if the good Lord makes it so, I'd be truly grateful."

Then she said, "If you're done poking around inside my private parts, do you think you can help this ole girl back up? Then, after I put my clothes back on, maybe we can sit in a nice office together, and I'll finish telling you about my situation."

The doctor laughed out loud. This was one feisty woman. He suspected she had just said what every other one of his patients would have liked to say, but most never dared to articulate.

A short while later, as Priscilla had requested, the two of them sat in his book-lined office.

Now that she had committed to both trust and action, Priscilla got right to it.

She told him about the abortion she had had after being raped back in graduate school, how she had fallen in love with Carlton, and how happy they were together. Then she went deeper into the effect of that rape on her.

"You see, Doc," she said, "after I had that horrible abortion, I sort of took on a self-enforced atonement. I told myself that I would never be blessed to give life because I took a life. Then, as the years progressed, I believed my own party line, as it were. That I was barren. Meanwhile, I pretty much forgot that I'd even had my tubes tied, and I certainly never imagined they could be *untied*." She looked intensely at the gynecologist and asked, "Does any of what I just said make sense?"

The gynecologist nodded.

"Ms. Austin-Bernhardt, I've seen and heard a lot more horrific stories. But I declare that none are as heartrending as women like you who have terminated a pregnancy after a sexual assault. It's as if you secretly bear a burden of guilt for something you did not bring about."

Then he surprised Priscilla even more when he said, "I remember seeing your television interview back when you told the entire world that you had been raped. I have to tell you, I felt for you."

Priscilla sensed sincerity in his eyes.

"But I never *ever* imagined," he added, "that you would become one of my patients. And when my colleague, Dr. Shoemaker, gave me your referral, something told me that you might benefit from my experience. I've previously worked with other women who sustained sexual assaults *and* had abortions—and convinced themselves, as you have, that somehow you are unworthy of giving life. But I implore you, please, let it all go. Let's begin anew. From what you have told me, your husband loves you. The two of you have so much life ahead of you."

Then the doctor took hold of both of Priscilla's hands and said, "You see, young lady, there's nothing more precious than the gift of life."

Priscilla flushed. She felt the hairs standing up not only on the back of her neck but on her whole body.

As their conversation neared an end, she thanked the kind and thoughtful gynecologist for his advice and words of encouragement.

Then he turned the discussion to the actual scheduling of the procedure. "I suggest the sooner, the better," he said, "How's January 6?"

She gulped. "So soon?"

"The sooner, the better," he repeated.

"Alright, then, January 6, it is." Priscilla smiled at the gynecologist, shook his hand, and left his office without as much a second thought.

Why, she did not even consider sharing this news with her darling Carlton.

"Not just yet," she told herself. "Let's see what comes of all this."

Priscilla kept a few other appointments for promises she had made to Lady Chelsea and Father, one of which involved speaking to a group of women who worked with Lady Chelsea on her many charitable projects. When Priscilla had asked what they might want to hear, her mother-in-law had answered, "Just tell them a little about yourself. You know, where you're from, your family, and your college and graduate school years." Priscilla had thought that much of her life experiences would be boring compared to the lives of the wealthy and prominent people she addressed. But when she finished telling what she kept calling "the boring details of my life," the women cheered and applauded. One of them had even come up to her afterwards and said, "Ms. Austin-Bernhardt, your life is so interesting, you ought to write a book."

Priscilla had heard that suggestion before, yet she still felt this woman was blowing smoke up her skirt, figuratively speaking.

But then, finally, the day came. Still new to marriage, Priscilla had assumed that she would ask Shelton to take her to her appointment because the gynecologist had cautioned that she would need someone to drive her home after the procedure. So when she walked outside the foyer and stood under the portico waiting for Shelton, she was surprised to see Carlton pulling up in his sports coupe.

"Oh, Carlton, my darling," she said, somewhat surprised, "what happened to Shelton? I'm sure you're busy."

But Carlton reminded her, "*I'm* your husband, Missy. Remember. You're a married woman now," he said with a big grin on his face. Why, even he knew that Priscilla still sometimes behaved like the independent woman she was.

After she kept her appointment with the gynecologist, who performed the procedure to reverse her tubular situation, she thought no more about it.

She and Carlton both, however, did remember the gynecologist's parting words: "Don't forget, young lady, call me if you experience any discomfort, especially any pain. Otherwise, give yourself a couple of weeks before any sexual activity."

The couple looked at each other and laughed. But Priscilla caught the shine in Carlton's eyes. His hopes had already risen as high as they could go.

Before January ended, Priscilla got an unexpected two-day visit from Laverne, whose healing from her injuries sustained in the Balkan adventure had thankfully continued. A highlight from that visit was the two of them watching a videotape of the masquerade ball. They had a grand time, screaming and hollering as they watched and laughed and munched on junk food and drank beer. As they had done when Macy had visited and shared her good news about her marriage to Ron, Father and Lady Chelsea and Ramses were so pleased to see Priscilla making herself so at home at Bow Lake. They took particular delight at how far she had come in accepting the Bernhardts as her new family.

Meanwhile, Priscilla kept a couple of other speaking engagements that her in-laws had arranged. Students and staff alike seemed captivated by her stories about her family's history in the South and her college and graduate school experiences at a Bow Lake High School assembly. She had a similarly warm reception with the Merrimack Rotary International gathering, especially when she told them that her father Nelson had once invited her to speak at the Prendergast Rotary International.

"Wow!" some of the Merrimack Rotary International members said.

"Young Ms. *Austin*-Bernhardt, your story is so interesting, you ought to write a book," the president said.

"Hmm," Priscilla eventually said to herself. "Maybe these people are onto something, after all. A book?"

Epilogue

Around the end of January 1990—three weeks after her tubular procedure—Priscilla and Carlton enjoyed one of their most sensual experiences ever. They'd always enjoyed making love. But Priscilla had always held something back, and Carlton had always known that way about her, too. But not this time.

This time, Priscilla accepted that she was, in fact, finally *in love*. Silently she prayed: *Dear Lord, please let me love this man, my darling Carlton.* And so it was that Priscilla opened up her mind, her body, and her soul. In the heat of it all, she felt a warm titillating sensation, a tingling throughout her body, like nothing she had ever before experienced.

And Carlton: well, he was moved to tears when he rolled over on their bed.

"My God, Missy, what just happened? I feel so, man alive, I feel good." He felt that Priscilla had finally let go of that last layer of defense that had so long shielded her heart from him, or anybody else, for that matter. Mostly though, Carlton felt Priscilla reaching out to him, welcoming him into her life entirely.

Then he said, "Missy, that was the best it's ever been."

That was saying a lot because Priscilla and Carlton always enjoyed a perfect sex life. But this time, it was more than about sex. This time it was about love.

In February, the second week, Priscilla was to deliver the keynote address for the Founders Day Program at her undergraduate alma mater. So she and Carlton headed to Salisbury, North Carolina.

As so it was that this part of Priscilla's journey was ending much as it had all begun. Or was it just beginning? Or continuing round and round? Life, she reflected, was so full of surprises, so abundant. Just as she thought everything was settled and predictable, doors opened, and wonders happened! There were her yeasty years in the Ohio Senate, learning so much from so many. Then bad things happened on the day she thought she would marry Jonathan, and she'd found herself whisked off to southern Africa to discover a new world of good things and high adventure. Then her American opportunities had surprised even her, first with working on that presidential election campaign, then marrying her Darling Carlton, not to mention embarking on another new life as an intelligence agent. And finally, most recently, having an inside look inside the corrupt world of art fraud, as well as living her dream in New York City, with escapades on a yacht in the Greek isles and a fashion show on the Hudson.

She wondered what was next. She smiled as she thought of people telling her that maybe she should create a fashion line of her own or even write a book—a memoir.

She had another thought. *Nah.* She refused to let her mind go there.

And then she thought again of "Jules, Ma'am. I'm called Jules McCorkle." Would their paths ever cross again?

She peered out of the window of the Bernhardt family jet. She remembered that nearly two decades ago, her father—the late Reverend

James Nelson Austin, a Methodist minister and consummate politician—had accompanied her on her first flight ever as she commenced her undergraduate studies at Livingstone College. They had flown to the Charlotte Douglas International Airport on Allegheny Airlines and rented a red Corvette to drive to the nearby college campus. Along the way, they had driven past rows upon rows of pine trees. Priscilla even remembered asking, "Daddy, why're you dumping me off in the backwoods of this state?" But this time, she was accompanied by her husband, not her father.

Later that morning, in the rented convertible that was so like Carlton's own car back at Bow Lake, she leaned over and planted a warm kiss on his cheek.

"What was that for?" her Darling Carlton asked.

"Was just wondering about how my daddy would feel if he could see me now."

"I can take an informed guess," he said with a knowing smirk.

"Oh-h, what's that?"

"There's just no telling what mischief that brat's up to these days! Never can tell with Missy." Then he laughed a hearty laugh as he sped north on Interstate 85 towards Salisbury.

Shortly, Carlton changed the subject. He could not help noticing how radiant his wife looked this morning. Although it was cold, the sun shone ever so brightly against her tan complexion. Then he asked her about something he had noticed earlier in the month, although Priscilla had not seemed to have given this any thought.

"Say, Missy, I couldn't help noticing that you haven't been using any of those tampon things you women use." He raised his eyebrows. "Don't you usually use them around the first of the month?"

Priscilla, still not on the same wavelength as her husband, lightly slapped his face.

440

"Ouch!"

"Shut up, you twerp."

Then, as she thought about the apparent implication of what her husband had just said, she nearly screamed his ears off.

"Do you think? Could it be? Oh, Carlton, my darling!" And now that she thought about it, she did feel a little different. But Priscilla could not even dare to say the word "pregnant," but what she did say was, "I could not be any happier."

Then she added, "You know something, Julia was right, I am so blessed. God has been so good to me."

Carlton was intimately aware of Priscilla's upbringing. She was a daughter who had been raised like a son, and if they had a girl, Priscilla would raise her much as she had been raised, imbuing her brand of feminism.

Two of them! Carlton thought: *I could live with that*!

"Oh, Miss Prissy," her Darling Carlton said, "I'm sure even you know how proud your father would be of his beloved Miss Prissy. Yes, Sirree, Bob! His beloved Miss Prissy is finally living her life for herself."

But then he had another thought: *Was she really*? Or, as Lady Chelsea had suggested to him sometime earlier, "Is Missy trying to please her husband now?" That, he realized, was something that even her father, Nelson, had cautioned her against so many years ago. But so be it. That was maybe a story for another time.

For now, Carlton was happy, so Priscilla was happy.

There was that smirk again.

Acknowledgments

This go-round, I put Priscilla in high cotton in the world of highly valued works of art, my first attempt at writing about something somewhat amusing with a bit of intrigue in the mix. In so doing, it occurred to me, where else to situate the story than the famed Metropolitan Museum of Art and the Montmartre arrondissement—the companion site—the latter? In this place, legendary figures mastered their artistic and creative writing crafts.

Although I grew up in the Snowbelt of western New York and loved my life there, I remain fascinated with the City—New York City, that is. So, in addition to featuring The Met, I also provide glimpses into the fashion industry and life in Harlem in early 1990.

This book is also a belated effort to improve my final grade in an Art Appreciation and History course that I almost flunked in college. I trust that I will receive a better grade this time around.

Thanks to my editor, Laurie Devine, for helping me to bring Priscilla to life. But since I make changes after my editor, any errors are mine.

This book is dedicated to the memory of my mom, Hazel B. Owens Simms—the first published author in our family and my inspiration for writing. She died before this book's publication, as did my darling husband,

Odinga Lawrence Maddox I, which left a massive gap in my foundation. Both of them were unyielding in their support for my writing.

Thank goodness for my friends and colleagues, including, but certainly not limited to, P. Jane Splawn, Elinettie Chabwera, Michael D. Connor, Hilton Kelly, Helen Turner, Marie Umeh, Ada White Taylor, Stephanie Jones, Carolyn Wilkerson Duncan, and Virginia Phiri. I am forever grateful to them for their constructive criticism of my work and their encouragement to continue writing. So, stay tuned, because there is more to come in the Priscilla series.

Blessings.

About the Author

Indie author M. J. Simms-Maddox, Ph.D., created The Priscilla Series, mainly mysteries and thrillers portraying a modern-day, self-assured Black female protagonist of diverse ancestry.

The South Carolina native grew up in the Snowbelt of western New York and currently resides in North Carolina.

She earned her doctorate in political science from The Ohio State University, has served as a legislative aide in the Ohio Senate, operated a PR firm, and taught political science for over thirty years. She also travels extensively, all of which plays prominently in the Priscilla series.

The author found her passion for writing fiction somewhat late in life. She has primarily written mysteries and thrillers since 1999.

She is affiliated with the African Literature Association, the Chanticleer Authors' Conference, the North Carolina Writers' Network, and the Surrey International Writers' Conference.

Apart from writing novels about contemporary, self-assured professional women with agency, she enjoys all-things-books, traveling, and working in her yard.